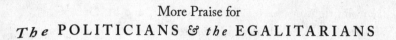
More Praise for

The POLITICIANS *&* *the* EGALITARIANS

A *St. Louis Post-Dispatch* "50 Best Books of 2016" selection

A *Kirkus Reviews* "Best Books of 2016" selection

"Sean Wilentz of Princeton is one of the best American historians of his generation. . . . For those readers eager to be introduced to Wilentz's work, *The Politicians & the Egalitarians* is a good place to start."
—Michael Beschloss, *Washington Post*

"Sean Wilentz is a rare historian who writes with confidence about the entire scope of American history and who does so in a way accessible to a broad reading public. *The Politicians & the Egalitarians*, like his previous books, is sure to command attention." —Eric Foner

"This stimulating book provides a major new interpretation of the alliance between egalitarian social movements and partisan politics to achieve some of the most notable liberal victories in the American past. Sean Wilentz has done more than anyone else to blend social and political history in a manner that offers powerful new insights."
—James M. McPherson

"Wilentz gets it. One of America's great modern historians, and also a devoted and outspoken liberal who writes left-leaning columns on the side, Wilentz happily joins the little-d democratic fight for equality and against privilege. . . . [T]his engrossing and deeply enriching book is both history and argument . . . and you should read it."
—Mickey Edwards, *Los Angeles Times*

"A shrewd and engaging assessment of the variable American tradition of egalitarianism, particularly as manifested in the political lives of Thomas Jefferson, John Quincy Adams, John Brown, Abraham Lincoln, right up through Lyndon Johnson and his Great Society—scrupulously detailed, elegantly written, incisively argued, and effectively combative."   —Philip Roth

"Wilentz evinces a vast knowledge of the American past while exploring, in his unique way, the interplay between raw party politics and the ebb and flow of reform efforts. In offering his take on pivotal figures from Jefferson to Du Bois, Lincoln to LBJ, Wilentz challenges us to debate history and ideas in a way that honors the best of the democratic system he has written about so provocatively throughout his career. Even when I most disagree with him, his arguments are always vigorous and passionate, lively and engaging."
                                                        —Henry Louis Gates Jr.

"Wilentz, author of the Bancroft Prize–winning *Rise of American Democracy* and professor of history at Princeton University, once again proves himself to be among America's most skilled (and pugilistic) historians with this brisk, hard-hitting book. . . . The result is wonderfully readable and the best kind of serious, sharp argumentation from one of the leading historians of the United States."
                                                        —*Publishers Weekly*

"It is a pleasure to be in the hands of an individual who can write compellingly about such a range of American history. Reading *The Politicians & the Egalitarians*, one comes away with the sense that historical debates *matter*. Whether the subject is Lyndon Johnson or Thomas Paine, Wilentz's vivid prose renders the debates as high-stakes."
                                —Jordan Michael Smith, *Christian Science Monitor*

"Sean Wilentz's provocative, engaging and well-written new book should be required reading for students of American politics."

—Erik J. Chaput, *Providence Journal*

"A stern, thoroughly satisfying harangue on the realities of politics in the United States by the veteran, prizewinning historian."

—*Kirkus Reviews*

"Wilentz offers a vigorous and convincing rebuttal to the notion that real progress toward equality comes from anything but patient, practical, experienced and—yes—at times flexible political leadership."

—Jim Kaplan, *National Book Review*

"Wilentz is a clear and graceful writer, and his judgment on historical matters is unfailingly carefully considered and backstopped by a life of research. He is a liberal's liberal, both in the classical sense and in the current meaning of the term in American political life."

—Tod Lindberg, *National Interest*

The POLITICIANS *&* *the* EGALITARIANS

The POLITICIANS
& the EGALITARIANS

★ ★ ★ ★ ★ ▬▬▬▬▬▬

The Hidden History of American Politics

SEAN WILENTZ

W. W. NORTON & COMPANY
Independent Publishers Since 1923
NEW YORK   LONDON

For information about permission to reproduce selections from this book,
write to Permissions, W. W. Norton & Company, Inc.,
500 Fifth Avenue, New York, NY 10110

For information about special discounts for bulk purchases, please contact
W. W. Norton Special Sales at specialsales@wwnorton.com or 800-233-4830

Manufacturing by Berryville Graphics
Book design by Lovedog Studio
Production manager: Julia Druskin

Library of Congress Cataloging-in-Publication Data

Names: Wilentz, Sean.
Title: The politicians & the egalitarians : the hidden history of American
politics / Sean Wilentz.
Other titles: Politicians and the egalitarians
Description: First edition. | New York : W.W. Norton & Company, 2016. |
Includes bibliographical references and index.
Identifiers: LCCN 2016009662 | ISBN 9780393285024 (hardcover)
Subjects: LCSH: United States—Politics and government. | Equality—
United   States—History. | Partisanship—Political aspects—United
States—History. | Political culture—United States—History. | Politicians—
United States—Biography. | Political activists—United States—Biography. |
Social reformers—United States—Biography. | Political parties—United
States—History. | Social movements—United States—History.
Classification: LCC E183 .W547 2016 | DDC 306.20973—dc23 LC record
available at http://lccn.loc.gov/2016009662

ISBN 978-0-393-35413-3 pbk.

W. W. Norton & Company, Inc.
500 Fifth Avenue, New York, N.Y. 10110
www.wwnorton.com

W. W. Norton & Company Ltd.
15 Carlisle Street, London W1D 3BS

1 2 3 4 5 6 7 8 9 0

To John Lewis

Contents

Preface to the Paperback Edition   xiii

Introduction   xix

I. TWO KEYS *to* AMERICAN HISTORY

   1. *The Postpartisan Style in American Politics*   3

   2. *America's Forgotten Egalitarian Tradition*   31

II. *The* POLITICIANS *and the* EGALITARIANS

   3. *Thomas Paine: The Origins of American Egalitarianism*   69

   4. *Life, Liberty, and the Pursuit of Thomas Jefferson*   84

   5. *John Quincy Adams: Slavery's Arch-Enemy*   125

   6. *John Brown: The Temptation of Terror*   148

7. *Abraham Lincoln: Egalitarian Politician*   170

8. *Democracy at Gettysburg, 1863*   213

9. *The Steel Town and the Gilded Age*   233

10. *W. E. B. Du Bois: A Heroic Education*   250

11. *Theodore Roosevelt: Politics and Folly*   267

12. *The Liberals and the Leftists*   280

13. *The Cold War and the Perils of Junk History*   295

14. *Lyndon B. Johnson: The Triumph of Politics*   307

Bibliographic Notes and References   333

Acknowledgments   347

Index   349

"It may be well for the statesman to know that statesmanship easily degenerates into opportunism and that opportunism cannot be sharply distinguished from dishonesty. But the prophet ought to realize that his higher perspective and the uncompromising nature of his judgments always has a note of irresponsibility in it. Francis of Assisi may have been a better Christian than Pope Innocent III. But it may be questioned whether his moral superiority over the latter was as absolute as it seemed. Nor is there any reason to believe that Abraham Lincoln, the statesman and opportunist, was morally inferior to William Lloyd Garrison, the prophet. The moral achievement of the statesman must be judged in terms which take account of the limitations of human society which the statesman must, and the prophet need not, consider."

Reinhold Niebuhr, 1929

PREFACE TO THE PAPERBACK EDITION

WRITTEN IN EARLY JANUARY 2016, THE INTRODUCTION TO *The Politicians & the Egalitarians* contended that the Great Crash of 2008 led to the resurgence of a long-dormant egalitarianism, "compelling Republicans as well as Democrats to decry the massive and growing divergences between the wealthiest Americans and the rest of the country." Discontent over economic inequality clearly was roiling the impending presidential nomination contests inside both major parties. No one, though, could have envisaged how those contests would turn into two more-or-less hostile takeover bids, and how the success of one of these bids would lead to the election of Donald J. Trump to the White House. Nor could anyone have foreseen the unprecedented events of the 2016 campaign, which pummeled basic American democratic norms.

There had been, to be sure, dirty, bitter, and irregular races before. These included four elections—in 1824, 1876, 1888, and 2000—in which the winner of the popular vote failed to carry a majority of the Electoral College, thereby clouding the legitimacy of the incoming administration. But no previous election had seen direct interference by a major adversarial foreign power commensurate with the Russian Federation's systematic computer hacking and related online operations in support of Trump—operations that Trump, on the campaign trail, at one point loudly encouraged. Never before had an FBI director gratuitously ignored official regulations and guidelines and harmed the reputation of one candidate, as James Comey did publicly with respect to Hillary Clinton and her email server, even as he remained silent about his agency's investigations of grievous wrongdoing by the other candidate. Whether these startling interventions actually turned the election, as many of Clinton's supporters insisted they did, is impossible to know for sure and probably always will be. Without question, though, these actions, amplified by the sensationalizing effects of social media and the sheer vitriol of the campaign, assaulted the integrity of democratic politics.

Aside from the wrenching anomalies, the election did in some respects affirm the continued importance of partisanship and the egalitarian tradition in American politics, albeit in odd, sometimes distorted, and deeply ironic ways. Although weakened institutionally and badly divided, the parties as ever became at once the chief battlegrounds and the main vehicles for expressing all sorts of political distempers. On the right, the real estate mogul and reality TV star Trump successfully commandeered a large portion of the long-frustrated, hyper-polarized Republican Party base by demonizing illegal immigration from Mexico along with international trade deals like the North American Free Trade Agreement. On the left, Senator Bernie Sanders, an independent, self-described democratic socialist running as a Democrat, aroused support among younger voters, especially on and around college and university campuses, by attacking the same trade deals as Trump did, as well as unregulated campaign contributions by large corporations and billionaire donors. Although Sanders considered running as a third-party candidate, he, like Trump, decided that contending inside one of the two major parties would do far more to advance his candidacy and his cause. Post-partisanship appealed to neither man, even though both of them vilified establishment politics as usual; instead of eschewing the parties, they would try to take them over.

To the astonishment of the political pundits and Trump's Republican rivals—sixteen in all—Trump won the Republican nomination handily;

and in time he won the endorsement of most of the GOP leadership, including some men he had humiliated and others who had called him unfit for high office. Sanders, by contrast, failed to capture most Democratic base voters, roughly two-thirds of whom cast their votes for Hillary Clinton, but he gained a passionate following among independents who in numerous states were eligible to participate in the Democrats' nominating process. The Sanders insurgency rattled Clinton, especially in caucus primary states, and pushed her marginally toward some of Sanders's positions, notably on trade policy. It also persuaded millions of voters that she was a corrupt lackey of Wall Street, a tag that, despite Sanders's endorsement of her in mid-July, severely hobbled the Clinton campaign in the general election.

Harping as they did on international trade gave both Trump and Sanders a wedge issue inside their respective parties, where different versions of liberal trade policies had taken hold as commonsense approaches to a globalizing economy. Bashing freer trade became a simplified, even demagogic, but highly effective way for the self-designated outsiders to appeal to white working-class voters as well as enthusiastic, idealistic so-called millennials. In truth, the hollowing out of much of traditional industrial America began decades before NAFTA and other liberalizing trade agreements were put in place. Economists generally agree that changes in the terms of international trade, intended to create new jobs, had little to do with further depressing certain sectors of the industrial workforce compared with more important factors, automation above all. But by singling out trade policy and especially NAFTA—"one of the worst deals ever made of any kind signed by anybody," according to Trump; "a disaster for the American worker," according to Sanders—the challengers provided a focus for popular insecurity and outrage that implicated the much-derided establishment of both major parties. (Trump's attacks on illegal immigrants became another focus, as did Sanders's and his supporters' diatribes against Clinton as a neoliberal epigone of "the billionaire class.") Rebutting these charges would have required arguments more complex than a sound bite or a slogan; in any event, neither Trump's Republican rivals nor Clinton succeeded in blunting these lines of attack.

And so the election concluded in a stunning irony: a campaign whose rhetoric had turned largely on rising economic inequalities yielded a billionaire president who proceeded to stuff his cabinet with super-rich men and women—the $14 billion cabinet, one commentator called it—thereby rounding out what loomed as the most plutocratic executive branch ever in our history.

How much that result would change the nation's basic political and constitutional structures was uncertain as Trump took office—an uncertainty whose very existence bespoke the campaign's disorienting effects. Had any other Republican candidate won the presidency, and had the GOP retained control of the Senate as well as the House, domestic and foreign policy could have been expected to take a sharply conservative, even reactionary turn, reinforced by highly conservative appointments to the Supreme Court and the rest of the federal judiciary. Trump's success seemed to augur exactly this sort of turn with respect to most domestic policies as well as to judicial selections.

But Trump's evident admiration of and even closeness to the Russian autocrat Vladimir Putin, along with his dismissals of NATO and the European Union, broke not only with long-established Republican positions but with what remained of the bipartisan foreign policy consensus that had emerged after World War II. His offhand remarks during the campaign about nuclear proliferation and other touchy subjects unnerved ordinary citizens as well as experts all across the political spectrum. His cavalier observations about bedrock constitutional freedoms and long-standing court precedents raised questions about his understanding of the Constitution that he would pledge his honor to preserve, protect, and defend. Trump's lax view of possible conflicts of interest with his sprawling and often obscure global business interests fed concerns about flagrantly unethical dealings and even violations of the Constitution.

The campaign as well as Trump's victory also suggested that the partisanship and egalitarianism that had long shaped American politics may have been, at the least, severely deflected. Trump was not the only non-politician without experience in elected office to have won the presidency, but the previous examples had been army generals like George Washington, Ulysses S. Grant, and Dwight D. Eisenhower who had served their nation and its government (and in Grant's and Eisenhower's cases, their presidential commanders-in-chief) with great distinction. Trump was a very different sort of figure, a businessman celebrity whose willingness (let alone capacity) to undertake even the most conventional political tasks required of any president was dubious. Even less clear was the future of the Republican Party which, although for the moment all-powerful in Washington and in most of the states, remained seriously divided, its fervent base now devoted to a professed anti-politician with at best ephemeral party ties. Likewise, the Democratic Party, now shut out of power and recovering from its own rancorous primary fights, emerged from 2016 battered and without clear direction.

Then there was the state of the egalitarian tradition. *The Politicians & the Egalitarians* discusses different kinds of egalitarianism, including the racist egalitarianism that proved so powerful in the eras of Reconstruction in the 1860s and 1870s and the so-called Second Reconstruction of the 1950s and 1960s. In 2016, though, there emerged a curdled egalitarianism akin to what the late historian Richard Hofstadter called "the paranoid style" in our politics, chiefly on the right but also on the left. That style, according to Hofstadter, proclaimed the restoration of a bygone mythic era of national greatness and was founded on a few key elements: "the idea of a golden age; the concept of natural harmonies; the dualistic version of social struggles; the conspiracy theory of history; and the doctrine of the primacy of money."

The paranoid style has been a perennial element in American political history, sometimes conflated misleadingly with populism. It came closest to winning the presidency, by Hofstadter's reckoning, when Barry Goldwater won the Republican nomination in 1964. Goldwater, of course, was crushed by the incumbent Lyndon B. Johnson, which some observers took to mean that political paranoia had been repudiated once and for all, and consigned to the political margins. But Hofstadter was not so sure, and he ended up being prescient. Donald Trump's campaign extolled virtually every element of the paranoid style. In particular, Trump's propaganda singled out for attack the corporate beneficiaries of free trade arrangements and a supposed dark conspiracy of internationalist bankers and financiers (all of those identified being Jewish)—the latest moneyed, cosmopolitan bogeymen of the paranoid imagination. With the election of Trump, the politics of paranoia, no longer on the margins, would now inhabit the Oval Office.

In the 2016 campaign and election, partisanship and egalitarianism, the driving forces of American politics that had been hidden from historians for so long, were hidden no longer. The hard, glaring reality in the days before Trump's inauguration was that the accumulation of abnormalities around those forces had caused a profound break, creating a regime unlike anything previously known in American political history—a presidency born of an authoritarian temper and impassioned appeals to divisiveness that the framers of the Constitution had deeply feared and worked intensely to check. For better or worse, or so it appeared, nothing would ever be the same.

S. W.
January 15, 2017

INTRODUCTION

THERE ARE TWO KEYS TO UNLOCKING THE SECRETS OF American politics and American political history. Current historians, in their enthusiasm for insight of a new and attractive sort, have mislaid these keys, and now they are hidden from sight. Once recovered, though, and put to use, the keys quickly demonstrate their usefulness.

The first key is to recognize both the permanent reality and the effectiveness of partisanship and party politics. Americans have been loath to believe these things. The founding generation distrusted parties. The framers of the Constitution designed a national government they hoped would avoid partisanship's debased ambitions and destructive tendencies. More than a hundred years later, reformers of the Progressive Era similarly distrusted parties and tried to replace them with nonpartisan elections and independent commissions of experts. Americans in our own time think likewise. We deplore partisanship. We want government conducted in a lofty manner, without adversarial confrontation and chaos. But more than two hundred years of antipartisanship has produced nothing.

This is because, despite their intentions, the framers built a political system which inspired partisan politics. After some badly-needed constitutional tinkering, the system soon fostered the rise of professional, mass-based, national parties. A nation as large and diverse as the United States has required parties both to turn discontent into laws and institutions and to prevent chronic political breakdown. Americans devised election rules that hand victory to the winner of a plurality of votes, which according to the axioms of political science virtually assures a two-party system in which third parties do not last. Possibly partisan politics is built into human nature. It is certainly built into the American version of human nature.

And partisan politics has survived because, in the United States, it has worked well, or well enough. Historians nowadays dismiss this basic truth. They regard the political parties as hindrances to democracy, and glorify political outsiders and social movements. They point with justice to the countless and unending episodes of partisan politicians corrupting our politics and sustaining social wrongs. Yet the great issues in our history have been settled not from friction between politicians and egalitarians but from the convergence of protest and politics. Party democracy has succeeded even in addressing the most oppressive of all American problems, which was slavery, and which in the end could only be settled in blood. Impeded by a party system designed to keep slavery out of national politics, antislavery partisans and politicians built parties of their own; and the carefully rigged party system fell apart; and the election to the presidency of one of the antislavery party politicians, Abraham Lincoln, forced the crisis that led to the slaveholders' rebellion and, in time, emancipation. Ever since, all of the great American social legislation, from the Progressive Era to the New Deal to the Great Society, has been achieved by and through the political parties.

The second key to American political history is the recognition that, from the very start, Americans have proclaimed—and sometimes been consumed by—the need to combat economic privilege and to strengthen what Walt Whitman called "the true gravitation-hold," "a vast intertwining reticulation of wealth." The struggle against economic inequality has been a great subterranean river in our political past, sometimes breaking through the surface, sometimes returning underground. Americans have fought endlessly about the meaning of democracy, and about government authority, and about rights and social justice. Running through these fights has been a recurring insistence that vast material inequalities directly threaten democracy.

This, too, we have been reluctant to see. The founding generation did not proclaim economic equality, as the founders believed that sound political institutions would sustain a just and harmonious society. We do not read about it in the Declaration of Independence, the Constitution, or the Bill of Rights. We do read about it, though, in numerous pamphlets and speeches, as well as in the correspondence of Thomas Jefferson and James Madison, and conflicts over economic privilege dominated American national politics from the battles between Jefferson and Alexander Hamilton to the furious clashes of the era of Andrew Jackson.

Slavery first stunted and then deformed American democracy, and its racist legacy has complicated, distorted, and sometimes disrupted the politics of economic inequality. Not only does white racism sustain and deepen great disparities of wealth; it has stamped American history so strongly that economic inequality has become symptomatic of racial injustice. To talk about one has often meant talking about the other. Thus, when antislavery forces attacked human bondage as immoral, they also attacked it as the cornerstone of hateful economic and political privilege, as exercised by the aristocratic Slave Power and its Northern accomplices. The war to crush the slaveholders' rebellion became a war of emancipation, but it was also, from the start, a fight to vindicate American democracy against a domineering and finally secessionist slaveocracy, its wealth and power concentrated in the hands of a tiny elite.

After the egalitarian impulses of the Civil War years dissipated, an ideology of rugged individualism, white supremacy, and the blessings of big business subdued all talk of inequality. Efforts by blacks and their supporters to lay full claim to the egalitarian tradition were crushed after the overthrow of Reconstruction, and trade unionists in a new class of industrial workers suffered harsh repression. The so-called Progressive movement and, even more, the New Deal brought the issue of economic inequality back front and center, as, in time, did Lyndon B. Johnson's Great Society, which transcended the New Deal by joining the fight for economic equality to the one for racial justice. But by the late 1960s, the egalitarian politics unleashed by the Great Depression and then recast by the civil rights movement began losing steam—and losing its way.

The long conservative era heralded by the election of Ronald Reagan to the presidency in 1980 seemed a repudiation of Great Society egalitarianism. Conservatives advanced regressive economic and fiscal policies and launched a divisive and politically devastating culture war based on race and religion. Dissenting egalitarian politics became framed by claims of racial identities and sexual affinities. Pundits wondered why so many ordinary Americans seemed so willing to vote against their own economic interests. Historians tried to explain the shortcomings and continual failures of economic egalitarianism in American politics.

Yet the issue of economic equality has been the great perennial question in American political history. This has come back into focus since the Great Crash of 2008, compelling Republicans as well as Democrats to decry the massive and growing divergences between the wealthiest Americans and the rest of the country. How long the refocusing will last is hard to tell. But it does prompt us to look where we have not wanted to look when considering past politics in the United States, and to see things that we have failed to see.

With these two keys—the primacy of party politics and the eternal underlying question of economic privilege and inequality—the whole of American political history begins to emerge more clearly. In the beginning, democracy in America rested on the proposition that vast inequalities of wealth were threatening and intolerable. Securing that proposition since then has required fitting it into party politics, which has not always been easy to do. Political leaders otherwise hostile to economic privilege have been crippled by their connections to slavery and Jim Crow segregation. At times, neither national party has been alert to widening gaps of wealth and power, or to the policies and institutions which abetted those gaps. Relations between party politics and protest politics have sometimes been fraught, and, in the absence of capable leadership, they have become destructive.

Still, the driving force in American political history has been the effort to curb the power of concentrated wealth, whether the power of the slaveholders or the power of industrial plutocrats. Often, egalitarians berate politicians as slow-moving wafflers, and politicians despair of egalitarians' obliviousness to the burdens of democratic government. But just as it is crucial in a democracy for egalitarians to agitate, so is it vital that politicians do all they can to advance equality within the limits of public opinion and the Constitution—sometimes to the point of amending the Constitution, as with the final destruction of slavery. American political history can be understood as the fitful history of the politicians and the egalitarians, and of the fateful occasions when their labors converge.

Doing full justice to this interpretation would require a book many times longer than this one. In fourteen chapters, I can only skim the surface. The bulk of these chapters dwell primarily on party politics; some focus on aspects of the tortured history of racial inequality and American democracy. An adequate accounting would consider an infinitude of experiences, some of them barely touched upon here and others absent completely—the history of women and feminism, or of the enormous Hispanic and Latino presence in American life. Set against that vastness, this book can offer only what Whitman once called (in considering the art of biography) "a few hints, a few diffused clews and indirections." All right: more than hints, more than clues. But these chapters are meant as a beginning. If I am correct in what I have to say here, it ought to be possible to make better sense of all of American political history.

★   ★   ★

RECOVERING THIS HISTORY REQUIRES confronting what is now the conventional historical wisdom on major topics. One way or another, each chapter in *The Politicians & the Egalitarians* does so. Thomas Paine and Thomas Jefferson were the most consequential egalitarians of the Revolutionary Era, one a pamphleteer, the other a political leader, president, and philosophe. Yet if historians have served Paine relatively well, the public has largely forgotten his contributions, and historians have mistreated Jefferson and his supporters to the point of caricature. John Quincy Adams bridged the period from the Revolution to the Civil War more auspiciously than any other political figure, but his emergence as the leading anti-slavery voice in national politics is improperly understood. Current studies of the abolitionist terrorist John Brown fundamentally misstate the political situation of the 1850s and gloss the temptation of political violence. Abraham Lincoln's apotheosis by historians as a man who rose above sordid politics and heeded the wisdom of the abolitionist radicals would, I imagine, have elicited from Lincoln a belly laugh and a long tall story about political purists. Yet Lincoln, the master party politician, also thought deeply about great political themes, above all the vindication of democracy and equality in a hostile world of kings, aristocrats, and treasonous slaveholders.

After the Civil War, trade unionists in expanding heavy industry, as at the giant Homestead works outside Pittsburgh, fought successfully for workers' rights, in part by adapting victorious antislavery principles to their own cause; and, in alliance with local politicians, they built their own democratic and egalitarian institutions—only to be crushed by governments, state and federal, that were friendly to the new corporations. As race relations descended into what historians would later call the "nadir," the young W. E. B. Du Bois wrote *The Souls of Black Folk*—a great and classic work but also a peculiar one, which struggles to understand the spiritual dimensions of racial subjugation. Although born to privilege and a code of noblesse oblige, Theodore Roosevelt became, more than his biographers recognize, a cunning and, when necessary, merciless partisan politician who fought to reduce some of the excesses of those he called "malefactors of great wealth"—until his own political instincts failed him.

The coming of the New Deal under TR's even cannier cousin, Franklin Delano Roosevelt, rearticulated the American egalitarian tradition, building on but also vastly enlarging the democratic nationalism of the Lincoln Republicans and TR's Square Deal. But for today's historians—I focus on a prominent book by Michael Kazin—the New Deal is yet another example of how party politicians, with self-interested aims of their own, heeded and then thwarted the radical egalitarians. A different line of argument holds that the advent of the Cold War after FDR's death and the end of World War II followed from small-minded, cynical politicians shoving aside the visionary Henry Wallace—a fallacious view which, thanks to a book co-authored by Oliver Stone, has now made its way into popular culture. Lyndon B. Johnson, another master political manipulator, tried to fortify the egalitarianism of the New Deal and entwine it with historic civil rights reform, and his early presidency demands reevaluation in the light of Robert A. Caro's multivolume biography.

The first two chapters, written in a different register from the others, cover the sweep of American political history from different perspectives and bring the threads of egalitarian politics forward from the 1960s to the present. These chapters, in describing the missing keys, also take issue with the current wisdom, both with regard to specific events and personalities and to the framing of the larger issues of partisanship and egalitarianism.

S.W.
January 2016

I.

**TWO KEYS *to*
AMERICAN HISTORY**

1

★ ★ ★ ★ ★ ═══════════

The Postpartisan Style in American Politics

THE AMERICAN DREAM OF POLITICS WITHOUT CONFLICT, and of politics without political parties, has a history as old as American politics. Anyone carried along on the political currents in recent years, however, might be forgiven for thinking that the dream is something new—and for thinking that a transformative era was finally at hand, in which the old politics of intense partisan conflict, based on misunderstanding, miscommunication, and misanthropy, might be curbed if not ended. After the hyper-partisan presidency of George W. Bush, Barack Obama hoped to usher in a new era of postpartisanship. He had arrived on the national stage with his speech at the Democratic National Convention in 2004 proclaiming that there was "not a liberal America and a conservative America—there's the United States of America." As president, Obama would not only reach across the aisle, listen to the Republicans, and credit their good ideas, but also demonstrate that the division between the parties was exaggerated if not false, as many Americans, younger voters above all, fervently believed. Divisive and hot-tempered partisanship would give way to healing and temperate leadership, not least by means of the new president's eloquence, rational policies, and good faith.

Yet after his first year in office, the Gallup poll registered that Obama was the most polarizing president in his first year in its recorded history. After Obama's second year, Gallup found that he was the most polarizing in his second year. The parties were more divided, and partisanship was more ferocious, than ever. Subsequent debates over extending the Bush tax cuts and raising the nation's debt ceiling affirmed and deepened the partisan divide. As his presidency's seventh year began, the partisan division over Obama was roughly as bad as that over George W. Bush's White House after Bush's early popularity imploded.

There are many reasons for this phenomenon, not least the radical transformation of the Republican Party over the last four decades. Clearly, though, the prospect that parties and partisanship would soon be diminished, let alone overcome, has receded. That prospect originated in an intense wishfulness, but it sprang also from unfamiliarity with the origins of this strand of American political history: the politics of postpartisanship, a political style that flourished in different ways under different names at various points in the nineteenth century and dates back to the nation's founding. The rage for a modern postpartisanship has failed to distinguish between sincere if wrongheaded antiparty rhetoric and attacking parties as a partisan ploy— distinct uses of antipartisan politics that have sometimes overlapped. And modern postpartisanship has also ignored the historical reality that partisanship, although often manipulated and abused, has been Americans' most effective vehicle for democratic social and political reform.

★ ★ ★

ANTAGONISM TO POLITICAL PARTIES ran deep in Anglo-American political culture through the era of the American Revolution, yet the prevalence of antiparty ideas before 1800 did not mean that early America was an idyll of impartiality and selflessness. Factional intrigues and battles, fought with sophisticated electioneering techniques, appeared throughout the colonies, most famously in the battles between the Proprietary and Quaker parties during the 1740s and 1750s in Pennsylvania, in which Benjamin Franklin cut his political teeth. In America as in Britain, antiparty statements as often as not amounted to cant—efforts, as the historian Richard Hofstadter described them, by "partisan writers and political leaders who [were] actually appealing to a general distrust of the idea of party" in order to assail their opponents. Such antiparty partisanship motivated Lord Bolingbroke, the great British advocate of antiparty politics in the 1730s. And it lay behind the most important antiparty statement by the most important antipartisan spokesman of the early American republic, even as that statement projected a sincere consensual political ideal.

President George Washington's Farewell Address of 1796 would prove to be a locus classicus of American antiparty thought, but its historical context suggests a more political story. Soon after the new government established by the Federal Constitution gathered in New York in 1789, sharp divisions appeared in Congress, particularly over Treasury Secretary Alexander Hamilton's fiscal proposals. In 1792, James Madison, the head of the congressional opposition, published several anonymous and highly partisan newspaper essays, including "A Candid State of Parties," which cut through antiparty conceits. Two parties were "natural to most political societies," Madison wrote, and two parties now existed in America: an antirepublican party aligned with the rich and influential that controlled national power, and his own opposition party, which represented the great majority but was out of power due to the wealth and stratagems of its opponents. Madison could not tell which party would ultimately prevail, but he was reasonably confident that the conflict would not end anytime soon.

The ensuing four years, strained further by bitter debates over foreign policy, saw the rise and fall of the so-called Democratic Republican societies, followed by the creation of formal party machinery dedicated to electing former secretary of state Thomas Jefferson to the presidency. Beginning in 1795, Washington started dropping hints that he would not accept reelection. He privately informed his anointed successor, Vice President John Adams, of his decision the following March, and by summer Jefferson's supporters had begun gearing up for a tough campaign. But Washington publicly stepped aside only in September, with his Farewell Address. So the great address, coauthored with Alexander Hamilton and commonly viewed as an Olympian statement about uniting in the national cause, was in fact deeply political—"a signal," Fisher Ames, the conservative Federalist leader from Massachusetts, called it, "like dropping a hat, for the party racers to start." It was also the latest highly partisan appeal delivered as an attack on partisanship and on the low demagogues who fomented it. Yet that attack was also genuinely motivated by a patrician ideal of politics without parties.

Washington's address never explicitly mentioned Jefferson or his supporters, but its attack on organized political opposition was plainly directed against them. As if replying to Madison's "Candid State of Parties," Washington stated that parties were not "natural" but "artificial" and intolerable—"of fatal tendency," and wholly illegitimate. Led by "artful and enterprising" men determined to impose despotism atop the ruins of liberty, parties would distract "the constituted authorities" from serenely producing "consistent and wholesome plans digested by common councils and modified by mutual interests." Supporting the Jeffersonian opposition, Washington implied, threatened the republic.

In an organic, well-ordered society, Washington contended, there supposedly existed a natural harmony of interests which, after reasonable deliberation by the delegated authorities, would produce at least an agreeable concord, if not a perfect unanimity, on political matters. "For the mass of our citizens," Washington wrote to the Virginia Federalist John Marshall the year following his address, "require no more than to understand a question to decide it properly." Outside of elections, ordinary citizens ought not to express themselves in any organized manner on the issues of the day, but should instead leave government to the wisdom of their elected governors. "After all," George Cabot, the esteemed Massachusetts Federalist, observed in 1795, "where is the boasted advantage of a representation system . . . if the resort to popular meetings is necessary?" The opposition party's basic aim, supposedly, was to disrupt that tranquil order and create conflicts that would not otherwise occur—or, as the Farewell Address put it, "render alien to each other those who ought to be bound together by fraternal affection." Out of those artificial conflicts, power-hungry demagogues might well crush public liberty and assume dictatorial powers.

Jefferson lost by a whisker in 1796, but his narrow victory in 1800–01 marked a stunning defeat for the organic, antipartisan conception of politics. The antiparty animus did not suddenly evaporate, of course. Jefferson's famous "postpartisan" declaration in his inaugural address—"We are all republicans, we are all federalists"—directly appealed to the old antiparty presumptions. Yet Jefferson's appeal was also a ploy, which he had designed to win over the more moderate Federalists and conquer his opponents by dividing them. The Federalists were not deceived. Some had faith that the besotted electorate would come to its senses after the certain chaos of Jeffersonian rule and restore disinterested patriots such as themselves to power. Other Federalists, though, abandoned the idea that organized politics should cease between elections. "We must consider whether it be possible for us to succeed," Alexander Hamilton observed in 1802, "without, in some degree, employing the weapons which have been employed against us."

During the decade after Jefferson's election, Federalists emulated the Jeffersonians by creating their own caucuses, county and ward committees, benevolent societies, and party newspapers (including, in 1802, Hamilton's own New York *Evening Post*). They also adjusted their rhetoric, embracing some of the majoritarian vocabulary of democratic politics. "We must court popular favor," the Massachusetts Federalist Theodore Sedgwick remarked.

But the Federalists' new majoritarianism simply inverted Jeffersonian rhetoric and rehashed the patrician antipartisan avowal in Washington's Farewell Address. The Jeffersonians' democracy, the Federalists argued, was in fact an aristocracy, imposed on honest farmers, merchants, mechanics, and the rest of the decent majority by self-serving adventurers who stirred up the mob in order to upset the harmonious natural order of things. The worst thing about politics, the Federalists contended, was politicians, described by one New Hampshire newspaper as "*Office-holders, Office-seekers, Pimps . . .* this Host of worse than Egyptian locusts, now preying upon the very Vitals of the public [who] must starve or steal or cheat."

The Federalists sometimes sounded as if they had embraced what Madison had called, in 1792, the cause of the plebeian many against the wealthy and privileged few. But now the Federalists articulated the cause of the many not against wealth and privilege, but against the new class of clever, grubby Jeffersonian politicians. Those politicians and, by extension, democratic politics were the real problem as far as the Federalists were concerned.

Siding with the many compelled some Federalists to drop their high-flown Burkean rhetoric about the swinish multitude in favor of more calibrated attacks on the dregs of society as the politicians' pliable dupes. But the more candid Federalists knew the game that they were playing and said so, at least in private. Some still used the terms "mob" and "people" interchangeably in their correspondence. And Fisher Ames, one of the stiff-necked conservatives who now courted the voters' favor, had little respect for those voters, and viewed them as merely a means to regain power—thereby encouraging, for his own ends, the kind of demagoguery that the Federalists accused the Jeffersonians of deploying. "Their love and hate, their hopes and fears are only to be addressed," Ames told an associate. "Logic is not worth chopping." The Federalists held on to their expectation that, once they had snatched fickle popular favor away from the Jeffersonians, they would return as the nation's natural, disinterested rulers and eliminate sordid, divisive political parties.

★ ★ ★

THE FEDERALISTS NEVER overcame the elitist "monocratic" reputation fixed on them by the Jeffersonians in the 1790s. The collapse of the Federalists after the War of 1812 persuaded Jeffersonians that national unity could now be proclaimed on a truly Republican basis. The shoe was on the other foot—and many Republican leaders now proclaimed that political parties were anathema to American government. "Equally gratifying is it to witness the increased harmony of opinion which pervades our Union," President James Monroe declared at his first inaugural in 1817. Eight years later Monroe's successor, John Quincy Adams, remarked that the country had uprooted the "baneful weed of party strife." The so-called Era of Good Feelings had apparently created precisely the sort of unity that Washington had once proclaimed, but on entirely Jeffersonian and not Federalist terms.

Yet many Jeffersonians suspected that the new harmony was a dangerous delusion. Jefferson himself, who said contradictory things about parties during his presidency as it served his purposes, eventually settled down to the idea that, as he told Lafayette in 1823, "In truth the parties of whig and tory are those of nature." He was dismayed by the policy, initiated by Monroe and continued under Adams, known as "amalgamation," of appointing to positions of responsibility men deemed virtuous and talented regardless of their political views or affiliations. "The common division of whig and tory, or according to our denominations of republican and federal . . . is the most salutary of all divisions," Jefferson wrote to William Short in 1825, "and ought therefore to be fostered, instead of being amalgamated." Not only would clear-cut party lines prevent a stealthy resurgence of Federalism; Jefferson also feared that, were the division between Republican and Federalist to fade, "some more dangerous principle of division will take its place"—above all, it went without saying, sectional division over slavery.

Fostering the division between Republican and Federal—redrawing the old party lines—became the chief object of New York's early machine

politician Martin Van Buren and the neo-Jeffersonians who designed
and built the Jacksonian Democratic Party in the late 1820s. In part,
Van Buren and the Jacksonians wanted to expel the crypto-Federalist
heresies about concentrated financial and political power, which they
believed were creeping back under Monroe and, especially, Adams.
In part, they wanted to stem a precipitous decline in popular interest in elections that had begun after the war, and halt a proliferation
of fierce personal factions, which, Van Buren wrote, had overrun the
country and "moved the bitter waters of political agitation to their
lowest depths." And in part, following the Missouri Compromise
crisis from 1819 to 1821, they wanted to remove issues concerning
slavery and its expansion from national debates in order to silence
what Van Buren called the irresponsible Northern "clamour ag[ains]t
Southern influence and African Slavery" and prevent the rise of parties arrayed on portentous sectional lines.

★ ★ ★

THE JACKSONIANS' DESIGN for a national party—a disciplined,
even quasi-military organization that demanded the subordination
of personal views and interests for the good of the whole—was far
more comprehensive than the Jeffersonians' organizations had been.
With their direct, continuing involvement of ordinary citizens, the
Jacksonians were also more democratic than the Jeffersonians. Still,
there were some remarkable similarities between the Jeffersonian
and Jacksonian parties. The Jeffersonians—the aging Jefferson not
alone among them—at least groped after an idea of a permanent
opposition party as a benefit to themselves as well as the nation. And
the Jacksonians, no less than their predecessors, believed that they
were the leaders of a natural national majority. Above all, the Jacksonian partisan rationale stemmed from their belief that conflict and
not consensus was the natural order of politics. In that conflict, they
insisted, the many needed the party as a political instrument to prevent what Van Buren called "the establishment of a moneyed oligar-

chy, the most selfish and monopolizing of all depositories of political power," as well as to stem sectional strife.

Even more striking than these continuities, though, is how the Jacksonians' various opponents recycled the antiparty, anti-politician arguments of an earlier day. Whig Party spokesmen cited Washington's Farewell Address, and especially its strictures against parties, like holy writ. They singled out Monroe's administration for praise as the nation's "one period of comparative repose . . . when all parties were apparently blended in a common mass." And they attacked the Jacksonians almost exactly as the Federalists had attacked the Jeffersonians—as the progenitors of a new aristocracy of corrupt politicians and officeholders who flattered the masses and, with party patronage, bribed loyalty out of men at every level of society—"from the President to the chiefs of office under him, from them to his subordinates, and from the subordinates to their shoeblacks," one Whig newspaper declared.

Although the Whigs certainly organized to defeat their opponents, and even formed what they called a party, they claimed that there was a great difference between party men and patriots who, one Whig publicist declared, "adopt party organization, and sustain it, not as an *end*, but as a *means* to an end." So, they asserted, they were a postpartisan party. The Jacksonian partisans, by contrast, formed what a resolution by New York's Whigs called "a conspiracy, which seeks to promote the interests of the few at the expense of the many." The many, for the Whigs as for the Federalists, were the honorable, upstanding farmers, merchants, and mechanics. The few, as one Ohio Whig newspaper explained, consisted of "the organized corps of office holders," their judgments subordinated to their political superiors, their livelihoods gained from the perquisites, emoluments, and corruption of their patronage-fueled party tyranny. In place of the selfish few, the Whigs would substitute natural aristocrats whose qualifications were "of the highest order and most arduous attainment," free from the imperative to "express the will of 'the party' whether it be their own individual will or not." As one writer for the Whigs' *American Review* put it, "Intelligence and virtue, must also, as a matter of fact, maintain the controlling interest in spite of universal suffrage."

This elitist tone never completely disappeared from the Whigs' appeals, especially in the circles that wrote for and read the *American Review*. But so long as both their theory and their practice of patrician antipartisan politics dominated, the Whigs would remain, as the New York politico Thurlow Weed remarked in 1834, "doomed to fight merely to be beaten." Weed was one of the younger emerging Whig leaders—and later the boss—of New York state politics who, with his ally William Henry Seward, understood that his party needed to learn the political lessons of the Federalists' failure. And so, in the late 1830s and early 1840s, a more hard-headed cadre of New School Whigs, including Weed, built local, state, and national party organizations that at least approximated the Democratic ones, dropped their air of lofty distinction, and donned and mounted down-home election trappings in the triumphant "Log Cabin" presidential campaign of 1840.

As the Whigs made their peace with partisanship, the antipartisan impetus turned up more empathically elsewhere on the political scene. Northern nativist groups attacked political parties as evil instruments to mobilize alien Catholics for subversion of the republic. Radical abolitionists, led by William Lloyd Garrison and committed to moral suasion instead of political campaigning, berated electoral politics as hopelessly immoral. The abolitionist's duty, the Eastern Pennsylvania Anti-Slavery Society resolved in 1840, was "to convert men of all parties," and "to make abolitionists of partisans, and not partisans of abolitionists." After the Whig Party collapsed due to sectional antagonisms in 1854, nativism briefly flared as a national antiparty party, the Know Nothings, only to be itself overwhelmed by the crisis over slavery. Instead, the antislavery Republican Party—which was very much a political party—became the sectional alternative to the pro-South Democrats. Among its leaders was a consummate partisan politician, the former New School Whig Abraham Lincoln.

A more elaborate version of antiparty politics in the 1830s and

1840s emerged from the opposite pole from Garrisonian abolition-ism. John C. Calhoun had risen to national office by mastering the peculiar political culture of South Carolina, guided by an older, aris-tocratic style of managing personal and intra-state factions. The emer-gence of party Northern "spoilsmen" such as Van Buren—men who allegedly hungered for the spoils of office—disgusted Calhoun. But the rise of the Democratic Party loomed more dangerously in the 1830s and after, when Calhoun turned to defending slavery against what he saw as incendiary Yankee assaults and developed his theory of the concurrent majority. The doctrine, which gave political minorities the authority to thwart the will of national majorities, would foreclose the possibility that a national party could be captured by antislavery Northerners and turned against the South's peculiar institution.

Calhoun's theory turned on his contempt for, and fear of, politi-cal parties and patronage—and Jacksonian democracy. Calhoun sin-gled out the parties as the instruments with which spoilsmen might enhance federal power and especially the power of the executive to attack slavery head on. He also feared that demagogic party leaders would stir up other conflicts that would rip apart the social fabric. The check of a concurrent majority, by allowing the South in effect a veto of federal laws, would stifle party formation and artificial strife, encourage the election of enlightened men to office, and usher in a truly ordered and fraternal republic. "Instead of faction, strife, and struggle," Calhoun wrote, "there would be patriotism, nationality, harmony, and a struggle only for supremacy in promoting the com-mon good of the whole." Washington and Monroe were both slave-holders, but Calhoun had turned their vision of non-partisan unity and good feelings toward a full-blown defense of slavery, in ways that neither Virginian could have imagined, let alone condoned.

★   ★   ★

By 1860, the principled partisanship of the Republican Party, as practiced by Abraham Lincoln, the master party politician, had fully superseded antiparty abolitionism, and it went on to elect Lincoln to the White House. In the South, Calhoun's reformulation of the idea of politics without parties became one of the cornerstones of the Confederate States of America—the most elaborate attempt at consensual, partyless government in our history. The Confederacy chiefly stood, of course, for what its vice president, the former Whig Alexander Hamilton Stephens, called "the great truth that the negro is not equal to the white man; that slavery, subordination to the superior race is his natural and normal condition." But alongside that "great truth," the Confederacy's architects believed that partisanship and party politics were dangerous vices.

The paradoxes were enormous. The South had shared in the national democratic political developments of the 1820s and after, and Southern votes were largely responsible for bringing Andrew Jackson and his party to power. Thereafter, state and local organizations of Democrats and Whigs arose throughout the region. Within the autocratic presumptions of racial slavery, the Southern states produced—for their white male citizenry—some of the most democratic constitutions in the world. "Nowhere in this broad Union but in the slaveholding states," Albert Gallatin Brown, governor of and senator from Mississippi, was able to claim, "is there a living, breathing exemplification of the beautiful sentiment, that all men are equal."

Yet party democracy struck shallower roots in the South than in the North. Calhoun's singular quasi-aristocratic South Carolina, always at the forefront of sectional and disunionist politics, had virtually no political parties along national lines. But even in the more democratic Southern states, partisan operations and loyalties were less robust than in the North. Party organizations arose in the South later than in the North, and they always tended to be more diffuse. A relatively lower number of competitive elections, a relative lack of government patronage jobs, and drastically lower literacy rates inhibited the spread of party machinery, including a partisan press, that were essential to Jacksonian party operations.

Above all, Southern slave society's ideals of honor, community, disinterested virtue, and harmony (especially on the soundness of slavery) coexisted uneasily with the imperatives of partisan politics. In 1850, a typical article in the *Southern Quarterly Review*, contrasting the South and the North, lambasted "the systematic immoralities of political parties, and the utter shamelessness with which they grasp at power, in the teeth of principle." Instead of obedient partisans and their political bosses, Southern spokesmen would elect and appoint gentlemen of independent mind and judgment who would divest themselves of what another writer for the *Review* called "the degrading livery of party."

The Confederate constitutional convention, which met in Montgomery in February 1861, backed the antiparty temper with the force of law. Although the delegates largely copied the federal constitution which they had just spurned, they also made key alterations aimed explicitly at inhibiting parties and partisanship as well as guaranteeing the right to own slaves. Beware "that devil that vexes us—party spirit," a writer for the New Orleans *Daily Picayune* observed as the delegates gathered. The drafters limited the Confederate presidency to a single six-year term with no possibility of reelection, thereby curtailing electioneering as well as democratic accountability. The new constitution also shifted a good deal of the appropriation power from Congress to the president, the better to restrict partisan congressional logrolling as well as extravagance and, as one Georgia newspaper observed, "keep the body politic in a healthy condition." As Robert H. Smith of Alabama (later a Confederate congressman) observed in the single most thoughtful explication of the convention's work, the advent of political parties had ruined the framers' noble system of 1787 and turned the presidency in particular into an instrument "not so much for the wisdom and the good of the people as for the triumph of party." Curbing party domination, Smith argued, would help prevent the Confederacy from degenerating into something "much worse than . . . a pure democracy . . . a mere oligarchy, and that not of intelligence and virtue but of low ambition."

Postpartisan purification, though, bred political torpor in the Confederacy, and, finally, chaos. An Atlanta newspaper mangled Jefferson's inaugural address by declaring that "we are all slaveholders—all Southern states," while it reminded readers, when electing their representatives to the new government, to remember Washington's Farewell Address on the subject of party divisions. Little has been written about those Confederate elections precisely because, absent party organizations and with so much of the voting-age male population in uniform, they were desultory affairs. In a sham election without a campaign or an opposition in November 1861, Southern voters dutifully ratified the provisional government's selection of Jefferson Davis, who had already served as president for ten months, and his sitting vice president, Alexander Stephens. Gubernatorial and state legislature races, as well as the two sets of congressional elections in 1861 and 1863, were marginally livelier, but according to one recent study, they were also badly factionalized, "a crazy quilt of idiosyncratic, almost apolitical contests conducted before a largely apathetic though sometimes angry electorate."

The lack of parties also severely harmed the operation of the Confederate government. With no clear party lines to demarcate friends and adversaries, President Davis had great difficulty in assembling a cabinet that was loyal to him in the least, let alone stable. Due to chronic resignations, the CSA had five secretaries of war, five attorneys general, and four secretaries of state during its brief existence. Although the antiwar Copperheads of the Democratic opposition in the North turned fractious and even treasonous, the War Democrats provided useful though not uncritical help to Lincoln. In the South, by contrast, opposition to Davis had no partisan focus, which led to crises of legitimacy when states rights' purists, led by Georgia's governor Joseph E. Brown and North Carolina's governor Zebulon Vance, refused to comply with directives from Richmond over taxes and conscription.

After Appomattox, Southern apologists turned the disarray of Confederate politics into a ready excuse for the rebellion's defeat. Many ex-Confederates, defending Davis as the hero of the Lost Cause, blamed the disaster on fractious leaders such as Brown and the persistence of divisive partisan habits. Davis's close aide, the unfortunate army commander Braxton Bragg, charged that too many "old, trading politicians and demagogues" (that is, Davis's critics) had occupied themselves by "dividing spoils not yet secured." Yet the enlistment of antipartisanship as an element of the Southern myth of the Lost Cause was not the largest irony in the history of antiparty politics to emerge out of the Civil War.

★ ★ ★

BARELY A DECADE after the Confederacy had put them into practice, the antipartisan principles of Washington's Farewell Address were revived once more—now by upper-class Northern reformers, based largely in the Republican Party. In 1879, an article in the reform-minded *Atlantic Monthly* noted approvingly that the "ultra-democratic" ideas fostered by the partisan Jeffersonians and Jacksonians were suddenly under siege. "When the war closed," the writer observed, "the last class government in the United States had been swept away by the destruction of the slave power, and men found themselves face to face with a pure democracy from one end of the country to another"—a horrifying sight. No serious reform of the nation's ills would occur, Henry Adams wrote in 1876, "until they are attacked at their source; not until the nation is ready to go back to the early practice of the government and to restore to the constitutional organs those powers which have been torn from them by the party organizations for purposes of party aggrandizement."

Beginning late in the 1860s and continuing for the next quarter of a century, these elite reformers formed a loosely knit group that operated under different names: "liberals," "educated men," Liberal Republicans, Mugwumps. Pro-Union Republicans during the war, they gravitated thereafter to a cluster of beliefs identified with classical liberalism. Laissez-faire, including limited government and free trade, headed the list. Deeply alienated by the activist civil rights policies of President Ulysses S. Grant, they led the démarche of respectable Northern opinion away from Reconstruction. While upholding the political claims of the white South, they derided the radical Southern governments as fiscally irresponsible and as—in the words of one of the reformers' premier journals, E. L. Godkin's *The Nation*—"a queer aristocracy of color . . . with the rich Congo thief on top and the degraded Anglo-Saxon on the bottom."

Professing disgust at the scandals of the Grant years, real, imagined, and exaggerated, the genteel liberals seized upon corruption and spoilsmanship as the cardinal sins of the age, and pushed hard for civil service reform. They feared that the resumption and then the growth of mass immigration would strengthen party rule and what *The Nation* called "the severance of political power from intelligence and property." But the anti-immigration effort achieved little, and so Northern reformers' efforts to restrict party politics and government became all the more pressing.

Some extreme antiparty liberals, such as the New York lawyer Albert Stickney, a friend of Henry Adams, dwelled in a political netherworld and called for the extirpation of political parties. More practical reformers attacked only what one of them, R. R. Bowker, called "the abuse of organization, which is stigmatized as 'the machine.'" The chief rationale for such abuse was the hateful concept of strict party loyalty and obeisance to party leaders that had been fundamental to political partisanship since the Jacksonian period. "A reform movement cannot succeed which starts off under the auspices of trading politicians," said the Democrat-turned-antislavery-Republican-turned-Liberal Republican Lyman Trumbull in 1872.

Early efforts by reformers to break with orthodoxy and run their own candidates against the party regulars and bosses enjoyed some local successes, but they ended poorly nationwide with Horace Greeley's disastrous Liberal Republican campaign against Grant in 1872. Thereafter the reformers carved out a stance of what they called "independency" within the major parties, applying pressure and establishing themselves as the vital balance of power in politics and government. Henry Adams called them a "party of the centre."

The independents scored what looked like their greatest triumph in national electoral politics in 1884, when defections of the so-called Mugwumps from the Republicans' presidential candidate, the spoils-man James G. Blaine, appeared to tip the election in favor of the conservative Democrat, Grover Cleveland. But Mugwumpery would prove to be the zenith of independent liberalism. By the mid-1890s, the reform impulses that had arisen during the postwar era had slowed, in part because of the acceptance of some of their ideas (in civil service, currency, and ballot reform), in part because of their fail-ures (in immigration restriction, proportional representation, and tar-iff reform). Although powerful concerns about parties and the purity of government persisted, especially in the states, national politics focused increasingly on the bewildering dynamics and injustices of a new industrial era, highlighted by the rise and fall of movements such as the Knights of Labor and the People's (or Populist) Party. The first national party leader of a fresh wave of reformism, Theodore Roo-sevelt, came out of the ranks of elite liberal reform in New York City, but by the time he reached the White House, he had made peace with more conventional forms of partisanship.

In 1884, as a young New York assemblyman, Roosevelt fought James G. Blaine's nomination but stuck with Blaine and his party in the general election, believing that high-minded indifference to party loyalty (he would write soon after) was "not only fantastic but abso-lutely wrong." He would later call the Mugwumps dangerous elitists who "distrusted the average citizen and shuddered over the 'coarseness' of the professional politicians." Roosevelt also rejected the laissez-faire dogma of the liberals, looking back for inspiration to the democratic nationalism of the Lincoln and Grant era.

Both before and during his presidency, Roosevelt would press for major reforms regulating the new industrial economy, including many that disturbed his more conservative fellow Republicans, in line with what he called "social efficiency." In pursuit of those reforms, he appealed not to antiparty ideals of "pure democracy" but to the exercise of presidential might. And to gain power and preserve it, he would strike and sustain the requisite alliances with party chieftains— becoming, in the White House, the greatest chieftain of all, controlling state party organizations all around the country.

Yet if the elite liberal reformers failed to uproot or even reshape the political parties they so despised, they still had an enormous impact—not simply on the course of antipartisan politics, but on the place of those politics in American life. Driven by severe class anxieties, incapable in the North of formally excluding the poor and the uneducated from politics, they aimed instead to change other rules of the political game. By founding various independent clubs and quasi-learned societies, they sought to educate the electorate properly. Instead of denouncing parties outright, the elite liberals, with their political style of "independency," appeared to be inside the parties but also above politics. The independent style rejected the old party flim-flam—including a stridently partisan press—in favor of a cooler, more detached politics, free of the old emotional partisanship. It was spiritually more akin to scientific enterprise, or even to one of the new corporate bureaucracies, than to the old parties of saloon assemblies and crossroads stump speeches. "The voters have been reading, not shouting," the reformist *Minneapolis Journal* claimed, hopefully, in 1892, "but their ballots will be just as numerous and far more intelligent in the aggregate." These high-minded politics, a new form of antipartisanship, would long outlast the liberal reform crusades of the Gilded Age.

★   ★   ★

THE BROAD TRENDS and developments in the history of antipartisan politics over the last century show how persistent those politics have been, and how they continue to affect us today. The wholesale attacks on the party system during the Progressive Era, often made in the name of "direct democracy," are staple subjects in the history of American politics. Efforts to weaken the party system gained popular support for reforms including direct election of senators and primary contests as supplements to party conventions, as well as initiative, referendum, recall, and other methods of "pure" democracy. Partisan newspapers fell into disfavor, displaced by a self-consciously independent and "objective" press, and by muckraking journalists commissioned by national magazines appealing to a new urban middle class.

The flood tide of the renewed antiparty politics was the Progressive Party campaign of 1912, in which an embittered and schismatic Theodore Roosevelt ran for president. In the historian Barry Karl's words, the campaign was "as much an attack on the whole concept of political parties as it was an effort to create a single party whose doctrinal clarity and moral purity would represent the true interest of the nation as a whole." "We hold with Thomas Jefferson and Abraham Lincoln," the Progressives' platform declared, "that the people are the masters of their Constitution."

That the antiparty Progressive Party—the political party to end all political parties—would invoke one of the chief inventors of the first American political party along with perhaps the craftiest and most complete of all nineteenth-century American party politicians was one of the movement's smaller, if more amusing, historical ironies. The greatest irony, of course, was that Roosevelt, who had run in 1904 as a thoroughgoing party politician, had, in his anger at his hand-picked successor William Howard Taft's supposed betrayal of reformism, transformed himself into his opposing image in an attempt to wrest back power.

Successful though the Progressive movement was in gaining some notable reforms intended to diminish political parties, the two chief instruments for change—Theodore Roosevelt and Woodrow Wilson—were practiced party politicians who also believed strongly in the exercise of presidential power, as leaders of their parties as well as of the nation. Roosevelt's unsuccessful third-party candidacy in 1912 ironically corroborated his more considered party alignments. By permanently damaging Roosevelt's standing with Republican regulars, and thereby foreclosing his renomination and likely reelection in 1916, his Bull Moose adventure helped cede the GOP to laissez-faire pro-business conservatives—Republicans whose policies, in the Coolidge era, laid the groundwork for the Great Depression.

It would take a Democrat whom Roosevelt despised, President Woodrow Wilson, to secure some of the reforms advanced by the Bull Moose Progressives in 1912, including votes for women, the establishment of a federal income tax, and laws that the national labor leader Samuel Gompers described as a "Magna Carta" for working people. Wilson, who became an equally skillful partisan politician, began as a theorist as well as a practitioner of what became known as "responsible" party politics and government. He in time recognized what he called "the extraordinary part political parties have made in making a national life." Efforts to provide local "non-partisan" government, he remarked, "always in the long run fail."

Progressivism had run its course by 1919, when Wilson's campaign for American entry into the League of Nations crashed and burned. Yet the president who most thoroughly embodied the Progressive movement's values of efficiency and expertise—and its distrust of partisanship—reached office a decade later. I am referring to Herbert Hoover, who was considered the most qualified man of the age not least because he was seen as above party. He came to public life after a career as a professional mining engineer, writer, and translator, and owed virtually nothing to party politics, having risen to prominence as secretary of commerce under Harding and Coolidge. His chief devotion was to the so-called Efficiency Movement, which held that nonpartisan professional experts were best positioned to eliminate the epidemic of waste and fraud that was ruining American government and business. His election as a Republican was heralded as the transcendence of bad partisan politics and celebrated as the beginning of a golden age of permanent prosperity. That, of course, was not to be—and as one of his most thoughtful biographers, Joan Hoff Wilson, has noted, "he did not really become a regular party man until after he was no longer president," which is when he became the indelible symbol of old guard Republican Party dogmatism.

Franklin Delano Roosevelt, of course, was an attentive, rigorous, and skilled party leader, strongly influenced by Wilson's presidency, especially by his failures in politics and policy. He was perfectly at home with James A. Farley, the quintessential machine pol whom he appointed postmaster general and chairman of the Democratic National Committee, as he was with Rexford Tugwell, the Columbia University professor who exemplified the bright young men he recruited into his Brains Trust. Even before he reached the White House, FDR had won the affection of his fellow New York Democrats for his ability to excel at party politics and carry the entire party with him come election day. One Brooklyn district leader, Hymie Schorenstein, explained to local government candidates why he was sending his political funds to Roosevelt, who was running for governor, rather than to those lower down on the ticket. Had they ever seen the Staten Island Ferry sliding into its slip, never alone but dragging in "all the crap in the harbor behind it"? Then Schorenstein paused for his punch line: "FDR is our Staten Island Ferry."

Franklin Roosevelt did attempt to remake the Democratic Party into a bastion of what he called "militant liberalism," even as his expansion of executive administration redefined party loyalty. His famous effort to purge the party of its hidebound conservatives, particularly in the Jim Crow South, which began in earnest in 1938, was an all-out attack on certain retrograde party structures. So was his shift in patronage preferences away from the regular party organization overseen by Farley and toward New Dealers in the executive headed by White House aide Thomas Corcoran. While FDR succeeded in some anti-conservative reforms, the purge largely failed. The Democratic Party emerged as a new coalition of an expanded liberal base, including organized labor, blacks, Jews, and women's rights advocates, alongside segregationist Southern Democrats who remained a powerful force in the party's counsels. The Southerners formed their own coalition with conservative Republicans out of the disastrous midterm elections of 1938 to block much reform until 1964. Still, Roosevelt's intention was not to destroy his party, or party government, but to sharpen the ideological divide. Something like that sharpening would eventually occur in the 1960s, although it would bring political results very different from those Roosevelt had expected.

The New Deal party coalition remained so powerful for so long that it appeared to have led to a new bipartisan consensus in the 1950s—to an end of ideology. President Eisenhower's "modern Republicanism," with its acceptance of many New Deal programs and ideas as well as internationalist foreign policy views, encouraged the presumption that the nation had entered an age of consensus, a new Era of Good Feelings. Yet bubbling just beneath the calm, and sometimes breaking the surface, were the turbulent political elements that would define the 1960s: the civil rights movement, first and foremost, but also sharp reactions against both modern Republicanism and civil rights reform, ranging from the Dixiecrat revolt of segregationist Democrats in 1948 to the right-wing anti-Communist crusades associated with Senator Joseph McCarthy—the reactions that would in time produce the presidential candidacy of Barry Goldwater and a coup within the GOP by its most conservative forces.

The turbulence of the 1960s and early 1970s did not destroy the political parties, but it did shatter the parties as the nation had come to know them. John F. Kennedy, like Lyndon B. Johnson, was hardly a nonpartisan or antipartisan president, despite his touting of the "best and the brightest." But Kennedy's—and then, more expansively, Johnson's—embrace of civil rights sent an already discontented conservative white South firmly into the Republican Party, where it eventually turned the party into a Southern-controlled organization not completely unlike the Democratic Party of the 1850s. Johnson's escalation of the Vietnam War opened divisions inside the Democratic Party, not just between hawks and doves but also between party regulars and so-called New Politics reformers, who echoed in some ways the affluent antiparty reformers of a century earlier.

Those splits helped to elect Richard M. Nixon president in 1968—a figure of partisanship above principle. After a moment of posing as an American Disraeli, Nixon set about trying to get not just his party but the government to stand behind what he called the "New American Majority" or the "Silent Majority," exploiting racial turmoil and resentments, consolidating the revived Dixiecrat constituency of George C. Wallace, and concentrating power in the executive as never before with a strident political agenda. Now the leader of the Republican Party, he attempted to remake the party in his own image and under his iron control. Watergate—the pursuit of Nixonian partisanship by any means necessary—destroyed Nixon, and with him his meta-partisan plan; it also blew a hole in the center of the Republican Party, which finally allowed the party's Goldwater wing to recapture control of the GOP once and for all, under the aegis of Ronald Reagan.

The Democrats, pushed by their New Politics reformers, reacted to the debacle of 1968 by revising their rules and shifting power over presidential nominations away from party bosses and toward voters in presidential primaries. Then, in response to Nixon's crimes, the Democrats selected for the presidency an idealistic but detail-oriented engineer in the Southern antiparty Progressive tradition. Jimmy Carter promoted himself as a moral man who would never lie, would end politics as usual, and would rely on brains, virtue, and talent: "Why Not the Best?" He was, in a way, the Democrats' version of the Progressive ideal, their own Hoover, although the similarities never crossed their minds.

Carter's travails paved the way for Reagan's admixture of a conventionally partisan, ideologically extreme, and peculiarly pragmatic administration that unevenly advanced the new conservatives' quest to push the sum and substance of government far to the right. Democrats countered by flailing about for a decade, first attempting to revive the spirit of New Deal liberalism with Walter Mondale, Carter's vice president, carrying the burden of the distant and recently rejected past, then returning to neo-Progressive expertise with Michael Dukakis, who in his most famous statement declared: "This election isn't about ideology. It's about competence." Eventually the Democrats found success with Bill Clinton, a new sort of partisan Democrat who tried to rebuild the party and relieve it of its accumulated political handicaps, from isolationism in foreign policy to knee-jerk defensive reactions to any criticisms of what had become the nation's welfare state.

Since 1980, there have been three important third-party campaigns in the antiparty tradition: the moderate Republican John B. Anderson's run in 1980, perceived as a high-minded moderate option for Republicans alienated by Reagan conservatism and liberals offended by what they saw as Carter's creeping conservatism; the eccentric entrepreneur Ross Perot's self-funded campaign in 1992, pitched as the chance to substitute a hard-headed, commonsensical private citizen in place of the corrupt politicians; and the modern muckraker Ralph Nader's left-wing anticorporate Green Party campaign in 2000, dedicated to the proposition that there was not a dime's bit of difference between the Democrats and the Republicans, between Al Gore and George W. Bush. All these candidacies supposedly heralded yet another fresh start for American politics after the events of the late 1960s and 1970s had loosened voters' attachments to the major parties: an era—the term was now gaining currency—of postpartisanship. In all three cases, antiparty candidacies did nothing to prevent the election of partisan administrations, including the radically partisan White House of the younger Bush. Indeed, Nader's run ensured Bush's presidency.

★   ★   ★

THE YOUNGER BUSH'S PRESIDENCY brought its own postpartisan ironies, although in retrospect they were superficial. Bush ran in

2000 on the theme of "compassionate conservatism" and promised to be "a uniter, not a divider"—building on his father's pledge of "a kinder, gentler" America while trying to blame the acidic partisanship of the Newt Gingrich–Tom DeLay Republicans on both political parties. He said that he would change the tone in Washington. It was a transparent campaign tactic, although the Democrats did a poor job of saying as much. From the start, Bush's administration was marked by efforts to use events, not least the terrorist attacks of September 11, to forge what Bush's political "architect" Karl Rove believed would be a permanent Republican Party majority, the fulfillment of Nixon's partisan dream.

It should have come as no surprise that after eight years of George Bush (much as after almost six years of Nixon), American voters would be receptive to antipartisan or postpartisan appeals, from a fresh, articulate Democrat untouched by recent conflicts, who said he wanted to put aside divisive rhetoric and divided government, a Democrat even willing to say admiring things about Ronald Reagan as a "transformative" president. Commentators naturally focused on the postracial aspects of Barack Obama's successful candidacy, and how, as the candidate himself put it, he "doesn't look like all those other presidents on the dollar bills." Yet Obama broke the mold in another crucial way: he became one of the only presidents in modern times— Jimmy Carter being the other outstanding example—who explicitly and sincerely ran for office promising not simply to unite the country but to transcend partisanship, substituting a spirit of thoughtfulness, expertise, and integrity above party and politics.

Obama's postpartisanship had great strategic and tactical advantages, in helping him to secure his party's nomination and then running against the partisan impasse of the previous eight years. And in his first term, he managed, against monolithic Republican opposition, to win an economic stimulus to help offset the financial disaster of 2008, as well as historic health care reform and major reform of financial regulation. Yet as he would show repeatedly in his first term, culminating in his doomed efforts to reach a "grand bargain" with congressional Republicans over fiscal issues, Obama also believed in the postpartisan idea, much as his most fervent supporters saw in him the idea's embodiment, a break with the corrupt party-driven politics of the past. The mirage seemed finally to lift following Obama's reelection in 2012. By 2015, after resurgent and unapologetically obstructionist Republicans had recaptured control of the Senate, Obama had mostly scuttled the postpartisan illusion. He bypassed Congress to advance various policies, including immigration reform, through executive order. In his 2015 State of the Union address, he presented a strong and even defiant agenda for liberal government.

As it happens, though, the postpartisanship trumpeted in 2008 and 2009 and pursued thereafter was nothing new. It was an updated variation of a very old theme in American politics—a theme, with the endless fascination of our political history, that connects George Washington to E. L. Godkin, John Adams's Federalists to Grover Cleveland's Mugwumps, James Monroe to John Quincy Adams, and Adams to his grandson Henry Adams—and strangely enough, all of these figures to the Confederate fire-eaters as well as, for a time, to the first African American president. What those earlier leaders, parties, and factions shared—in marked contrast to Thomas Jefferson, Andrew Jackson, Abraham Lincoln, Theodore Roosevelt (before and after 1912), Woodrow Wilson, Franklin D. Roosevelt, John F. Kennedy, Lyndon B. Johnson, Richard M. Nixon, Ronald Reagan, and Bill Clinton—was an antipathy to partisanship. It was an antipathy that failed to prevent the rise of parties or to dislodge them from what became their central place in American political life.

More important, that antipathy invariably ensured ultimate political defeat and even catastrophe, no matter whether the cause being advanced came from the right or the left. The antiparty current is by definition antidemocratic, as political parties have been the only reliable electoral vehicles for advancing the ideas and interests of ordinary voters. Every era of fundamental reform in our history, from the

Jeffersonian Democracy of the early nineteenth century through the triumph of the Lincoln Republicans, the Square Deal of TR and the New Deal of FDR, on to the Great Society of Lyndon Johnson to the counterreformation of the age of Ronald Reagan, has involved partisan politicians advancing basic and far-reaching political principles. The Tea Party activists who emerged in 2010, for all their proclaimed alienation from both major parties, understood this from the start: they did not whine about the evils of partisanship, they worked on it and, with great success, used the party system to advance their hard-right agenda as a wing of the Republican Party.

Whenever political leaders have presumed that their expertise and their background make them special repositories of wisdom above the wheeling and dealing and "spoilsmanship" of democratic politics, the result has been a fatal disconnection between themselves and the citizenry. And not just the citizenry—for without the trust and continuing cooperation born of strong party loyalties, it has been impossible for presidents to work closely with Congress to enact legislation, or to construct an effective executive branch.

President Kennedy is sometimes cited as an antipartisan who held party hacks in disdain—or so a few writers and historians such as the late James MacGregor Burns persuaded themselves. But Kennedy relished being his party's chieftain, and astutely understood the imperatives of party and party leadership, which he explained as well as anyone has. "No president, it seems to me, can escape politics," Kennedy observed in 1960, as he began his quest for the Democratic presidential nomination. "He has not only been chosen by the nation—he has been chosen by his party. And if he insists that he is 'president of all the people' and should, therefore, offend none of them—if he blurs the issues and differences between the parties—if he neglects the party machinery and avoids his party's leadership—then he has not only weakened the political party as an instrument of the democratic process—he has dealt a blow to the democratic process itself." Kennedy went on to say that he preferred the example of Abraham Lincoln, "who loved politics with the passion of a born practitioner."

What has distinguished Obama, like Carter, is that he has operated in an era in which, paradoxically, party ties among the voters have supposedly weakened but the parties themselves have become bitterly ideological. Carter became president in an earlier part of this cycle, which has become more intensely polarized under Obama than ever before. But as contentious as the current tone and substance of our politics has become, the oasis of postpartisanship, by whatever name you choose to call it, has proven to be as much a mirage today as it has ever been. The mirage persists in some high-minded circles, where it remains fashionable, as Theodore Roosevelt put it, to revile "the 'coarseness' of professional politicians." But the beautiful dreamers of this generation, who yearn for an American politics without partisanship, have proven and will prove no more successful than those of all the generations that have gone before. The longer they persist, the more they will damage their greatest political hopes.

2

★ ★ ★ ★ ★ ═══════════

America's Forgotten Egalitarian Tradition

IN THE UNITED STATES, DEMOCRATIC POLITICS HAS BAT-tled against two sets of inequalities, distinct but closely related. One set arises from the bigoted exclusion and subjugation of racial minorities, women, and other stigmatized groups, the other from economic inequality and the privilege exercised by a plutocratic few. American politics after the 1960s revolved in part around the first of these, framed as battles about rights, in conflicts over racial equality, sexual equality, matrimonial equality, and more. For several decades, though, beginning in the 1970s, economic inequality, however sorely felt by ordinary Americans, passed virtually unnoticed in our national politics. To judge from public debates, most Americans found nothing unjust or politically dangerous about staggering and surging disparities of wealth, so long as every citizen had even a slim chance to prosper.

The financial crisis of 2008, the worst since the Great Depression, along with the continuing battles over the Affordable Care Act of 2010—the most comprehensive piece of national social legislation since the 1960s—revived controversy over economic inequality. Leading Democrats, from President Barack Obama on down, denounced the fraying of the New Deal and Great Society social compact and the creation, in Obama's words, of "an economy that's become profoundly unequal." But Republicans, too, after they failed to prevent Obama's reelection, began lamenting economic inequality, which, unsurprisingly, they blamed on Obama's policies.

For Republicans as well as Democrats to speak this way marked a large shift in political perceptions. In one national opinion poll taken in mid-2015, two-thirds of the respondents agreed that the distribution of money and wealth in America ought to be more even. Whether this view would last was difficult to know. But the focus on economic inequality did beg questions about why the issue had long been absent—for, as it happened, that absence was highly abnormal. The revival of arguments over economic inequality was just that, a revival, bringing back into public debate matters once at the core of American politics. By fits and starts, Americans had begun recovering an egalitarian tradition that dated back to the eighteenth century.

★   ★   ★

AT THE NATION'S FOUNDING, most Americans agreed that misdistribution of wealth could wreck their experiment in republican government. In a letter to his friend James Madison in 1785, Thomas Jefferson famously decried the "numberless instances of wretchedness" that stemmed from gross inequalities of property. Jefferson recognized that "an equal division of property is impracticable." He objected, on another occasion, to taking property arbitrarily from well-off men, or the sons of well-off men, and giving it to others who had "not exercised equal industry or skill." Nevertheless, Jefferson observed, "enormous inequality" produced "much misery to the bulk of mankind"—so much misery that "legislators cannot invent too many devices for subdividing property, only taking care to let their subdivisions go hand in hand with the natural affections of the human mind."

Jefferson's sometime ally and sometime antagonist, the conservative-minded John Adams of Massachusetts, broadly agreed, and noted that concentrations of landed wealth in the hands of the few ultimately bred tyranny over the many. "The balance of power in a society," Adams wrote in 1776, "accompanies the balance of property in land." Only by making "the acquisition of land easy to every member of society . . . so that the multitude may be possessed of landed estates," could power be secured "on the side of equal liberty and public virtue."

Similar formulations appeared throughout the infant republic, cutting across lines of party, region, and ideology. Noah Webster of Connecticut, writing in staunch support of the new Federal Constitution in 1787, claimed that "a general and tolerably equal distribution of landed property is the whole basis of national freedom," and "the very *soul of a republic*." One year later, a Virginian writing under the pseudonym "The Impartial Examiner" attacked the proposed constitution precisely because, he contended, it would enable "a few men— or one—more powerful than all others," to "obtain all authority, and by means of great wealth." The wealthy would thereby have the means "perhaps totally [to] subvert the government, and erect a system of aristocratic or monarchic tyranny in its room [that is, in its place]."

There were, of course, exceptions—political thinkers and leaders who asserted that great economic inequalities between the few and the many were inevitable and even, some said, desirable. In general, however, Americans of otherwise clashing political beliefs agreed with the pseudonymous New Jersey writer Eumenes that, in a republic, "there should, as much as possible, be . . . something like an equality of estate and property."

This egalitarianism originated in the eighteenth-century antimonarchial politics that culminated in the Revolution. These politics reflected a largely rural world where most wealth was produced directly, on farms and plantations and in artisan workshops, and where even urban mercantile wealth was expressly personal, based on long-standing relationships. The politics contained two powerful and connected assumptions: first, that human labor is the creator of all wealth; and second, that social and economic disorders are the consequence, and not the cause, of political disorder, and therefore require political reforms. As these assumptions are largely alien to modern readers, it can be difficult to discern let alone comprehend the original American egalitarian tradition.

The doctrine that the value of all property is determined by and owed to the human labor that created it—known to historians and political economists as the labor theory of value, or, more precisely, the labor theory of property—claimed an enormous array of supporters from the early national era down to the Civil War. The concept lay at the core of John Locke's theory of property, as stated in the second of his *Two Treatises on Government*. Diverse Enlightenment writers including David Hume, Adam Smith, and the Comte de Volney took the idea for granted. So did American political agitators and public officials ranging from Samuel Adams and John Rutledge in (respectively) revolutionary Massachusetts and South Carolina to Andrew Jackson, John C. Calhoun, and Abraham Lincoln.

A major reason for the theory's ubiquity was an ambiguity that could render it at once oppressively hierarchical and profoundly egalitarian. At one level, the labor theory drew distinctions that barred dependent persons from claiming the fruits of their labor as their own. Locke, for example, formulated the theory in ways that permitted, indeed encouraged, the subjugation of a variety of "nonproductive" persons, be they nomadic hunters and gatherers or dependent African slaves. American slaveholders—their property in human beings fully legitimate in all thirteen rebel colonies in 1776—assumed that, as black slaves were themselves property, so their white masters owned the full product of their labor. Slaveholders and non-slaveholders alike discounted the labor of other bound workers, including indentured servants, as well as the labor of wives and children, subsuming and attaching the wealth created by their dependents' labor to themselves. To the vast majority of settlers, the hunting and fishing economies of the Native Americans plundered resources but produced nothing.

On the other hand, the labor theory accorded all free citizens property rights that arose, as the Pennsylvanian George Logan observed in 1791, "from the labor we have bestowed acquiring [it]." America thus seemed, to the free white men who settled and resided there, a place that could sustain unprecedented general prosperity. Because the vast preponderance of American wealth came from the land, because American land was plentiful, and because (compared to the Old World) ownership of the land was widely distributed, it followed that America would escape the inequities of past civilizations. Of course, all would not be perfectly equal, even among the freeborn. Equal rights to obtain property did not translate into the kind of radical equality of property that Jefferson thought "impractical" and that later genera- tions would call "agrarianism." Some citizens, by dint of extraordinary labor, rare skills, or good fortune, would always obtain more property than others. The lazy, unskilled, or unfortunate would obtain less. But nature placed limits on what the land could produce, and so there were natural limits on how far the wealthiest free citizen could rise above the poorest. A visionary ideal took hold of a nation where liberty was secure, "so long as Property . . ."—meaning land, Ezra Stiles wrote to Thomas Jefferson in 1786—"is so minutely partitioned and transfused among the Inhabitants."

The available historical statistics on American inequality, to be sure, depict a very different reality, quite apart from slavery and the conquest of Indians' lands. On the eve of the Revolution, according to the findings of Alice Hanson Jones, as reported and updated by Jeffrey G. Williamson and Peter H. Lindert, the richest 1 percent of free Americans held slightly more than 10 percent of the nation- to-be's wealth, while the richest 10 percent owned roughly half of that wealth. But these figures need to be understood in their larger context. Compared to later periods in American history—and com- pared to Great Britain and Europe in the 1770s—the degree of eco- nomic inequality among non-slaves in Revolutionary America was remarkably low. Local studies of the colonial era strongly suggest that American inequality worsened dramatically only just prior to the

Revolution—a worsening that Americans blamed on what the historian John M. Murrin has called the "Anglicization" of colonial society during the two decades before 1776.

Free Americans did not live in the classless utopia described by some patriots and some astonished foreign visitors, but they could easily consider America the closest thing in history to such a utopia, so long as they deemed dark-skinned slaves and Indians inferior castes outside society. Even Thomas Paine, an antislavery man, could write in 1782 that "[t]here are not three millions of people in any part of the universe, who live so well, or have such a fund of ability, as in America." In this providential setting, Americans interpreted rising inequality among freemen as a by-product of artificial political manipulations by the British and their American allies, as well as of the persistence in the New World of certain repugnant Old World institutions.

Here, American views on labor and equality conjoined with another conceptual distinction common in eighteenth-century Anglo-American political thought, between society and government. On this view, social relations, including trade and commerce, were wholly natural, and they tended strongly, especially in America, to promote equality. Gross inequality, it followed, was unnatural, the product of laws and customs imposed on society by government, by which they meant hereditary monarchy and aristocracy. To American patriots, one historian observes, commenting on Paine, "[t]he cause of . . . wretchedness" was "political, not economic," while "the existence of poverty"—the most glaring indication of economic inequality— implied that, in Paine's words, "something must be wrong in the system of government."

This explosive mixture of the Lockean labor theory of value and anti-aristocratic politics propelled the American radical and reformist movements of the second half of the eighteenth century and the early decades of the nineteenth, beginning with the movement for independence. The idea that the British fed off the sacrifices and labor of their productive colonial subjects cropped up all across Revolutionary

America, notably in Jefferson's *Summary View of the Rights of British America* in 1774: "America was conquered, and her settlements made, and firmly established, at the expence [sic] of individuals and not of the British public," Jefferson wrote, ". . . and for themselves alone they have a right to hold." The same egalitarian impulse also led Americans to repudiate some of what they considered the most egregious of their own traditional and inherited political and legal arrangements, not least the laws of entail and primogeniture. By abolishing these practices, Jefferson boasted, Americans "laid the axe to the root of Pseudo-aristocracy."

The Revolution, above and beyond securing American independence, meant throwing off the heavy weight of exploitative privilege, deference, and dependence which characterized monarchy and aristocracy. Whereas monarchists, the patriots endlessly charged, lived in idle luxury off the labor of others, to be the citizen of a republic came to mean being engaged in productive labor, geared toward sustaining a world of "mediocrity," by which they meant a middling, egalitarian society without extremes of wealth and poverty. "Monarchy," the Connecticut pamphleteer, orator, and political leader Abraham Bishop wrote in the Revolution's aftermath, "delights in taking from the great body of labouring people their rank in being, by making the idle few so wealthy and powerful, as to sink mediocrity into contempt." A republic, by contrast, was associated with "the industrious part of the community," what the unschooled Massachusetts farmer William Manning called the great mass of citizens, those "that Labour for a Living."

★   ★   ★

LIKE ALL MODERN REVOLUTIONARIES, the American patriots came to blows quickly after they won their revolution. Those battles, first between supporters and opponents of the federal Constitution, then between Federalists and the supporters of Thomas Jefferson (also known as Republicans or Democratic-Republicans), led to the greatest struggles over the egalitarian tradition prior to the Civil

War—struggles that, like the Revolution itself, entailed fundamental questions about how society ought to be organized.

Contrary to most of the other American revolutionaries, the Federalist Alexander Hamilton, the new nation's first secretary of the treasury, understood inequality neither as an artificial political imposition nor as something to be feared. He saw it as an ineluctable fact—"the great and fundamental distinction in society," he declared in 1787, which "would exist as long as liberty existed" and "would unavoidably result from that very liberty itself."

Hamilton's program of national debt assumption and a national bank aimed to turn inevitable inequality toward national prosperity and greatness by raising a powerful moneyed interest. Hamilton saw agrarian America as deplorably and even perilously underdeveloped, its financial credibility strained, its sense of national unity stunted, and its armed defenses deficient. By attaching the purses (and thus the loyalties) of the moneyed few firmly to the federal government, he believed, their wealth would be channeled toward enlarging the new government's financial and military capacities, thereby creating an innovative, dynamic, truly strong and united America.

It was a matter not simply of favoring wealthy Americans but of augmenting particular forms of wealth that aligned with national power. In Hamilton's view, the mass of wealth in Revolutionary America consisted of things that were difficult to move, difficult to manage, and costly to maintain, whatever the prestige attached to them: land and livestock, products of the land (as well as rents), and, especially in the South, human beings owned as chattel. The moneyed interest stood apart, its wealth derived from long-distance trade, financial dealings, and speculative investments, at once more expansive and more flexible than landed wealth. Crucially, this moneyed wealth rested on properties, particularly the debts of the federal government, whose very reality depended on the legal guarantees of the fledgling national government. If properly managed, the moneyed interest, unlike the landed or mercantile interests, would be tied ineluctably to the emerging American nation-state.

Jeffersonians (and even some Federalists, like John Adams) were shocked. To them, Hamilton's proposals represented not a bold new departure but a reversion to corrupt, artificial, state-centered, quasi-aristocratic favoritism. The offense, they charged, lay not simply in worsening inequality but in creating a moneyed inequality in partnership with the national government—a partnership in which the moneyed interest, separate from and unaccountable to the great body of the citizenry, was both the beneficiary and the corrupting agent. In 1788, during the debates over the ratification of the Constitution, James Madison observed that political instability gave an "unreasonable advantage . . . to the sagacious, the enterprising, and the moneyed few over the industrious and uninformed mass of the people." Four years later, standing in opposition to Hamilton's policies, he criticized worsening "the inequality of property, by an immoderate, and especially an unmerited, accumulation of riches," and commended "the silent operation of laws which, without violating the rights of property, reduce extreme wealth towards a state of mediocrity, and raise extreme indigence toward a state of comfort."

Looking back thirty years later, Thomas Jefferson regarded his Federalist opponents as a privileged few who favored—some more, some less—the oppressive doctrines of Great Britain and the rest of the Old World:

[T]o constrain the brute force of the people, they deem it necessary to keep them down by hard labor, poverty and ignorance, and to take from them, as from bees, so much of their earnings, as that unremitting labor shall be necessary to obtain a sufficient surplus barely to sustain a scanty and miserable life. And these earnings they apply to maintain their privileged orders in splendor and idleness, to fascinate the eyes of the people, and excite in them an humble adoration and submission, as to an order of superior beings.

Against these oppressions and "the inequalities they produced," Jefferson wrote, the Democratic-Republican opposition "believed that men, enjoying in ease and security the full fruits of their own industry, enlisted by all their interests on the side of law and order, habituated to think for themselves, and to follow their reason as their guide, would be more easily and safely governed, than with minds nourished in error."

The division, it needs emphasizing, was not over agrarian stasis versus commercial growth but over clashing agendas for economic innovation and expansion, connected to clashing ideas about government. Had the Jeffersonians failed to win the Congress, and Jefferson the presidency, in 1800–1801—and had Hamiltonian Federalism carried the day—a federal government responsive to moneyed creditors would have overseen national economic development. A more speculative, centralized, top-down American economy would have been founded on the immediate interests (and to the peculiar profit) of a national financial and mercantile elite. In power, the Jeffersonians pursued a very different vision. They opposed neither commerce nor banking, but sought to promote a more egalitarian form of market economy, based on the dispersion of wealth across the general population of farmers, artisans, and shopkeepers, rather than its concentration among a moneyed few. Their goal was to foster local power centers that would then take an equal place at the national table, not beholden to a coastal elite that could know little of their interests.

Jeffersonian leaders, above all President Jefferson's secretary of the treasury Albert Gallatin, grasped the necessity of furnishing new resources to agriculture and commerce, and they understood government's role in promoting economic development. Unlike Hamilton, though, they sought to promote wealth creation and investment less through federal means and federal men than through the chartering of state banks and corporations. (In 1800, there were twenty-eight banks in the United States; in 1810, there were 327.) The federal government continued to sell land at regulated prices, and state governments encouraged speculative investment by granting licenses, franchises, and bounties, but "public authority," as the historian Joyce Appleby has written, "appeared merely as the handmaiden of private enterprise."

★　★　★

THE FEDERALIST PARTY, rocked by the Jeffersonians' ascendancy in the opening years of the nineteenth century, died as a national political force after the War of 1812, leaving the egalitarian economic ideals of the Revolution to stand virtually unchallenged. Those ideals would survive for another three generations, although in curiously fractured ways.

A market revolution transformed the United States after 1815, creating the foundations for an integrated national economy and pulling the nation from the margins closer to the center of international finance and commerce—but deepening inequality accompanied national prosperity. In 1860, according to Lindert and Williamson, the richest 1 percent of Americans held nearly 30 percent of the nation's wealth, more than twice the percentage of the Revolutionary Era. Whereas in 1774 the richest 10 percent owned 50 percent of the nation's wealth, by the outbreak of the Civil War the equivalent portion of the population controlled nearly three-quarters of the nation's total assets. Much of this concentration of wealth was based in slaveholding: almost two-thirds of the richest Americans, worth $110,000 or more, resided in the South. But in the great cities of the Northeastern seaboard as well as smaller urban centers which were the engines of commercial development, the unequal distribution of wealth, already manifest in the 1820s and 1830s, worsened during the antebellum decades—a trend that began even before the arrival of large waves of propertyless immigrants from Ireland and Germany after 1845. In New York City, the emerging national metropolis, the top 1 percent of the population controlled 29 percent of the city's non-corporate wealth in 1828, whereas in 1845, the same percentage controlled 40 percent.

The shift did not go unnoticed. Between 1815 and 1860, a host of dissenting movements—including organized working men in trade unions and working men's parties, radical abolitionist societies led by, among others, William Lloyd Garrison, and utopian communities like New Harmony and Brook Farm—denied that America's basic economic and social relations were sound. In electoral politics, issues concerning economic justice and inequality exploded with a force that matched that of the 1790s. The "one-party" system controlled by Jeffersonian Republicans shattered in the mid-1820s, and two competing parties emerged: one, which coalesced under the leadership of Andrew Jackson, took the name Democrats; the other, a shifting alliance of Jackson's opponents, was known initially as the National Republicans and then as the Whigs. The parties fought bitterly over issues of economics and national development. Strikingly, however, they both honored the egalitarian tradition, albeit in sharply opposed versions.

The fullest restatements of the established anti-aristocratic egalitarianism appeared in the policies and pronouncements of the Jacksonian Democratic Party. Firm believers in the labor theory of value—"Labor the Only True Source of Wealth" was a Jacksonian battle cry—the Democrats lambasted wealthy, nonproductive, moneyed drones as "aristocrats" who lived off the labor of others by the grace of charters and other privileges granted by the federal and state governments. A severe financial panic in 1819 had triggered the first truly national economic depression; that panic had been worsened by the operations of a new national bank, chartered three years earlier to replace the Hamiltonian original.* The disaster brought outcries that well-connected moneyed insiders had tainted the broadened, more democratic commerce originally envisaged by the Jeffersonians. "Monopoly" became the Jacksonians' catchword, the demiurge of inequality.

The Democrats aimed to remove the aristocrats' hands from the levers of economic power and restore what they considered "natural" com-

---

* The Jeffersonian Congress allowed the charter for Hamilton's Bank of the United States to lapse in 1811. The near ruination of the nation's finances during the War of 1812 led Congress to charter a Second Bank of the United States in 1816.

merce by arousing the great democratic majority of the (newly enlarged) white male electorate. The central Democratic anti-monopoly struggle was President Jackson's war with the Second Bank of the United States. The key document of that struggle—Jackson's message vetoing the bank's re-chartering in 1832—was a manifesto of Democratic egalitarianism, containing all of the old revolutionary and Jeffersonian-era ideals and language virtually intact. Calling the bank a "monopoly," Jackson explained at length his constitutional reasons for blocking the charter, then launched a powerful peroration:

> It is to be regretted that the rich and powerful too often bend the acts of government to their selfish purposes. Distinctions in society will always exist under every just government. Equality of talents, of education, or of wealth cannot be produced by human institutions. In the full enjoyment of the gifts of Heaven and the fruits of superior industry, economy, and virtue, every man is equally entitled to protection by law; but when the laws undertake to make the rich richer and the potent more powerful, the humble members of society—the farmers, mechanics, and laborers—who have neither the time nor the means of securing like favors to themselves, have a right to complain of the injustice of their government. There are no necessary evils in government. Its evils exist only in its abuses. If it would confine itself to equal protection, and, as Heaven does its rains, shower its favors alike on the high and the low, the rich and the poor, it would be an unqualified blessing. In the act before me there seems to be a wide and unnecessary departure from these principles.

The gist of Jackson's message could well have been written by a Jeffersonian Republican in the 1790s.

Jackson's opponents viewed the president's attacks on the bank (as well as on bank money and protective tariffs) with horror, as assaults on commerce and property rights that were bound to ruin the nation's expanding market economy. Yet unlike Hamilton and the High Federalists of the 1790s—who were in many respects their spiritual ancestors—the National Republicans and the Whigs of a generation later advanced programs in terms agreeable to the egalitarian tradition.

Fundamental to the reconciliation to egalitarianism of the National Republicans/Whigs was their success in exploiting some of the ambiguities in the labor theory of value. Jeffersonians and Jacksonians tended to define "labor" narrowly, to mean manual labor or, in the case of Southern planters, direction of the labor of slaves. Other occupations—whether they involved living off accumulated fortunes, trading commodities, or speculating—were far more suspect. Bankers, financiers, and bondholders struck Democrats as parasitic, quite apart from their monopolistic proclivities—moneyed men who produced nothing, but who made considerable fortunes by living (as John Taylor of Caroline, among many others, had put it) "upon the labour of the other classes."

By expanding the concept of labor to include all gainfully employed persons, however, the National Republicans and Whigs presented themselves as the true friends of the toiling masses. Invidious distinctions between producers and nonproducers, the National Republican manufacturer Tristam Burges declared in 1830, only excited "hostile feelings among men, all equally engaged in one great community and brotherhood of labor for mutual benefit." Lacking a formally titled aristocracy, the United States was a land of unlimited opportunity, where wealth, Edward Everett, the Whig governor of Massachusetts, remarked, "may be traced back to industry and frugality," and where "the wheel of fortune is in constant operation, and the poor in one generation furnish the rich of the next." Everett declared himself "at some loss to account for the odium which at times has been attempted to be cast on capitalists as a class." Just as every workingman was a capitalist in classless America, so, the argument followed, every capitalist, like every planter, was a workingman; indeed, as one anonymous writer put it in 1833, in America, "all men are workingmen."

Inequality, according to the National Republicans and Whigs, stemmed not from imagined corrupt privilege but from individual moral differences and the Democrats' disastrous class-based rhetoric and policies. Drenched in the evangelical ethical righteousness of the Second Great Awakening, these anti-Jacksonians blamed poverty on bad individual choices and on the refusal by some men to practice the basic virtues of industry, economy, and temperance. Government, they insisted, had a duty to help the people achieve their individual self-improvement, by enacting temperance reform and by building reformatories, asylums, and new-model prisons (all of which required public taxation). In order to widen economic opportunities and promote equality, government needed to help accelerate economic development from the top down, by chartering a national bank and funding internal improvements—orderly innovations that would, they claimed, benefit all industrious citizens.

The great political emblem of this egalitarian anti-Jacksonianism was the protective tariff. Jacksonians tended to regard protectionism as but another form of unnatural monopoly, granted by government to select elite interests. Like any other monopoly, it transferred wealth artificially from hand to hand, and helped establish what one New Hampshire Democrat called "the basest, most sordid, most groveling of aristocracies . . . a moneyed aristocracy." For National Republicans and Whigs, however, tariff protection ratified the harmony of interests between capital and labor. It laid a foundation for economic growth and military security that would combat what the protectionist writer Daniel Raymond singled out as a great evil: "a too unequal distribution of wealth."

The Whigs turned the tables on the Jacksonians by also squaring themselves with political democracy. Having denied Democratic charges of "aristocracy," they countercharged that a reborn monarchism, under the executive tyrant Jackson and his minions, was ruining the nation's economy by running roughshod over the Constitution and offering special favors to Jackson's political cronies. Again, Jackson's war with the Bank of the United States became the flashpoint.

Supposedly, by disregarding both Congress and the Supreme Court during the bank struggle, "King Andrew I" had usurped authority, trampled on the people's liberties, and funneled power and property to his own corrupt coterie. The basic conflict was not between the nonproducing few and the producing many, but between despotic, patronage-glutted Democratic rulers and the mass of the people. The Whigs, accordingly, were the true democrats, who offered laboring Americans what the publicist Calvin Colton called "the democracy which does them most good; which gives them food, clothing, and a comfortable home, instead of *promises*."

And so, amid the market revolution, the egalitarian tradition survived, but fractured now, and propounded in distinct and competing versions. Americans continued to believe in the necessity of restraining gross disparities of wealth. They continued to believe that productive men deserved to enjoy the full fruits of their labor. They continued to believe that special interests in politics—either selfish aristocratic monopolists or immoral monarchical demagogues—were chiefly responsible for deepening inequality. By the mid-1840s, these two versions of the egalitarian tradition could claim closely matched electoral support nationwide. At that very moment, though, westward expansion forced Americans to confront fully the institution of slavery and its implications for both morality and economic justice.

★   ★   ★

CHARGES THAT CHATTEL SLAVERY grotesquely contradicted and endangered American equality dated back to the Revolutionary Era. The most radical voices agreed with one writer (purported by some to have been Thomas Paine) that slaves, as human beings, were entitled to freedom and to enjoy "the fruits of their labors at their own disposal." The great ambiguity in the Revolution's egalitarianism, they charged, could not stand: if all men truly were created equal, slavery had to be destroyed. Other critics, North and South, blamed slavery for encouraging an aristocratic love of luxurious leisure and a despotic temperament among the slaveholders. Still others charged that slavery produced a backward economy, controlled by a small opulent elite that discouraged the wide diffusion of property among non-slaves.

In the North, a combination of egalitarian fervor among antislavery whites, antislavery activities by free blacks, and resistance from the slaves brought constitutional and judicial elimination of slavery as well as the first legislative acts in history aimed at gradual emancipation. Yet many Southerners also condemned slavery's degradation and recognized, as the historian David Ramsay of South Carolina noted in 1789, that slave system had "led to the engrossing of land, in the hands of a few," in marked contrast to the mostly free North. Only after the revival and vast expansion of Southern slavery caused by the post-Revolution cotton boom, did a coherent proslavery argument forcefully emerge across the slaveholding South. Only then did clashes over slavery become truly dangerous, signaled in national politics by the furious debates in Congress over the admission of Missouri as a slave state in 1819 and 1820.

The rise of the cotton kingdom deepened a political and moral revulsion in the North against slavery that challenged the basic terms of American egalitarianism. Yet, except for the brief period of "one-party" government that followed the War of 1812, the national political system was largely impervious to antislavery impulses. For all their talk of protecting the "many" against the "few," the Jeffersonians and Jacksonians were led by Southern slaveholders. Especially after the Missouri crisis, many of these planters saw limiting central government as, in part, a means to fend off any political attacks on human bondage. Criticism of slavery was much more common among Federalists, National Republicans, and Whigs from the Northern states, who saw their opponents' power inflated by the concessions given to slavery under the Constitution. They objected above all to the increasingly notorious three-fifths clause that counted slaves for inflated representation of the Southern states in Congress and the electoral college. Yet Federalists and Whigs also counted among them some of the wealthiest and most fervently proslavery Southern slaveholders, which checked the respective parties' antislavery enthusiasm and pushed them to agree to keep issues connected to slavery out of national debates.

The issue of slavery was forced only through the persistence of abolitionist politics, begun amid the struggles for emancipation in the late-eighteenth-century North, accompanied and pushed forward by the activism of free blacks and the resistance of Southern slaves. Within the folds of supposedly egalitarian American politics emerged clear-cut antislavery and proslavery political currents. Both sides tapped into the egalitarian tradition, promoting its own version while accusing the other of trying to tyrannize the nation.

Political opposition to slavery reached maturity in the new Republican Party formed in the mid-1850s, an amalgam of antislavery Whigs from the North (whose national party had collapsed), dissident antislavery Democrats, and political abolitionists. Befitting the party's mixed origins, the Republicans' antislavery variant of the egalitarian tradition borrowed elements from Whig and Democratic thinking, as well as from long-established abolitionist arguments. Like the Whigs, Republicans vaunted free labor as a harmony of interests in which the humblest industrious man enjoyed what, in 1860, the ex-Whig Abraham Lincoln called "an equal chance to get rich with everyone else." Slavery, by contrast, suppressed what Lincoln called "the true system" by enriching a small group of slaveholders and by declaring slaves chattel property, thereby denying them, with every other freedom, the chance to improve their condition.

From the antislavery Democrats, the Republicans absorbed a critique of the slaveholders as an aristocracy that, by aggressive political action, warped American society to advance its peculiar, immoral, and oppressive institution at the expense of all ordinary Americans, slave and free. In 1839, the Ohio antislavery Democrat Thomas Morris observed that the moneyed aristocracy of the North, which he called the Money Power, had forged a fresh alliance with the Southern slaveholders, which he called the Slave Power, "both looking to the same object—to live on the unrequited labor of others." (For his pains, Morris was officially excommunicated from the Democratic Party.) Whereas orthodox Jacksonians described slaveholders as honorable producers, dissident and beleaguered antislavery Democrats such as Morris considered the slaveholders aristocratic tyrants.

Political abolitionists including Salmon P. Chase, Gamaliel Bailey, and other veterans of the short-lived, schismatic abolitionist Liberty Party of the 1840s, added a powerful antislavery constitutionalism, which confronted spurious claims by slaveholders that the framers of the Constitution had enshrined slavery in national law. In fact, Chase and the others insisted, the Constitution purposefully refused to recognize slaves as property in areas under national jurisdiction. Accordingly, Congress was empowered to commence slavery's destruction by barring it from entering the national territories—the issue upon which the Union would finally crack in the 1850s.

Republican Party attacks on the immoral Slave Power went hand in hand with a vindication of their vision of a free-labor society dominated by what one Ohio Congressman called the "middle class of intelligent farmers, artisans, and mechanics, who make the real wealth, and are justly the pride and glory of the free states." Lincoln, like Jefferson, cautioned against reckless attacks on affluence and money-making. "I don't believe in a law to prevent a man from getting rich," he said in 1860. But Lincoln's envisaged America was chiefly a land of prosperous, middling, independent producers, with poverty "rarely in extremity." As "[l]abor is prior to and independent of capital," and as "capital is only the fruit of labor," he observed, then "labor is the superior of capital, and deserves much the higher consideration." Lincoln's "true system" was one of equal opportunity and easy mobility, firmly rooted in the economic egalitarian tradition, in which the hired laborer would before long go on to work for himself "and hire men to work for him!"

In his momentous debates with Stephen A. Douglas in 1858, Lincoln plainly and pointedly outlined the Republicans' inclusive labor theory of value, which, he said, guaranteed to all, black and white, the "right to eat the bread, without the leave of anybody else, which his own hand earns." Slavery, Republicans said, robbed slaves of their just rewards and degraded the dignity of all labor by turning some laborers into chattel, constrained by force. Slavery in turn concentrated wealth and deepened economic inequalities between the haves and the have-nots, the latter including the vast majority of whites as well as the abused slaves—creating a world, one New York Republican observed, in which "[g]reat wealth or hopeless poverty is the settled condition."

Proslavery spokesmen, assembled after 1854 in the commanding Southern wing of the Democratic Party, faced enormous difficulties in trying to adapt the established egalitarian tradition to their cause. In promoting slavery as a positive good, they often found themselves repudiating the natural rights legacies of John Locke and Thomas Jefferson. Some openly praised the virtues of aristocracy, although they made clear that they opposed hereditary aristocracy. Any honest defense of slavery required an admission that certain inequalities were inevitable and, indeed, decreed by God—that, as the ardently proslavery Virginian Abel Upshur asserted, "one portion of mankind shall live upon the labor of another portion."

Yet despite their aristocratic pretensions, slavery's advocates, the most reactionary American political force of the nineteenth century, also tried to mold the egalitarian tradition into an explicit defense of slavery, in part to rebut antislavery Northerners and in part to secure the support of the Southern white majority of non-slaveholders. They did so by turning the Revolution's ambiguous egalitarianism into a brief for bondage as the main bulwark of social and political equality for white men. Repeatedly they described the slave South as more egalitarian—for whites—than the supposedly "free" North.

George Fitzhugh, perhaps slavery's most thoroughgoing admirer and propagandist, sharply attacked economic injustice and inequality in the North. Although Yankees boasted of their adherence to the labor theory of value, Fitzhugh declared, in fact, under the free labor system, "Labor makes values, and Wit exploitates and accumulates them." Northern "freedom," Fitzhugh proclaimed, amounted to forsaking all sense of responsibility and permitting non-laboring employers to earn their livelihoods off the sweat of their workers, while compelling the workers to accept subsistence wages—on pain of joblessness and starvation. Under slavery, Fitzhugh asserted, the slaves, as valuable property, were assured of a decent living standard, while Southern whites supposedly lived in something far closer to economic security than wage-dependent Northerners.

Yet if Fitzhugh's writings vaunted slavery's superiority to free labor, their unapologetic hostility to all forms of egalitarianism, for whites as well as blacks, made them unusual. Slaveholders more generally praised slavery on the grounds that it conformed far better to American egalitarian principles than did the free-labor society of the North. The prominent South Carolina political leader James Henry Hammond, who like Fitzhugh accepted the idea that slavery created an aristocracy, went on to describe that aristocracy as a remarkably large and democratic one, consisting of every white man: "Be he rich or poor, if he does not possess a single slave, he has been born to all the natural advantages of the society in which he is placed, and all its honors lie open before him, inviting his genius and industry."

Just as antislavery forces moved slaveholding planters from the category of "producers" to "nonproducers," so the proslavery forces retained the idea, older than the Constitution, that enslaved blacks fell outside consideration as part of American society proper and formed what Hammond called a "mudsill" class of inferior beings—a class whose submission guaranteed white freemen's equality. Slavery also promoted a variation of what Northern Whigs and Republicans liked to call an underlying harmony of interests, in the supposedly organic connection between white master and black slave but also between white equals. A sharp-edged racist egalitarianism emerged in slavery's defense. So long as the planters preserved the suffrage rights of non-slaveholders, so long as the white majority of non-slaveholding yeomen were permitted to enjoy the full fruits of their labor, so long as tax burdens remained light, and so long as the non-slaveholders raised no objections to slavery, there would be no exploitation of whites by whites. All whites would share the privileges of their race, independent non-slaveholders would be spared oppression by the grasping Yankee moneyed class, and masters would live in paternalist harmony with their human chattel.

Seen through this lens, even the slaveholders' familiar stance on states' rights could be presented as a variation of the egalitarian tradition, rooted in the idea that economic and social injustice arose from political tyranny. According to John C. Calhoun, the foremost and ablest proslavery political theorist, the framers had designed "a democratic federal republic" in which the states "retained their separate existence as independent and sovereign communities." Unfortunately, Calhoun claimed, the work of the framers was flawed by their failure to provide the states with an explicit veto power over federal legislation, thereby allowing pro-consolidation Federalists, beginning with Alexander Hamilton in the 1790s, to advance what he called "the national impulse." Allegedly, in the 1830s, the National Republicans/ Whigs had turned themselves into the numerical balance of power in national politics and compelled the Jacksonian Democrats—led by Andrew Jackson himself, one of Calhoun's bitterest foes—to abandon the South and the animating spirit of the Revolution.

The federal government, Calhoun charged, had aggressively usurped power, and created "a great national consolidated democracy . . . as absolute as . . . the Autocrat of Russia, and as despotic in its tendency as any absolute government that ever existed." The South's blessed slaveholders' democracy was under siege by a corrupt and hypocritical Northern absolutism. And when, a decade after Calhoun's death, the voters swept Lincoln and the Republicans into national power, Calhoun's followers led the way in dissolving the Union rather than submit to the hated Yankees—dictatorial, self-described democrats who presumed to deny what the slaveholders speciously proclaimed was their absolute right and liberty, under the Constitution, to hold human beings in perpetual bondage.

★ ★ ★

AS THE CONTROVERSIES in the 1850s over slavery and the territories intensified, so the Jacksonian political alignments crumbled, and civil war proved unavoidable. In the midst of that war, the Republican Congress, freed from the constraints of Southern Democrats, enacted numerous measures directed at widening economic opportunity as well as stabilizing national finances, ranging from the Homestead Act and the Morrill Act (establishing and funding land-grant colleges) to the National Banking Acts and the Pacific Railway Act. The admixture of Whig and Democratic politics inside the Republican Party created a forthright democratic nationalism, emboldening the federal government, for a time, at once to stimulate economic development and broaden its benefits. In the war's aftermath, the victorious Union made the last great effort in our history to vindicate the old egalitarian tradition inherited from the Revolutionary Era, by securing to the ex-slaves, through forceful federal intervention, their natural right to the fruits of their labor.

As the former Confederate secretary of the treasury Christopher G. Memminger noted soon after Appomattox, Reconstruction turned mainly "upon the decision which shall be made upon the mode of organizing the labor of the African race." To Republicans, moderate and radical, the only possible solution was to organize the ex-slaves' labor along the lines familiar in the North, by eradicating the slaveholding aristocracy and ensuring that every freed person would receive the full harvest of his or her labor. Mudsills no longer, the ex-slaves were now fully entitled to the basic property rights accorded to all freeborn Americans.

In the broadest terms, ex-slaves agreed. "[W]e . . . understand freedom," a mass meeting of blacks in Petersburg, Virginia, resolved in June of 1865, "to mean industry and the enjoyment of the legitimate fruits thereof." But reinventing the egalitarian tradition in order to include the ex-slaves proved to be an overwhelming task. Radical Republicans, led by Thaddeus Stevens, believed that only comprehensive economic and political reform, including mass redistribution of slaveholders' lands to the freedmen, would suffice—proposals that, not surprisingly, met with intense opposition from the white South.

In the North as well, calls to redistribute Southern land ran afoul of what most Republicans and old-line Democrats considered acceptable under the egalitarian tradition, with its insistence on the inviolability of legitimate private property. Worse, Northern businessmen pointed out, redistribution would play havoc with the staple-based agriculture that was the foundation of Southern prosperity and (not incidentally) a source of Northern profits. Worse still, land redistribution in the South might encourage increasingly restive Northern workers to undertake some similar sort of revolution against property.

There was, however, one area in which radical and more moderate Republicans, as well as freed slaves, could agree: the imperative of black suffrage in the South as a means to secure economic equality. And in this respect, Reconstruction was in line with the basic concepts of the old egalitarian tradition. Without black suffrage, George Julian, a leading Republican from Indiana, observed, former slaveholders would reassume political power and make "the condition of the freedmen more intolerable than slavery itself." As long as the political monopoly of the slaveholders was broken, enfranchised blacks would have the power to prevent the reemergence of aristocracy and inequality.

The guarantee of black voting, proclaimed the black Republican Oscar J. Dunn of Louisiana, preserved the essence of America's revolutionary legacy, which was to abolish all "hereditary distinctions" and bar the door from "the institution of aristocracy, nobility, and even monarchy." If black suffrage would not have the sudden dramatic effect on the distribution of wealth that radical redistribution would have, it would at least open up the strong possibility of further change, and of greater economic equality, in the South. Black suffrage, lamented one ex-Confederate political leader, was nothing less than a revolution, "and nobody can anticipate the action of revolutions."

A rapid slackening of Republican reform, though, amid the economic depression of the 1870s, and the violent overthrow of radical state governments in the South, marked a shattering defeat for the prewar Republican version of the egalitarian tradition. Resurgent racism fed charges that the black-supported Reconstruction governments were hopelessly corrupt; Southern blacks became entangled in a sharecropping system that meant virtual debt peonage; political reaction eventually halted the revolution of black suffrage in the South and, in time, institutionalized disenfranchisement and imposed Jim Crow segregation. Hopes of extending the egalitarian tradition to the ex-slaves in a free-labor South crumbled.

Thereafter, the emergence of enormous new business corporations and trusts and the rise of an all-too-conspicuous American plutocracy battered existing egalitarian assumptions. Suddenly, basic verities— that American abundance and free government would guarantee workers the full fruits of their labor; that respect for competition, private property, and contracts would, in America, foster a rough equality— were dashed. A gigantic force unknown to earlier generations—what the eminent economists John Bates Clark and John Maurice Clark, father and son, would call "the devil of private monopoly"—was now in the saddle.

A revolution in economic thought, begun in the 1860s and 1870s, both hastened and justified the emergence of the new economic order. The labor theory of value, fundamental to formal political economy and to popular thinking about economic justice before the Civil War, proved irrelevant to understanding vital aspects of the monetized corporate economy, from the setting of prices to adjustments in the money supply. More important, economists in step with the new order accepted the rise of huge corporations as perfectly natural, an inevitable outcome of technological breakthroughs rather than of political or entrepreneurial changes. Indeed, economists effectively divorced the corporate economy from politics altogether, belying the fact that laws necessarily organized markets. Whereas earlier monopolies had been the creatures of government, the modern corporation—or what some experts called "cooperation"—now arose strictly out of objective market forces. Economics, as a self-regulating sphere of its own, supplanted the old egalitarian versions of political economy: "This," wrote one of the popularizers of the new economic doctrine, Charles R. Flint, known as "Father of Trusts" and founder of the company that became IBM, "is the difference between monopoly and cooperation, between government favoritism and natural law."

By the 1920s, prevailing views of economic inequality had changed utterly. Above all, the old association between inequality and political privilege dissolved. Far from an unnatural distortion of the invisible hand, caused by political favoritism, gross inequality now turned out to be a perfectly natural result of market forces. Limiting government became the touchstone of the new economics and of conservative pro-business doctrine, based on the resurgent principle that inequality was not only inevitable, but also rational and just. Government regulation, on this view, would only distort the natural operations and just outcomes of the market by preventing talented and fortunate Americans from accumulating and possessing as much wealth as they could.

This transition—what the great reformer of the new century Robert M. La Follette would call the "vast revolution in economic conditions"—fitfully transformed the American egalitarian impulse. Agrarian protests of the 1880s and 1890s, culminating in the rise of the Populist Party, revived the Jeffersonian-tinged anti-monopoly rhetoric of the old egalitarianism, asserting, as the Populists' founding Omaha platform of 1892 declared, that "[w]ealth belongs to him who creates it." The Knights of Labor, reaching the peak of their power and membership in the strife-torn 1880s, likewise proclaimed the by-now traditional principle that every worker was entitled to "the full fruits of his toil." But just as federal action underwrote Reconstruction until its overthrow, so hard-pressed farmers and workers turned to government, state and national, as never before to propose all sorts of interventions, from price regulation and nationalization of the railroads to limitations on working hours and the enactment of a graduated national income tax. The agrarian movements, however, fell victim to political manipulation and the rampant, violent, racist egalitarianism that accompanied the rise and consolidation of Jim Crow. The labor movement was crippled by corporate-backed official repression, in a crescendo of labor violence unmatched in the rest of industrializing world.

★   ★   ★

IT WOULD TAKE the Progressives and later the New Dealers of the first half of the twentieth century to shape a national government that turned a revived American egalitarian tradition into laws and institutions. The Progressive writer Herbert Croly, at once an admirer of Theodore Roosevelt and a shaper of TR's politics, famously described these efforts as using Hamiltonian means to reach Jeffersonian ends. They also represented a return to and updating of the democratic nationalism of the Lincoln Republicans, using national power to stabilize a volatile national economy while providing ordinary citizens with the means to better their lives.

Basic elements of the older egalitarian tradition, above all the labor theory of value, had disappeared. In their stead, the Progressives and New Dealers, fully accepting modern capitalist enterprise, used federal authority toward many ends: to curb the unregulated business excesses that had caused repeated economic panics and depressions, to legitimize organized labor and collective bargaining, to outlaw profit-making practices that endangered the health and safety of workers and consumers, to increase federal spending on public works projects, including improvements in transportation and expansion of environmental conservation, and, more broadly, to assess a progressive income tax on individuals, intended initially as an effort to rein in the wealth of the super-rich.

During the 1920s, political reaction to the Progressive reforms achieved under TR and Woodrow Wilson led to an interregnum of pro-business Republican government, which turned the laissez-faire doctrines of an earlier time into a successful assault on rapidly expanding progressive taxation and federal regulation—the forerunner of what would later become known as supply-side economics. Guided by the financier Andrew Mellon—treasury secretary to presidents Warren G. Harding, Calvin Coolidge, and Herbert Hoover—the new dispensation held that government was, in Mellon's words, "just a business, and can and should be run on business principles."

The economy grew, but so, starkly, did inequality: by 1928, the share of wealth owned by the top 1 percent of American households, which had declined substantially at the end of the Progressive Era, surged to more than 50 percent, whereas the share owned by the bottom 90 percent, which had been rising, plunged to around 15 percent. Combined with reckless and unchecked speculation by businesses, banks, and well-off individuals flushed with cash, the imbalances produced the catastrophic depression that followed the stock market crash of 1929. The revised laissez-faire economic creed quickly fell into disgrace, where it would languish for more than two generations.

Revisions of the egalitarian tradition, meanwhile, recommended many-fold under the New Deal and culminated in President Franklin D. Roosevelt's call in 1944 for a "second bill of rights." Profound economic changes, FDR argued, had rendered the political rights won by the American Revolution "inadequate to assure us equality in the pursuit of happiness." To provide the citizenry with what the Revolutionary generation would have called a "competency," and which Roosevelt called "security," would require public efforts to guarantee full employment at decent wages and, among other things, "adequate medical care and the opportunity to achieve and enjoy good health."

Even as Roosevelt called for further action, the New Deal and the mobilization for World War II had begun producing what, through the 1970s, would prove to be the sharpest and most profound reduction in economic inequality in all of American history. The economic historians Claudia Goldin and Robert Margo first described the shift as the "great compression": "When the United States emerged from war and depression," they observed, "it had not only a considerably lower rate of unemployment, it also had a wage structure more egalitarian than at any time since." Subsequent studies by, among others, the economists Thomas Piketty, Emmanuel Saez, and Gabriel Zucman, have revealed similar trends regarding the concentration of wealth. Whereas during the brief conservative period between the Progressives and the New Dealers, the share of total income received by the top 10 percent surged to 46 percent, it began falling—unevenly after 1929, then dramatically after 1937—to around 33 percent in 1945, and then it dipped below 10 percent for much of the 1950s through the 1960s. Far from hobbling the national economy, the great compression accompanied the great postwar boom in economic growth. Between 1947 and 1973, the annual rate of growth of a typical family's real income was 2.7 percent, compared to a growth rate of 0.7 percent from 1980 to 2007.

Yet for all of its effectiveness, the great compression of the New Deal era could only mitigate the failure after the Civil War to expand the egalitarian tradition to include the ex-slaves and their descendants. By the 1930s, the Democratic Party had become an uneasy national coalition of the one-party white South, descended from the antebellum Slave Power, allied with a rising wing of Northern liberals, with its strongest base among urban ethnic working-class voters. Not until the late 1940s did liberal Democrats, including President Harry Truman, begin directly to confront the issues of segregation and racial equality in national politics, which prompted the so-called Dixiecrat schism of 1948 led by Senator Strom Thurmond of South Carolina. Much as in the early nineteenth century an American egalitarianism could coexist with slavery, so, in the 1930s and 1940s, New Deal reform coexisted with Jim Crow. But just as, in the 1840s and 1850s, confrontations over slavery in the territories forced a reckoning over the immorality of human bondage and the limits of equality, so the rise of the modern civil rights movement, pioneered by the African American labor leader A. Philip Randolph and advanced by the Rev. Dr. Martin Luther King, Jr., forced a reckoning over segregation, disenfranchisement, and racial subjugation.

By the early 1960s, prompted in part by the growing black presence in Northern cities, the national Democratic Party was ready—albeit, at first, tentatively—to embrace civil rights reform. A turning point of sorts came in June 1963 when, in the wake of a federal showdown with arch-segregationist Governor George C. Wallace of Alabama, John F. Kennedy delivered the strongest address on racial equality of any president since Abraham Lincoln. Following Kennedy's assassination five months later, President Lyndon B. Johnson vowed to gain passage of a pending civil rights bill bottled up in Congress, which he did; and in March 1965, after the bloody events at Selma, Alabama, Johnson placed his administration squarely in alliance with the civil rights movement, and gained enactment of the Voting Rights Bill.

Johnson's Great Society agenda marked what at the time looked like a momentous breakthrough in American politics, a fateful joining of the abiding struggles for economic and racial justice. At one level, LBJ committed himself to achieving all that Franklin Roosevelt had marked out two decades earlier as the essential American economic rights. With the help of an overwhelming liberal majority in Congress elected in 1964, he was remarkably successful in doing so, winning major legislative victories in areas ranging from health care and public housing to rural development and the environment. But by linking these reforms to landmark civil rights legislation, Johnson also picked up the burden laid down at the overthrow of Reconstruction. He would have the nation renounce, once and for all, the idea that American equality could exist to the exclusion of subordinate classes, above all African Americans—indeed, that American equality somehow *required* such exclusion. In close concert with African American agitators and organizers like Randolph and King, he would also approach racial equality and economic equality as inalterably linked, certain that just as civil rights would be empty without a more general expansion of economic security and opportunity, so the expansion of opportunity required putting racial division in the course of extinction.

To Americans who came of age in the 1950s and 1960s, the predominance of updated New Deal-era egalitarianism seemed to be the normal state of American politics. Soon enough, though, that egalitarianism would be shoved to the political margins.

★ ★ ★

THE DEMISE OF New Deal–Great Society liberalism seemed to come suddenly, leaving many of its defenders perplexed and disoriented, but its origins had deep historical roots, some of which lay outside of American history. The era of World War I, which destroyed the confidence and complacency of the nineteenth-century Old World, brought revolutionary changes with lasting implications. The Bolshevik Revolution and the rise of Communist dictatorship in the name of a proletarian utopia, the harsh terms of Germany's defeat leading to the genocidal horrors of National Socialism, the breakup of empires and the assertion of national and ethnic self-determination, all shifted the terms of egalitarian politics. But while these global changes played a part, the receding of the American egalitarian tradition owed most to currents of the American past.

Conservative political reaction, held in check during the New Deal and its immediate aftermath, began in earnest with the Dixiecrat schism of 1948 and the white South's "massive resistance" to civil rights reform in the 1950s. As the centennial of the Civil War approached, segregationists sounded, sometimes strikingly, like the propagandists of the Confederacy, stoking a racist egalitarianism directed against both blacks and elite Yankee outsiders, defending Jim Crow as an organic, traditional, harmonious order, and lambasting federal authority as despotic and illegitimate. If they would not go as far as secession, segregationist leaders did raise the specters of state interposition and nullification. And as the national Democratic Party became the party of civil rights, the old solid Democratic white South became, by 1964, the solidly Republican white South.

An accumulation of political disasters and tribulations in the late 1960s and 1970s—including the Vietnam intervention, the Watergate scandals, recurring oil-price crises, and the idealistic but ultimately ineffectual presidency of Jimmy Carter—reinforced public skepticism nationwide about politics and government. The conservative movement inside the Republican Party, with its roots in the corporate anti–New Deal reaction of the 1930s and now joined by whites hostile to the civil rights movement, rallied behind the figure of Ronald Reagan. Reagan, in turn, projected a sunny optimism that promised resolve and recovery, which he tied to a demonization of the federal government as powerful as any in American political history since the era of Reconstruction. The anti-aristocratic, antimonarchial egalitarianism of the American founding—including Thomas Paine's phrase in *Common Sense* about beginning "the world over again"—became, in Reagan's reformulations, appeals to dismantle the New Deal and the Great Society and retreat from civil rights legislation.

Whereas nineteenth-century Americans believed that the federal government would unjustly transfer wealth from the middling classes to the wealthy, the late-twentieth-century right charged, with great political success, that the federal government was unjustly transferring wealth from the wealthy and the middle class to the poor (especially the minority poor). The imagery of parasitic nonproducers became affixed, in this new vocabulary, to the bottom of the social ladder instead of the top. The true monarchs and aristocrats in Reagan's America became the so-called "welfare queens" and their patrons, elitist, bleeding-heart "brie-and-Chablis," "radical chic," "limousine liberals." Collective solutions to ordinary individual problems—through labor unions, civil rights groups, and other movements—became disgraced as the distorting influence of entitled "special interests." Collective efforts by private corporations, even those reliant on the government, to secure their own interests passed unnoticed—or won approval as the natural operations of free enterprise.

The effects of Reagan's economic policies were predictable. By backing the anti-inflationary measures of Federal Reserve chairman Paul Volcker (appointed by Carter), Reagan was able to revive economic growth, in what was rightly called the Reagan boom, at the cost of a severe but brief recession. But over the long term, that growth was meager compared to the postwar boom years, and it accompanied a sudden and startling reversal of the great compression—what the economist Paul Krugman has called the great divergence. Stable through most of the 1950s until the end of the 1970s, the share of total income going to the top 10 percent increased dramatically over the quarter century after the mid-1980s, reaching 50.6 percent in 2012, higher than any year on record since 1917. Inside that elite, a super-elite also emerged. In 1982, according to figures gathered by Emmanuel Saez, the highest-earning 1 percent of households received 10.8 percent of all pretax income, while the bottom 90 percent received 64.7 percent. Three decades later, the top 1 percent received 22.5 percent of pretax income, while the bottom 90 percent's share had fallen to 49.6 percent. And that super-elite contained a rising plutocracy of the top 0.1 percent, whose share of total household wealth, which had fallen to around 7 percent in 1978, grew to around 20 percent thirty years later.

To be sure, there were some important fluctuations. The Reagan boom of the 1980s, fed by expanded federal spending on defense and infrastructure, boosted the incomes of all but the oldest sectors of the workforce. That growth dissipated in the late 1980s, then revived even more strongly during the 1990s. But it stopped abruptly in 2002, after which the incomes of most households stagnated or declined for a decade, with the incomes of the less educated sectors of the workforce suffering a devastating falloff.

These trends, long-term and short-term, only fitfully reawakened the egalitarian impulse in national politics. Conservative anti-government arguments put latter-day egalitarians on the defensive, scrambling for some redefinition of purpose. Through the 1980s, Democratic leaders either restated the old New Deal verities or rejected political ideas altogether, taking refuge in expertise and claiming (as presidential candidate Michael Dukakis did in 1988) that politics was not about ideas or ideology but competence. After his grand efforts to revive liberal government in the area of health care came to naught, President Bill Clinton was forced to declare that, although laissez-faire was discredited, "the era of big government is over." Liberals, when not fending off attacks on progressive taxation and other achievements of earlier decades, looked to specially targeted programs and indirect redistribution (through tax credits) to improve opportunities for middle-class and poor Americans.

In a remarkable political performance, Clinton was able to outfox an increasingly radical Republican congressional majority led by Speaker Newt Gingrich, and, without promoting any programs on the scale of the Great Society, reverse the trend toward inequality, overseeing dramatic decreases in unemployment and increases in real wages, while turning an immense national deficit into a national surplus. But the Supreme Court's decision of the 2000 presidential election brought, with the administration of George W. Bush, a return to and acceleration of policies that deepened inequalities, including massive tax cuts skewed to the top. As the political scientist Larry M. Bartels explained in 2008, Clinton presided "over higher average income growth across the board and substantially higher average growth for people of modest means," while Republican control of the presidency, especially under the second Bush, produced sharp increases in broad-based inequality.

The financial crisis in the late summer of 2008, abetted by the Bush administration's retrenchment of regulation, all but assured the election of Barack Obama to the White House. But Obama, who hoped to move government away from bitter partisanship and gridlock, confronted a Republican Party committed from the start to obstructing his every move. Doggedly, the Obama administration won a historic victory with the Affordable Care Act, a major step toward fulfilling FDR's proposed guarantee of universal medical care, as well as the Dodd-Frank reforms of financial regulation. In 2012, candidate Mitt Romney's unguarded remarks about the Democrats' constituency of good-for-nothing takers helped secure Obama's reelection. By 2015, the economy had recovered to the point where, in his State of the Union message, Obama was able to declare that "the shadow of crisis has passed," and to propose an ambitious and frankly egalitarian social agenda, including a substantial raise in the minimum wage, immigration reform, and making community college education tuition-free.

With Republicans holding strong majorities in both the House and the Senate, the chances of passage for almost all of these proposals ranged from slim to none. Yet by making them at all, Obama laid down markers for some future Democratic administration and laid out the elements of a revived egalitarian politics. The rush, during the months after Obama's address, by Republicans as well as Democrats to declare economic inequality one of the great pressing issues of our time suggested that the nation's politics had turned a corner.

Whatever egalitarian politics emerge in future will necessarily differ from Lyndon B. Johnson's Great Society, just as the Great Society differed from the New Deal and the New Deal differed from its predecessors. The American egalitarian tradition has remained vital only insofar as it has adapted to and helped advance momentous social and economic changes and risen to face fundamental moral issues, none greater than the contradictions of slavery and Jim Crow. It has had to overcome the various strains of racist egalitarianism that have tapped into popular anxieties and resentments and directed them against nonwhites, especially African Americans. The old egalitarianism of the Revolutionary Era and after was profoundly altered by the trauma of the Civil War; reconstructed, it proved incapable of meeting the challenges of modern corporate capitalism. An entirely new form of egalitarianism had to replace it—one that, a century later, was besieged and nearly overwhelmed by post-Reagan conservatism, turning New Deal themes on their head. But if the old egalitarian thinking about political economy was rendered obsolete, its legacy endured, in the embattled idea that democracy's fate rested on a large and prosperous middle America, reflecting a basic equality in the distribution of the nation's wealth.

Into the first quarter of the twenty-first century, much as in the 1790s, the 1850s, and the 1930s, it became clear that those who would salvage and modernize this American tradition had better be about their work. They would do well to consider more closely the political history of American egalitarianism, starting with the lives and writings of Thomas Paine and Thomas Jefferson.

II.

★ ★ ★ ★ ★ ===================

The POLITICIANS
and the EGALITARIANS

3

★ ★ ★ ★ ★ ══════════

Thomas Paine:
The Origins of
American Egalitarianism

THOMAS PAINE DIED LONELY AND REVILED AND TODAY IS largely unremembered by the public, but it was not always so. Beginning in 1825, sixteen years after Paine's death, hundreds of Jacksonian workingmen and deists turned out annually for birthday festivities in cities from Albany to Cincinnati, celebrating Paine as a freethinking friend of labor. After 1850, immigrant freethinkers picked up the tradition, joined by native-born democrats such as Walt Whitman, who addressed the Paine commemoration in Philadelphia in 1877. Later in the century, however, the Paine cult dwindled, as radicals found more modern heroes to honor and as the old Enlightenment currents of militant anticlericalism evaporated. Paine would occasionally resurface in rebel circles as a sort of all-purpose emblem of American dissent—among free-speech advocates and sex radicals at the turn of century, among Popular Front Communists in the 1930s and 1940s (notably in Howard Fast's *Citizen Tom Paine*), and even in one of Bob Dylan's more obscure lyrics from the late 1960s—but on the left in general Paine's legacy faded. Conservative Americans, if they recalled Paine at all, did so uneasily, mindful of Theodore Roosevelt's characterization of the man as a "filthy little atheist."

Interest in Paine revived around the time that one of President Ronald Reagan's speechwriters began citing him by name and placing patriotic snippets from *Common Sense* and *The American Crisis* into the president's major addresses, heralding supply-side economics as a glorious effort "to begin the world over again." Suddenly the stigma that earlier generations of conservatives attached to Paine disappeared. At least some liberals, meanwhile, still recalled him as a great egalitarian, and in 1994, with bipartisan support, Congress authorized the construction (with private funds) of a Paine memorial in Washington on or near the National Mall. But the money never got raised, and the authorization expired.

The Thomas Paine Memorial Association still looks after the cottage in New Rochelle, New York, on the farmland given to him by the state of New York in appreciation of his revolutionary services. In tandem with nearby Iona College, the association has established an Institute for Thomas Paine Studies. Groups of admirers still gather in New Rochelle to honor him on his birthday at a memorial erected in his honor in 1839. Barack Obama quoted a passage from *The American Crisis* in his first inaugural address, although, unlike Reagan, he did not mention Paine's name. As far as honoring Paine goes, that's been about it. We live in an era of so-called Founders Chic, when the great men of the Revolution are treated to best-selling biographies, HBO specials, and even a hip-hop Broadway hit musical about the resolute anti-egalitarian Alexander Hamilton. But Thomas Paine is absent.

Scholars have not been so neglectful. In 1995, the Library of America effectively canonized Paine by publishing a volume of some of his major writings. Since then, there has been a steady stream of books about Paine, including two full-dress biographies, a thorough, so-called "political biography," and at least a dozen monographs on everything from Paine's deism to his place in American literary history. Yet even then, Paine doesn't quite fit in. Over the years, historians have tried to arrange the political ideas of the Revolutionary Era into an assortment of tidy categories. According to one school, Revolutionary Americans divided up into planter democrats and capitalist elitists. According to another school, the basic division pitted egalitarian back-country localists against market-oriented urban cosmopolitans. There are historians who say that the Revolution sprang from classical republican fears of corruption, and there are historians who say that it sprang from Lockean liberalism, and there are historians who charge that the Revolution's democratic stirrings were paradoxically linked to slavery and white racism.

Paine cannot be understood according to any of these descriptions. He was a democrat and an egalitarian, but he was neither a nostalgic agrarian nor a narrow-minded localist. He spoke the language of disinterested virtue and commonwealth proclaimed by eighteenth-century republican writers, but he was a liberal with respect to individual rights and commercial expansion. His democratic vision was hardly predicated on the subjugation of blacks; indeed, he abhorred slavery, hoped for its eradication, and was at least briefly a member of the Pennsylvania Abolition Society. As J. G. A. Pocock has observed, Paine's writings simply do not fit "any established radical political vocabulary" of the late eighteenth century. If we were to judge matters solely from Paine's output, virtually every major existing interpretation of American revolutionary political ideas would collapse.

None of this would be troubling if Paine were not so important. He was, without question, the American Revolution's most popular and consequential pamphleteer. *Common Sense*, published in January 1776, sold 150,000 copies in cheap editions in its first year, an astounding figure for the time, and it was widely credited with galvanizing pro-independence opinion. *The American Crisis*, Paine's series of wartime political commentaries, was read by troops and civilians alike, and emboldened the patriot effort at its most difficult moments. (In the second of the essays, published at the beginning of 1777, Paine described the country as "the United States of America," a phrase which, even if he was not the first to utter, he helped place into common currency.) Paine's influence expanded many-fold when, after his return to his native England, he published his famous two-part reply to Edmund Burke on the French Revolution, *Rights of Man* in 1791 and 1792.

Nor was Paine merely a best-selling agitator and publicist. His contributions, political and intellectual, were more profound, changing the very substance of revolutionary politics in an era of democratic revolutions. Reflecting in 1806 on the "Folly, Vice, Frenzy, Brutality, [and] Daemons" that beset his own long political career, the aging John Adams wrote curtly, "Call it the Age of Paine." Coming from the conservative-minded Adams, it was an embittered observation, but it was not a wholly unwarranted one.

To be sure, Paine lacked Madison's realism and originality as a political theorist or Hamilton's at times frightening genius for finance. In his occasional role as a practical politician and officeholder, he performed assiduously but not terribly auspiciously. Yet in his finest writings, particularly in *Common Sense*, Paine, better than any other patriot leader, defined the revolutionary cause as ordinary Americans came to define it—not as a transatlantic tax revolt or merely a struggle for independence but as an epochal effort to give birth to an entirely new social and political world, a cause for all mankind. Later, in *Rights of Man*, he delivered the most influential defense of democratic principles to appear in his lifetime. And as a delegate to the revolutionary National Convention in Paris, his speeches and articles on behalf of moderation (especially in opposition to the execution of Louis XVI and to the Terror) offered eloquent, if in the short run doomed, testimony on the barbarity of capital punishment and the necessity for radical regimes, above all, to respect the rule of law.

How Paine wrote was nearly as important as what he wrote. The style of Paine's work was a considerable part of its substance. Not that his literary efforts were completely unprecedented. Before Paine, numerous Americans took time off from their usual employments to compose political pamphlets. The modern arts of political insult and satire that Paine practiced so brilliantly had a long history, dating back to the city-states of the Renaissance. (Defoe and Swift were two of the more obvious influences on Paine's style.) But Paine was the first notable American writer to live solely by his pen. And he was the first important American pamphleteer to reach beyond the elite eighteenth-century political nation in order to address directly a new audience of farmers, craftsmen, and laborers on the principles of government. To his detractors, like Adams, Paine was a guttersnipe whose writing lacked literary merit, "with no felicity of remark, no extent of research, no classical allusion, nor comprehension of thought," as the polemicist James Cheetham put it. But these supposed vices of Paine's were precisely what impressed his largely plebeian readership. They embodied his political thinking as much they conveyed it.

The pithy phrases that still make Paine irresistible—"these are the times that try men's souls"; "government, like dress, is the badge of lost innocence"; and (ridiculing Burke's apologies for the French aristocracy) "he pities the plumage but forgets the dying bird"—created a new democratic style of political talk. Anyone could understand it. Its power was inversely proportional to its erudition. As Paine himself suggested, he crafted his style to puncture the verbiage of his pompous antagonists. (Paine on Burke: "How ineffectual, though gay with flowers, are all his declamation and argument.") With its plain metaphors and its limpid logic, Paine's writing proclaimed that the mysteries of politics were not so mysterious, that supposedly rude men could comprehend public affairs and act reasonably upon their comprehension. Paine thus opened channels of democratic persuasion that at their worst have inflated clever demagogues but at their best have inspired some of our finest political leaders, most notably Abraham Lincoln, who as a young man greatly admired Paine's writings.

Paine's prose style as well as his politics derived from his fundamental belief in the power of human reason, and his generally optimistic view of the possibilities of human progress. Such optimism, although common in enlightened American circles high and low, cut against eighteenth-century Calvinist America's widespread assumptions about human depravity. Not that Paine ignored humanity's darker side: government, he observed in 1776, was necessitated "by the inability of moral virtue to govern the world"; and twenty years later, in the wake of the Jacobin Terror, he repeatedly remarked on how, without a self-limiting constitution, democracy would degenerate into tyranny. For the most part, though, the freethinking Paine took a more generous Enlightenment view of human perfectibility, rejecting gloomy cyclical interpretations of history while insisting that progress would come from mankind's own efforts, not through Providence.

Apart from his friend Benjamin Franklin, Paine's closest counterpart inside the nation's political leadership was Thomas Jefferson. In 1792, Jefferson warmly praised *Rights of Man* and declared himself Paine's "sincere votary" and "ardent well-wisher"; a decade later, as president, Jefferson arranged for Paine's return from virtual exile in France and welcomed his political advice. Among prominent Americans, only the rationalist Jefferson equaled Paine in his belief that, as Paine put it, "human nature is not of itself vicious," and that men's reason could lead them to transcend their passions and narrow self-interest and make a better world.

Still, Paine was not exactly an Enlightenment Jeffersonian. Although he eventually came to move in some of the highest political circles in three countries (counting among his friends Washington, the Marquis de Lafayette, Charles James Fox, and, before he broke with them, John Adams and Edmund Burke), Paine spent his first thirty-seven years in utter obscurity, as a humbly born, small-town British corset-maker, sailor, shopkeeper, and excise officer. When he moved to America in 1774, aided by a modest reference letter from Benjamin Franklin, he gravitated to Philadelphia's plebeian taverns and debating clubs. It was in that world, and not in the drawing rooms of the urbane American philosophes, that his ideas and his vocabulary took shape. His chief associates were, like himself, self-educated men of the practical arts, whose appreciation of science and reason owed as much to their every-day workshop experiences as to their reading. They were city men, not rural squires (or, for that matter, back-country yeomen), mercurial men of improvement, commerce, and trade, not Jefferson's stolid, self-reliant tillers of the soil.

The difference, as historians have noted, was fundamental to Paine's politics. Jefferson, for all his faith in reason and progress, retained some of the classical fear that rapid commercial and material improvement would breed moral corruption and decline. The Jeffersonian ideal of a republican empire of liberty envisaged independent small farmers occupying the vast expanses of the American West, re-creating as nearly as possible the pristine egalitarian social order that had supposedly existed in bygone Anglo-Saxon times. To be sure, Jefferson was not an anti-commercial agrarian, as he is sometimes wrongly portrayed. But his image of a bustling, broadly-based market economy always placed virtuous, self-reliant farmers at its center. Paine's vision, by contrast, was thoroughly dynamic and anti-nostalgic. It regarded commerce, like science, as a civilizing force that would help release men from their mental and material fetters. It regarded history and tradition as oppressive weights to be challenged at every opportunity and, if found unreasonable, to be cast aside.

At the same time, Paine's politics had a sharper democratic edge than the republicanism of the Jeffersonian gentry. In ways that Jefferson and his peers could only imagine, Paine and his constituency felt the enormous and unending condescension of hereditary aristocracy as a matter of personal insult. Those on top (even in America) scorned men like Paine as "meer mechanicks" (or as part of, in Burke's notorious phrase, "a swinish multitude"). And yet, Paine demanded, had he and other ordinary men not been endowed by nature with the same reasonable faculties as their privileged betters? Indeed, he continued, had the productive artisans and farmers of America and Britain not contributed far more to the public good than the well-born ladies and gentlemen who had never produced a thing in their lives? "Male and female are the distinctions of nature, good and bad the distinctions of heaven," he wrote in *Common Sense*, "but how a race of men came into the world so exalted above the rest, and distinguished like some new species, is worth inquiring into." Those inquiries constantly led Paine to mock the absurdities of aristocracy and to proclaim the axioms of what he called "representation ingrafted upon democracy": simple government, minimal government, government beholden to a broad democratic citizenry, government subordinate to society, and not the other way around.

It was the vehemence of Paine's polemics, his utter rejection of the old regime, that most shocked his detractors and aroused his followers. No previous American pamphleteer had written as boldly as the author of *Common Sense*:

> England, since the conquest, hath known some good monarchs, but groaned beneath a much larger number of bad ones; yet no man in his senses can say that their claim under William the Conquerer is a very honorable one. A French bastard landing with an armed banditti, and establishing himself king of England against the consent of the natives, is in plain terms a very paltry rascally original. It certainly hath no divinity in it. However, it is needless to spend much time in exposing the folly of hereditary right; if there are any so weak as to believe it, let them promiscuously worship the ass and the lion, and welcome. I shall neither copy their humility, nor disturb their devotion.

Such effrontery was unheard of even in opposition circles, and it sent conservatives into sputtering rages against what Adams called Paine's "yellow fever." Whereas earlier British political reformers (and even most American ones) had hoped to restore some idealized version of a balanced British constitution, Paine called for sweeping away the entire mess and beginning anew, with a wholly republican government freed from any traces of those "two ancient tyrannies," monarchy and aristocracy. "Lay then the axe to the root," he declared in *Rights of Man*, "and teach government humanity."

Paine was sketchier when he discussed the structure of his envisioned republican government. He did outline some fundamentals in *Common Sense*: unicameral state assemblies based on a broad franchise, a national legislature, frequent elections, and a "Continental constitution" written by a democratically elected national convention that would secure individual rights, including rights to property and religious freedom. (Here, Paine anticipated Madison, Hamilton, and the other framers of the U.S. Constitution by a decade.) Paine also took a hand in some practical constitution-making, first in Pennsylvania in 1776 and then in Paris in 1793. And in the second part of *Rights of Man*, and later in his pamphlet *Agrarian Justice*, he devised specific government programs to alleviate the conditions of the British and European poor, writings which ought to embarrass and discredit modern conservatives who claim Paine as one of their own. Still, compared to Madison and the other American founders, men who were engrossed with the intricacies of state-building, Paine was relatively uninterested in such matters. Paine's apparent lack of insight, though, was not just a matter of temperament. It was linked to his most basic ideas about republican government, and his radical take on the common distinction between government and society.

Left to its own devices, Paine believed, humankind was harmonious. Individuals entered into relations with one another in order to fulfill individual desires; the sum of those relations was what he meant by society, a wholly natural and reasonable entity ever attentive to the common good. It was government, as established by a parasitic hereditary caste—a caste that stood outside society—that was the cause of human misery: "Society is produced by our wants and government by our wickedness; the former promotes our happiness positively by uniting our affections, the latter negatively by restraining our vices. The one encourages intercourse, the other creates distinctions. . . . Society is in every state a blessing, but government, even in its best state, is but a necessary evil."

Madison and the other founders saw things differently. Society, on their view, was wracked with divisions of class and sectional interest, which republican government needed to balance and mediate—hence their absorption in the complexities of constitutional architecture. For Paine, however, the major problem was to liberate society from superstitious and oppressive monarchical government. Once that was achieved, elaborate government structures beyond a democratic legislature and (he came to add) a judiciary would be unnecessary, indeed harmful. Hence his relative reticence about constitutional details, apart from his insistence that democratic constitutions were indispensable to keeping even the simplest republican governments in line.

★   ★   ★

PAINE'S CONTRAST between society and government appeals to contradictory political impulses today. There is plenty in Paine's writings to encourage latter-day liberals and leftists, from his contempt for privilege and tradition to his humanitarian concern for the poor and disenfranchised (that "mass of wretchedness," he wrote, which had "scarcely any chance than to expire in poverty or infamy"). The common sense in *Common Sense*—published months before the drafting of the Declaration of Independence—took equality as its primary maxim: "Mankind being originally equal in the order of creation," Paine wrote. Since he attacked government as the cause of human wretchedness, however, selections from Paine's writings have been abstracted and construed, from another angle, as precursor texts of contemporary conservatism, including its angrier populist strains, by publicists who equate eighteenth-century monarchy with modern American liberalism. And since he believed that republican America had freed itself from the Old World's political and social vices, Paine often projected a cheerful view of this country as a classless society of unbounded opportunity (with "the generality of people living in a style of plenty unknown in the monarchical countries")—the sort of exceptionalist rhetoric that has become a standard conservative reply to critics of America's enduring inequalities. Reagan, or his speech-writer, didn't latch on to Paine simply because of a sonorous one-liner or two.

The paradoxes and ironies of Paine's life add to his aura of ambiguity. At one level, he was the archetypal freebooting internationalist radical—a man always in motion, disheveled, prone to drink, consumed by politics. Yet he was also a determined American nationalist, generally supportive of the federal constitution that many of his fellow democrats opposed. In the 1780s, he allied himself with some of America's most conservative financiers, the sponsors of the Bank of North America, in order to save the Revolutionary cause from financial ruin; and he wrote on behalf of banking. Having delivered what remains the most memorable defense of the French Revolution, he wound up paying for his troubles by languishing for nearly a year in a Jacobin prison, where he only barely escaped the guillotine. For all of his celebrated contributions to the Atlantic revolutionary epoch, the condemnations by the respectable of his anti-Christian views helped keep him stranded in France until 1802. He died destitute in Manhattan seven years later, his funeral attended by a Frenchwoman, her two sons, an Irishman, and two African Americans.

Making sense of it all, and making sense of Paine's legacy, is a large assignment, made all the more difficult by the absence of any sizeable collection of Paine's papers and correspondence, most of which were accidentally destroyed in a fire more than a century ago. Not surprisingly, historians and biographers have been tempted to interpret him in their own image, or to conflate a part of his thinking—his anti-Christian deism, for example—with the whole of his thinking. If they are not careful, even the most thoughtful writers can fall into the trap of judging Paine's contributions in light of present realities, as in one biographer's observations about how Paine thought in "remarkably modern" ways about the necessary balance of market economics and "nonmarket support mechanisms"—that is, public debate and government intervention—in sustaining a healthy democracy.

Paine's abiding relevance can be better judged not by elevating him as a beacon for today but by setting him once again alongside his contemporaries. Jefferson and Paine developed two versions of American antimonarchial republican politics, and Paine's republicanism meshed closely with the ideas of other men who boldly wrote for the ages, but whose visions were circumscribed by their times. In particular, Paine's ideas bear close resemblance to those in another work commonly misread as prophecy, the other great book published in 1776 (along with Edward Gibbon's history of the Roman Empire), *The Wealth of Nations*.

At first glance Adam Smith and Thomas Paine may seem an unlikely pairing. Smith, the Oxford-educated Glasgow ethics professor, had some republican and rationalist sympathies, but he was largely uninterested in the political affairs that were the sum of Paine's existence. And on some basic philosophical matters, Smith and Paine disagreed. For Smith, the individual pursuit of self-interest would create the greatest social good. Paine championed the pursuit of reason. Smith saw society as a constant collision of competing individuals that produced harmonious results. Paine saw society as a harmonious whole, held together by recognized common interests.

Yet the two men's modes of thought, as the historian Eric Foner has noticed, were essentially alike. Both considered themselves practitioners of Enlightenment science. Despite their differences, they both believed in an underlying accord of human interests. They both defended the primacy of society—and in particular commercial society—against meddlesome government. They both opposed established institutions and customs such as primogeniture and state churches, which they believed interfered with society's natural workings. They both ripped away at the prevailing traditional systems of authority as wasteful and parasitic, and sought to replace them with a new order of liberty. And they both encouraged new engines of prosperity (such as, in Paine's case, the Bank of North America), to widen commercial opportunities for ordinary men.

But Paine was no more a prophet of modern democracy than Smith was a prophet of modern capitalism. Both men could not help but think of human liberation in terms of a society of small independent producers, where the intensification of commerce would dissolve social privilege, encourage perfect competition, and check the growth of glaring inequalities. Paine's revolution, at once political and economic, would, like Smith's revolution, destroy the government racketeers and unproductive classes forever and put in their place the unrefined, industrious, productive common citizenry.

That revolution did not completely succeed anywhere in the world. In the United States, where it succeeded far more than elsewhere, the growing importance of chattel slavery as a bulwark of commercial society in the early nineteenth century deeply corrupted (and greatly distorted) the natural workings of democracy; and even a century and a half after its violent abolition, slavery's crippling heritage endures. To be sure, Paine could not have foreseen the vast expansion of cotton slavery and the rise of what his later admirer Lincoln would regard as the Slave Power. Yet even to the extent that the revolution Paine propounded succeeded, it prepared the way for a society very different from anything he imagined: a new world of divided political parties, of national and international corporations, a world consisting chiefly not of independent producers but of wage earners and salaried employees, a world of new sorts of connections and patronage and birth privilege, less rigid than the monarchical society of old but hardly a world of perfect competition and equality of opportunity.

The irony, of course, is that the ideas of simple government and laissez-faire that Paine exemplified are now invoked by the chief beneficiaries of this new world (and their political allies) in order to ward off any attempts to interfere with their power—and their bottom line. Worse still, since the mid-nineteenth century, the liberating individualist doctrines of 1776 have been used regularly to cloak a callous disregard for the poor. While reading Paine's words, there is a temptation to turn the tables on this cynical rhetoric, to revive a different usable Paine, the friend of the despised common man, the radical who once remarked (puckishly quoting James I) that "a rich man makes a bonny traitor."

But not so fast. Paine offers only so much consolation to those who would seek to lessen the inequalities of modern American democracy. In particular, his optimistic view of republican society as a web of cooperation has proven hopelessly inadequate, even naive. When, in *Rights of Man* and *Agrarian Justice*, Paine dared to broach the divisive politics of property and interest—what Madison called, in "The Federalist, No. 10," "the most common and durable source of factions"— he did so strictly with reference to the Old World, secure in his belief that the United States would escape such strife thanks to its republican governments. When, at the very end of his life, he began to notice some growing inequalities in America, he blamed them on Federalist plotters who wished to restore the old monarchy, not on any ills intrinsic to American society. Yet those ills, not limited to human slavery, existed, and some continue to exist; and most of the better moments in our democratic history have come about not through the workings of a consensual republican general will, but from the clash of interests. Those interests have been more profoundly antagonistic than Paine imagined, and organized politically as separate interests in ways that Paine would have abhorred. However attractive his desires, however humane his sympathies, Paine's principle of republican harmony has not stood up well in American history.

Still, there is much to remember and to honor about the man and his labors. His questions, if not always his answers, are of enduring significance. His bounding, forward-looking egalitarianism helps to put the American Revolution in its full and proper light, as a genuinely radical revolution, a thorough break from the past. His skepticism about received truths, if overly optimistic about human reason, is a powerful antidote to the lure of dogma. For all their ambiguities, Paine's writings helped to change the world forever. They unleashed ideas about privilege, equality, and democracy that have resounded ever since.

Curiously enough, the old Paine memorial near the cottage in New Rochelle sums up Paine's fate quite well, though it does so in the style of the ironic God that Paine the deist could never quite comprehend. The monument, a battered old bust set upon a shaft, stands near the spot where Paine was buried. But there he no longer lies.

In 1819, the British political writer William Cobbett, who had been one of Paine's fiercest opponents but later converted to radicalism, arranged to have his remains covertly dug up for transportation back to Britain and reburial. Somewhere along the line, the bones were lost. They were never recovered. So Paine rests nowhere. Or better, he is everywhere.

4

★ ★ ★ ★ ★ ▬▬▬▬

Life, Liberty, and the
Pursuit of Thomas Jefferson

ESPECIALLY DURING HIS TROUBLED SECOND ADMINISTRA-
tion, President Thomas Jefferson received a lot of hate mail. "You have
sat aside and trampled on our most dearest rights bought by the blood
of our ancesters," one angry correspondent snarled at the height of the
embargo crisis in 1808. Another letter began, "thomas jefferson, You
infernal villain," and still another saluted the president as "You red-
headed son of a bitch." Jefferson affixed his own laconic endorsements
to these messages ("abusive," "bitter enough") and quietly filed them
away, but he could not hide his growing annoyance. "They are almost
universally the productions of the most ill-tempered & rascally part of
the country, often evidently written from tavern scenes of drunken-
ness," he wrote angrily to his secretary of state, James Madison (who
was also a target of poison pen letters).

Were he alive today, Jefferson could be forgiven if he regarded modern American historians as a bitter, rascally bunch. To be sure, he
remains a sainted figure to millions of ordinary Americans, enshrined
in popular culture as the author of the Declaration of Independence.
Academic historians are hardly of one mind about him. Yet Jefferson
has been subjected to intense attack over the past fifty years by numer-

ous important scholars and distinguished writers, more so than any other leader of the American Revolution.

In 1963, the legal historian Leonard W. Levy damaged Jefferson's reputation as a civil libertarian by describing how, as president, he tolerated the suppression of opposition editors with selective prosecutions for seditious libel. Soon afterward, several leading historians, including Winthrop D. Jordan, David Brion Davis, and Edmund S. Morgan, challenged the authenticity of Jefferson's antislavery professions and emphasized his disturbing writings about blacks. Conservative and leftist writers have been discovering common anti-Jefferson ground on issues ranging from Indian removal to the Haitian Revolution, and they have adopted an increasingly acidulous tone. Whereas pro-Hamiltonians such as Forrest McDonald denounce Jefferson as a "wild-eyed political quack," left-leaning historians such as Michael Zuckerman describe him as "the foremost racist of his era in America." In perhaps the most thorough denunciation, the late Conor Cruise O'Brien, attacking from the left and the right simultaneously, linked Jefferson's legacy to the Jacobin Reign of Terror, the Ku Klux Klan, Pol Pot, the architect of South African apartheid Hendrik Verwoerd, and the right-wing militia movement in contemporary America.

To a certain extent, all these vicissitudes of reputation are just the familiar academic boom-and-bust cycle. Undervalued by historians in the nineteenth century (when pro-Federalist New Englanders dominated the field), Jefferson enjoyed a revival in the 1920s and 1930s, when he was celebrated as a liberal champion of the Enlightenment and a patron saint of democratic reform. The dedication of the Jefferson Memorial in Washington, DC, in 1943, presided over by President Franklin D. Roosevelt, signaled Jefferson's enduring stature in the public mind; and thereafter a series of scholarly monuments, above all Dumas Malone's admiring six-volume biography, which appeared between 1948 and 1981, ratified Jefferson's greatness inside the nation's history departments. In recent years, inevitably, there has been a corrective, anti-Jefferson reaction. But this alone cannot explain the shrillness of some of Jefferson's current critics, or why so many of them are leftists or liberals, formerly Jefferson's champions against the Hamiltonian plutocracy.

Somewhat paradoxically, Jefferson's fate has paralleled that of twentieth-century American liberalism. There was always something absurd about describing Jefferson, the agrarian anti-statist, as one of the forerunners of Progressive reform and New Deal reform. Jefferson's writings on religious liberty gave the argument a certain plausibility in the 1920s, which saw the Scopes trial and a revival of anti-Catholic nativism. A decade later, New Deal Democrats pointed with pride to their party's distant genealogical connections to the Jeffersonians. Much more influential, though, was the notion Herbert Croly had popularized back in 1909, that modern reformers were trying to use Hamiltonian means to achieve Jeffersonian ends. (That is, it was Jefferson who inspired latter-day government efforts to rein in the malefactors of great wealth, and subordinate wealth and property rights to human rights and the nation's well-being.) "If Jefferson would return . . . ," FDR told an audience of Democrats in 1932, "he would find that while economic changes of a century have changed the necessary methods of government action, the principles of that action are still wholly his own." With that presumption, the reputations of Jefferson and modern liberalism crested at about the same time, from the 1930s to the 1950s. Yet as the twentieth century dragged on and became the twenty-first, and as American liberalism suffered through its own intellectual and political crises, it has become harder to sustain Jefferson's reputation as any kind of liberal forerunner.

The great triumphs of the civil rights movement posed the greatest problems for Jefferson's reputation. In the 1930s and 1940s, the New Deal coalition of liberal Northerners and the segregationist Solid South could comfortably admire a contradictory Virginia slaveholder who proclaimed that all men were created equal. In the 1960s, as the New Deal coalition collapsed under the weight of civil rights agitation and reform, so did many liberals' and leftists' admiration of Jefferson.

Despite his exquisite pain about slavery as "an abominable crime," Jefferson remained a slaveholder his entire life, owning at one point as many as two hundred slaves. Alert to the returns from his human chattel, he arranged for the manumission of fewer than ten of his slaves, while thousands of his fellow Virginians, including George Washington, freed theirs (although in Washington's case only upon the decease of his wife). For all of his egalitarianism, Jefferson proffered, in his *Notes on the State of Virginia,* some hair-raising, pseudo-scientific personal observations about the innate mental and physical inferiority of blacks, including his notion that Negroes prefer whites "as uniformly as is the preference of the Oran-ootan for the black women over those of his own species."

When he registered his deep objections to slavery, as he also did in *Notes on the State of Virginia,* Jefferson always sounded more troubled by the institution's degrading effects on whites than by its oppression of the slaves. Until his dying day, Jefferson doubted that blacks and whites could ever coexist peaceably as American citizens; indeed, he believed that slavery's terrible travails made racial segregation mandatory, and he looked forward to the eventual disappearance of blacks from these shores, preferably through emancipation, deportation, and colonization.

On similar grounds, of course, almost every politically prominent white Southerner of Jefferson's time (with notable exceptions, such as Jefferson's law teacher, George Wythe, and the Virginia jurist and emancipationist St. George Tucker) could be excluded from being honored in ours. As one of Jefferson's most effective modern critics, Robert McColley, has observed, Jefferson's hypocrisy in the matter of legislative plans for emancipation was typical of the enlightened "antislavery" Virginia slaveholder gentry of the Revolutionary Era. Yet it is Jefferson who gets singled out, and it is easy to understand why: he wrote, in the opening lines of the Declaration of Independence, the most famous summary of the American egalitarian creed. Plainly, there was less to those great words than met the eye, for they were written by a slaveholder who believed in, or at least hypothesized about, shockingly, the racial superiority of whites.

Precisely because of his egalitarian professions, Jefferson fell out of fashion faster and harder than other Founding Fathers did. Indeed, by the 1990s, with the arrival of what some critics have called "Founders Chic," biographers helped rehabilitate John Adams, Alexander Hamilton, and other leading conservatives of the Revolutionary Era by pointedly contrasting them with their adversary, the wretched Jefferson. The most celebrated of these books, David McCullough's biography of Adams, contrasts McCullough's doughty, forthright, admirable second president and a fugacious, narcissistic Jefferson without spending much time at all on Adams's conservative-minded republicanism and its differences with Jeffersonian democracy. Another anti-Jefferson book, Ron Chernow's flattering biography of Hamilton, miscasts its hero as an "ardent abolitionist" while it travesties Jefferson's democratic politics as the inert vision of a duplicitous "populist slaveholder."* Meanwhile, as academic historians reinterpreted the past along the grid of race, class, and gender, and as identity and affinity politics effaced other forms of politics, Jefferson appeared less as an egalitarian democrat purposefully if tragically entwined with slavery and more as a privileged, deceitful, slaveholding racist, a forerunner of John C. Calhoun and Jefferson Davis.

Interestingly, many black American reformers and radicals since Jefferson's time have been able to own the contradictions between his words and his deeds, and between some of his words and others. In 1829, three years after Jefferson's death, the fiery free black pam-

---

* Although he was a founding member of the antislavery New-York Manhattan Society and served briefly as the group's president, Hamilton never publicly or, apparently, privately advocated slavery's abolition, much less do so ardently. Indeed, he consistently supported property rights over the slaves' natural rights to freedom. See Michelle Du Ross, "Somewhere in Between: Alexander Hamilton and Slavery," *Early American Review* 15 (2011), available at http://www.earlyamerica.com/early-america-review/volume-15/hamilton-and-slavery/.

phleteer David Walker angrily (and lengthily) refuted the racism in *Notes on the State of Virginia*, calling the book "as great a barrier to our emancipation as any thing that has ever been advanced against us." Walker's fury and disgust at Jefferson's Negrophobia precluded any consideration of the book's antislavery passages. But Walker also regarded Jefferson as a great man, "a much greater philosopher the world has never afforded." He held up Jefferson's Declaration of Independence as an unfulfilled charter for racial equality, to be secured by any means necessary. And more than a century later, Dr. Martin Luther King, Jr.—speaking at the Lincoln Memorial and not the Jefferson Memorial—echoed Walker's Jeffersonian themes (although not his violent overtones) by quoting the Declaration at the March on Washington in 1963.

Still, black Americans have always been unlikely to harbor illusions about an American patriot who was also a slaveholder, which may explain why figures such as Walker and King have been able to approach Jefferson's legacy with (in Walker's case) angry reproach but also a certain ironic detachment. "I'm a forgiving man," the late historian John Hope Franklin remarked in Ken Burns's PBS documentary *Thomas Jefferson*, "therefore, I forgive him for what he did. But I remember that what he did was a transgression against mankind." By contrast, much current historical writing on Jefferson has acquired a single-minded peevishness that turns into truculence that turns into fury. On slavery and race, as on other matters, Jefferson disappoints many modern liberals and leftists, and that disappointment has led to outrage, and so a new anti-Jefferson left has joined up with the traditional anti-Jefferson right, flinging around invective and accusations that make "red-headed son of a bitch" sound mild.

★ ★ ★

IT WAS ODD to see Conor Cruise O'Brien, some twenty years ago, enter the arena in the guise of an intrepid Jefferson debunker. All of the major pieces of evidence that O'Brien's book, *The Long*

Affair, marshals against Jefferson—including the egregious passages on blacks in *Notes on the State of Virginia*, and a notorious sanguinary letter that Jefferson wrote in praise of the French Revolution in 1793—had been familiar to scholars for decades. Most of O'Brien's specific charges about Jefferson's political chicanery and opportunism were validated long before he began his assault. They were and are accepted by scholars who remain, withal, Jefferson's admirers. But O'Brien's contortions of Jefferson's faults created a horrific image of the man that contributed to making him, as the historian Joseph Ellis has put it, one of the prize "trophies" in the continuing culture wars.

O'Brien spends a good deal of time lambasting biographers and historians he calls starry-eyed "liberal Jeffersonians," whom he accuses of suppressing and falsifying documentary evidence, among other crimes against scholarship. When not simply abusive, these attacks turn out themselves to be outrageous, as when O'Brien accuses Dumas Malone of willfully ignoring Jefferson's controversial letter extolling the French Revolution—which Malone evaluated at length. Still, it is Jefferson, not the historians, who receives the roughest handling in *The Long Affair*.

According to O'Brien, Jefferson's attachment to his privileged social station and his singular contempt for blacks (apart, perhaps, from his concubine, Sally Hemings) overrode whatever abstract criticisms he made of slavery. The Piedmont philosophe lived well enough off black slave labor. Virtually all of Jefferson's public life and much of his private life, as O'Brien reads them, were shaped by a deep-seated defensiveness attached to his slaveholding. On this view, Jefferson's famous battles against Hamilton's financial and military plans arose not (as most historians have contended) from his fear of an encroaching, British-style corruption of the new republic, but from his desire to shield slavery from Federalist criticism and Northern-style economic development.

O'Brien claims also that Jefferson's racism and his slaveholder's anxieties explain his abiding and "almost manic" support for the French Revolution. Yet Jefferson's record on the French Revolution has long been established. As the American envoy to France, Jefferson was caught by surprise by the revolutionary crisis in 1789, but he immediately welcomed it as an extension of America's revolution and a mighty blow against a rotten old regime. His early political advice to his French comrades, on the eve of the fall of the Bastille, was to persuade Louis XVI to issue a charter of rights—a fairly modest, even conservative proposal that would have left the monarchy intact (and which O'Brien fails to discuss).

Only after his return home late in 1789, as George Washington's secretary of state, did Jefferson's rhetoric about the revolution become more heated, in part as a symbolic aspect of his larger domestic battles with the Anglophile Hamilton. As those domestic battles over banks and national finance grew nastier, Jefferson became ever more enthusiastically pro-revolution, even after he received news of the September Massacres and other outrages. Finally, on January 3, 1793, writing to William Short (his former personal secretary and now the American minister to The Hague), Jefferson fell into arguing that the revolution's glorious ends justified apocalyptic means: "My own affections have been deeply wounded by some of the martyrs to this cause, but rather than it should have failed, I would have seen half the earth desolated. Were there but an Adam & an Eve left in every country, & left free, it would be better than as it now is."

Excerpted, it is an appalling passage when read today, after two more centuries of dictators and apologist intellectuals who have countenanced slaughtering the innocent for the sake of perfecting mankind. It was here, O'Brien contends, that Jefferson exposed his truest self, as a fanatic proponent of utopian genocide, addled by what Burke called "the wild *gas* of liberty." Link up that fanaticism with Jefferson's racism, and you have largely summarized O'Brien's case that Jefferson foreshadowed the Klan and today's right-wing militias.

The case is worse than feeble. Never mind that Jefferson was prone in his private correspondence to passing flights of flamboyance, what his friend Madison called "a habit in Mr. Jefferson as in others of great genius of expressing in strong and round terms, impressions of the moment." It takes a mean-spirited imagination to conclude that Jefferson's remarks show he condoned, much less relished, mass slaughter. Moreover, by the end of 1793—that is, by the time the Jacobins had launched the Reign of Terror—Jefferson's feelings about revolutionary France had cooled considerably, in part because of the embarrassing efforts by the French envoy, Edmond Genêt, to undermine the Washington administration's neutrality policy. Two years later (as O'Brien does note but fails to account for), Jefferson denounced what he called "the atrocities of Robespierre"; thereafter, the notorious XYZ Affair, whereby Talleyrand and the French Directory attempted to exact tribute from three American diplomats, alienated Jefferson from the Jacobins' successors. Looking back in his late seventies, he repeated his original hope that Louis XVI could have been retained as a limited monarch, thereby staving off "those enormities which demoralized the nations of the world, and destroyed, and is yet to destroy, millions and millions of its inhabitants."

Despite these disavowals, O'Brien insists that Jefferson retained a fondness for the revolution in Paris at its most atrocious—as, of all things, a pretext for protecting slavery and alleviating white Southern guilt. Without fear (and without evidence), O'Brien proposes that Jefferson and other Virginians used their loyalty to what he calls the "Cult of the French Revolution" as a ploy to fend off the antislavery jibes of Hamilton and other Northern Federalists, projecting their guilt over slavery onto Northerners, whom they charged with insufficient ardor for France's extension of the American Revolution. Weary of being lectured about slavery, Jefferson supposedly tried to turn the tables by making loyalty to the French cause the measure of one's loyalty to human liberty, including American liberty.

★　★　★

EVERY POINT IN this argument is tendentious at best. Ascribing support for the French Revolution to Jefferson's projections of guilt ignores that much of the loudest support for the French came from

Northern Jeffersonians, who held no slaves and in some cases were firmly antislavery. Any account of Jefferson's views on slavery must take seriously his (admittedly wishful) insistence, in 1774, that "the abolition of domestic slavery is the great object of desire in those colonies where it was unhappily introduced in their infant state." Then there is Jefferson's committee's proposal to Congress a decade later to exclude slaves from the western territories after 1800. Had Jefferson died in 1784, his modern critic David Brion Davis allows, he would be remembered as "one of the first statesmen in any part of the world to advocate concrete measures for restricting and eradicating Negro slavery." By contrast, Davis goes on to observe, O'Brien's beloved Edmund Burke drafted a bill for the improvement of the conditions of West Indian slaves in 1780, preparatory to their emancipation— but Burke kept the idea secret for twelve years, out of fear of dividing the Whig Party.

Jefferson's views on slavery followed a tragic trajectory. When, for example, *Notes on the State of Virginia* (which Jefferson did not originally intend for general circulation) was printed in a small private anonymous edition in Paris in 1785, it was, as Jefferson feared, the antislavery passages that caught people's attention. John Adams, one of O'Brien's Burkean heroes, read the book immediately and congratulated Jefferson, claiming that his remarks on slavery were "worth Diamonds" and would "have more effect than Volumes written by mere Philosophers." Thereafter Jefferson, rattled that his views had been published, would be scrupulously circumspect about his opinions on slavery, to the point of maintaining a virtual public silence on the subject. But Jefferson's retreat from his more youthful convictions is a historical and biographical problem in need of an explanation, one more exacting than O'Brien's scurrilous description of his attachment to slavery as "a classical case of Odi et amo."

To be sure, Jefferson never became anything like a liberal on race, even by late eighteenth-century standards, a failing for which authorities ranging from the Abbé Henri Grégoire to various Northern

Federalist editors took him to task. Jefferson's racism rendered him consistently hostile to the legal rights of Virginia's free blacks, notably during the debates over revising Virginia's legal codes in the 1770s and 1780s. As late as the 1820s, when he acknowledged that the size of America's slave population was too great to allow for a summary deportation of blacks, Jefferson was still cooking up colonization schemes whereby the federal government would buy all newborn slaves from their owners and eventually ship them to Santo Domingo.

It would be a travesty to portray Jefferson as a proponent of the sort of interracial American democracy that is a cardinal principle of modern liberal politics. But it is also unfair to portray Jefferson as O'Brien portrays him, as the prophet and the patron of racist evil. One can find racist statements from some of Jefferson's Southern antagonists (and even from some Northerners) that are just as damning as Jefferson's and also justify the institution of slavery, which Jefferson never did. The proslavery racism that later helped to propel Southern secession had less in common with the ideas of Thomas Jefferson (whom the more thoughtful Confederates rejected as a foolish egalitarian) than with those of figures like the South Carolina Federalist William Loughton Smith, who declared in the House of Representatives in 1790 that slavery was a fit, indeed beneficial status for members of an "indolent," "improvident" race, "averse to labor," who, if emancipated, "would either starve or plunder."

Jefferson, by contrast, struggled with his racial assumptions. Searching the papers of Washington, James Madison, James Monroe, John Marshall, and the rest will produce nothing similar to Jefferson's at times uneasy writings about slavery and race. In a letter explaining himself to Grégoire in 1809, Jefferson wrote that his ideas about blacks in the *Notes* "were the result of personal observation on the limited sphere of my own State," that he expressed them "with great hesitation" and earnestly wished to see their "complete refutation," and that, in any case, superior natural talents could not justify granting anyone superior legal or civil rights. ("Because Sir Isaac Newton was superior to others in understanding," Jefferson noted, "he was not therefore lord of the person or property of others.")

Although Jefferson was profoundly pessimistic about social relations between whites and freed blacks, his beliefs about linking emancipation with colonization were far from extreme in his time. Indeed, when Jefferson died in 1826, many white pro-emancipationists (and even some free blacks), unable to imagine true harmony ever existing between the races in America, favored some sort of colonization scheme. In the North, especially outside New England and the Yankee cultural outcroppings of the Old Northwest, such views persisted into the Civil War era, even among some implacable antislavery partisans. In December 1862, President Lincoln declared to Congress that "I strongly favor colonization," by which he meant finding the freed slaves new homes "in congenial climes, and with people of their own blood and race." (Soon after, he dropped his backing of colonization.) Three years earlier, Lincoln had proposed "[a]ll honour to Jefferson" for declaring as a self-evident truth that all men are created equal. Would O'Brien have cast Lincoln, too, as a precursor of Hendrik Verwoerd or merely as an early, muddle-headed "liberal Jeffersonian"?

Domestic politics do help explain why pro-French sentiment tended to run stronger in the South than in the North—but not as a twisted defense of Southern slavery, which most Northern Federalists were happy enough to leave alone and even protect. Pro-French Southerners chiefly feared (as expressed in Jefferson's numerous writings about the "Anglican monarchical aristocratical party") that the Francophobic Federalists were about to impose a centralized state in order to prop up a Northern financial aristocracy. And the documentary sources from the 1790s show that the affections of some Federalists for an American elective monarchy, and their skepticism about popular government, were all too real. In order to block Jefferson from the presidency, Alexander Hamilton for one favored official repression, and, in time, he proposed making blatant, retroactive changes in voting laws that would have reversed the outcome of the election of 1800. No wonder Jefferson and his supporters were apprehensive.

As for the supposed proslavery origins of Jefferson's pro-Jacobinism, the most forthright proslavery elements of the Southern slaveholding planter class in fact supported neither Jefferson nor the French Revolution. They were political allies of the Northern Federalists, and sworn enemies, as John Rutledge, Jr., of South Carolina declared, of "this new-fangled French philosophy of liberty and equality," in part because it threatened slavery. Jefferson, according to the ardently proslavery Federalist William Loughton Smith, was among the "*pretenders* to philosophy" who would coolly justify "the most atrocious and *sanguinary cruelties*, provided they are a means to a certain favorite *end*."

Was Jefferson ever really the unhinged fanatic O'Brien (echoing the anti-Jefferson reactionary slaveholders) claims he was? As it happened, American support for the French Revolution remained remarkably strong and enthusiastic even after the execution of Louis XVI in January 1793 and the onset of the Reign of Terror later that year. Much of the frenzied millennial rhetoric in the everyday debates over the French Revolution made Jefferson's passing comments in the "Adam and Eve" letter to William Short sound almost meek by comparison. In 1794, for example, just as the Reign of Terror was gearing up and Jefferson was tempering his views, Ezra Stiles, the gentle and venerable Congregationalist president of Yale College, called with full-throated antimonarchial enthusiasm for "more Use of the Guillotine yet" in France, to mow down "hurtful and poisonous Weeds" so that "Right Liberty and Tranquillity can be established." Given the fragility of republicanism in a world of monarchs and aristocrats, it would have been remarkable had public emotions not reached such a pitch. And when their own political moment of truth came in 1800–1801, of course, Jefferson and his supporters erected no guillotines and launched no insurrections. Instead, they organized an electoral opposition that defeated the Federalists and conducted a peaceful, indeed conciliatory, transfer of power.

None of this, to be sure, extenuates or excuses Jefferson for writing two chilling sentences to William Short, or for retreating from his early antislavery stance, or for advancing hideous racist theories. Apologizing for Jefferson is no less offensive to history than diabolizing him. But ripping portions of Jefferson's writings out of context and extrapolating them nearly two hundred years into the future in order to turn Jefferson into the political ancestor of Timothy McVeigh is worse than caricature. One cringes to think what O'Brien might have written about Jefferson and Dylann Storm Roof.

A failed exercise in biographical annihilation, *The Long Affair* brings to mind the remark of one Jackson-era politician that it is sometimes possible to kill a man too dead. A lighter touch would have served O'Brien better—as it would another distinguished writer, Garry Wills, in his sounder yet complementary study of slavery and what used to be called Jeffersonian democracy, *"Negro President."*

★ ★ ★

WILLS DISAPPROVES of O'Brien's effort to, as he puts it, render Jefferson "more a friend to despotism than to freedom." He avows that, unlike O'Brien and other Jefferson bashers, he greatly admires the man. That admiration clearly animated Wills's *Inventing America*, published in 1978, which carefully re-creates Jefferson's authorship of the Declaration. Yet if Wills is more measured than O'Brien, he dedicates *"Negro President"* to the proposition that Jefferson's political career, as well as the success of the political party he inspired and led, rested on "protection and extension of the slave power" which exploited the Constitution to entrench human bondage. And in exposing Jefferson's proslavery politics, Wills also aims, in the manner of the Founders Chic biographers, to rehabilitate his Federalist adversaries, including his most scabrous foes.

Wills takes his title from a letter written by the book's hero, Timothy Pickering, the High Federalist from Massachusetts and one of Jefferson's sharpest antagonists. Cast by Wills as a principled antislavery fighter—indeed, as an "abolitionist"—Pickering invented the term "Negro president," in Wills's telling, to refer to the infernal extra representation that the Constitution gave to the South under the three-fifths clause, which permitted the slaveholders to strengthen and to expand their evil. In 1804, the high-minded Pickering, alarmed over the ascendancy of the nascent Slave Power, wrote to his fellow Federalist Rufus King about the seeming inevitability of "negro Presidents and negro Congresses."

Here is the full story behind that letter. In 1804, Pickering was in a panic over the gains being made by pro-Jefferson Republicans in Federalist New England, including in his home state. He had good reason to fret: Jefferson would carry Massachusetts in his landslide reelection campaign later that year, and in 1806 the Jeffersonians would gain control of the Massachusetts legislature. And so Pickering tried to organize a conspiracy to get New England, and if possible New York and New Jersey, to secede from the Union. He explained to his would-be recruits the grounds for separation: Jefferson had given no patronage to Federalists; Jefferson and his supporters had tried to debase morals and religion (not least, as his friends knew, in the Congregationalist theocracy of Connecticut); and above all, the Jeffersonians had tried to make government more democratic, thereby ending, as Pickering wrote, "the protection of the best." Curbing democracy and preserving Federalism—with not a word about slavery—was reason enough to dissolve the Union.

On March 4, Pickering sought to enlist the moderate Federalist Rufus King in his plot. "I am disgusted with the men who now rule," he began, and especially with "the cowardly wretch at their head," who, "like a Parisian revolutionary," enjoyed "prating about humanity" while actually endeavoring to destroy "integrity and worth" and install "Jacobinism." Pickering's letter seethed with hatred—not of slavery but of democracy. On and on Pickering went about the inferior Jacobins whom Jefferson was appointing to office—including one Virginian, Pickering observed with revulsion, "who could not now get credit

in Richmond for a suit of clothes!" Nothing about slavery or its cruelties turned up—except (in what had become a familiar sour-grapes
excuse among Federalists for their national political failures) how the
three-fifths clause aided the wretched Jacobin Jeffersonians. "Without
a separation," Pickering wrote, "can those states ever rid themselves of
negro Presidents and negro Congresses, and regain their just weight in
the political balance?"

King saw the conspiracy for the sordid thing that it was and
strongly objected, as did Alexander Hamilton and, less strenuously,
the others to whom Pickering wrote. John Quincy Adams, still a
Federalist, complained about the "party grounds" on which the Pickering's maneuvering was founded—"the victory of professed democracy over Federalism," which Adams, taking the Federalist line, said
had indeed been enabled by the triumph of "the slave representation
over the purely free." The Federalists, that is, chafed at the sectional
advantages that the three-fifths clause secured for the South, but for
partisan reasons. King, Hamilton, and Adams detected no antislavery
purport to Pickering's attack on the monster Jefferson and his vulgar
Jacobin hordes, chiefly because Pickering had offered none. So it is
important to recognize that Wills's title comes not from some lofty
antislavery tract, but from a letter advancing ultra-Federalist, antidemocratic secessionist propaganda, proposing a plan that eminent
Federalists considered harebrained and ludicrous.

How did Wills come to such an unfortunate pass? His main argument is the old Federalist claim that the three-fifths clause in the
Constitution was the reason that Thomas Jefferson was elected president in 1800–1801, and that the Democratic-Republicans won and
then sustained a majority in Congress. The voters, it seems, did not
really reject the Federalists in 1800; although constitutionally correct,
the so-called Jeffersonian Revolution of 1800 lacked democratic legitimacy; far from a blow for egalitarian politics of any kind, Jefferson's
election marked the first victory in a national election for the Slave
Power, "a great tipping point in American history," according to Wills.

Rooting Jefferson's career in national politics in the three-fifths clause is problematic from the start. Jefferson was in Paris, serving as American minister to France, during the Federal convention in 1787, so he had nothing to do with the clause's formulation or inclusion in the Constitution. Among the convention delegates most involved was the proslavery South Carolinian Charles Cotesworth Pinckney, who, along with his younger cousin Charles Pinckney and Pierce Butler, pushed the convention to grant even greater representation on the basis of owning slaves. After agreeing to the three-fifths compromise, they would cleave to that extra representation for the rest of their political lives. The younger Pinckney, who came to be known as "Blackguard Charlie," would go on to betray his original Federalist allegiance and become a key backer of Jefferson. Butler, nominally a Federalist, proved a maverick, especially on foreign policy. But Charles Cotesworth Pinckney would become a steadfast Federalist foe of Jefferson and the Jeffersonians. Indeed, the Federalist Party would nominate Pinckney for the vice presidency in 1800, then nominate him against President Jefferson in 1804, and then run him again for the presidency against James Madison in 1808. Connecting the three-fifths clause and Jeffersonian politics is not, it turns out, so simple.

Still, if the slaveholder Jefferson did not create the three-fifths clause, Wills contends that he and his supporters decisively benefited from it. Thanks, supposedly, to the extra representation, Jefferson's Republican supporters—led by slaveholders and their political fortunes entwined with slavery—were able to pass legislation that protected human bondage and permitted its expansion. "On crucial matters," Wills writes, "the federal ratio gave the South a voting majority." That influence lasted long after Jefferson left office; among other things, according to Wills, it prevented the exclusion of slavery from Missouri in 1820 and, in the late 1840s, it doomed the Wilmot Proviso, which would have banned slavery from territories grabbed from Mexico. The main political beneficiaries were Jefferson, his party, and their slaveholding successors, who were opposed prophetically but unsuccessfully by Federalists like the unsung hero Timothy Pickering.

There are so many errors in this argument, factual and interpretive, that it is hard to know where to begin. The three-fifths clause certainly inflated Southerners' power in the House, not simply in affecting numerous roll-call votes—roughly one in three overall of those recorded between 1795 and 1821—but also in shaping the politics of party caucuses and, later, party conventions, as well as patronage and judicial appointments. Yet even with the extra seats, the share held by the major slaveholding states in the House actually declined between 1790 and 1820, from 45 percent to 42 percent, and, according to one quantitative study, the clause's effects on House roll-call votes dropped dramatically after 1800. Although the three-fifths rule carried some major bills through the House before 1820, none of those listed in the study concerned slavery, whereas in 1819, antislavery Northerners, most of them Jeffersonian Republicans, rallied a clear House majority to halt slavery's expansion.

Strikingly, in one of the most significant congressional struggles prior to 1820 where the three-fifths rule proved decisive (according to the same quantitative study) its effect was not at all proslavery— but it was momentously anti-Jeffersonian. Before 1820, the rule most frequently affected voting in the House during the Fifth and Sixth Congresses, in 1797–99 and 1799–1801. In both congresses, the extra slave representation made the difference in more than half the total number of recorded House roll-call votes. Yet the study identifies only two major pieces of legislation that passed during these years because of the clause (apart from the act that established the Department of the Navy in 1798, the Bankruptcy of 1800, and the Judiciary Act of 1801): the Alien Act and the Sedition Act, both approved in 1798. These notorious repressive measures—two of the four laws known collectively as the Alien and Sedition Acts—were advanced by, among others, the stalwart Federalist slaveholders John Rutledge, Jr., and Robert Goodloe Harper, in order to destroy Jefferson and his political supporters. If the voting figures are correct, and had the laws achieved their intent, historians would now be writing of how the three-fifths clause helped strangle the Jeffersonian opposition in its cradle.

The three-fifths clause guaranteed the South a voting majority on some but hardly all of the "crucial matters," later in the nineteenth century, that Wills singles out. Indeed, the congressional bulwark of what came to be known, rightly, as the Slave Power proved to be not the House but the Senate, where the three-fifths clause made no difference whatsoever—which is one reason why the slaveholders fought as hard as they did, through the 1850s, to admit as many new slave states as possible to the Union and keep parity in the Senate with the North.

In the very first Congress, and the very first fractious debate over slavery, the House actually crushed, by a margin of three to one, an effort by angry lower-South slaveholders to reject an antislavery petition from the Pennsylvania Abolition Society, signed by the group's president, Benjamin Franklin, which the Southerners charged was unconstitutional. "[A]lass—how weak a resistance against the whole house," the South Carolina Federalist William Loughton Smith wrote to a friend. The Southerners, fighting back fiercely, managed to tone down severely an extraordinary ensuing special committee report (which encouraged the abolitionists and their "humane objects"), but they could not render slavery untouchable under national law. Three years later, Congress did pass a fugitive slave law, but by so large a majority in the House—48 to 7 with 14 abstaining—that the three-fifths rule was irrelevant.

After Jefferson's election in 1800–1801, one of the most "crucial matters" (as Wills puts it) debated in Congress and connected to slavery concerned the so-called Hillhouse amendments—and the story of those amendments tells a great deal about the reliability of the scholarship in *"Negro President."* Early in 1804, the Connecticut Federalist James Hillhouse proposed alterations to a territorial organizing bill, including one that would have ended slavery in the newly acquired Louisiana Territory. But the issue was decided not by the House but the Senate, so the three-fifths clause made no difference. The same had held true for the approval of the Louisiana Purchase treaty two years earlier—an essentially proslavery move in Wills's eyes, which is a view that Rufus King, Alexander Hamilton, and John Quincy Adams, although concerned about the three-fifths clause, did not share.

Meanwhile, the roll call of the vote defeating the Hillhouse proposal in the Senate is highly revealing. Although Hillhouse was a Federalist, the bulk of his support came from Northern Jeffersonians, who divided six to four in favor of the amendment, whereas the Northern Federalists split right down the middle, three to three. So much for the Democratic-Republicans as the tool of the slaveocracy, at least regarding slavery in Louisiana. More to the point: had four more of the eighteen Northern senators voted with Hillhouse and against the slaveholders, the emancipationist amendment would have passed, which would have been a momentous, possibly pivotal occasion in early antislavery politics. Among those who instead voted with the South were the two Federalist senators from Massachusetts: John Quincy Adams and . . . Timothy Pickering!

The three-fifths clause certainly did not prevent the House from voting to exclude slavery from the new state of Missouri in 1819. The House twice passed, by substantial margins, antislavery resolutions proposed by the Republican James Tallmadge, Jr., with the largely Republican Northern majority founding its case largely on Jefferson's Declaration—the "definition of republican government," in one congressman's words. The antislavery effort died in the Senate, where, again, the three-fifths clause made no difference.

It demanded protracted and furious efforts by House leaders including Speaker Henry Clay, with behind-the-scenes support from President James Monroe, to chip away at the Northern majority and eke out a deal in which the House finally agreed, in March 1820, to admit Missouri as a slave state. Here Wills has a point: without the three-fifths clause, it almost certainly would have been impossible for Clay and the others to keep slavery in Missouri. But if Clay had failed, the Senate, the slaveholders' true redoubt, would have simply continued to block any antislavery provision, prolonging the stalemate. Finally, Wills evades the really important point, that permitting slavery in Missouri required the slaveholders to grant what many of them considered an intolerable concession concerning congressional authority over slavery—barring slavery from the Louisiana Purchase lands outside Missouri that lay north of 36° 30', in the famous Missouri Compromise. In time, slaveholders' resistance to that concession, culminating in the notorious Supreme Court ruling in the *Dred Scott* case in 1857, would lead directly to secession and civil war.

A quarter century after the Missouri crisis, in a virtual reprise, the Jacksonian Congressman David Wilmot added a proviso to a military appropriations bill, barring slavery from any territory gained in the continuing war with Mexico. "It caused a great flutter; but it stuck like wax," Abraham Lincoln, then a young Illinois Whig Congressman, would later remark. Lincoln lasted only one term in the House; still, he recalled, the proviso "or the principle of it, was constantly coming up in some shape or other, and I think I may venture to say I voted for it at least forty times; during the short term I was there." He exaggerated the number, but on numerous occasions, Lincoln joined with a crushing Northern majority in the House to pass the measure, only to have the Senate reject it. The Senate (and the Slave Power) did finally prevail after long and furious debate, when, thanks to Northern Democratic defections, the House approved an enlarged appropriations bill without the proviso, not unlike the vote over Missouri in 1820. But the idea that the three-fifths clause in itself doomed the Wilmot Proviso is simply mistaken; and the conflict reinforced the growth of antislavery politics in the North, leading to the formation of the Free Soil Party in 1848.

The core of Wills's argument on the three-fifths clause, though, concerns not the House and Congress but the Electoral College and the presidency. Above all, Wills confidently reports as outrageous fact the Federalist canard that, except for the three-fifths rule, John Adams would have defeated Jefferson and won reelection in 1800. Contrary to Jeffersonian propaganda, dutifully repeated by their historian admirers, the Federalists remained the majority party, not the Republicans. The so-called Revolution of 1800, celebrated by Jeffersonians and described by historians as a popular repudiation of the Federalists and Federalism, was a fraud.

Based on a quick look at the numbers, the argument seems to have merit. With the three-fifths rule in effect, Jefferson defeated Adams in the Electoral College by seventy-three votes to sixty-five. The historian William W. Freehling, on whom Wills relies, calculates that without the rule, Adams would have won reelection with sixty-three votes to Jefferson's sixty-one. So it was only the extra representation given to the slaveholders that elected Jefferson president. But this overlooks the Federalists' deliberate suppression of the Jeffersonian vote in key Northern states.

In Massachusetts, for example, the Federalists simply rescinded popular voting in 1800 in some of the larger towns with sizeable Jeffersonian constituencies. More important, the Federalists' shenanigans in heavily Jeffersonian Pennsylvania, blocking legislation to organize the presidential voting, led to Adams getting as many as seven more electoral votes, and Jefferson getting seven less, than they respectively deserved. (The Federalists knew that Jefferson would win Pennsylvania in a landslide, as he had swept the state in 1796; in 1800, Republicans routed the Federalists in Pennsylvania's state and congressional elections, winning upward of two-thirds of the votes cast.)

Federalist manipulation cleared the way for Adams to run as well as he did. Eliminate both the three-fifths rule and the Federalists' perversions of democracy and Jefferson still would have defeated Adams by anywhere from six to ten electoral votes. Without the three-fifths rule but with the perversions—Freehling's and Wills's fancied hypothetical outcome—the Jeffersonians could have charged that the Federalists had stolen the election, and they would have been correct.

Charging instead that the Slave Power stole the election and that the outcome in 1800 was the wrong one also flies in the face of the plain shift in political alignments that had begun in 1796, when Jefferson won the popular vote for president in Pennsylvania. After gaining their first congressional majority in 1800, the Republicans did even better in 1802, and better still in 1804, making sizeable gains in New England as well as the middle Atlantic states. And in 1804, the same year that Timothy Pickering wrote the bitter letter about "negro Presidents" from which Wills takes his title, Jefferson, running for reelection, carried all of New England except Connecticut, and every other state except slaveholding Delaware and Maryland. The "Negro President," indeed. There was a genuine Jeffersonian revolution; the three-fifths clause had nothing to do with it; and four years after electing Jefferson president, that revolution had consolidated a massive nation-wide popular majority.

★ ★ ★

ABOVE AND BEYOND the three-fifths clause, Wills rearranges the early political history of slavery in order to make Jefferson and his supporters look as bad as possible and his Federalist foes look as good as possible. He notes, correctly, that Jefferson cast a cold eye on the Haitian revolutionaries, but he fails to mention that most Federalists, Northerners and Southerners, tried to exploit the revolution by blaming it on the spread of Jefferson's political principles. He notes, again correctly, that slavery was more of an issue in national debates than some pro-Jefferson historians have been willing to allow, but he repeatedly gets the politics wrong.

In 1798, for example, the Massachusetts Federalist congressman George Thatcher proposed an amendment to ban the spread of slavery into Mississippi Territory. Thatcher, devoutly antislavery, hoped also to embarrass the Republican slaveholders amid the continuing struggle over the Alien and Sedition Acts, and announced that he was offering a motion "touching on the rights of man." Yet the only two members who spoke on the amendment's behalf were both Republicans, including Albert Gallatin, Jefferson's future secretary of the treasury. In joining the vast House majority against the amendment—the three-fifths clause was not required to defeat it—the Federalist stalwart Harrison Gray Otis declared haughtily that he "would not interfere with the Southern states as to the species of property in question," and that "he really wished that the gentlemen who held slaves might not be deprived of the means of keeping them in order." And one of the most powerful and effective voices counseling Congress to permit slavery in Mississippi Territory was none other than Secretary of State Timothy Pickering.

In 1807, the Republican congressional majority, with Jefferson's strong support, approved the closing of the Atlantic slave trade at the earliest possible date under the Constitution. Revisionist interpretations have held that Jefferson and other Virginians supported the closing because it suited their material interests. Especially after 1793, when the cotton boom gave slavery a new lease on life, Virginia slaveholders stood to make huge profits by selling off their redundant slaves to the cotton planters. Allowing the continued importation of new slaves from Africa, so the argument goes, would only have depressed the domestic market in human beings.

Wills bypasses Congress's closing of the trade, but leaves the strong impression that the revisionists are correct. Immediately following the Louisiana Purchase, he writes, Jefferson supported closing the newly acquired lands to the international slave trade because Virginia "was the leading seller of slaves in the domestic market." By shutting off the trade, Wills argues, Jefferson turned Louisiana into "a bonanza to people anxious to unload their slaves at high prices"—including, Wills charges, Jefferson himself.

This is economic determinism so crude that it makes the old works of Charles A. Beard look like exercises in idealism. It is also, regarding the Atlantic slave trade, out of sync with the evidence. Long before the cotton boom, long before the prosperous interstate slave trade—indeed, years before Virginia had even become a state—Jefferson and others denounced the trade. In his original draft of the Declaration of Independence, Jefferson sharply attacked it as "piratical warfare, the opprobrium of infidel powers." At the federal convention in 1787, George Mason demanded that Congress be empowered to abolish the Atlantic trade, which he eloquently denounced as a "nefarious traffic" driven by "a lust for gain."

Then, in 1807, Jefferson faced stern opposition from Southerners—Republicans and Federalists alike—especially in South Carolina and Georgia, where more Africans had been imported over the previous twenty years than during any previous twenty-year period. (Some of these Southern opponents, repeating allegations made in 1787, charged that Jefferson and other Virginians were simply out to make a profit on their excess slave population; and so, modern revisionists have ended up backing the cynical and polemical accusations of slavery's and the slave trade's most fervent supporters.) Yet Jefferson stuck by his long-standing principles, backed the Northern Jeffersonians who initiated the abolition bill in the House and Senate, and finally congratulated Congress for ending the "violations of human rights which have been so long continued on the unoffending inhabitants of Africa, and which the morality, the reputation, and the best interests of our country have long been eager to proscribe."*

Wills does make some valid and interesting points about Timothy Pickering's openness to the Haitian revolutionaries during his tenure as John Adams's secretary of state, which may have been his finest hour, although it is debatable how much Pickering sympathized with

---

* Southern slaveholder interests did manage to extract some concessions over Northern objections, including the defeat of an amendment, offered by the Massachusetts Jeffersonian Barnabas Bidwell, which would have forbidden the sale of any persons "confiscated" as a result of enforcement of the abolition of the slave trade. A tie-breaking vote cast by House Speaker Nathaniel Macon of North Carolina settled the issue. Although Wills exaggerates, the three-fifths clause certainly mattered in early American politics, and would loom even larger in the 1850s when, among other things, it ensured passage of the Kansas-Nebraska Act, as Wills notes correctly.

the oppressed blacks of Saint-Domingue and how much he simply wanted to weaken France. Without question, Pickering disliked
the slaveholders and slavery, which he called in private an "evil," and
he appears to have been remarkably less afflicted by racial prejudice
than most white Americans of his time. Pickering's record on slavery
was not at the forefront of his career, but that record was nobler than
those of Thomas Jefferson and virtually any other slaveholder, even if
it was not nearly as noble as Wills claims (To contrast Jefferson with
an exemplary antislavery Federalist, Wills might have done better
to choose an actual antislavery activist like John Jay, who served as
founding president of the New-York Manumission Society and who,
as governor of New York, helped oversee the enactment of the state's
gradual emancipation law.)

But there were also ironies about Pickering's antislavery commitments, even when set against Jefferson, which Wills elides. In 1783,
Pickering, as quartermaster general of the army, devised an idle scheme
to create an entirely new state for war veterans in the Northwest Territory, from which slavery would be immediately and irrevocably barred.
Somehow, to Wills, this scheme overshadows a formal proposal made
the following year by a committee inside the Confederation Congress
headed by Jefferson which would have banned slavery in *all* American
territories after 1800—a plan which, had it won approval, would have
kept slavery from enduring in what would become Alabama, Mississippi, Tennessee, and Kentucky. The proposal by Jefferson's committee,
which infuriated Southern delegates, failed by one vote, but it became
one of the bases for the famous Northwest Ordinance barring slavery
in 1787. Wills makes much of how Pickering's scheme would have
eliminated slavery in the fancied veterans' state right away, and how
Pickering continued to push for slavery's exclusion in the 1780s, even
though Pickering had nothing directly to do with the Northwest Ordinance's passage in 1787, and even though it is unclear that his influence
in shaping the Northwest Ordinance was nearly as great as Wills suggests. (Wills disregards how, in the actual debate, proponents of the

ordinance cited the Declaration of Independence.) Wills then states that, thereafter, Pickering was "consistently on the side of excluding slavery" from the territories, overlooking his determined and successful efforts to open Mississippi Territory to slavery in 1798 as well as his vote against Hillhouse's Louisiana amendment five years later.

In setting aside Pickering's increasingly rancorous ravings against democracy, Wills inflates Pickering's and (more generally) the Northern Federalists' antislavery avowals, and slights how much, especially after 1800, they amounted to partisan efforts to enhance the Federalist Party's political prospects. Granted, some Federalists and their supporters, men like George Thatcher and Theodore Sedgwick of Massachusetts, expressed egalitarian views on both human rights and slavery that were well ahead of their time. Individual Federalists, especially in New York and Philadelphia, were far more conspicuous than Jeffersonian Republicans in the nation's first effective antislavery organizations through the 1790s and into the new century.

Yet as James M. Banner, Jr., persuasively demonstrated back in 1970, the antislavery streak in New England Federalism was "cautious and restrained," and occupied "a marginal position in the Federalist ideology." The assaults upon the three-fifths clause were designed to win "not the abolition of slavery but the abolition of Negro representation." Southern manumission, as Banner explained, would only have increased Southern representation and further diminished Yankee Federalist influence, exactly the opposite of what Pickering and his fellow Federalists wanted: "Freed, it appeared, the Negro was more of a political threat than enslaved."

In his angry disappointment at Thomas Jefferson, and his wish to provide a foil, Wills fabricates a Timothy Pickering who never existed. Although he claims no special fondness for the man—"I suspect I would have found his company irksome," he writes—he is puzzled by the unflattering portraits of his champion that were painted by previous historians. But there is no puzzle here. Outside of his cramped circle of ultra-Federalist cronies, contemporaries regarded Pickering as a conniving, vindictive, partisan ideologue, a loathsome, simpleminded mediocrity whose chief political purpose was to thwart democracy and, after 1801, to embarrass Jefferson by any means possible, including secession. A vehement foe of egalitarian politics, Pickering gained a lasting reputation as John Adams's secretary of state with his obsessive enforcement of the Sedition Act, ferretting out and jailing democrats he deemed subversive, and otherwise turning himself, the historian Jeffrey L. Pasley remarks, into "the J. Edgar Hoover of the 1790s."

The moderate New England Federalist William Plumer was an antislavery advocate with no personal or political ax to grind; and he did find Pickering honest enough. Yet Plumer also found Pickering's manners so "disgusting," and his public vituperations so "personal & very gross," that he broke off all but the most formal relations with the man. Pickering's passions, Plumer believed, were as destructive as other men's wickedness. Those passions, as reported by Plumer, had nothing to do with slavery or antislavery and everything to do with suppressing democracy.

★   ★   ★

IN THE FINAL ANALYSIS, Wills, like O'Brien, reveals nothing about Jefferson and the politics of slavery that even Jefferson's admirers have failed to concede. Certainly, though, Jefferson's record on slavery weighs far heavier than some of those admirers have wanted to admit. Jefferson's vow of public silence about slavery from the mid-1780s on infuriated some of his younger followers, most famously his Virginia neighbor (and James Madison's private secretary) Edward Coles, who in 1814 beseeched him to endorse publicly gradual emancipation. (Jefferson replied, lamely, that, though he approved of such a plan, and though "the hour of emancipation is advancing, in the march of time," he was now too old to take up the cause.) In his private correspondence, Jefferson always held that slavery was evil and that its days were numbered—that, as he wrote in 1805, "interest is really going over to the side of morality."

But Jefferson was wrong about where slavery was headed in 1805, and the ignorance he displayed in his letters then and over the remainder of his life could only have been willful. The cotton boom that few in the Revolutionary generation foresaw was underway by the time he left the presidency, and it took off after 1815, reviving slavery on a scale of profitability and mass bondage that, soon enough, would exceed anything previously imagined. Yet until his dying day, Jefferson clung to his older perceptions of slavery's decline and certain doom. He also clung to his dark suspicions, born of the struggles of the 1790s, that the rising antislavery fervor in the North was really inspired by cunning Federalists who wanted to distract the country and regain national power. As a result, Jefferson could claim, sincerely enough, that he hoped for abominable slavery's eventual abolition, while he also tolerated and even, at times, encouraged slavery's expansion. He became, in effect (and more so as he grew older), an anti-antislavery slaveholder.

Jefferson's duplicity reached the point where, in 1819 and 1820, when Northern Republicans in Congress were fighting, largely on Jeffersonian grounds, to get rid of slavery in Missouri, Jefferson, ironically, opposed them firmly—wary that the antislavery Northerners were the tools of crypto-Federalists, and insistent that admitting Missouri as a slaveholding state would diffuse the overall slave population, which would in turn promote emancipation. His fears of Federalist resurgence were artificial; the cotton boom had long since proved that the diffusion idea, once favored by some humanitarians, had become thoroughly specious. But Jefferson hung on to illusions born decades earlier—illusions that, in the fullness of time, look more like an Enlightenment slaveholder's comforting self-delusion.

And so he lived out his life; indeed, just as telling as any of Jefferson's political positions was how he presided over his Palladian plantation Monticello, the enlightened patriarch amid his books, his wine, his gadgets, and his guests—but with almost all of his slaves (the privileged Hemings family excepted) living and working out of sight, further down the mountainside or on one of his remote estates. "[T]here were no Negro and other outhouses around the mansion, as you generally see on [other] plantations," Jefferson's overseer Edmund Bacon recalled. That is, Jefferson at Monticello did as much as he could, physically and psychically, to distance himself from the fact that he owned, bought, and sold other human beings. In his rural seat of Reason, unreasonable slavery, and the blackness that was its emblem, could not be expelled, and so Jefferson concealed them as best he could.

The contradictions of a willfully ignorant man of reason are hardly less glaring than those of an egalitarian slaveholder. Thomas Jefferson was both; worse, he articulated a standard for equality that neither he nor the early republic matched, and that the nation is still struggling to match. He is, in other words, an abiding torment. By his best examples and his worst, he still eats at American consciences. At one level, he singularly exemplifies the essential historical contradiction of American equality and American slavery at the nation's founding, from which it is tempting to conclude either that American equality is, always has been, and can only be a lie, or that its vindication requires the obliteration of Thomas Jefferson. At another level, the egalitarian Jefferson is the lasting messenger of the bad news about the nation, the stubborn monitor of America's truancies, the hard if human teacher against whom we sin, collectively and individually. Who would not wish to have that message complicated or qualified or (mis)interpreted out of its stringency and its reproach? Who would not wish to think better about ourselves by demonizing the contradictory Jefferson and the political party which he inspired and led?

Interestingly, the writing about Jefferson which has done the most to resist this torment has concerned the most explosive issue of all regarding Jefferson and slavery: his long sexual relationship with his slave Sally Hemings. Jefferson inherited Hemings from his father-in-law James Wayles, who was almost certainly her father, which would have made her the half-sister of his wife, Martha. Martha died in 1782 from complications following childbirth; Jeffferson is alleged to have begun his relationship with Sally some years later. The story of that relationship first gained widespread notice in 1802, when the vituperative (and racist) journalist James Callender, a disgruntled former Jefferson supporter, reported in the Federalist press that President Jefferson and his "wench Sally," "the African venus," had parented five children. Callender based his account on rumors that had been making the rounds in Virginia for years, and he made little effort to distinguish gossip from fact. Callender was known as a scurrilous exaggerator. But he was not an outright liar; and Sally Hemings had given birth to children whose father was obviously white, and who physically resembled Jefferson.

Down through the centuries, Sally Hemings's offspring and their descendants, beginning with her son Madison Hemings, affirmed that she had stated that Jefferson was the father of her children. And down through the centuries, Jefferson's white descendants, with the help of several generations of historians, offered a variety of explications for why the Hemingses' claim was absurd. Now and again, anti-Jefferson writers would revive the Hemings story as a lurid tale, in order to show that, atop everything else, Jefferson was a moral monster. (The case duly appears in O'Brien's *The Long Affair*.) In 1974, the historian Fawn Brodie offered a somewhat clunky psychological interpretation of the evidence affirming the story, although without the sensational indictments of Jefferson's character. The reaction against Brodie, though, was fierce, and virtually until the end of the twentieth century, the most prominent authorities agreed that everything we knew about Jefferson made the story impossible.*

The legal historian Annette Gordon-Reed, though, began toppling those authorities in 1997 with her book *Thomas Jefferson and Sally Hemings: An American Controversy*. Working with the same evidence as her predecessors, Gordon-Reed, a scrupulous investigator, found their work marred by logical lapses and unacknowledged inferences.

---

* Like most historians, it needs saying, I believed them.

None of their explications, especially those which tried to tie the paternity of Sally Hemings's children to someone other than Jefferson, were consistent with the available evidence. But one set of facts (which Dumas Malone had reported) truly was compelling, and it had to do with proximity.

After his return from Paris with his young slave Sally in 1789, Jefferson spent only occasional stretches of time at Monticello (except for the hiatus between his resignation as secretary of state in 1793 and his inauguration as vice president in 1797), until he completed his second presidential term in 1809. Yet repeatedly, some months after Jefferson did visit his beloved homestead, Sally Hemings, who was constantly in residence, gave birth. Gordon-Reed summarized: "The relationship was so strong that it can be described as creating a pattern. The pattern went like this: Jefferson comes home for six months and leaves. Hemings bears a child four months after he is gone. Jefferson comes home for six weeks. Hemings bears a child eight months after he is gone. Jefferson comes for two months and leaves. Hemings bears a child eight months after he has gone. This went on for fifteen years through six children. He was there when she conceived, and she never conceived when he was not there."

It seems highly unlikely that some other purported father's fertility would be so exactly linked, for a decade and a half, to Jefferson's presence at Monticello. And when Gordon-Reed connected these facts to the rest of her supporting evidence, the case seemed probably true. (Hemings and her children, for example, were the exceptional slaves freed by Jefferson at his death, based, according to Madison, on a "treaty" between them. The Hemingses also lived apart from the other slaves, in closer quarters with Jefferson.) Yet even after Gordon-Reed's book appeared, most professional historians resisted; and some continued to resist even after the announcement, a year later, that a Y-DNA test, once thought impossible to perform, revealed a match between a descendent of the Jefferson male line and a descendent of Eston Hemings, Sally's youngest son.

Only around 2001, when the Thomas Jefferson Foundation at Monticello released its own study that affirmed Jefferson's paternity of at least one of Hemings's children and probably all of them, did the scholarly consensus shift. Resistance, to be sure, has continued; to wit, a book published in 2009, *In Defense of Thomas Jefferson*, by the attorney William G. Hyland, Jr., which fingers Jefferson's younger brother Randolph as a likely culprit. In the main, though—and as sustained by the Smithsonian Institution, the United States Parks Service, and the Jefferson Foundation, as well as the great preponderance of professional historians—the longtime struggle for recognition by the Hemings descendants, and the scholarly tenacity of Annette Gordon-Reed, have been vindicated.

The truly remarkable thing, however, has been not the revelation that Jefferson almost certainly fathered children with one of his slaves, but the reaction to that revelation, shaped in no small part by Gordon-Reed's first book and her succeeding volume, *The Hemingses of Monticello*, which was awarded a Pulitzer Prize in 2009. To this day, the tone of those who would deny Jefferson's liaison with Hemings remains defensive, as if Jefferson's reputation was in danger of being debased, discredited, and even ruined. And for two centuries, the tone of many of those who have advanced the story, from James Callender to Conor Cruse O'Brien, has been harshly accusatory, aimed precisely at ruining Jefferson. But that is not what the Hemings descendants, beginning with her son Madison Hemings, have been saying for well more than a century. They have simply wanted acknowledgment, against condescending (at the least) Jeffersonian tradition and stubborn scholarly presumption, that what they believe to have been true about Sally Hemings and Thomas Jefferson—and what has emerged was almost certainly true—was and is true.

Gordon-Reed is no more accusatory than the Hemingses. As much a historian as a legal scholar, she cuts to the heart of the myths that still govern our thinking about miscegenation under slavery. Those myths lead us to imagine that an omnipotent Thomas

Jefferson, the white master, must have imposed himself on the powerless Sally Hemings, the black slave girl, in scenes of more or less forcible rape. Without question, rapes commonly occurred under slavery. Still, as Gordon-Reed observes, the evidence in the case of Thomas Jefferson and Sally Hemings does not support a story involving "thirty-eight years' worth of nights of 'Come here, gal!'" Nor, given the courtship norms of the eighteenth-century Virginia gentry, would there have been something terribly unseemly about a forty-five-year-old male establishing a sexual or emotional attachment with a fifteen-year-old female.

Instead, we are left with a less sensational and more poignant story, along the lines that Madison Hemings first outlined to an Ohio newspaper reporter in 1873. It is the story of an apparently faithful match that lasted several decades, that began with a middle-aged, widowed white statesman (who had pledged to his dying wife that he would never remarry) and a young, fair-skinned African American female. The female was almost certainly the half-sister of the widower's late wife—and she was also the widower's slave. But enslaved though she was, by assenting to the match she gained enough influence over the widower to extract the promise that he would free her children, and years later she held him to his promise. Bound though he was by the rules of his class to keep the relationship secret, the widower, a vigorous man who had never abjured female companionship, sustained some semblance of connubial connection, at least when he was back on his Virginia mountainside.

The cruel facts of slavery, compounded by the widower's earlier pronouncements against miscegenation—pronouncements he continued to make until late in his life—and by his need to sustain his respectable position in politics and society, rendered the relationship absurd, beyond the point of hypocrisy and almost to the point of tragedy. No matter how much decorum, let alone affection, may have sustained the relationship, any such connection between owner and owned was constrained and tortured and imbalanced. But neither Thomas Jefferson nor Sally Hemings could undo those facts, and so they lived with them as best they could.

This is not a happy story, but neither is it grotesque. In *The Hemingses of Monticello*, Gordon-Reed tries to dispel the presumption that Jefferson's relations with Hemings were cruelly exploitative, and challenges the idea that romantic love between white and black in the context of slavery was impossible; she may go too far in the direction of suggesting the connection was indeed a star-crossed romance. On the emotional character of their intimate relations, the sources are basically silent. But withal the bizarre vagaries, it is almost impossible to imagine that the relationship was an inhumane one. Jefferson and Hemings plainly established, within the boundaries of their time, more than a modicum of decency with each other. That such decency existed even in conditions of brutal racial oppression is, if not redemptive, at least hopeful; it establishes a small marker of decency for the bettered but still troubled conditions in which we now live. And although it absolves the slaveholder Jefferson of nothing—indeed, although it only deepens his entanglement in slavery's horrors—it does help lift him out of the hateful place to which too many historians have tried to consign him.

★　★　★

JEFFERSON WILL SURVIVE the latest historians' bashing. Never monolithic, recent prominent writing on Jefferson includes some contrarian assessments, ranging from Joyce Appleby's concise but rich book focused on Jefferson's presidency to Jon Meacham's full and skillfully composed biography, with special insight on Jefferson's formidable political skills. Indeed, the time to worry will come when Jefferson is no longer vexing and oppressive—when he becomes so untroubling, so safe, or so reviled that nobody bothers to attack him anymore. When that happens, our democracy, and not just Jefferson, will have expired of its own complacency.

But where should we place Jefferson in the American political tradition? The Civil War, followed a century later by the Second Reconstruction, exploded Jefferson's mixed legacy on slavery and his consistent legacy on race. But so too the era of high industrialism, mass immigration, and urban growth at the turn of the twentieth century destroyed what remained of his vision of a homogenous agrarian America. The New Deal, and then the Cold War, enlarged the lineaments of national political and military power beyond anything Jefferson would have thought possible or desirable. The mechanistic natural laws on which he based his views of man and society no longer stand. "The entire mental universe in which Jefferson did his thinking has changed so dramatically," Joseph Ellis has written, ". . . that any direct connection between then and now must be regarded as a highly problematic enterprise."

What survives of Jefferson's philosophy exists most prominently in strange combinations, right and left. The conservative wing of the Republican Party upholds a nostalgic version of the Jeffersonian idea that the government that governs best governs least—except, perhaps, when it comes to government imposing upon the moral life of the citizenry. Modern liberals and Democrats are all for the promotion of equality, but with ideas about positive state action, regulation, and protected rights that Jefferson associated with monarchy and aristocracy. Perhaps it would be well for these partial Jeffersonianisms to cease and to desist. Perhaps Jefferson cannot provide political guidance, apart from his famous injunction to Madison that "the earth belongs in usufruct to the living," and that we must truly be the masters of our own fates.

Yet Jefferson remains pertinent, and in some ways he is exemplary. Americans still honor, for example, his fundamental belief in individual sovereignty as a starting point for thinking about democratic government. As Ellis has noted, Jefferson, more than any other political leader or thinker of his time, based his ideas about justice and happiness on individual sovereignty, with government poised between protecting individual rights and liberties and minimizing its interference in individual lives. Illusory though that image of sovereignty might be, it endures as a legitimizing principle and even a core conviction of American politics, liberal and conservative. On the right, it has become a license for the unfettered pursuit of self-interest. On the left, it has appeared as what Abraham Lincoln, in 1859, called Jefferson's "superior devotion to the personal rights of men, holding the rights of property to be secondary only, and greatly inferior." We are not, in any way, a consensual people, but most of the time, our conflicts revolve around how best to secure the individual sovereignty that Jefferson proclaimed.

Although he sometimes spoke of overarching unifying principles, meanwhile, Jefferson well understood that conflict was indeed inevitable in a nation that had cast itself upon what he once called "the boisterous sea of liberty." In the face of that certainty, he singularly tried to put high democratic principles into practice at the highest levels of politics. No philosophe anywhere in the Atlantic world succeeded as Jefferson did in turning the supreme values of the Enlightenment into living realities. (His friend Madison, so vital to framing and then defending the Constitution, came close, but he proved to be a less capable political leader than Jefferson.) The practice of democratic politics, however, required forsaking the kind of consistency that the world demands of a philosophe—or expects from a philosophical polemicist like Thomas Paine.

Jefferson preached equality, not purity. Successfully translating philosophy into politics meant that he had to compromise and guard his political viability. His self-protecting circumspection over slavery has earned him posterity's condemnation. Otherwise, though, his political side served him and the country well. As president, beleaguered by his critics, he observed to a friend that "what is practicable must often control what is pure theory." This, in turn, meant that he would expose himself to charges of contradiction and cunning, from future generations as well as from his contemporaries—but that price had to be paid to make ideals into realities.

Jefferson in turn had to learn how to lead a new nation of squabbling sovereign individuals who, coming out of their revolutionary experience and their rejection of monarchy, were preternaturally suspicious of government. He had no practical example on which to draw for this style of leadership—certainly not those of his presidential predecessors Washington and Adams. To hold the country together under his presidency after the bruising battles of the 1790s—battles that some reasonably thought would degenerate into either tyranny or civil war—required a protean quality that was the very opposite of what his enemies beheld as unprincipled.

In his famously conciliatory—and devious—first inaugural address, Jefferson told the country that "we are all republicans, we are all federalists," then proceeded to govern as a Republican, yet not so dogmatically that he would entrap himself (as when he overcame his own strict reading of the Constitution's limits on executive power and approved the Louisiana Purchase). He would not compromise easily (as when he rejected his treasury secretary Albert Gallatin's advice to retain, for a time, much-hated federal internal taxes), but he knew well enough to back off when necessary (as he did with regard to undoing or even restricting Hamilton's national bank). He would never win over the likes of Timothy Pickering, and he never expected to do so, but he would advance his principles while allowing different constituencies to see in him what they wanted to see, and this allowed him to lead while appearing to be a follower. For all of his talents, he could not sustain his own success amid the international intrigues of his second presidential term, when his own idealism in dealing with the warring great powers, France and Great Britain, got the better of him; he would return to Monticello feeling like a man freed from prison. But at his best, Jefferson more or less invented and then pursued a style of democratic leadership that remains essential to our political life.

Finally, though, Jefferson's abiding importance is in his contribution to democracy itself. Recent historians who have refused to grapple with the democracy in the Jeffersonian Republican impulse—or have rendered it, clumsily and anachronistically, as a "populist" cloak for white supremacy and slavery—have entirely missed what made Jefferson important in his own time, and makes him important in ours.

When Federalist polemicists and intriguers denounced Jefferson as a slaveholding hypocrite, it was not a battle cry for emancipation. It hardly could have been, given that so many of slavery's most extreme defenders were in their own partisan ranks. What Federalists across sectional lines—the Pickerings and the Pinckneys—did agree upon was that Jefferson and his supporters' attacks on aristocracy, intolerance, and deference threatened to undo the natural order of things, and to topple what the Massachusetts Federalist Fisher Ames called government by "the wise, and good, and rich." The very word "democracy" gave Federalists the shivers; their aim, said the Federalist newspaper the *Port Folio* of Philadelphia, was "to present democracy in its native deformity." This is what made Jefferson so dangerous; and this is what drove the Federalists to distraction at the mere thought of a Jeffersonian America, envisaging guillotines at every crossroads, or, as the Connecticut Federalist Theodore Dwight predicted, moral catastrophe, "the ties of marriage . . . destroyed; our wives and our daughters . . . thrown into the stews; . . . a world full of ignorance, impurity, and guilt; . . . without worship, without a prayer, without a God!"

Jefferson and his party were steeped in Enlightenment liberalism. This, too, frightened the Federalists, who took Jefferson's devotion to science and his insistence on the complete separation of church and state as further proof of his depravity. And the American Enlightenment's devotion to science and rationality went hand in hand with the most democratic politics in the new nation. Jeffrey L. Pasley has reminded us that, although the Jeffersonian Republicans had strong bases in the South and West, their crucial struggles for power occurred in the mid-Atlantic states, including the plebeian wards of New York and Philadelphia, where Jefferson's supporters also embraced Thomas Paine and William Godwin, and denounced every kind of human slavery, and endorsed reforms ranging from public education to the abolition of imprisonment for debt. To these Jeffersonians, it was no surprise when, days after assuming the presidency, Jefferson warmly invited Paine to return to the United States—a gesture of solidarity with the reviled infidel radical that Federalist newspapers swiftly denounced as proof positive that Jefferson was unfit for high office.

Jefferson's appeal to the city democrats was no ruse. A slaveholder in slaveholding Virginia, Jefferson—unlike the illiberal slaveholders who despised him and his vulgar, infidel supporters—was attuned to the democrats' egalitarian impulses, and he helped change forever the sum and substance of American life at many levels. In reforming the mercantilist political economy engineered by Alexander Hamilton, in which the favored moneyed few would be government's chief pillar, Jefferson opened the way for a more egalitarian commerce. But possibly his greatest contribution was to advance democratic political principles we now take for granted.

The Federalists believed that as soon as election days were over, the voting citizenry's participation was over, and that they should thereafter defer to their chosen representatives. (Some thought even that much, with the jarring of personalities and interests, was troublesome: "Elections, my dear sir, elections to offices which are great objects of Ambition, I look at with terror," the ever blunt John Adams wrote to his then-friend Jefferson in 1787.) Jefferson and his supporters, on the contrary, built the prototype of a modern political party, with clubs and newspapers and political discussion and criticism year-round. Jeffersonians pushed at the state level, especially in the North, for widened access to the vote, including the reform or elimination of property qualifications. As a result of Jefferson's and his supporters' party-building efforts (in time imitated by the Federalists), the opening years of the nineteenth century brought some of the most intense campaigning and popular participation in all of American history.

Ten days before he died, in the last letter he ever wrote, Jefferson contended that "the general spread of the light of science" had "laid open to every view the palpable truth, that the mass of mankind has not been born with saddles on their backs, nor a favored few, booted and spurred, ready to ride them legitimately by the grace of God." Before Jefferson and his revolutionary generation, those saddles and those spurs were fully legitimate. They are legitimate no more, even if they have not all been fully destroyed. We are still far from fulfilling the Declaration's creed about equality before the law. Nor have we provided equality of opportunity to all to gain a modest prosperity: if wealth is the measure of opportunity in America, we have become more unequal in recent times. Although Jefferson's egalitarianism paradoxically helped lead to slavery's destruction, slavery's legacy still disfigures national life. By his actions and inactions—and with his words on race—Jefferson created the paradox that stains his memory, living off human bondage and its unmetaphorical whips and chains, the legitimacy of which he denied and which mocked his Declaration. And yet, over the centuries, more and more Americans have also ridden the ride of which Jefferson dreamed—more than Jefferson ever thought possible—by the grace of God, if you will, but also by the grace of Jefferson.

5

★ ★ ★ ★ ★ ▬▬▬▬▬▬▬▬▬

John Quincy Adams: Slavery's Arch-Enemy

WHEN CONGRESSMAN JOHN QUINCY ADAMS DIED IN FEBRU-
ary 1848, masses of Americans mourned. At the Capitol, where Adams
was fatally stricken and where his body lay in state, untold thousands
of citizens lined up to file past his velvet-draped coffin. Many thousands more crowded alongside the railroad track all the way from
Washington to Boston to witness the train carrying Adams's remains
home. Some of Adams's oldest and fiercest political antagonists, from
the conservative Whig Daniel Webster to the hard-money Democrat
Thomas Hart Benton, delivered tributes. Even the Southern leaders of
what Adams in his later years contemptuously called "the slaveocracy"
paid chivalrous tribute to the departed patriarch.

To be sure, not every slaveholder forgave Adams. Some recalcitrants
and fire-eaters praised him grudgingly as, in the Virginian Henry
Wise's words, "the acutest, the astutest, the archest enemy of Southern slavery that ever existed." One member of the Virginia House of
Delegates decried an official resolution of regret because, he declared,
"the course pursued by Mr. A in the Congress of the United States
was in utter violation of the interests and rights of the South." Other
slaveholders politely said nothing. Nor was every antislavery Northern

overcome by sadness at the Whig Adams's passing. Shortly after the funeral, the free-soil Democratic editor Walt Whitman (temporarily working in New Orleans) remarked that although Adams was "a virtuous man, a learned man . . . he was not a man of the People."

Yet Adams, the anxious and austere failed president, had gained something that had eluded the other anxious and austere American president of the early republic, his father: he had gained, thanks to his antislavery activities, popular favor. Nearly five years before his death, in the summer of 1843, Adams basked in a tumultuous response, in town after town, when he toured antislavery areas of western New York and Ohio; even more remarkably, he received similar receptions when he headed back east through northern Kentucky and Pennsylvania. The public reaction to his death five years later marked, along with respect for a venerable departed president, sadness at the loss of an antislavery hero.

Popularity came as a delightful surprise to the old man. Shortly before his controversial election to the presidency in 1824–25, Adams remarked, with good reason, that the public perceived him as "a gloomy misanthropist." He never claimed to have mastered the common touch, and for most of his life he took a dim view of those who had. How, then, could such a man surmount the disappointments and the deep melancholy of his White House years and become not simply a respected former president but a beloved political maverick congressman and a cagey crusader against evil? It is one of the more perplexing and important puzzles of early American political history.

Beginning with his participation in 1781, when he was fourteen, in the Continental Congress's legation to the court of Catherine the Great, and ending with his final mumbled vote in the thirtieth United States Congress against a routine measure connected with the war against Mexico, Adams resided at or near the pinnacle of national politics. His long and prominent public career, as recorded in his huge and magnificent diary (itself a neglected treasure of American letters), perfectly exemplifies the transition from the Federalists' elitist, deferential republic to the mass-based, democratic republic of the Democrats and Whigs. Understanding Adams's unlikely popularity requires understanding how he negotiated this transition, especially after his crushing defeat at the hands of Andrew Jackson in 1828. Adams's transition in turn sheds light both on the changing character of American government and on the democratic origins of the Civil War.

It also helps to unravel the political enigma that is John Quincy Adams. No American political life of the early republic was, on its surface, more paradoxical than Adams's, and no political personality was more mysterious. As James Monroe's brilliant secretary of state, Adams was among the most important of the new nation's expansionists—but he went on to denounce the annexation of Texas, the war against Mexico, and what became known as Manifest Destiny, ascribing them to the malevolent designs of the hated Slave Power. An early supporter of nationalist sectional compromise, he would wind up trying to check and obstruct the power of the slaveholders. Adams's first success in electoral politics came in 1802, after his embittered father, turned out of the presidency by Jefferson two years earlier, had decided to retire from politics and let the Jeffersonians ruin the country. His first failure came a few years later, after he had appeared actually to have joined forces with the Jeffersonians (a step that, in the long run, probably saved his political career). Later, as secretary of state, Adams put his political future at risk by defending a bellicose American military commander over an incursion into what was then Spanish Florida—his future nemesis, General Andrew Jackson.

The longer Adams lived, the more the paradoxes and mysteries of his life seemed to multiply. He was one of the only genuine intellectuals ever to occupy the White House, and he was one of his era's most high-minded opponents of party strife and demagogic electioneering; but in 1828, he allowed his political friends to take the low road in his reelection campaign against Jackson by printing scurrilous and inflammatory campaign propaganda. (The stuff was so clumsy and outrageous that one of Adams's captains, Thurlow Weed of New York, a true pol, refused to distribute it to the voters of his district lest it lose Adams votes.) Thereafter, humiliated by defeat, he withdrew behind what his son Charles Francis Adams called his "Iron Mask," the forbidding demeanor that sometimes made him a cipher even to friends and family—only to emerge in the 1830s and 1840s as a witty, prickly, and resourceful spokesman for a cause he had hitherto avoided: antislavery. He was man of books and sometimes visionary ideas, yet he was not, Ralph Waldo Emerson wrote in his journal, a "literary gentleman" but "a bruiser," an "old roué who cannot live on slops, but must have sulphuric acid in his tea."

In short, John Quincy Adams's political life does not seem to add up. Yet such a life is neither ironic nor contradictory in the ways that sometimes confound and generally displease modern scholars. Adams's achievement was to contain within himself things that are not supposed to go together, and to do so with high seriousness and not a whit of cynicism. Among the things that he contained after 1828 was a newfound appreciation for the possibilities of democratic politics as a vehicle for his overriding political ambition, which was to be regarded as a courageous, enlightened, and virtuous statesman, a great and good man in the classical mold. He resolved his apparent contradictions by becoming, in effect, America's egalitarian Cicero. He did so not by his own lights alone, but thanks to his connections, never simple, with the sorts of democratic stirrings that, early in his career, he would have found disreputable and even dangerous.

★   ★   ★

PAUL C. NAGEL'S BIOGRAPHY, *John Quincy Adams: A Public Life, A Private Life*, examines how Adams's emotional life hampered and animated his public career. This is psychobiography of a fairly unreconstructed sort. Still, it illuminates Adams's political personality, arguing persuasively that, until the 1830s, Adams suffered from chronic bouts of what today would be called clinical depression. To reach that conclusion, Nagel closely studied, from start to finish, the manuscript of Adams's diary, which has yet to be published in its entirety. As the historian Allan Nevins observed, in his drastically edited edition of the diary published in 1928, "in all American political literature, there is no record of the kind which approaches [it] in value and interest." Nagel's book, if nothing else, highlights the diary's abiding literary as well as historical allure.

Nagel quotes regularly from Adams's sometimes mordant, sometimes charming observations about matters small (the punctilious revelries of the Russian court, where "everything moves like a piece of clockwork"; church singing in Washington that "lap'd me in Elysium") and large (the negotiation of the Treaty of Ghent; the Missouri Compromise; Jackson's election). Above all, though, Nagel is interested in its most tortured passages, which he renders as the portrait of a struggling depressive.

Adams certainly had reasons to be depressed, in ways common to talented young men of great expectations. He was born in 1767 at the family house in Braintree (now Quincy), in Massachusetts, John and Abigail Adams's eldest son. The tumults of the American Revolution, instigated and led by his father and his father's friends, dominated his early childhood. (When he was five, he witnessed with his mother from a Braintree hillside the distant battle of Bunker Hill, which was the scene of the glorious death of Dr. Joseph Warren, who happened to be the Adams family physician.) In 1778, he accompanied his father to Paris, where John Adams was posted as minister to France. Thereafter, he and his father moved to Amsterdam and Leyden, in accordance with changes in the elder Adams's assignments.

Johnny Adams's serious demeanor and excellent command of French led to his appointment, in 1781, as secretary to Francis Dana, the American minister to St. Petersburg (where all courtiers and diplomats spoke French). Following a journey through Scandinavia and northern Germany, he rejoined his father in 1783, and served as a secretary during the treaty negotiations in Paris that completed American independence. Two years later, young Adams returned home to complete his college education at Harvard. In 1790, after three years of study with the eminent jurist Theophilus Parsons, he began his own legal practice. And throughout these years, and for years to come, Adams's parents made it harshly clear that they would tolerate nothing less than greatness from their fortunate firstborn son. "You came into life with advantages which will disgrace you if your success is mediocre," John Adams warned in 1794, adding that "if you do not rise to the head not only of your profession, but of your country, it will be owing to your own *Laziness, Slovenliness*, and *Obstinacy*."

JQA (as he began to style himself, to avoid getting confused for his father) sometimes hinted that he would have preferred a quiet, bookish existence to a career in law and politics; and some of the happiest and most fruitful times in his life would come from his reading, writing, and teaching. With his translations of Christoph Martin Wieland and Friedrich von Gentz, and his traveler's account, *Letters from Silesia*, Adams established, virtually on his own, the serious study in the United States of German language and literature. Although he would never complete the literary masterpiece that he thought was in him (unless one counts the diary as his masterpiece, which it was), he did write plenty of competent, second-rate verse as well as some strong pieces of dramatic and literary criticism, showing a special affinity for Shakespeare. A stint as the first Boylston Professor of Rhetoric and Oratory at Harvard, from 1805 to 1809, brought him great satisfaction (although he initially found his students ignorant, his lecturing chores burdensome, and the Harvard treasurer inept at disbursing his salary on time).

JQA's literary talents also recommended him for diplomatic and political leadership in the fledgling republic. His pseudonymous "Publicola" essays—written in 1791 to defend his father and his father's alter ego, Edmund Burke, and the principles of orderly government, from the democratic diatribes of Jefferson and Paine—were so artful and learned that many if not most readers assumed that John Adams had written them. Subsequent essays by the young polemicist, attacking the erratic French envoy Edmond Genêt and defending the Washington administration's foreign policy, gained President Washington's admiration, and in 1794 (to Vice President Adams's delight), JQA, aged twenty-seven, was appointed America's minister to Holland. At Washington's insistence, Adams remained in the diplomatic corps even after the elder Adams ascended to the presidency in 1797. (Father and son had fretted over the appearance of favoritism.) Only after Jefferson's election in 1800–1801 did JQA again come home— where he quickly threw himself into politics, winning election to the Massachusetts state senate in 1802 and to the United States Senate a year later.

Under the burden of his parents' desires (and, after 1797, under the burden of a tense marriage to Louisa Johnson, the daughter of an American consul), JQA went to pieces from time to time. The evidence in the diary, as retrieved by Nagel, is unmistakable. Beginning in 1788, when his miseries forced him to withdraw temporarily from Parsons's law academy ("God of Heavens . . . take me from this world before I curse the day of my birth"), Adams repeatedly succumbed to fits of anxiety and remorse. He would reproach himself mercilessly for the tiniest of slips: for boastful remarks at dinner, for the mishandling of a minor piece of diplomatic correspondence. His imperfections plunged him into sleepless nights, when he despaired over his worthlessness. In some of his blackest moments, he would copy out excerpts from his favorite poets and playwrights, including these lines from *Henry IV, Part 2*: "Oh gentle sleep / Nature's soft nurse, how I have frighted thee / That no more wilt weigh mine eye lids down / And steep my senses in forgetfulness."

Adams battled his depressions with valerian root tea and quinine, and with rising early in the morning and exercising strenuously. (He became an avid swimmer.) As he grew older, he also mastered a public demeanor of icy restraint. Nagel finds that, contrary to the conventional historical wisdom, the private JQA, surrounded by close friends and family members, was an amiable and appetitive man, with passions for good drink, good conversation, and good (conjugal) sex. Outside his inner circle, however, Adams acted aloof and irritable. Sometimes, while on diplomatic missions, he ate evening meals alone, in order to avoid his colleagues' postprandial bad wine, cheap cigars, and vulgar talk. At other times, when, as he put it, he was not "master of myself," he would lash out at any stupidity or apparent slight. Quick to anger, he would hold grudges for years, even decades, against those whom he believed had treated him disrespectfully.

Exquisitely aware of his "over-anxious" disposition, Adams admired the "deliberate coolness" and the "real self-command" he observed in others; and he did his best to hold his emotions in check, donning the Iron Mask that left the rest of the world wondering what was actually on his mind. The Mask proved a valuable tool in political and diplomatic negotiations. In 1807, Federalists became furious at his support of Jefferson's embargo—the president's doomed effort to assert American maritime rights against warring Britain and France with a complete boycott of international trade. Forced to resign from the Senate, Adams stoically delivered his lectures and licked his wounds at Harvard, only to be persuaded the following year by Jefferson's successor, James Madison, to take charge of the American ministry in Russia. Thereafter, JQA's career turned into a string of brilliant triumphs: as a commissioner to the Ghent treaty negotiations, as American minister to Great Britain, as secretary of state (and architect of important treaties with Britain and Spain, as well as of the Monroe Doctrine), as victor in the fractious presidential campaign of 1824.

If, as Nagel argues, JQA's successes owed something to his overcoming of himself, they also owed a great deal to his political ideas. Simply put, Adams was the boldest and most consequential American nationalist of his time. It was his belief in the United States's destiny as a world power that first led him to break with his Anglophilic Federalist colleagues and support Jefferson's embargo. The same belief inspired his greatest achievements as secretary of state, including the Spanish cession of Florida and the enunciation of the Monroe Doctrine (which might be more properly called the Adams Doctrine) that "the American continents are no longer subjects for any new European colonial establishments"—though the United States could intervene in the Western Hemisphere as it saw fit. The same belief led him, as president, to propose a startlingly ambitious program of federal spending on roads, canals, observatories, and a national university, the better to unite the country's various regions, accelerate commerce, and improve the national intellect.

Closely linked to Adams's nationalism was his patrician conception of American politics. Although he gradually backed off from the quasi-Burkean traditionalism of his youth, Adams never put much faith in the political wisdom of the common man, and he put even less in the machinations of professional politicians. Not that he abjured political conflict. Repeatedly, in his diary and in his letters, JQA displayed his enthusiasm for the political fray. In 1811, he actually declined Madison's offer of a seat on the Supreme Court because, he wrote privately, "I am . . . and always shall be too much of a political partisan for a judge." But Adams's vision of orderly politics was a high-minded one, in which enlightened, patriotic gentlemen from around the nation—gentlemen such as himself—would assemble at the capital, and then tug and pull and settle American policy. He was a partisan for his ideas, not for any political party. He despised electioneering and logrolling congressional deals and the corruption known as patronage. He appeared to think of politics and government as drawing-room diplomacy by other means.

Here lay the cruelest twist in Adams's career: the patrician nationalism that had served him so brilliantly as an ambassador and as secretary of state proved disastrously out of touch with the nation's democratizing realities when Adams was in the White House. In 1824, Adams ran for president against three other nominally Jeffersonian Republican candidates: Henry Clay, the Speaker of the House; secretary of the treasury William H. Crawford of Georgia; and General Andrew Jackson, the war hero. Jackson won a convincing plurality of the popular vote, with Adams running second, but the Tennessean failed to gain a majority in the Electoral College, leaving the outcome to be decided by the House of Representatives. After some hesitation, Clay threw his support in the House to Adams, thereby ensuring JQA's election, and shortly thereafter Adams named Clay as his secretary of state.

Adams saw his choice of Clay as a healing act of statesmanship, and, on a similar lofty note, he spurned patronage requests from his own supporters. But this left him vulnerable to vicious charges by Jackson and his friends that he had reached a "corrupt bargain" with Clay, as well as to charges of disloyalty from his erstwhile political friends. The Clay affair badly damaged Adams's presidency even before he was sworn in. Not much later, JQA's pursuit of an idealistic, nationalist domestic program sealed his administration's doom.

In the mid-1820s, the United States was still recovering from the devastating effects of the financial panic of 1819 and the ensuing commercial depression, as well as from the political crisis that surrounded Missouri's admission to the Union as a slave state in 1821. Workingmen, shopkeepers, and small farmers, ruined by the panic, blamed their distress on centralized federal policies, especially the policies of the quasi-public Second Bank of the United States. Southern slaveholders, meanwhile, wary of rising Northern aggressiveness over restricting slavery's expansion, regarded almost any expression of national power as a pretext for slavery's abolition. Yet here was a freshly inaugurated president—a New Englander who had won barely 30 percent of the popular vote, and not much more of the electoral vote—calling for federal improvement programs on a dazzling scale. Not surprisingly, Adams's proposals got nowhere in the Congress. His support for U.S. participation in a Pan-American conference called by Simón Bolívar—a gathering that included governments which had abolished slavery—became a pretext for further galvanizing congressional opposition.

Bitterly disappointed and more certain than ever that history would judge him a failure, Adams fell into yet another severe depression. Haggard in visage, his appetite gone, his clothes hanging on him like sacks, he endured his last months in office and his reelection effort thanks mainly to his reserves of family pride, his adamantine sense of duty, and a determination that someday, somehow, he would get even with his traducers.

John Quincy Adams's politics and his ideas about politics, with their exalted nationalism, proved as costly as his gloomy psychology in the late 1820s. And it was also politics (and ideas about politics) that would help him revive his reputation and his amour propre after 1830, when he emerged as an antislavery hero. That revival, however, was the result of an unlikely and important turn of events—Adams's involvement in a now largely-forgotten political cause, the anti-Masonic movement.

★ ★ ★

ADAMS'S FORMAL INVOLVEMENT with anti-Masonry began in 1831, just as he recovered from the worst torments of his much-tormented life. His final year as president had been a misery, as political setbacks and public ridicule dragged him down. His long-foreseen defeat—outside of New England, he carried only New Jersey and, just barely, Maryland—actually brought him a measure of relief; but that relief was dashed the following spring by the outbreak of a controversy concerning his alleged condemnation of some prominent old New England Federalists, followed by the final breakdown and suicide of his deranged eldest son, George Washington Adams.

Heartbroken once more, and nearly broke, Adams gradually pulled himself together by indulging in his natural aptitude for political maneuvering. He was unable, as his wife later remarked, "to bring his mind to the calm of retirement . . . without risking a total extinction of life." In 1830, at the urging of his fellow anti-Jacksonians (by now known as National Republicans), and with the support of the local offshoot of the burgeoning anti-Masonic movement, Adams won a congressional seat in a landslide. "My election as President of the

United States," he wrote in his diary, "was not half so gratifying to my inmost soul."

Within weeks, Adams found himself having finally to make up his mind about the anti-Masons, a growing movement intent on uprooting Freemasonry, the clandestine Old World brotherhood dedicated to liberal principles and religious toleration that had gained a considerable following in the new republic. Anti-Masonry had first arisen at the end of the 1790s as an enthusiasm of conservative New England Federalists. Roughly equivalent to the anti-Masonic and anti-Illuminati currents in Europe that blamed the French Revolution on secret-society plots, American anti-Masons, led by the Massachusetts minister and geographer Jedidiah Morse, raised a scare campaign charging that Jefferson, too, was the tool of a dark Illuminist conspiracy. Quite apart from the lack of evidence, Jefferson's victory and his decidedly non-Jacobin presidency discredited Morse and his hyperimaginative associates. Along with George Washington, who was both a Federalist and a Mason, John Adams rejected the anti-Masonic charges.

Almost thirty years later, anti-Masonry was again on the march, with a different and far more powerful political charge. The upsurge had begun with the mysterious disappearance in 1826 of a dissenting Mason, William Morgan, in Batavia, New York, and the alleged cover-up of his alleged murder. This time, the evidence of wrongdoing was more compelling. By tapping into a pious, rural anti-elitism that had been fueled by the Second Great Awakening, as well as by the secular tensions of rapid commercial development, anti-Masonry swept from western New York into New England. Anti-Masonic organizers, including the young newspaper editor Thurlow Weed, turned justified suspicions and resentments over the Morgan affair into a full-fledged popular cause, attacking Freemasonry as a sinister aristocratic conspiracy against American liberties and Christian morals—and denouncing, among others, the active Mason and the former Grand Master of the Grand Lodge of Tennessee, Andrew Jackson.

In the election of 1828, the aggrieved anti-Masons, now organized into the Anti-Masonic Party, tried to deliver their support to the non-Mason candidate, President John Quincy Adams. Eager to gain anyone's backing, JQA took anti-Masonry seriously enough to issue a denunciation of secret societies and even promised to divulge the dark secrets of Phi Beta Kappa, while Jackson stoutly defended his Masonic membership. But there were numerous Masons inside his own campaign, and so Adams refrained from attacking the Masonic order by name, and a formal alliance between grassroots Anti-Masons and the Adams forces failed to develop. The Anti-Masonic Party nevertheless gained a considerable following, becoming the chief opposition to the Jacksonians in New York state. Over the next four years, the new party broadened its appeal in Pennsylvania and the New England states, and began gearing up for the presidential campaign in 1832.

In Massachusetts, where, unlike in New York, support for the Jacksonians was feeble, the Anti-Masons became the National Republicans' main rivals. By 1831, just after Adams's election to Congress, the divisions in Massachusetts between National Republican insiders and Anti-Masonic insurgents had turned into a full-fledged political brawl. Adams, unexpectedly, threw in his lot with the insurgents. In 1831, he attended an Anti-Masonic convention in Faneuil Hall; four months later, he described himself as "a zealous Antimason," and he began producing energetic pamphlets and newspaper essays denouncing Freemasonry and its secret oaths as antirepublican and anti-Christian.

Anti-Masonry, although largely contained to the Northeastern states, gained followers from across lines of class and occupation. Still, there was something odd about John Quincy Adams—a one-time Harvard professor and member of the American Academy of Arts and Sciences—joining a movement that was happy to proclaim, in the words of one Anti-Masonic editor, that it represented "the lower classes . . . for in this country the lower classes are the head of all." There are some unintentionally amusing passages in

Adams's diary from 1831, detailing his travels from Quincy to attend Anti-Masonic meetings in Boston, where he was surrounded by plain and even rough-hewn men whom he knew not at all and where "none of the aristocracy was present." It was not the sort of political meeting that the Massachusetts mandarin was accustomed to attending. Nor does it appear to have been more than an accident that Adams was not himself a Mason. (His father had failed to join, but not out of a principled objection, and had the father become a Mason, it is reasonable to suppose the son would have followed suit.)

To some extent, Adams's newfound Anti-Masonic loyalties may have been (as his son Charles Francis Adams feared they would be perceived to be) the product of cold political calculation. Anti-Masonic candidates had captured absolute majorities in eleven of the twenty-four towns located in Adams's congressional district, and enjoyed considerable support in the others. At the national level, the Anti-Masons would help keep opposition to the Jacksonians from coalescing behind Adams's once and future rival, Henry Clay. But if Adams expected that political Anti-Masonry would advance his own career, he was disappointed. Although he flirted with gaining the Anti-Masonic presidential nomination in 1832 when contacted by Weed and Weed's New York protégé, William Henry Seward, the party passed him over. Adams did gain the Anti-Masonic nomination for the Massachusetts governorship in 1833, but after winning one-third of the vote in a three-way race and running well behind the National Republican candidate, he withdrew. Meanwhile, despite these defeats, Adams continued his attacks on the Masons through 1835, when the Anti-Masonic enthusiasm began to wane, and he would never retract those attacks.

Adams's delayed but ardent conversion to the Anti-Masonic cause was not merely tacking with the political winds. That conversion must be judged sincere, chiefly because he found Anti-Masonry so compatible with his own well-established political, social, and ethical views. Although he was, by any reasonable standard, a member of the New England elite, a reserved man steeped in old-fashioned classicism,

Adams was in many ways the least pompous of the early presidents. He was the first to wear trousers instead of knee-breeches, and he thought nothing of swimming nude in the Potomac. His national development politics promised to quicken the sort of top-down economic changes that so many grassroots Anti-Masons feared, but Adams was no pro-business National Republican. He was preeminently a moralist, who declared that economic privilege and government by wealth were terrible things, and who viewed national economic improvement as an instrument for national mental and moral improvement.

Adams's religious outlook—a deep, postmillennial, morbidly self-examining liberal Calvinist piety—merged easily with the "new measure" evangelicalism and "effort Calvinism" that were sweeping through Anti-Masonic strongholds in New England and New York. (Charles Finney, the great evangelist of New York's Burned-Over District, broke with the order and denounced it in terms similar to Adams's, strongly enough to provoke threats on his life.) Armed with that reformist piety, Adams beheld (like the grassroots Anti-Masons) an American political order that, under Andrew Jackson and his friends, has been corrupted by secret cabals of unprincipled spoilsmen and hacks, men who spread party strife in order to advance their personal fortunes at the expense of the public good.

By these lights, Adams did not interpret the anti-Masonic movement and the party it produced as many old-line ex-Federalists did, as crude and noisome threats to virtuous and orderly government. For Adams, anti-Masonry was the vindication of virtuous and orderly government. He objected with special force to the order's secret initiation rites, its secret oaths, and its punishments for divulging those secrets—seemingly innocuous but in practice unpatriotic and unChristian regulations, binding Masons to a peculiar loyalty that would indulge the most wanton crimes, like the murder of William Morgan. "Masonry *ought* forever to be abolished," Adams wrote in 1832. "It is wrong—essentially wrong—a seed of evil, which can never produce any good."

The Anti-Masonic Party had the additional merit of melding perfectly with Adams's injured pride. As he regained his political footing after 1828, Adams cultivated his rage against three groups of local and national foes: old-line New England Federalists, especially in Boston (few of them Masons), who had regarded him as an apostate ever since he supported Jefferson's Louisiana Purchase; pro-Jackson slaveholders and their Northern sympathizers (many of them Masons) who had turned him out of the presidency; and his longtime rivals among the leadership of what had become the National Republicans, chief among them the Mason Henry Clay.

Thinking about these villains sometimes drove Adams to distraction. "Among the dark spots in human nature which, in the course of my life, I have observed, the devices of rivals to ruin me have been sorry pictures of the heart of man," he thundered in his diary in November 1835. In a presentiment of modern-day enemies lists, Adams proceeded to name names:

> [F]rom the day I quitted the walls of Harvard, Harrison Gray Otis, Theophilus Parsons, Timothy Pickering, James A. Bayard, Henry Clay, Jonathan Russell, William H. Crawford, John C. Calhoun, Andrew Jackson, Daniel Webster, and John Davis, W.B. Giles, and John Randolph have used up their faculties in base and dirty tricks to thwart my progress in life and destroy my character.

Politically, it is a strikingly disparate collection of antagonists, running all the way from Boston Federalist snobs to Andrew Jackson—but political Anti-Masonry gave Adams a means to fight them all at once.

By the time Adams drew up his catalog of demons, however, political Anti-Masonry was on its last legs. Success quieted the movement, as New England legislatures took steps to curtail the giving and the receiving of Masonic oaths, and lodge membership figures plummeted. In Massachusetts, meanwhile, Daniel Webster secured the political predominance of the mainline anti-Jacksonian opposition, now known as Whigs, when he crushed an Anti-Masonic effort to elect Adams to the Senate in 1835—a move that led some embittered Adams supporters, including Charles Francis Adams, to advocate backing the Jacksonian Martin Van Buren for the presidency the following year.

Adams could not bring himself to support Jackson's handpicked successor, and he stayed neutral in 1836. Thereafter, realizing that Anti-Masonry had no political future, Adams, like most of his fellow Anti-Masons, joined Webster and Clay in the newly organized Whig Party. The alacrity of his switch has led some historians to conclude that Anti-Masonry was nothing more than a fleeting political dalliance for Adams, "an outlet," as his greatest biographer Samuel Flagg Bemis wrote, "for his compulsive genius for political contention." In reality, Adams's Anti-Masonic interlude (like that of so many Anti-Masons) was a profound transition that would mark him for the remainder of his life. Joining the Whigs hardly led Adams to abandon the antiparty political moralism that had drawn him to Anti-Masonry in the first place, and that the movement impressed upon him all the harder. Indeed, Adams's distaste for what he called "mere partisanship" distanced him, at first, from some of the more democratic innovations which former Anti-Masons helped introduce to Whig politics. He recoiled, for example, at what he deemed the Whigs' rabble-rousing, much of it coordinated by men like Weed of New York and Thaddeus Stevens of Pennsylvania, which far exceeded what his National Republican friends had attempted in 1828—the gargantuan rallies and "ball rollings," the endless rounds of stump speeches by candidates and their supporters, along with what he called, amid the Whigs' famous Log Cabin campaign of 1840, the "immense unwieldy mass of political machinery" that "accomplish[ed] nothing."

Inside Congress, meanwhile, Adams continued to fancy himself an elevated, independent man of principle, whose course had put him (as he told Charles Francis Adams in 1835) "to the ban of *all* Presidential parties." For all of his hauteur, however, Adams had learned, as an

Anti-Mason, to work with resourceful democratic organizers, and, in Congress, to work with fellow representatives toward contesting for power and toward mobilizing public opinion on behalf of a patriotic ideal. Although he voted with the Jacksonians on a few occasions, 90 percent of his roll-call votes in Congress were in line with the rest of the opposition; Adams obeyed what he called "the bugle horn of party" far more consistently than most of the supposedly disciplined Jacksonians did. Along with other rock-ribbed "antiparty" Whigs, Adams gradually softened his stance about political parties in elections. As the *American Review* put it in 1845, whereas a "party" was organized around principles, and hence was something noble, a "faction" was organized solely for patronage and hence was corrupt. (Needless to say, the *Review* went on to explain that the Whigs constituted a party and the Jacksonian Democrats a faction.)

With this distinction in mind, Adams became a much more fervent Whig in the early 1840s, delivering unvarnished partisan speeches, telling his constituents that he gloried in the name "Whig," and even (in the 1844 election) taking to the stump on behalf of the Whig national ticket. Unlike the Democrats, he declared, the Whigs had principles, and the great principles for which the Whigs stood, as Adams saw things, were free speech and antislavery. And those were the principles which had become Adams's political passions, in his fight against the notorious gag rule blocking the acceptance of abolitionist petitions in the House of Representatives, and in his legal work on behalf of thirty-nine African rebels who, in 1839, had violently seized and commandeered a Cuban slave ship, the *Amistad*, and steered it to Long Island.

★   ★   ★

PRIOR TO 1831, Adams publicly displayed no interest in promoting or even defending any antislavery cause. His parents, and especially his mother, had certainly passed along to him their strong antislavery views. In 1820, during the debates over the Missouri crisis, he did have some fascinating conversations with John C. Calhoun, after which he remarked in his diary on the perversion and the hypocrisy of the slaveholders, and noted that "if the Union must be dissolved, slavery is precisely the question upon which it ought to break." Yet Adams the nationalist ended up endorsing the Missouri Compromise, thereby adding to a long public record of seeming indifference to slavery and its spread.

If Adams had died in 1831 instead of going to Congress, the historian Leonard L. Richards has observed, "he might have come down in the history books as a fence straddler, or even a proslavery Northerner, rather than an antislavery man." Nor, after his arrival in Congress, did Adams think highly of the radical immediatist abolitionist movement, least of all William Lloyd Garrison and Lewis Tappan, whom Adams regarded as fanatics dedicated to destroying political decency, social stability, and the nation itself. Adams did refrain from publicly joining the anti-abolitionist chorus of old-line Whigs and racist Democrats. But as late as October 1835, he assured his constituents, and himself, that he had no intention of getting mixed up in what he called the "Slave and Abolition whirligig."

It was not slavery per se that first galvanized Adams; it was the gag rule over abolitionist petitions that was instituted only weeks after his "whirligig" remark. Beginning in the mid-1830s, the newly formed American Anti-Slavery Society, inspired largely by Garrison and headed by Arthur Tappan, organized huge congressional petition drives demanding, among other things, the abolition of slavery and the slave trade in the District of Columbia. Southerners, furious at what they perceived as Yankee arrogance and worried that the abolitionists might stir up slave insurrections, demanded retaliation, and in December 1835, Congressman James Henry Hammond of South Carolina (a close ally of Calhoun's) initiated an effort that led to the adoption of a House rule automatically tabling all abolitionist petitions.

Horrified at the Southern onslaught against the people's right to petition their representatives, and seeing it as a manifestation of the slaveholders' unbridled will to power, Adams fought back from the floor. For the next eight years, he was the moral and logistical leader of the anti-gag rule forces inside the House, ending his opposition only when the rule was finally overturned in 1844. The gag rule fight was well-suited to Adams, as it allowed him to vent his moral and political objections to the slaveholders—and, by extension, his detestation of slavery—without raising an issue that contradicted his nationalist principles or in any way questioning the authority of the Constitution of the United States, as some of the abolitionist radicals had begun to do. As a result, a historical image of JQA has emerged, based partly on hasty readings of his diary, as the lonely congressional voice of conscience—not truly an abolitionist, but enough of a defender of free speech to defend the abolitionists' right to dissent.

This image is misleading. For one thing, Adams was not really alone, even inside the House. From the very beginning of the gag rule fight, he was joined by a small group of little-known but determined Northern Whigs, including William Slade of Vermont, who consistently spoke up and voted against the gag rule. Significantly, these men were not mainstream Clay–Webster Whigs, but men with Anti-Masonic backgrounds like Adams's, who represented districts where Anti-Masonry had been particularly strong. Adams also began a fruitful working relationship with the influential, pragmatic abolitionist radical Theodore Dwight Weld, who, having relocated to Washington, served as Adams's secretary and research assistant, and came to adore the feisty ex-president. Together, these men (with Adams working as their chief spokesman) managed to gain the support of the large majority of Northern Whigs, opening up a wedge of sectionalism that would widen in the coming years.

Adams's reverence for the Constitution always kept him from supporting the Garrisonian abolitionists, but his thinking and writing increasingly concentrated on the slaveholders and their Northern friends as a new conspiracy against American liberties. The Slave Power, headed by Calhoun—"the high priest of Moloch," JQA wrote in his diary, "the embodied spirit of slavery"—had displaced the Masonic Power as the great political evil of the day. Numerous historians have remarked that the Anti-Masonic Whigs remained moralistic crusaders, and that they imparted to Northern Whiggery a strong antislavery spirit. That imparting had its earliest and most significant effects in Adams's and his colleagues' fight against the gag rule.

Never one to squander a political opportunity, Adams made the most of the controversy, baiting his Southern colleagues, pulling oratorical and procedural stunts on the floor of the House—knowing all the while that, although he might be ruled out of order or even shouted down, his performances would be reported to the country, burnishing his name and rallying support for his cause. As in his Anti-Masonic days, he had found an issue—and, as he saw it, a political conspiracy—that gathered together all of his enemies, from Jacksonian Democrats to conservative Whig gentlemen of property and standing. He quickly began to reinterpret his own life to reflect that issue, charging in his diary that it had been the "Sable genius of the South" that undid his presidential administration.

The *Amistad* affair was an important further step in Adams's antislavery career. At first, when approached by Tappan and other abolitionists, JQA begged off from joining the legal team to defend the Africans. He was too old, he told them, his eyesight was failing, and his memory was weak. Yet here again, as in the gag rule fight, Adams had the opportunity to fight the Slave Power without compromising his nationalism or attacking the Constitution. And once again, after taking the Africans' case, he played the Ciceronian role to the hilt, working long hours to prepare oral arguments once the case reached the Supreme Court, delivering those arguments with a flourish (before a jammed courtroom that had turned, according to one onlooker, into "a theater of great interest"), and after the justices ruled in the Africans' favor, helping to distribute around the North published versions of his nine-hour concluding speech to the court in order to advance the antislavery movement.

But Adams said and thought and did all of these things in a political world that was very different from the one in which he had grown up. In the new world, clever and even demagogic appeals to the people had become an essential part of everyday politics. In his own Olympian way, Adams had learned to participate in that world—certain that he was standing up for principle and not "mere partisanship." This he would continue, accomplishing the repeal of the gag rule in 1844, fighting the annexation of Texas in 1845, and opposing the war with Mexico. And so his efforts, and those of the other so-called Conscience Whigs, would arouse a growing Northern antislavery constituency, leading to the formation of the Republican Party in the 1850s.

These events, crucial as they are in understanding the most traumatic issue in American history, also hold the key to the enigma of John Quincy Adams. Adams's recovery in the 1830s can be explained only in part as the result of his mastering his depressive disorders. Nor was it chiefly a matter of Adams lashing out gleefully in his old age against his old enemies (although there was an element of that). His achievements were finally neither psychological nor narrowly political. By means of his involvement in Anti-Masonry, Adams made the transition into the new political world of the democratic republic—and in that new context, he made the best use of his authority and his skills in service to a mighty cause that was at once moral and political. It was enough to make him a popular hero; and it was enough to make him deserve to be one.

Adams's story is an illuminating part of the larger national story of the rise of American democracy. The emergence of Jacksonianism was the outstanding part of that history—but so, in time, was the emergence of political currents that were or became fiercely opposed to the Jackson Democrats, including the rise of political antislavery, all of which raised the expectation of voters about politics and about the role of the people in the governmental process.

As the example of John Quincy Adams makes clear, those efforts touched every level of American politics, including at least a few men whose entire political careers had made them suspicious of the people. In time, the effects would be revolutionary. To be sure, the designers of the party system that arose in the 1820s and 1830s did not have revolutionary intentions, least of all about slavery, but the democratic impulses that helped create the new politics, and that the new politics in turn encouraged, could not be easily controlled. Attempts to do so, with gag rules and other repressive measures, only inflamed the body politic more, to the point that antislavery Northerners formed parties of their own, which eventually led to secession, civil war, and emancipation.

John Quincy Adams had prophesied as much in the late 1830s and 1840s. He noted in his diary that American democracy could never permanently tolerate human slavery, and that the democratic politicking of the new partisans would eventually tear the country apart. "Where will it end?" he wrote of the electioneering of the 1840 campaign. "These meetings cannot be multiplied in numbers and frequency without resulting in yet deeper tragedies. Their manifest tendency is to civil war." He was right. And, despite his abiding nationalism, he would play his part in making it so, not in any manner he could have foreseen: neither as John Adams's driven, precocious son nor as a demoralized president of the United States, but as the singular antislavery Whig politician he eventually made himself into.

After Adams's death, his cause would be carried on by younger politicians of far less exalted backgrounds than his, self-made men who had risen in the partisan political world to which Adams had had to adapt, principled men but born practitioners of democratic party politics. The greatest of them, the Illinois Whig congressman Abraham Lincoln, apparently never met the old man, but in Congress he fully supported Adams's opposition to the war against Mexico. As it happened, Lincoln was present on the floor of the House when Adams fell stricken, and he then served on the committee of arrangements for Adams's funeral. As far as we know, these were the only conclusive connections between the two men, and Lincoln would not emerge as a political figure of national importance for another decade. But when he did, Lincoln would build on Adams's crusade and in effect become Adams's successor, as slavery's acutest and astutest arch-enemy in American politics. This was the patrician rebel's greatest legacy.

6

★ ★ ★ ★ ★ ▬▬▬▬▬▬

John Brown:
The Temptation of Terror

JOHN BROWN WAS A VIOLENT CHARISMATIC ANTISLAVERY terrorist and would-be insurrectionist, capable of cruelty to his family as well as to his foes. Every one of his murderous ventures failed to achieve its larger goals. His most famous exploit, the attack on Harpers Ferry in October 1859, actually backfired. That backfiring, and not Brown's assault or his later apotheosis by certain abolitionists and Transcendentalists, contributed something, ironically, to the hastening of Southern secession and the Civil War. In a topsy-turvy way, Brown may have advanced the antislavery cause. Otherwise, he actually damaged the campaign against slavery, which by the late 1850s, led by the Republican Party, was a serious mass political movement contending for national power, and not, as Brown and some of his radical friends saw it, a fraud even more dangerous to the cause of liberty than the slaveholders.

This accounting runs against the grain of the usual historical assessments, pro and con, and also against the grain of what David S. Reynolds calls his "cultural biography" of Brown. The interpretations fall, roughly, into two camps. They agree only about the man's unique importance. Writers hostile to Brown slight the enormity of slavery and describe him as not merely fanatical but insane, the craziest of all the crazy abolitionists whose agitation drove the country mad and caused the catastrophic, fratricidal, and unnecessary war. Brown's admirers describe his hatred of slavery as a singular sign of sanity in a nation awash in the pathologies of white racism and African-American bondage. Alone of the Northern white abolitionist leaders, they say, Brown was willing to put his life on the line by taking up arms alongside blacks against the accursed institution, and in doing so he fired the shots that triggered the Civil War. Unlike inconsistent moderates such as Abraham Lincoln (who, Brown's champions assure us, had no interest in destroying slavery at the war's outbreak, only in saving the Union), Brown saw slavery for the enormity that it was, and fought for racial equality as well as emancipation. He was, as W. E. B. Du Bois wrote in a celebratory biography, "the man who of all Americans has perhaps come nearest to touching the real souls of black folk." Most important, Du Bois concluded, "John Brown was right."

The strongest portions of Reynolds's stimulating and argumentative book trace the evolution of this second, pro-Brown line of thought. Until recently, Reynolds maintains, it was largely restricted to black Americans. True, soon after Brown's capture at Harpers Ferry, and even more after his execution, a cult of the man arose, celebrated most intensely by white abolitionists. But in the despairing period that followed Reconstruction's demise and eventually led to the establishment of Jim Crow, a racial divide opened over John Brown's career and legacy. Black writers and political leaders lionized Brown's memory. Frederick Douglass, who refused to join Brown in the attack on Harpers Ferry, proposed in 1881 that Brown's act made him "our noblest American hero." Whites, however, with a few radical exceptions such as Eugene V. Debs and Mother Jones, vilified Brown. Even the impressively detailed biography of Brown written in 1910 by the staunch liberal Oswald Garrison Villard (William Lloyd Garrison's grandson and a founder, with Du Bois, of the NAACP) found deep fault with Brown's violence and political dreams.

Brown's legacy was mostly laid aside during the early, hopeful days of the modern civil rights movement. It was revived amid the angrier, pessimistic black nationalist vogue of the late 1960s, when Malcolm X, H. Rap Brown, and others hailed Brown as the one white American in history worthy of respect. This time, the esteem for Brown appeared among white radicals and liberals as well, sometimes wracked with ambivalence (as in Stephen Oates's fine biography, *To Purge This Land with Blood*, which appeared in 1970), and sometimes not (as in the terrorist Weather Underground's slogan, "John Brown, Live Like Him / Dare to Struggle, Dare to Win!"). It would appear, then, that Brown's reputation, although always strongest among black reformers and militants, has varied with the times as well as along the racial line, peaking when political frustration on the left boils over into rage against American politics as hopelessly corrupt and finally against America itself as irredeemably racist. According to that incensed view of our history, Brown stands alone as a model of purity, valor, and sacrifice.

The less persuasive parts of Reynolds's book try to validate the perception of Brown as an exemplary figure. Reynolds is a scholar, not a revolutionary, and his judgments are tempered. He plainly calls Brown's early bloody exploits during the struggle over Kansas in 1856 acts of "terrorism" and "war crimes." He leaves a strong impression of Brown as an overbearing and violent man, with an immense capacity for self-dramatization. Yet Reynolds weighs these matters against the calumnies of Brown's detractors and against the qualities that he believes make Brown so admirable today. Brown, he insists, was not insane, in his politics or in his strategies. Of all the white abolitionists, Reynolds asserts, Brown was the least racist and the most comfortable entering what he calls, abstractly, "black culture." Far more than "the Great Emancipator" Abraham Lincoln, and even more than staunch radicals such as William Lloyd Garrison, Brown embodied the egalitarian color-blind ideals of the present. Brown's prophecies that only rivers of blood would wash slavery away proved true, Reynolds observes; his denunciations of America's political and moral corruption were eloquent as well as valid. Reynolds, too, believes that John Brown was right.

Brown was also, Reynolds insists, a crucial figure in American history—nothing less than (according to the book's subtitle) "the man who killed slavery, sparked the Civil War, and seeded civil rights." Even allowing for publishers' hype, though, this extravagant description ought to raise eyebrows. Did John Brown really kill slavery? No, Abraham Lincoln, the Union Army, and the framers of the Thirteenth Amendment killed slavery. Did Brown's raid on Harpers Ferry spark Southern secession and the Civil War? No, the Republican Lincoln's victory in the election of 1860 did that, and would have done it regardless of Brown's assault. Was Brown the man who created the basis for the civil rights movement? No, uncounted thousands of other Americans did: women and men, blacks and whites who agitated for equal rights as well as emancipation long before 1865, and before Harpers Ferry. Reynolds is able to quote various abolitionist admirers of Brown to back up his assertions, but their remarks are metaphorical and eulogistic, not historical. As history, as opposed to metaphor, eulogy, and an expression of moral certitude, the book's claims and apologies for Brown are unconvincing.

★ ★ ★

As Reynolds makes clear, John Brown was not in any way a typical abolitionist radical. During the American Revolution and over the twenty years thereafter, abolitionism took root first among Northern slaves and free blacks as well as devoted groups of white reformers who attacked the ancient premise that some human beings could own other human beings as chattel. The organized antislavery labors helped produce, in the Northern emancipation that began in Pennsylvania in 1780, the first legislation in history aimed at destroying property in man. Their efforts complemented those of free blacks in the Northern cities who, through a variety of benevolent and church societies, railed against slavery, denounced the rising so-called colonization movement that aimed to send blacks back to Africa, and protested racial prejudice in the free states.

In the 1830s, when mainstream political leaders had pushed slavery out of national debates, Northern white reformers and free blacks took a more radical stand for the immediate elimination of slavery. Led by William Lloyd Garrison and the American Anti-Slavery Society (which Garrison helped to found in 1833), these antislavery radicals, the so-called immediatists, demanded the nation's full purging of any complicity with its original sin. Drawing on the Christian humanitarianism and perfectionism unleashed by the revivalist Second Great Awakening, Garrison and the immediatists also renounced violence and stressed the efficacy of moral suasion, in the belief that saving the nation's soul required transcending ungodly coercion.

John Brown was never committed to moral suasion, nonviolence, or redemptive Christian humanitarianism. Born in Torrington, Connecticut, in 1800, and raised chiefly in Ohio, he was trained by his devout parents in the old Congregational Calvinism, with its adherence to predestination and divine intervention. Other antislavery activists were moved by the evangelical promise of spiritual rebirth in Christ's merciful bosom. Brown, as comfortable in the Old Testament as in the New, worshipped an angry, vengeful God; his sword, like Gideon's, killed indiscriminately in the name of the Lord. As Brown grew older—wandering through Ohio, Pennsylvania, and upstate New York, following up one business venture with another—his hatred of slavery and his imagined kinship with abused blacks hardened.

Reynolds successfully rebuts previous claims that Brown's business setbacks drove him into the insanity that set him on the road to Harpers Ferry—in part, he shows, because some of his businesses proved perfectly solid. There were, to be sure, minor would-be Old Testament seers in pre–Civil War America, whose ups and downs in business seem to have been a prelude to religious dementia. But Brown appears to have taken his reverses as well as his successes in stride. In this, he was very much a Calvinist fatalist. Anyway, the insanity charge has always been a red herring, raised by historians who, wanting to explain away the causes of the "needless" Civil War, have found it necessary to dismiss Brown not simply as a good-for-nothing but as a madman.

Reynolds spends considerable time, perhaps too much, in establishing Brown's sanity. The important point is that it is entirely possible to be sane and rational and also, like Brown, a fanatic.

It is to Reynolds's credit that he takes Brown's Calvinism seriously, though he sometimes glosses over how it contributed to Brown's indifference to inflicting suffering on those he considered evildoers. Believing that, as a godly patriarch, he had to multiply the legions of the Lord, Brown fathered twenty children (by two wives), eight of whom either died soon after birth or in early childhood. Brown raised the survivors to live according to strict biblical principles. He did not request anything of his children: he commanded and expected complete obedience, much as his own father had done, and dealt swiftly with any infractions, more in sorrow, he said, than anger.

Reaching for his whip, Brown also kept a meticulous record of his paternal punishments, reflecting both his righteousness and his shame at his children's sinful recalcitrance. Reynolds quotes from the ledger, although he fails to note its similarity to a master's precise accounts of correcting his slaves:

John. Jr.
For disobeying mother 8 lashes
For unfaithfulness at work 3 lashes
For telling a lie 8 lashes

But Reynolds does make clear that Brown's patriarchal devotion to the merciless God of John Calvin and Jonathan Edwards was the keystone of his life. That makes it easier to understand how Brown could become a cold-blooded killer for the Almighty.

★   ★   ★

WHY BROWN CAME to direct his holy wrath against slavery is uncertain, even in Reynolds's account. Brown's father hated slavery, but he took no recorded measures to attack it. There is a story that, at age twelve, Brown witnessed a slave boy being beaten and swore then and there to wage war on the institution, but this sounds too much like other Parson Weems-ish accounts of the era about the youthful epiphanies of American heroes. Nor is it clear why Brown came not simply to sympathize with the slaves but also to identify with them, to talk as if every indignity and blow they absorbed had been inflicted upon him as well. A beaten child as well as a child-beater, he might well have felt a powerful identity with humans tortured for the "sin" of having black skin—but other old-line antislavery Calvinists endured and witnessed what Brown did without acting as he did, so there will always be some mystery about what goaded him. What is certain is that more than a decade before Harpers Ferry, Brown was mulling over plans to lead a great antislavery insurrection.

Given the political context of the time, Brown's mounting frustration and ferocity are understandable. In the 1830s, the Garrisonian abolitionists had enlisted hundreds of thousands of members and sympathizers, and sponsored many mass petition drives, only to slam into furious reaction from an obdurate Congress and scores of violent anti-abolitionist mobs. (One, in Alton, Illinois, killed a local antislavery editor, the Reverend Elijah Lovejoy.) The strain on the abolitionist movement showed, and in 1840 the American Anti-Slavery Society split over strategy and tactics. The minority faction, headed by Garrison, added causes such as women's rights to its agenda while continuing its nonresistant ethical crusade, abjuring resistance to authority in favor of moral suasion. Their adversaries turned to agitating in national electoral politics (which the Garrisonians dismissed as a corrupt snare) and formed the Liberty Party, which received only a tiny number of votes in the presidential campaigns of 1840 and 1844. (A more moderate Free Soil Party succeeded the Liberty men in 1848, raised a great deal of noise, expanded antislavery's ranks—and failed to make a dent on the election's outcome.) In response to abolitionist attacks, meanwhile, Southern slaveholders took an increasingly hard proslavery line, proclaiming their system a benevolent system ordained by God: "instead of an evil a good—a positive good," as John C. Calhoun told the Senate.

For many antislavery Northerners, developments within mainstream politics further augured the consolidated domination of what they called "the Slave Power." The annexation of Texas, followed by the Mexican War and the absorption of vast new territories, looked like a mere cover for the expansion of the slaveholders' economic and political power. The enactment of the Fugitive Slave Law as part of the so-called Compromise of 1850 to settle the territorial question was, for many antislavery Northerners, radicals and nonradicals alike, the last straw, and in 1850 and 1851 they undertook a series of spectacular rescues of captured slaves awaiting their return to bondage. Some of these episodes were violent: "Civil War—The First Blow Struck," one local newspaper reported after the bloodiest incident, outside Christiana, Pennsylvania. "The only way to make the Fugitive Slave Law a dead letter," snapped Frederick Douglass, still nominally a nonresistant Garrisonian, "is to make half-a-dozen or more dead kidnappers."

Against this dismal background, Brown began his own crusade. At a memorial meeting for the martyred Lovejoy, he rose and, with God as his witness, pledged his life to the destruction of slavery. A decade later, while living in Springfield, Massachusetts, he developed a plan for a guerrilla campaign, based partly on the Nat Turner rebellion of 1831 and partly on the Spanish resistance to Napoleon during the Peninsular Wars, whereby hit-and-run attacks would terrorize the slaveholders and liberate slaves. In 1851, in response to the Fugitive Slave Law, he formed a small all-black militia with himself at its head, the United States League of Gileadites, consisting chiefly of fugitive slaves and sworn to resist the new law through Brown's guerrilla operations. But the group came to nothing, as did another plan, hatched with the wealthy abolitionist radical Gerrit Smith, to establish a community for escaped slaves in the Adirondack Mountains.

After the Christiana affair, Northern resistance to the Fugitive Slave Law also petered out, overwhelmed by a counter-campaign mounted by Northern moderates and conservatives who held that the wicked abolitionists aimed finally to destroy the Union. The desire for sectional peace remained powerful; the Great Conciliator, Henry Clay, happily observed that "the patriotic obligation of obeying the Constitution and the laws" was now "almost universally recognized and admitted." In the fall of 1852, a so-called doughface Democrat from New Hampshire sympathetic to the South, Franklin Pierce, won the presidency. The antislavery movement looked thoroughly stymied.

★   ★   ★

THE KANSAS-NEBRASKA ACT of 1854 changed everything—and gave Brown the opportunity to kill his first Philistines. Pushed by proslavery hardliners, Illinois Senator Stephen A. Douglas's bill to organize Kansas and Nebraska territories repealed the Missouri Compromise of 1820, which by admitting Missouri as a slave state while also banning slavery in territories north of latitude 36' 30° had been the bulwark of sectional comity. Kansas bordered on Missouri and harbored many slaveholders as well as Yankee free-staters. It quickly became a deadly battleground. "Come on, then, gentlemen of the slave States," the antislavery New Yorker William Henry Seward bellowed on the Senate floor. ". . . We will engage in the competition for the virgin soil of Kansas, and God give the victory to the side which is strongest in numbers as it is in right." Discerning God's will would turn out to be a gruesome business, thanks in part to the newly arrived settler John Brown.

By the time Brown joined six of his sons in Osawatomie, a small settlement in eastern Kansas near Pottawatomie Creek, in the summer of 1855, the situation had degenerated into a virtual civil war between free-staters and proslavery men. Each side was determined to have its way over permitting or prohibiting slavery under the new territorial constitution, and Brown, now fifty-five, won an appointment as captain of the Pottawatomie Rifles company of the free-stater Liberty Guards. In May 1856, he and his men rushed to the pro-free-state capital in Lawrence to help fend off an attack by proslavery men, but arrived to find the place in smoldering ruins. A day later, Brown received word that a zealous proslavery South Carolina congressman had replied to an insulting speech by Senator Charles Sumner of Massachusetts by coolly walking up to Sumner on the Senate floor and beating him within an inch of his life. According to one of Brown's sons, his father went "crazy-crazy" upon hearing the news from Washington.

"Something must be done," Brown declaimed, "to show these barbarians that we, too, have rights." On a May night, Brown, four of his sons, and three other men, carrying broadswords, raided the farm of James Doyle, an anti-free-stater but not a slaveholder, near Pottawatomie Creek. The raiding party dragged Doyle and his two grown sons from their house and hacked them to pieces, sparing Doyle's wife and fourteen-year-old son. Then Brown and his band moved to the Wilkinson farm and abducted and killed the law-and-order man Allen Wilkinson, before ending their attacks at the home of James Harris, where they split the skull of another proslavery partisan, William Sherman.

Brown and his sons eluded capture; proslavery men destroyed the Brown homestead; and the massacre, combined with the Lawrence affair, escalated violence across the territory. Two hundred men (including one of Brown's sons) died in the renewed combat. Brown himself fought on uncaptured until the autumn, when he headed back East to raise money to provide fresh supplies, hard cash, and more Sharps rifles to the Kansas warriors. "You know what I have done in Kansas," he told a group of abolitionist sympathizers in New York. ". . . I have no other purpose but to serve the cause of liberty."

Reynolds sees Brown's Pottawatomie attack in the context of the convulsions in Bleeding Kansas—not simply an act of terrorism but also a war crime. The judgment is reasonable enough, though it is somewhat anachronistic. He also concedes that the attack utterly failed to achieve Brown's stated goal: to intimidate proslavery settlers into departing Kansas en masse. At the time, though, northern reaction to Brown and his atrocities was divided. Some antislavery editors idolized him as "Old Osawatomie Brown," while others looked away. Rumors circulated that Brown had not been involved, or that he had acted in self-defense. Brown was evasive and mysterious when questioned, denying nothing but admitting little. In any event, dispatches about the subsequent bloodshed in Kansas soon overshadowed Brown's massacre. By summer's end, attention had switched to presidential politics—and to a political universe drastically different from that of only four years earlier.

The Kansas-Nebraska Act had shaken the political system to its core. The Whig Party, already weakened by sectional divisions, collapsed when Southern Whigs supported Douglas's bill; antislavery Democrats, fed up with their party's long history of placating the slaveholders, bolted. In the autumn, the new antislavery Republican Party ran its first fledgling congressional campaigns and won a plurality of seats in the House of Representatives. Two years later, in the wake of the continuing bloodshed in Kansas, the Republicans ran John C. Frémont for the presidency on a platform that replicated the basic planks of the earlier Liberty and Free Soil platforms, denouncing slavery as one of the "relics of barbarism" and pledging to put the institution on the road to elimination by banning it in all American territories, Kansas included. Frémont wound up carrying eleven of the sixteen free states against the doughface Democratic victor James Buchanan, and the opposition retained a substantial, though reduced, presence in the House. "[T]he process now going on in the politics of the United States," one Republican newspaperman wrote, "is a Revolution."

Antislavery Northerners now had two revolutions to choose from, one peaceful and constitutional, the other violent and finally at war with the Constitution. The Republicans' revolution would remove the federal government from the grip of the Slave Power, allowing slavery to exist only where (as the Constitution stipulated) it already existed

and banning it elsewhere—a move which (Northerners and Southerners agreed on this point, although on nothing else) would hasten
slavery's extinction by halting its expansion. For Brown, however, this
amounted to nothing more, as he put it, than "talk—talk—talk."

Some antislavery radicals (including Garrison) believed that the
Constitution was an evil document, a covenant with the Devil approved
in Hell. And for some of those radicals, like Brown, slavery's continued
existence, anywhere, meant that the American republic deserved to die.
Only a violent upheaval of slaves and free blacks joined by white revolutionaries would free the oppressed. The rise of the Republicans did
nothing to dissuade Brown and his supporters. It only fixed their aims,
now set in opposition not simply to the Slave Power but also to the
milquetoast moderates who, in their pretended concern for the slaves,
only made the task of emancipation that much harder.

★　★　★

BY 1859, the Republicans' revolution was struggling hard against
mounting reaction. The momentous Supreme Court decision in 1857
in the case of *Dred Scott v. Sandford*, tried to squelch the Republicans'
efforts by declaring any federal ban on slavery in the territories unconstitutional, which only inflamed and reinforced Northern antislavery
opinion. Senator Douglas outlasted the Republican Abraham Lincoln and won reelection in 1858, but his debates with the challenger
turned Lincoln into a national figure. Continuing events in Kansas split the Democratic Party yet again, setting the moderate anti-
Republican Douglas against the Buchanan administration and the
proslavery fire-eaters who were striving to command the party's dominant Southern wing. Republicans and anti-administration Democrats
now held a majority in the House.

The revolutionary abolitionists, having forsaken politics, became
increasingly desperate. Even among Garrison's friends and loyalists,
peaceful nonresistance was losing favor. Gerrit Smith, who had been
an officer in the American Peace Society, declared that after Kansas he

was ready to pursue the Slave Power "even unto death with violence." The Bostonian Thomas Wentworth Higginson, a leader in the fight against the Fugitive Slave Law, devised plans to raise an armed force "for resisting the U.S. Government in Kanzas [sic], and sustaining such resistance elsewhere"; a year later, Higginson and his supporters met in Cleveland and passed a series of resolutions extolling slave uprisings. Another radical Bostonian, Wendell Phillips, scrutinized the new Republican leader Lincoln and pronounced him a "huckster" and "the slave hound of Illinois." And in Maryland, a mysterious bearded stranger named Isaac Smith rented a small and secluded farm near the Virginia border, where all through the summer of 1859 a trickle of black and white men took up residence.

Smith's visitors turned out to be a ragtag army, and Smith turned out to be John Brown. He had set his insurrection in motion a year earlier, laying out his plans to Gerrit Smith and Franklin B. Sanborn, a young protégé of Ralph Waldo Emerson, at Smith's estate in upstate New York. To their protests that the proposal was mad—"an amazing proposition,—desperate in its character," Sanborn later wrote, ". . . of most uncertain result"—Brown replied that he was determined to carry it out with or without their support. Awed by Brown's confidence, and by the possibility that even if the plan failed it might ignite a civil war, Smith and Sanborn agreed to help, and enlisted four other abolitionist radicals to form an advisory and fundraising committee, the so-called Secret Six.

Brown was ready to go by the fall of 1859—but despite his energetic recruiting efforts, his "army" wound up amounting to a pitiful twenty-one soldiers, only five of them black. With some members of the Secret Six growing jittery, Brown appealed to Frederick Douglass, an old friend in the antislavery struggle, to join him, but at a secret meeting of the two in August at a quarry in Chambersburg, Pennsylvania, Douglass refused. Brown had determined that his guerrilla war would begin with an assault on the federal armory in Harpers Ferry—a plan that Douglas warned was suicidal and "would array the whole country against us."

Douglass's military instincts proved sound. Harpers Ferry is situated on a point of land formed by the Potomac and Shenandoah rivers and surrounded by imposing cliffs—a "perfect steel-trap," Douglass called it. Once inside the town, Brown's little force would be easy prey for a counterattack, which is exactly what transpired. On the evening of October 16, Brown's men easily captured the armory by overcoming its single watchman. Brown sent out a patrol to spread the alarm among the slaves on neighboring plantations, then sat and waited for the rebels to arrive. He had made no previous contacts with those neighboring slaves to prepare them; he had planned no escape route out of Harpers Ferry; and even less explicably, he released a midnight train bound for Baltimore that he held hostage for a few hours, in the hope that it would take the word to a hostile outside world about what was transpiring in Harpers Ferry. The haphazardness of Brown's behavior suggests that, by the time the raid began, he knew it would be futile. But it is just as likely that he simply threw the dice and hoped that the slaves would join him—prepared, if they did not, to exchange the role of avenging commander-in-chief for that of martyr.

Less than a day and a half after it began, the raid was crushed. Armed townsmen, not content to wait for the Virginia and Maryland militia, picked off eight of Brown's men while losing three of their own. Brown, his surviving guerrillas, and some prisoners retreated inside a small but sturdy fire-engine house. After nightfall, a company of federal marines, commanded by Colonel Robert E. Lee and Lieutenant J. E. B. Stuart, joined the militiamen on the scene and prepared for the final assault, using a battering ram and their bayonets in order to avoid killing hostages. When the fighting ended, Brown, wounded in action, was taken captive. The combat had killed ten raiders (including two of Brown's sons), four townsmen (including the black baggage-handler at the railroad station, who was mistaken for a watchman), and one marine. Seven of Brown's men escaped, although two were later captured. One of the handful of confused and frightened slaves picked up by Brown's patrol was killed; the rest were sent back into bondage.

Now, in defeat, Brown had a second drama to perform, which would prove in many ways more important than the first. In his jail cell in Charles Town, charged with treason, Brown recovered from his wounds, wrote letters, and gave interviews with an impressive if highly calculated solemnity. In his courtroom testimony, he claimed he had not intended to raise an insurrection against the United States, but only to arm oppressed slaves—a hair-splitting defense that made no impact on the judge or the jury. But with his uncowed dignity and his uncompromising remarks about slavery, he became a public sensation, and he saved his best for last. In his closing speech before being sentenced to hang, Brown eloquently appealed to the laws of God and expressed contentment that, in a just cause, he would "mingle my blood further with the blood of my children and with the blood of millions in this slave country." On the morning of his execution, December 2, he wrote out with a steady hand his final prophecy, that "the crimes of this guilty, land: will never be purged away; but with Blood. I had as I now think: vainly flattered myself that without very much bloodshed; it might be done."

Governor Henry A. Wise, fearing an effort to free the prisoner, ordered 1,500 soldiers to Charles Town, which only heightened the tension. (Among the troops was John Wilkes Booth, an actor who enlisted in the Richmond Grays militia with the sole intention of seeing Brown die. Others in the hanging-day throng included the fire-eater Edmund Ruffin and Thomas J. Jackson of the Virginia Military Institute, who would soon earn the nickname "Stonewall.") Taken to the gallows in a wagon, Brown stared out over the Blue Ridge Mountains and remarked, "This is a beautiful country." After the deed was done and while John Brown's body dangled, a Virginia colonel intoned: "So perish all such enemies of Virginia! All such enemies of the Union! All foes of the human race!"

★   ★   ★

BROWN'S INSURRECTION was a total failure, but the drama was not finished. Southern reaction swerved, within a matter of weeks, from alarm to a mixture of reassurance and cocky pride. Even as Brown's men exchanged gunfire with the local citizenry, exhilarated crowds lined the railroad tracks from Baltimore to Harpers Ferry to cheer the federal forces on their way. Then a wave of hysteria hit the slaveholding states, amid rumors that Brown's raid was meant to signal massive uprisings on Southern plantations. Well into the autumn, reports circulated about imagined black rebellions and whole armies of abolitionists marching southward as reinforcements.

Vigilance committees sprang to life; the South Carolina legislature passed several measures further restricting slave movement and augmenting military preparations. But when the rumors faded and it became clear that no slaves had rushed to join Brown's insurrection or any other, relieved Southerners momentarily calmed down. The insurrectionists represented only a small number of monomaniacal Yankees. Some claimed that the events had actually vindicated slavery by proving that slaves everywhere were loyal and content. The raid itself, one Richmond paper observed early on, was "a miserably weak and contemptible affair."

Northern opinion passed through its own series of revisions and reversals. Initially, the raid shocked even some radical abolitionists—"misguided, wild, and apparently insane," Garrison said, though he would not renounce the terrorists. But Brown's gallantry in defeat quickly led to the rise of a virtually religious cult of the man in antislavery circles. At the hour of his hanging, church bells tolled from Boston to Chicago. Ministers preached special sermons on Brown's sacrifice; those in attendance at mass meetings bowed their heads in worshipful silence. Well before execution day, New England abolitionists and intellectuals were beside themselves: Thoreau wrote "A Plea for Captain Brown" and called him "a transcendentalist above all, a man of ideas and principles," and Emerson predicted that Brown would "make the gallows as glorious as the cross."

Illustrators churned out portraits of Brown and his exploits; hagiographies flew off Northern presses. And in the wake of Brown's apotheosis, a renewed wave of fury and fresh rumors washed over the South. How, one Baltimore newspaper asked, could Southerners any longer "live under a government, a majority of whose subjects or citizens regard John Brown as a martyr and Christian hero?" A virtual reign of terror ensued, in which touchy Southerners, persuaded that every Yankee was a potential John Brown, appropriated new funds for military preparations and committed random acts of violence against the Northerners in their midst. There were several reported lynchings.

According to Reynolds, Brown's ultimate historical importance lies in creating this wave of fear. For decades, Southerners had worried that Northern abolitionists would instigate a massive slave rebellion. From the alleged Denmark Vesey Conspiracy of 1822 through Nat Turner's bloody rampage nine years later, Southern proslavery leaders blamed Yankee agitators for slave unrest; and through the 1830s and 1840s, the Southern states built a virtual wall along the Mason-Dixon Line to keep out incendiary abolitionist preachings. John Brown was the slaveholders' worst nightmare come true, and even though he failed, the Northern celebration of him fed Southern panic and paranoia that led directly to secession and Civil War. Disunionism—which Reynolds claims was weak in the South, even in 1860—would have carried little weight except for the terror that followed the attack on Harpers Ferry. And although Reynolds allows that nothing could have prevented an eventual war over slavery, he insists that "Brown emerges as a positive agent for change because he forced a war that would have come anyway but could only have been worse than it was."

Describing John Brown as "a positive agent for change," a cliché in today's progressive lexicon, deflates the man it would defend. But in truth, Brown forced nothing. Disunionism was not weak in the South, especially the Deep South. John C. Breckinridge, the hardline Southern Democratic candidate for president in 1860, may have only carried 18 percent of the national vote—a figure that Reynolds emphasizes—but he swept the lower South, winning nearly 60 percent of the vote in Mississippi, 75 percent in Texas, and strong majorities and pluralities elsewhere. (Stephen A. Douglas, the only Northerner besides Lincoln in the race, ran dismally in the South, winning 4.8 percent in Mississippi and only .03 percent—a grand total of eighteen votes—in Texas.) After Lincoln won the presidency, Unionism prevailed for a time in the border South, but not in the secessionist heart of Dixie, where delegates to the state secession conventions divided mainly between those who preferred immediate disunion and those who preferred to wait until other Southern states had seceded. The panic that followed Brown's raid surely played into the hands of the most determined Southern disunionists, but the evidence favors the idea that much of the South would have seceded once Lincoln or any other Republican won the presidency.

Nor was Southern disunionism the product of paranoia stoked by Brown's raid. However moderate they seemed in comparison to the radical abolitionists, the Republicans hated slavery fiercely, and, unlike the abolitionists, they posed a clear and present danger to the future of the slaveholders' regime. Lincoln had pledged to undo *Dred Scott*, which he considered illegitimate. He and his party were committed to banning slavery in all of the nation's territories, thereby placing slavery, as Lincoln had said, "in the course of ultimate extinction." The nation, Republicans said, would cease to be a house divided, and they were dedicated to seeing that it would be a nation of freedom, not slavery.

As Lincoln proclaimed in his mostly conciliatory first inaugural address, the conflict was clear-cut, pitting "[o]ne section of our country [which] believes slavery is *right*, and ought to be extended," against "the other [which] believes it is *wrong*, and ought not to be extended." Secession, to be sure, might not have been the wisest response. Some slaveholders urged holding on at least until the midterm elections in 1862, when they could begin to roll back the Republican victory, and in retrospect, given what actually happened, this sounds like excellent advice. But once the Republicans had captured the White House along with a considerable House plurality, it was perfectly rational for slaveholders to believe that what the Georgian Alexander Stephens called the "corner-stone" of their civilization was doomed. It was also perfectly rational for the Northern Republican Charles Francis Adams to observe, after Lincoln's triumph, that "[t]here is now scarcely a shadow of a doubt that the great revolution has actually taken place, and that the country has once and for all thrown off the domination of the Slaveholders."

Brown's raid, instead of forcing the Republican revolution, actively damaged it, by linking antislavery with treasonous insurrection against the United States—an idea that, no matter how popular it was among the radicals of Boston, was politically dangerous in key states from New York westward to Indiana and Illinois. Indeed, had the attack on Harpers Ferry somehow succeeded (as Reynolds thinks it might well have done), the Republicans would most likely have lost the election of 1860. A prolonged military counteroffensive against Brown would have divided staunchly antislavery New England against the lower North, handing the Northern Democrat Douglas (most likely) the electoral votes of New York, Ohio, Illinois, and Indiana. This would have been more than sufficient to throw the election into the House of Representatives where, according to the one-state, one-vote rule, a pro-Southern candidate would almost certainly have prevailed. Fortunately for the Republicans, however, Brown failed in everything except captivating the hearts and minds of some overexcited New England intellectuals and causing a posthumous wave of sympathy in the North and terror in the South. Running, in effect, against Brown by upholding his antislavery but denouncing his assault as an act of treason, Republicans fared well in the off-year elections in 1859.

In only one paradoxical respect did Brown unintentionally advance the antislavery cause and hasten the coming of the Civil War. In late 1859, the odds-on favorite to win the Republican presidential nomination was William Henry Seward—a man considered even by many Republicans to be too much of a firebrand. After Brown's raid, Northern Democrats immediately singled out Seward as the true instigator of the uprising, which put him on the defensive and led him to announce that he approved of Brown's execution. Seward's rival, the more moderate-sounding Lincoln, was able to capitalize and draw a finer, vital distinction: although Brown "agreed with us in thinking slavery wrong," this alone "cannot excuse violence, bloodshed, and treason." Many factors led the Republicans finally to nominate Lincoln and not Seward, but the impact of Brown's raid was one of them. Ironically, President Lincoln proved, during the secession crisis in 1861, far more stubborn in resisting any compromise with the departing Southern states than the supposed hothead Seward, whom he had named his secretary of state.

Here lay Brown's largest political importance. By frightening the Republicans, he contributed to the nomination of the Kentucky-born moderate Lincoln—the radical abolitionists' "slave-hound of Illinois." Lincoln's combination of outward courtesy to the South and firmness on the issue of slavery's immorality allowed him to win the lower Northern states and thus the election, which Seward might not have been able to do. His election immediately sparked Southern secession, and his unyielding resistance to secession led to the Civil War.

So Brown played a role, though it was tiny compared with his grandiose expectations (and the grandiose claims of his admirers, then and now). He indirectly helped to elect Lincoln to the White House. A Civil War ensued—not the slave uprising that Brown had envisaged, but a sectional conflict. And in that war, the side that bore the onus of insurrection and treason to the American republic was not the antislavery North, but the Confederate States of America.

★   ★   ★

THE LEGEND OF JOHN BROWN remained. Northern soldiers did indeed sing "John Brown's Body" when marching to battle, although the song was originally meant as a joke directed against another John Brown altogether, a humorless Scotsman in the Massachusetts 12th Regiment. When Lincoln issued the Emancipation Proclamation in

1863, turning the war to end secession into a war to end slavery, Brown's surviving partisans quickly celebrated their hero as the true man of the moment—if not the Great Emancipator, then the Great Anticipator. And after the war, as the revolutionary hopes of equality faded, embittered Americans, and especially embittered blacks, looked to the example of Brown—sometimes alongside Lincoln's, sometimes alone—as a beacon of courage and integrity in reactionary times.

Something like this pessimistic mood and its periodic return may account for the persistent interest in Brown's legend, rooted in the chaotic radical politics of the late 1960s and early 1970s but spread more generally among liberal-minded Americans frustrated by their own impotence in electoral politics during the age of Reagan and after. "America," Reynolds writes, "has become a vast network of institutions that tend to stifle vigorous challenges from individuals. . . . America must be large enough to allow for meaningful protest, instead of remaining satisfied with patriotic bromides and a capitalist mass culture that fosters homogenized complacency." Even after the election of the first African American president in 2008, this remains a familiar sentiment in liberal circles, including academic liberal circles, and it sometimes hardens into cynicism. At its worst, it can revive the old cult of purifying violence that turned up here and there among the radical intellectuals of the 1850s and 1960s.

One problem with the wish for "vigorous challenges from individuals" is that, throughout American history, and especially since the Civil War, the politics of terror has served chiefly to uphold white supremacy. And in the years since the atrocities of September 11, 2001, one ought to have become careful about finding some deeper good in terrorist politics of any kind. Reynolds forthrightly addresses this problem, and claims that the scale of the slaughter unleashed by Osama bin Laden makes his acts different in kind from John Brown's—but this does lead one to wonder what Brown might have done if he had jet airliners at his disposal. In the matter of slaying defenseless persons for a higher political and religious cause, the body count is not an instructive marker between good and evil.

Since America is a democratic republic, and since that republic survived the Civil War, we are fated to confront the legacy of John Brown whenever normal politics seems too blocked, too slow, too deafened to the cries of injustice. It is not so much a contrast between radicals and moderates: plenty of radicals refused to join Brown's operation, no matter how much they celebrated him in later years. The contrast posed by Brown is between a savage, heedless politics of purity and a politics of the possible. In flat political times, when the possible seems shrunken and democracy seems hollow, Brown materializes, particularly among liberal intellectuals, as a noble figure, an egalitarian paragon, a man ahead of his time. David Reynolds's book, first published in the middle of George W. Bush's presidency, raises the matter once more, and for that it is worth arguing with—and for understanding all over again that John Brown was not a harbinger of idealism and justice, but a purveyor of curdled and finally destructive idealism. This is what Abraham Lincoln understood. John Brown deserves to live in American history not as a hero, but as a temptation—and as a warning about the damage wrought by righteous American terrorists, not just to their victims but also to their causes.

7

★ ★ ★ ★ ★ ▬▬▬▬▬▬▬

Abraham Lincoln: Egalitarian Politician

THE PAST THREE GENERATIONS OF HISTORIANS HAVE AGREED that Abraham Lincoln was probably the best president in American history and that Franklin Pierce was one of the worst. Pierce, from New Hampshire, was one of the so-called "doughface" Northern Democrats who gave political cover to slaveholders and their violent supporters in the 1850s. His softness on the slavery issue encouraged the Southern truculence that later led to secession and the formation of the Confederacy. Apart from their closeness in age—Pierce was a little more than four years Lincoln's senior—about the only things the two men had in common were their preoccupation with politics and their success in reaching the White House.

When Pierce ran for president in 1852, Lincoln, a Whig, naturally campaigned against him. (The Whigs, originally formed in opposition to Andrew Jackson, were a national coalition dominated by pro-business conservatives, humanitarian reformers, Christian evangelicals, supporters of federally-backed economic development, and moderate Southern planters. Lincoln remained a staunch Whig loyalist until the party crumbled in 1854.) But the cause of the Whig Party was extremely feeble in Illinois that year, so Lincoln limited himself to a long speech in

Springfield—it took him two days to deliver it!—which he abridged and repeated in Peoria. The speech did nothing to affect the outcome of the election, in Illinois or in the country at large. But it deserves to be remembered because it can be disturbing reading to anyone inclined to worship Father Abraham's every deed.

In defending the Whig presidential candidate, General Winfield Scott, Lincoln attacked Pierce—not as a slaveholders' tool, but as a Yankee who had flattered antislavery Northerners. Lincoln specifically charged that Pierce had expressed a "loathing" for the Fugitive Slave Law, which Congress had passed two years earlier to help masters and their hirelings retrieve runaway slaves who had fled to the North. This was the very law that had provoked an outraged Harriet Beecher Stowe to write *Uncle Tom's Cabin*, which portrays the slave Eliza making her daring escape to freedom across the Ohio River. Lincoln defended the law as perfectly constitutional, and charged that Pierce had taken a stance that was all too friendly to the real-life Elizas, and too dismissive of the rights of slaveholders and slave hunters. Pierce did so, Lincoln charged, in an effort to pick up antislavery votes outside the Democrats' proslavery base in the deep South. Lincoln even claimed that the Northerner Pierce's "efficacy" at winning antislavery votes "was the very thing that secured his nomination."

There was more. Lincoln charged that Pierce could win only by positioning himself as a peculiar kind of political progeny, born of a mating of Northern conservative Democrats and antislavery Free Soilers, "the latter predominating in the offspring." Pierce's contrived politics—which were entirely Lincoln's contrivance, in his effort to alienate racist voters from the Democrats—put Lincoln in mind of a sailor's sea chantey that had appeared in a book by the British writer Frederick Marryat: "Sally is a bright Mullater, / Oh Sally Brown— / Pretty gal, but can't get at her, / O Sally Brown." Were Pierce actually elected, Lincoln joked, "he will, politically speaking, not only be a mulatto; but he will be a good deal darker one than Sally Brown."

My point in retelling this story is not to try, yet again, to debunk

Lincoln's reputation for probity and sagacity, and for perfect enlightenment on racial issues. The defamatory image of Lincoln as a conventional white racist, whose chief cause was self-aggrandizement, is even more absurd than the ubiquitous awestruck hagiographies. My point is simpler and larger. It is that Abraham Lincoln was, first and foremost, a politician.

Lincoln hated slavery, and had said so long before 1852. But as a political leader as well as a lawyer, he had to admit that the Fugitive Slave Law, which he also hated, was technically and constitutionally correct. In the congressional deal known as the Compromise of 1850, the Fugitive Slave Law was just part of the price the Southern slaveholders exacted for sectional comity, and both major parties formally endorsed it in 1852. Lincoln knew that by assailing Pierce, a Northern man with Southern principles, as a conniver willing to play politics with the Fugitive Slave Law, he would sow doubts among Northern conservatives, Whig and Democratic, whose votes the Whigs badly needed.

Lightly infused with offhand racist humor, Lincoln's speech was hardly his finest political hour—but it was just that, a political speech. It was not, as some current writers imagine Lincoln's every utterance was, a foray into moral philosophy or social theory. Nor did his brief quotation from Marryat's book have much at all to do with race or sex, the major preoccupations of so much of today's academic scholarship, and it certainly had nothing to do with Lincoln's love of English literature. It had to do with ridiculing Pierce as someone who would say anything to win the election.

In 1854, when Lincoln began shifting his loyalties to the fledgling antislavery Republican Party, the tone as well as the substance of his speeches became grander, and the casual racism disappeared. Lincoln's politics developed as the Republican Party and antislavery public opinion in the North developed, and Lincoln helped develop both the party and Northern opinion. But it is important to understand that those later pronouncements of Lincoln's were no less political than his earlier ones, no less geared to achieving a particular political goal or set of political goals. Given the enlarged stakes of the sectional crisis and then the Civil War, Lincoln's goals were actually more political than ever. He was a shrewd and calculating creature of politics, and he achieved historical greatness in his later years because of, and not despite, his political skills. It was the only way that anyone could have completed the momentous tasks that history, as well as his personal ambition, had handed to him.

These points are not new. One of the great Lincoln scholars of our time, David Herbert Donald, made some of them in an essay published sixty years ago, "A. Lincoln, Politician." Yet many of Lincoln's latter-day admirers, the most effusive as well as the begrudging, prefer a fantasy Lincoln who experienced some sort of individual awakening or mystical conversion, who somehow transcended politics for a realm more pure.

Lincoln has never lacked for critics, ranging from pro-Confederates on the right to black nationalists and their sympathizers on the left. Yet he has inspired far more approval and even adoration than animosity among historians—including one admiring line of argument that can accommodate even his unsavory attack on Pierce in 1852. That interpretation runs roughly as follows. For most of his adult life, Lincoln was an enormously ambitious and partisan Whig Party organizer and officeholder who, after a single frustrating term in Congress, retired from politics in 1849 to become a highly successful lawyer in Springfield. Then the enactment of the Kansas-Nebraska Act five years later stirred his moral aversion to slavery and reawakened his political aspirations. Thereafter—his enormous human sympathy aroused, his conscience pricked by eloquent radicals such as Frederick Douglass, and, as president, his hand forced by ordinary slaves who flocked to Union lines during the Civil War—Lincoln the hack politician gradually turned into a philosopher-statesman and a literary genius.

This account appears in many different forms. It is consistent with— or can be made to be consistent with—a particular view of American political history that emerged out of the politics of the 1960s and is widely held today. On this view, elected officials, even the most worthy, are at best cautious and unreliable figures who must be forced by unruly events—and by outsiders—into making major reforms. Thus, Martin Luther King, Jr., and the civil rights movement had to compel the Southern wheeler-dealer Lyndon B. Johnson to support civil rights and voting rights for blacks. Thus, John L. Lewis and the left-wing Congress of Industrial Organizations had to push a reluctant Franklin Delano Roosevelt into making and then enlarging the New Deal. And thus, Frederick Douglass and the escaped slaves, not Abraham Lincoln, deserve the real credit for the Emancipation Proclamation.

Without question, what Lincoln called "public sentiment" is and always has been a key battleground, and insofar as agitators such as abolitionists affect that sentiment, they have a crucial role to play in democratic politics (as Lincoln also recognized). For a long time, historians too often either maligned the agitators as misfits and hotheads or ignored them altogether. But it is one thing to acknowledge the contributions of outsiders and radicals and quite another to vaunt their supposed purity in order to denigrate mainstream politics and politicians. The implication of this antipolitical or metapolitical narrative is that the outsiders are the truly admirable figures, whereas presidents are merely the outsiders' lesser, reluctant instruments. Anyone who points out the obvious fact that without a politically supple, energetic, and devoted president, change will never come runs the risk of being branded an elitist or worse. Lincoln may be the only one of these presidents who, having seen the light, went on to earn a kind of secular sainthood, but his redemption from grubby politics and self-interested prudence had to precede his martyrdom and canonization. That redemption came as a result of the words and the actions of uncompromising abolitionists and the dramatic resistance of heroic slaves.

Another, related current of interpretation, already present inside the vast historiography of Lincoln but newly restated, has further diminished the importance of party politics and government in his career.

This line of argument takes it for granted that Lincoln rose to a surpassing greatness. In one way or another, though, it locates Lincoln's chief distinction in his literary sophistication and his empathetic powers, making only passing glances at his political astuteness. Indeed, in some quarters, Lincoln's political successes before and during his presidency now seem to have come almost entirely from his writing and his oratory, in what might be called a literary determinist interpretation of history. Lincoln's apotheosis remains undisturbed; the difference according to this interpretation is that he was an archangel of belles lettres—or, as Jacques Barzun described him fifty years ago, a "born writer" with a hidden hurt who became a "literary artist, the maker of a style that is unique in English prose." Therein, supposedly, lay the basis, or at least one important basis, for his political importance.

Having already been mythologized, Lincoln is in some danger of being aestheticized: now he belongs to the English department. Combined with an abiding post-1960s' preference for radicals over politicians, this trend renders Lincoln the supreme giant of American politics because he had, as Barzun observed, "a style—clear, forcible, individual, and distinguished," and because his compassion, as well as the force of circumstances, led him to heed the wisdom of the militants and finally, as president, to transcend politics as usual.

Modern democratic politics are supposed to be immune to the kind of intense cult of personality common in authoritarian regimes, with their caudillos, patriot kings, and maximum leaders. James Madison and the framers of the Constitution designed a federal government to hinder the emergence of such an individual. But the United States—or, at least, historical writing about the United States—is not immune. We are given a Lincoln whose surviving everyday possessions, like his pocket watch or his stovepipe hat, are accorded the attention and invested with the properties otherwise associated with sacred relics. The historical Lincoln disappears and a wishful fantasy takes his place, symbolizing a politics that has been cleansed and hallowed, which is to say a politics that is unreal—a politics constructed out of words, just words.

Lincoln may have had his own purposes, like the Almighty, but those purposes always included gaining or maintaining political advantage, often enough by cagey and unexhilarating means. Although he was often unsuccessful, his political cunning was his strength, and not a corrupting weakness. Pure-hearted radicals did not manipulate him into nobility as much as he manipulated them to suit his own political aims—which, as president, were to save the Union and ensure that freedom, and not slavery, would prevail in the struggle of the house divided. Unless we understand this, none of Lincoln's philosophizing, and none of his spare, arresting, and moving rhetoric, makes any sense.

★   ★   ★

SOME RECENT STUDIES of Lincoln have, to be sure, taken his politics and his political career very seriously. Harold Holzer, a prolific writer on Lincoln, admires him enormously, but also understands that he was a political creature. His book *Lincoln President-Elect* is the closest study ever undertaken of the critical four months between Lincoln's election as president and his inauguration on March 4, 1861. It aims to correct what Holzer considers the unjust view—formulated by the young Henry Adams at the time, and supported by later scholars—that Lincoln acted unsteadily in the face of the growing emergency of secession, resorting to platitudes and trivialities in his public statements and otherwise giving an impression of weakness and indecisiveness.

For many pro-Lincoln historians, the transition months of 1860–61 offer an important baseline for judging his later growth in office—but Holzer insists that Lincoln was a brilliant leader even before the inauguration. If Lincoln appeared to be fumbling, according to Holzer, he intended as much, in order to cloak the momentous decisions that he was making about his administration's policies and personnel. On his long, circuitous train journey from Springfield to Washington, Lincoln would show his homely, newly whiskered face to the crowds and say a few innocuous words, so as to connect personally with the voters who had elected him. All the while, behind the scenes, he completed the delicate task of selecting his cabinet while writing the inaugural address that would make his views about the mounting crisis perfectly clear to all. What Adams had criticized as Lincoln's "masterly inactivity" was actually, Holzer writes, the "confident silence" of a master of maneuver.

Holzer rescues Lincoln from some familiar and powerful misconceptions, above all the claim that, as of 1861, he cared completely about saving the Union and not at all about slavery. Although cautious not to say so publicly lest he worsen the situation, Lincoln vigorously opposed all congressional efforts to thwart secession by reaching some sort of deal that would allow slavery to expand into the western territories. "Let there be no compromise on the question of extending slavery," he instructed his fellow Illinois Republican, Senator Lyman Trumbull. "If there be, all our labor is lost, and, ere long, must be done again." Given that allowing slavery's extension was the nub of the issue as far as the Southern secessionists were concerned, and given that Lincoln himself had long described slavery's restriction as the first step toward abolishing the institution entirely, this was, as Holzer recognizes, an unprecedented "show of power and influence" by a president-elect. Secession was evil, Lincoln believed—but he was not prepared to concede his party's core antislavery conviction, or turn it into a bargaining chip, in order to salvage the Union.

Two prominent recent biographies of Lincoln, like Holzer's book, also offer serious accounts of Lincoln's political career. Michael Burlingame, who has written or edited a dozen books on Lincoln, gained considerable notice in the world of Lincoln scholarship with a study, heavily indebted to Jungian psychology, that purported to describe and to analyze Lincoln's inner life. It was not the first time that a biographer or a historian has put Lincoln on the couch, if only to puzzle through Lincoln's famous chronic bouts of severe depression and to speculate about what some have seen as his burdensome marriage to an unstable woman. But Burlingame is deeply immersed in the sources on Lincoln, primary and secondary, so his judgments carry far more authority than the usual jerry-built psycho-histories.

Burlingame's labors have culminated in a massive two-volume life study so copiously documented that he and his publisher decided to make the full footnotes available only on the Internet (where they can be updated as any new documentation or relevant secondary literature becomes available). Burlingame reliably and astutely covers Lincoln's political career, and he grasps the subtleties of Lincoln's political machinations; for these contributions alone, his labors deserve praise. Still, reactions to this vast book will depend on how useful one thinks Jungian archetypes are in evaluating long-departed political leaders, and they will also depend on one's view of the arc of Lincoln's political life.

Burlingame's book fully accords with what might be called the standard "two Lincolns" approach—the line of argument that posits not simply that Lincoln's antislavery political convictions hardened over time, but also that Lincoln experienced a sharp and complete transformation in the deepest recesses of his soul. Burlingame naturally presents the shift in psychological terms, as a painful but productive midlife crisis, in which Lincoln laid aside evanescent ambitions and constraining loyalties, concentrated on the weightier aspects of life, curbed his ego, and became a fully individuated man. It is certainly plausible that Lincoln endured such a psychological trial. But in Burlingame's account, a common rite of passage approximates the grandiose mythological sequence in which the hero must pass through some sort of clarifying ordeal before he can be reborn as truly heroic.

So heroic, in fact, is Burlingame's Lincoln that he becomes quasi-sacred—and maybe not so quasi. "Lincoln's personality was the North's secret weapon in the Civil War," Burlingame remarks. His attainment of "a level of consciousness unrivaled in the history of American public life" made possible the Union's victory. Indeed, Lincoln was not simply a startling exception among petty politicians, with their clamorous egos. He also rose above the limitations of mere humankind. "Lincoln achieved a kind of balance and wholeness," Burlingame writes, "that led one psychologist to remark that he had 'more psychological honesty' than anyone since Christ." Burlingame finds the comparison apt, if one regards the Christian messiah "as a psychological paradigm."

There is no way to prove or disprove such an assertion: it is, about Lincoln as about Jesus, a matter of faith. Burlingame's final evaluation takes us back beyond the Lincoln Memorial, beyond the populist hero-worship of Carl Sandburg, to a level of unreality and hagiography not seen since the traumatized aftermath of Lincoln's Good Friday murder, when an outpouring from grieving ministers, editorialists, politicians, and ordinary citizens affirmed that, as the president's young personal secretary, John Hay, remarked in 1866, "Lincoln, with all his foibles, is the greatest character since Christ."

Ronald C. White, Jr.'s biography of Lincoln is another story of an evolving glorious hero who was plagued by doubt, including intense self-doubt. But White is chiefly interested in examining Lincoln's words and rhetoric, about which he is highly informative. If Burlingame's biography explores Lincoln's inner emotional life, White's biography studies his inner intellectual life, as grounded in Lincoln's reading of Shakespeare, the Bible, Blackstone's *Commentaries*, and poets such as Burns and Byron. An endless self-improver—at one point, he took on the task of teaching himself Euclidean geometry, the better to sharpen his own logic—Lincoln also got into the habit of composing personal memos of varying lengths, on which he would later draw in his public pronouncements. The notes form, according to White, a kind of running journal, which offers essential clues about not simply what Lincoln thought but also how he thought.

White's historical approach to Lincoln's reading, writing, and speaking enhances the record of the man and his career. Known by his associates more for intellectual thoroughness than for quickness or brilliance, Lincoln would spend weeks, months, even years taking the measure of a particular issue, jotting down his musings, refining his opinions, and finally honing his prose and its rhetorical structure. The famous "House Divided" speech of 1858 is a case in point. Most Lincoln scholars, following the memoirs of Lincoln's law partner, William Herndon, have believed that he composed the speech during the days before he delivered it. But White points to a lengthy memo written seven months earlier, in which Lincoln elaborated his belief (as he wrote in the memo) that "the government cannot endure permanently half slave and half free." Understood this way, Lincoln's prose remains arresting, especially after 1854, and most especially in contrast to the prolix billows that passed for fine oratory at the time. White's portrayal of Lincoln's deliberate approach to his reading and his writing usefully reinforces what historians and biographers have written about his deliberate nature in other realms of life, including politics.

White also sheds light on one of the perennial puzzles in Lincoln scholarship: the increasingly religious tone of Lincoln's speeches after 1862, culminating in his second inaugural address. Although not the first scholar to examine the connection, White shows how Lincoln's reflections on "divine attributes" outside human control or comprehension may have reflected the preaching of the Reverend Phineas Densmore Gurley of the New York Avenue Presbyterian Church, where Lincoln sometimes attended services during his presidency. A student of the redoubtable Charles Hodge at the Princeton Theological Seminary, Gurley imparted a faith that joined, somewhat ambiguously, the spiritual fatalism of his own Old School Presbyterians and the free-will "effort" Calvinism of the evangelical New School. Gurley bundled the two in a mysterious description of man as a rational, accountable moral agent who was nevertheless governed by the traditional American Calvinists' unknowable, omnipotent Providence. "Man proposes; God disposes," Gurley explained; and that paradox of human agency and divine sovereignty was, he insisted, the best way to begin to understand what he called "the probable fruits and conse-quences" of the continuing civil war.

Lincoln, an open skeptic in his youth who never actually joined a church, did not have to have become a believing Christian in order to kindle to these ideas. (In the second inaugural address, he seemed at pains not to identify himself as one of "the believers in a living God"; and the claims made by some historians that he had developed a personal Christian faith are based more on fancy than on evidence.) But Lincoln and his wife certainly did begin showing up for services more often after he became president, especially after the death of their young son, Willie, in 1862. Gurley's sermons offered lessons on human limitation and humility in the face of an inscrutable universe, with a quiet faith that the Union would finally prevail.

In sum, White shows that Lincoln was not, as some writers have portrayed him, America's redeemer, the inventor of a national civil religion that he built out of his torments and the nation's, and that became symbolized by his lofty words and, finally, by his murder. He was, rather, a Victorian doubter (and self-doubter) who found some comfort—and perhaps ways to question and at least partially to com-prehend the incomprehensible—in the preaching of a Presbyterian minister. He then borrowed some clerical language to express what he had found, as well as his continued uncertainties, from his beloved King James Bible, the book most widely read and studied by his countrymen.

★   ★   ★

THE MUCH GRANDER CLAIMS about Lincoln's prose—the work of Barzun's literary genius—rest on a very small body of writing. The historian Don E. Fehrenbacher assembled two lengthy volumes of Lincoln's speeches and writings for the Library of America in 1986, but the bulk of them consists of letters and minor speeches that are chiefly of historical and biographical interest, not examples of fine fin-ished prose. Several of Lincoln's speeches in Illinois during the 1850s (including some of his remarks during his debates with Stephen A. Douglas in 1858) qualify as literature, as does the Cooper Institute address that effectively kicked off his campaign for the Republican nomination in 1860. Thereafter, there are the powerful first and second inaugurals, the Gettysburg Address, and some passages in the first and second annual messages to Congress. In his letters, public and private, as well as in his conversation, Lincoln displayed a talent for sly metaphor and figurative language, reflecting his love of Aesop's *Fables* as well as his Westerner's wit. But that's about it. Apart from Jefferson, no American president has matched Lincoln's mastery of prose—but no other American author has enjoyed such a stellar reputation based on such a slender artistic output.

Fred Kaplan's study of Lincoln as a writer is a case of how literary analysis of this body of work can easily become strained and misdirected. On the one hand, Kaplan's book is sufficiently attuned to its subject's flops as well as his triumphs that it discusses Lincoln's marathon "mulatto" speech in 1852. Kaplan aptly describes the political background and practical purposes of Lincoln's remarks. But he is chiefly interested in the speech's literary artifice, its blend of burlesque and seriousness, its witty literary allusions to Oliver Goldsmith and Cervantes—and especially its concluding riff on Frederick Marryat and the sea chantey about the "bright Mullater" called Sally Brown.

In a brief and somewhat opaque analysis, Kaplan identifies Marryat's travelogue, *A Diary in America*, as Lincoln's exact source for "Sally Brown." Fixing on the political uses of "the language of race," Kaplan speculates about Lincoln's literary entitlements in quoting the song. He then shows how Lincoln bent the song's true meaning, which had to do with eros, not race, and he concludes that, at least in 1852, Lincoln shared in the dominant racialist discourse of his time. So the actual subject of Franklin Pierce and the speech's actual politics have receded into a thicket of words and Lincoln's misappropriated metaphors and the discursive practices of the 1850s. It is a small example of the much larger dangers of approaching Lincoln primarily as a writer.

More than any other president save Jefferson and John Quincy

Adams, Lincoln certainly loved, quoted, and alluded to great literature. As Kaplan argues, like Ronald White and many others before them, the graceful and condensed prose of Lincoln's finest efforts, especially after 1854, reflected his immersion in Shakespeare and the Bible, as well as his training in the law. There is justice in Kaplan's description of the second inaugural address as closer to a dramatic soliloquy than to the usual oratory at a presidential swearing-in. Weary, tormented, and uncertain, Lincoln was talking to himself as much as he was to the nation. Yet Kaplan goes much too far in making Lincoln a literary man, in connecting his prose to British literature, and in making Lincoln's use of words the key to his greatness.

Kaplan's indifference to the political context, and to Lincoln's immersion in the work of political writers as well as that of novelists, poets, and playwrights, can lead him badly astray. Consider an example. Analyzing Lincoln's powerful closing to his "House Divided" speech of 1858, Kaplan pauses over its description of a united Republican Party drawn from "strange, discordant, and even hostile elements," in contrast to the divided Democrats, who were "wavering, dissevered and belligerent." Here is a passage, Kaplan rhapsodizes, that "emulated the distinctive intensity of Shakespearean language," and represents "the best of literary English from Shakespearean oration to Tennyson's 'Ulysses.'" In particular, he claims, the speech's "distinctively original use of 'discordant' and 'dissevered' make this mission statement the most distinctively powerful by any American president." The trouble is, these words and lines came, in some cases directly, from Daniel Webster's famous second reply to Robert Hayne, delivered in 1830, one of Lincoln's favorite congressional speeches.* Lincoln's meaning was different, but his "original" prose was not Shakespearean, it was Websterian—not John, nor even Noah, but Daniel.

Lincoln was a politician, and he regularly looked for inspiration,

---

* From Webster's speech: "When my eyes shall be turned to behold for the last time the sun in heaven, may I not see him shining on the broken and dishonored fragments of a once glorious Union; on States dissevered, discordant, belligerent."

including literary inspiration, to his political predecessors. When composing his first inaugural address amid the mounting secession crisis, he asked to be brought copies of three works: public pronouncements by Andrew Jackson, Henry Clay, and Daniel Webster. The heart of Lincoln's address—which was to deny any historical, political, or philosophical justification for secession—was a gloss on Jackson's proclamation denouncing the South Carolina nullification movement at the end of 1832. When Lincoln spoke, in the first inaugural address, of American democracy and asked if there was "any better or equal hope in the world," or when he again spoke of American government, in his annual message in 1862, as "the last best hope of earth," his words owed nothing to Shakespeare and everything to Jefferson, whose first inaugural address referred to "this Government, the world's best hope."

Kaplan's vaunting of the literary reflects a deeper problem, which is to present Lincoln's words and rhetoric as his chief asset—even, at times, his only asset. Kaplan correctly observes that "for Lincoln, words mattered immensely." He has a point when he argues that Lincoln's "lifelong development as a writer" gave him "the capacity to express himself and the national concerns more effectively than any president ever had, with the exception of Thomas Jefferson"— although how strong that point actually is depends on what one means by "effectively." But to say that Lincoln "became what his language made him" is an English department conceit. Lincoln may have relied on his speaking and writing abilities more than some or even most, but like any self-made man—including stump-speaking politicians— he became who he became because of much more than his language.

To say, as Kaplan does, that, as president-elect, "the only weapon [Lincoln] had at his command was language" ignores the many weapons that Lincoln not only commanded but actually wielded before his inauguration, including his political clout and his ability to shut down efforts at compromise in Washington that conceded too much. Later, as if concerned that his readers might be getting the wrong impression, Kaplan draws back a little, and observes that "words could not prevent the war, and by themselves words could of course not fight the war." That such a ridiculous sentence even appears in Kaplan's book indicates how much it overvalues rhetoric.

Indeed, it was just as well for Lincoln, and the nation, that the Union's fate did not rest on the power of Lincoln's prose. If by "effective" one means effectual or consequential, instead of merely impressive or eloquent, then Lincoln's words had a mixed record indeed. His powerful speeches from 1854 through 1860, above all the Cooper Institute address and the "House Divided" speech, as well as the newspaper accounts of his debates with Stephen A. Douglas in 1858, were certainly crucial in making Lincoln a national figure and gaining him his party's presidential nomination. But the first inaugural address, even with its moving appeals to "the mystic chords of memory" and "the better angels of our nature," could not forestall the crisis at Fort Sumter—or prevent Virginia and three other Southern states from seceding in April and May 1861—thereby, as Kaplan admits, failing "in its primary purpose." The Gettysburg Address powerfully summarized what the Union cause had become in the aftermath of the Emancipation Proclamation; it won praise from various listeners and readers, including the day's main orator, Edward Everett; and it certainly accomplished its primary purpose, which was to dedicate a military cemetery—but it did not alleviate Northern weariness with the war, or prevent Lincoln's political standing from plummeting seven months later owing to the military stalemate and high casualties. (For several months thereafter, until Sherman's smashing victory in Atlanta in September 1864, it remained doubtful that Lincoln would win reelection.)

The second inaugural address—one of the shortest presidential inauguration speeches ever, composed with victory close at hand—superbly justified the Union effort and described the sin of slavery as the war's cause; and it did so with resounding Shakespearean as well as biblical overtones. Some at the time hailed it as the masterpiece that it was. Lincoln's murder six weeks later makes it impossible to know how the speech might have affected future events. Still, with Lincoln dead, the most frequent references to this speech over the decades to come, and even into our own time, skipped over the passages about "the bond-man's two hundred and fifty years of unrequited toil" and about "blood drawn with the lash," and moved directly to "with malice toward none; with charity for all"—which unreconstructed Southern whites turned into a plea for leniency and eventually used as a conservative pitch to obstruct racial equality. Strangely, the greatest effect of the second inaugural address, at least through the 1950s, may have been in helping to fabricate the pro-Southern Lincoln later inflated and favored by the novelist romanticizer of the Ku Klux Klan, Thomas Dixon, and put on the screen by D. W. Griffith.

By contrast, President Lincoln's most effective document was one of his least literary. Historians have gone back and forth over the years on the significance of the Emancipation Proclamation. Most are now inclined to agree with John Hope Franklin that, even with its limitations, the proclamation set in motion the train of events that led to the abolition of slavery under the Thirteenth Amendment: "The first step," Frederick Douglass called it, "on the part of the nation in its departure from the thralldom of the ages." Kaplan correctly describes the proclamation as "perhaps the single most consequential document of Lincoln's presidency," but neither he nor anybody else can call it a literary masterpiece or anything close—something that Kaplan tries to explain away as a paradox. As Richard Hofstadter once observed, the proclamation has "all the moral grandeur of a bill of lading." And yet words can be more than just words, even if they are dry legalisms—especially when they are backed up by the full force of the federal government, including the army and navy.

The point is not that presidential oratory makes no historical difference, especially in swaying or consolidating public opinion. Think of Andrew Jackson's message vetoing the recharter of the Second Bank of the United States in 1832 (which ensured his reelection), or his nullification proclamation (though that, too, was backed up with the threat of force). And think of Franklin Roosevelt's first inaugural address or his fireside chats. All were powerfully convincing in their own ways, although none of them approached the splendor of Lincoln's great addresses. Presidential rhetoric certainly can persuade, placate, or inspire people to action, whether the presidents actually write their own words (as Lincoln did) or rely on speechwriters and cabinet members. But just as presidential language need not be eloquent in any classic literary sense to get things done, so eloquence is no guarantee that the words will be effective, or even right.

★   ★   ★

FOR MANY YEARS, the literary scholar Henry Louis Gates, Jr., has been vigorously expanding and institutionalizing the study of African American literature and history, bringing to light forgotten but important writings by black authors, and serving as a link between the academy and an American mass audience. For the book *Lincoln on Race & Slavery*, Gates and his coeditor, Donald Yacovone, chose seventy writings by Lincoln and reprinted either key passages or the entire document, along with commentary and an extensive introduction by Gates. Originally published in connection with a PBS documentary, the book dwells on what Gates contends was Lincoln's supposedly imperfect stance on slavery and his even more imperfect stance on race.

In his introductory essay, Gates reports that he is especially struck by how Lincoln developed quite distinct lines of thinking about the two subjects—as well as about a third subject, colonization: the idea that blacks, once emancipated, ought to resettle voluntarily in Africa or in some other tropical destination far from the United States. Much of his discussion of these matters ably summarizes what historians have been saying over the last forty years.

The basic historical connections between slavery and racism before the Civil War are straightforward. Essentially, white Americans divided into four groups. Virtually all proslavery Americans believed absolutely in white supremacy, and thought that inferior blacks merited bondage. All Americans who believed in racial equality were adamantly antislavery. Most antislavery American whites believed, to one degree or another, that blacks were inferior. A fourth group, identified with Stephen A. Douglas and the Northern Democratic Party, expressed moral indifference to slavery and were firm white supremacists.

The first of these groups, the proslavery forces, dominated the South. The second group, the immediatist abolitionist radicals, represented a small minority in the North, and believed that slavery should be abolished immediately throughout the entire country. The third, the non-immediate antislavery forces, represented, by 1860, a majority of the North, and included a wide spectrum of views about race.

The most conservative of this third group were vicious racists who wanted to halt slavery's expansion in order to keep the western territories lily white. At the liberal end were those, like Lincoln, who believed that blacks, although inferior to whites, were human beings endowed with rights and should be emancipated. Antislavery Northerners, whatever their view of blacks, wanted to end slavery, but, unlike the immediatist abolitionists, they believed they could do it under the U.S. Constitution, despite the Constitution's protections for slavery where it already existed. As an important first step toward eliminating slavery nationwide, they fought for a congressional prohibition on the expansion of slavery into the territories, which they believed (and the proslavery forces denied) the Constitution allowed. Lincoln, after 1854, became a preeminent political leader of this broad antislavery group, with views on race that were decidedly at the more liberal end.

The colonization idea attracted some slaveholders in the upper South and, for a time, a few black activists in the North, as well as some non-abolitionist but antislavery white Northerners. Again, there was a spectrum of opinion about race among the pro-colonizationists. Racist conservatives wanted to encourage colonization simply to rid

the country of hateful subhuman blacks. Other supporters of colonization believed that, given the fierceness of white racial prejudice and
the long chain of abuses under slavery, it would be better for whites
and freedmen alike if they went their separate ways. (Some of these
supporters also saw colonization as a means to prevent interracial sex
and marriage, from which most white Americans publicly recoiled.)

Lincoln, following his first great political hero, the Kentucky Whig
slaveholder Henry Clay, held to the latter view, which as late as 1862
he said was the best possible solution to the nation's racial torment.
Anticolonizationists, meanwhile, included slaveholders and their
allies, who wanted to keep black bondmen enslaved and in America,
as well as white abolitionists who, along with the African Americans,
slave and free, wanted to bring racial equality to America.

Gates dispenses his lessons on these matters well. For the most
part, he places Lincoln correctly in these different groups and along
these different measures, even though it requires conceding that Lincoln fell far short of our own conceptions of justice and humanity. It
is refreshing to read an evaluation of Lincoln that refuses, as Gates
writes, to "romanticize him as the first American president completely
to transcend race and racism." Yet Gates presents also his own unper-
suasive version of the fanciful "two Lincolns" script, in line with those
historians who say that radicals and outsiders had to push Lincoln the
politician into greatness.

According to Gates, Lincoln's most "radical"—and therefore his
most admirable—achievement was to overcome Thomas Jefferson's
limitations and proclaim that blacks as well as whites should be
included in the Declaration of Independence's "self-evident" truth that
all men are created equal. Whatever he may have learned from Sally
Hemings, Gates remarks, Jefferson (although in principle antislavery)
believed that blacks were subhuman, and he did not include them
within his definition of men in 1776. Lincoln, by contrast, "most certainly and most impressively did," and although this "rather radical"
belief never led Lincoln to embrace full social and political equality

between blacks and whites, it did propel him to the point where, at the end of his life, he declared his limited support for black suffrage—the first American president to do so.

A correction is immediately required regarding Thomas Jefferson. In 1785, Jefferson did advance in his *Notes on the State of Virginia*—as "a suspicion only," he added—"that the blacks . . . are inferior to the whites in the endowments of body and mind," and he explained why, in terms that today are repulsive. Later in the *Notes*, though, Jefferson observed that slavery removed "in the minds of the people that [their] liberties are of the gift of God"—that slavery is a human usurpation of men's God-given rights to liberty. Years later, he told Abbé Henri Grégoire that he hoped that one day blacks would be placed "on an equal footing with the other colors of the human family." In short, it is false to claim that Jefferson the racist failed to recognize blacks' humanity. His thinking (though not his political action) ran a bit closer to the "rather radical" Lincoln than Gates allows.

On other points, Gates takes Lincoln to task. He is inclined to endorse Frederick Douglass's assertions that Lincoln hated slavery chiefly as an economic system that degraded all labor and hurt poor whites, and that it was for the good of whites, not blacks, that he fought slavery as he did. Now, it is without question that what the historian Eric Foner has called the "free labor" argument against slavery did form a part of antislavery's principled core (just as it deeply informed the more radical abolitionists' arguments), and Lincoln certainly shared this view. But it is unfair to slight Lincoln's repeated affirmations that he also considered human bondage a moral abomination, and that blacks, as humans, had the same basic rights as whites to life, liberty, and the pursuit of happiness. It is especially unfair to describe these broad rights to individual selfhood strictly as economic rights.

Much more besides race, meanwhile, affected Lincoln's political approach to slavery, above all the U.S. Constitution. For Lincoln, to destroy slavery while destroying the Constitution would have been no victory at all, as it would demonstrate to the world that the American Revolution and republican government were follies or frauds—impervious to dramatic reform. Yet in accord with most antislavery men, Lincoln held that, like it or not, the Constitution tolerated and even protected slavery in the states where it already existed. How, then, could Americans abolish slavery under the terms of their own constitution?

As of 1860, there was absolutely no possibility that two-thirds of Congress would pass, and that the states would ratify, a constitutional amendment banning slavery, which would have been the only peaceable and constitutional way for the federal government to outlaw bondage everywhere. Nor was there any possibility that the cotton states of the Deep South, or even the less slave-dependent states of the upper South, would abolish slavery on their own anytime soon. On that account, a minority of radical abolitionists, most conspicuously William Lloyd Garrison, concluded that the Constitution was irredeemably proslavery and hence morally bankrupt. But most of the antislavery forces, Lincoln among them, concluded that they would commence eroding slavery by attacking it where they believed the Constitution gave the federal government the power to do so, chiefly by barring slavery from the territories.

These antislavery advocates believed that, as an economic system, plantation slavery would have to expand or it would die. Halting its expansion thus amounted to a sentence of gradual death. (On this point, the slaveholders agreed.) Politically, the addition of new free states out of the vast territories added from the Mexican War, as well as the remainder of the Louisiana Purchase lands, would break the hammerlock that the South had long enjoyed in Washington over the slavery issue. This was what Lincoln meant when he spoke of putting slavery in the course of extinction—by containing it, as opposed to permitting its expansion which, he said, would put the nation "on the high-road to a slave empire."

Some historians claim that Lincoln conceded that the choking off of slavery that he had in mind would take a hundred years to complete—a poor reflection on Lincoln's antislavery zeal. Gates accepts the claim, and writes, cuttingly, that "at that rate, some black people born in my birth year, 1950, would have been born slaves." But Lincoln's actual remarks, delivered during his debates with Stephen A. Douglas in 1858, were nothing close to definitive, suggested a worst-case scenario, and were more like throwaway lines than position statements. They hardly endorsed the concept of a gradual emancipation protracted over the century to come.

But the key point is that until the Civil War, and even through the war's opening months, most Americans thought of emancipation in terms of one form or another of gradual emancipation. That was how slavery had ended in parts of the Caribbean and Latin America, as well as in most of the northern United States. And it was, by any definition, a revolutionary proposal, destroying and outlawing an entire class of property. In the North, it had proceeded without the owners' consent—offering them extended remuneration but, in itself, no compensation for the loss of their property.

Any proposal for gradual emancipation, in whatever form, in the United States was regarded as a fundamental attack on slavery's legitimacy, and had been since the first gradual emancipation measures were fought over and enacted in the Northern states in the 1780s. The slaveholders knew as much. Likewise, to them, the principle of nonextension was a radical threat to slavery's survival. Thus, Lincoln's election as president in 1860, to go along with a Republican plurality in the House, was sufficient to convince the Deep South states that they ought to secede from the Union.

Secession, which Lincoln called "the essence of anarchy," amounted to a strike against the Constitution—anathema to him and other antislavery non-immediatists. And so Lincoln, during his first two years as president, repeatedly told his abolitionist critics that he was fighting to save the Union and not to "put down slavery" or "upset slavery"—that is, to abolish slavery in the rebel states where it already existed. But this did not mean that Lincoln (as Frederick Douglass and other abolitionists suspected) had suddenly abandoned his belief that the work on dismantling slavery ought to begin. It meant that he wanted to restore the Union as it existed in 1861—with a democratically elected federal government that was determined to commence the process of emancipation by, among other steps, banning slavery's expansion. When, by the spring of 1862, it became clear to Lincoln that such a restoration was no longer viable, he began looking into emancipation using his powers as commander-in-chief.

So it is impossible to understand the seriousness of Lincoln's antislavery politics before 1862 without paying close attention to his ideas, and to the ideas of others, about the Constitution. And if it is mistaken to dismiss concerns about the Constitution's integrity as underhanded evasions, it is obtuse to complain (as Gates and many other current writers do, *pace* Henry Holzer) that Lincoln's true concern was the Union and the Constitution and not slavery. Between 1854 and 1860, virtually every speech Lincoln delivered, and every political letter that he wrote, made it clear that his basic goal was to commence slavery's destruction by halting its expansion. When he spoke in 1858 about a house divided against itself not being able to stand, he was not talking about the Union collapsing on its own accord, any more than he was talking about divisions over states' rights, or internal improvements, or the tariff. He was talking about slavery, just as the Republican platform on which he ran in 1860 was when it denied that the Constitution protected "an unqualified property in persons."

Lincoln's first inaugural address in 1861 defined the division between North and South as an essentially moral struggle in which "one section of our country believes slavery is *right* . . . while the other believes it is *wrong*." Was there any doubt that Dixie's secession, which triggered the war, did not chiefly concern slavery and Southern fears for slavery's future under Lincoln and the Republicans? One had only to read the official address that justified South Carolina's secession, which referred directly to "an increasing hostility on the part of the non-slaveholding states to the institution of slavery."

Lincoln did not, to be sure, go on, in his first inaugural address, to describe why he thought human bondage was cruel and intolerable, as he would in brief but powerful detail under the vastly different political circumstances of his second inauguration after four years of war. For sound political and constitutional reasons, Lincoln kept the suppression of the secessionist rebellion front and center throughout the fighting, and he framed the struggle in those terms at least through 1862. But before the first shot was fired, Lincoln certainly recognized that slavery was the origin of the conflict.

In effect, Gates endorses the assumption, widespread among current historians, that the radical abolitionist view of slavery and its immediate and total eradication is the only one worthy of respect, let alone serious consideration. This contention denigrates not just Lincoln but the core of the Republican Party's platform of 1860, that the containment of slavery would vindicate the proposition that all men are created equal. To Lincoln's critics, leading the Republican effort to end slavery without trashing the Constitution merely shows, as Gates writes—more than a little contemptuously—that Lincoln "could live with slavery if he had to." This may express a noble morality, but it is bad history: it fundamentally distorts and stigmatizes what Lincoln and the antislavery political movement actually believed, and how Lincoln and that movement—which eventually sparked secession and freed the slaves—actually developed.

Ironically, this neglect of the political and constitutional context can lead even a literary scholar like Gates to misunderstand how the political leader Lincoln used words. Lincoln's secretaries John G. Nicolay and John Hay once observed that to understand "as a whole" any utterance of Lincoln's, the surrounding "conditions . . . must continually be kept in mind." Gates, like so many of the historians whose work informs his own, does not heed the warning.

Consider a conspicuous example, one that has practically become a set piece in recent historical writing on Lincoln. In the late summer of 1862, amid a pressure campaign by the abolitionist radicals, the eccentric but influential left-wing Republican editor Horace Greeley criticized Lincoln for not pursuing emancipation more aggressively. Lincoln was happy to reply that he was determined to save the Union whether it would mean freeing all the slaves or freeing none of the slaves.

A close reader would have noticed that this marked the first time that Lincoln even hinted that he was contemplating freeing all the slaves. Instead, attention naturally fell on Lincoln's stubborn insistence about the primacy of the Union. Standing up, with these measured remarks, to the importuning left wing of the Republican Party was a surefire way for Lincoln to shore up his support among moderate and conservative Northerners—parsing his words carefully in order to sound cautious and responsible without in any way contradicting the constitutionalist antislavery views that he had proclaimed when running for president.

It was all the better—indeed, it was imperative—to do so because, unbeknownst to Greeley and his allies, Lincoln had begun drafting the Emancipation Proclamation more than a month earlier. He would sign and release to the public the preliminary version of the document only a few weeks later, when he thought the time was ripe—undercutting the radicals completely, while inevitably stirring up trouble among Northern moderates and conservatives.

Lincoln's reply to Greeley was not, in short, a white moderate's declaration of his cautious and even callous determination to ignore the slavery issue in order to advance the Union cause. It was an example of Lincoln shrewdly and successfully manipulating Greeley to suit his immediate political end, which was to calm conservative fears prior to issuing the Emancipation Proclamation. Gates's headnote covering Lincoln's reply to Greeley does appreciate the president's deeper political strategy better than some historians do, but also sneers at it as "a transparent attempt to disarm conservative political rivals" which heightened black leaders' distrust of Lincoln. Once again, the realities of politics—and the political realities that Lincoln faced—are trumped by an abstract moralism.

★ ★ ★

MORE THAN FIFTY YEARS AGO, the easily caricatured but politically gifted Senator Everett Dirksen, Republican of Illinois (then still a member of the House) observed that the first task of any politician is "to get right with . . . Lincoln." Today it sometimes appears that the first task of any American historian of the nineteenth century is to get right with Frederick Douglass. As an escaped slave turned abolitionist agitator, a scintillating orator, a fearless editor, a race man, an integrationist, a feminist (at least at Seneca Falls in 1848), and more, the admirable Douglass embodied, better than any American of his time, everything that today seems worthy of supreme honor. In scholarly writings, Douglass invariably gets cited positively. His words cast an aura of nobility that can shut down any dispute. Some historians still sanctify Abraham Lincoln, but for many, Frederick Douglass is now the era's true hero.

Another book by another literary historian, John Stauffer's *Giants*, is all about Lincoln and Douglass, and in many ways it exemplifies some prevailing scholarly trends. Stauffer's stated objective is to juxtapose the lives of two "giants," two great men who "stood at the forefront of a major shift in cultural history"—the shift that extended freedom and equality to blacks as well as whites. Yet even though he intends the book as in part a monument to Lincoln, he winds up maligning as well as misunderstanding Lincoln's antislavery politics. Somehow Lincoln keeps eluding his admirers.

In much of his writing on the Civil War era, Stauffer fixes on the emotional content of politics, with particular interest in friendships between black men and white men. His first book, *The Black Hearts of Men*, which served as a springboard for *Giants*, examined the connections and the activities of four uncompromising abolitionists, including Frederick Douglass and John Brown, who were brought together in the tiny and short-lived Radical Abolition Party in 1855. Stauffer was fascinated by their empathetic radicalism about race, which led one of the four, Gerrit Smith, who was also one of the richest men in the country, to declare that he would "make myself a colored man."

A century before Norman Mailer's "white negro," there arose at the radical fringes of the antislavery movement, as Stauffer discovered, a highly racialized sense of righteousness in the name of eliminating racial hierarchy. (Stauffer summarized his quartet's central belief, again in keeping with current humanistic usage, as the constructed "performative" self of an outsider: "The true spiritual heart was a black heart that shared a humanity with all people and lacked the airs of superiority of a white heart.") One member of Stauffer's group, the physician and literary critic James McCune Smith, who was the most highly educated black man in the country, called their sacred pursuits a form of "Bible Politics," which Stauffer describes as the belief that "the government of God and earthly states should be one and the same." The Radical Abolitionists, in short, undertook a millennial flight from politics. This is completely recognizable to anyone familiar with the radical fringes of the late 1960s, with their renunciation of "white skin privilege." Stauffer prefers to see it as a kind of failed transcendence.

Not surprisingly, the effort ended badly—in violence and in insanity. Smith, the party's mainstay, temporarily lost his mind after authorities identified him as one of the chief conspirators supporting his fellow "colored man" John Brown, after Brown's suicidal raid on Harpers Ferry in 1859. Once he had partially recovered, Smith decided that blacks truly were inferior to whites, and he endorsed colonization. One might easily conclude that Smith was drawn to extreme doctrines, noble and ignoble. Stauffer prefers psychology, speculating that Smith's racist turn was his way "to exorcise his feelings of guilt" over the deaths of innocents at Harpers Ferry—and that thereby, tragically, Smith "lost his black heart."

Stauffer's sympathy for performative cross-racial self-fashioning as a strategy to destroy slavery and racial injustice is in tune with what is known as "whiteness studies" among cultural historians and critics. This approach construes race as the primary identity of consequence in American politics, and it construes "whiteness" as something tantamount to original sin. It also conflates politics with culture and psychology, which is yet another way to sound deeply political while evading politics and political history. More traditional, though, are Stauffer's sympathies for the purity and the boldness of the radicals, in contrast to the moral flaccidity and the corruption of the world around them, including mainstream party politics. Those sympathies reappear in *Giants* and dominate its interpretations of Douglass and Lincoln.

The idea of pairing the two men has been in the air over the last several years. With great subtlety, James Oakes's exceptional *The Radical and the Republican*, which appeared in 2007, traces how two very different men, following fundamentally different sets of political imperatives, eventually converged. Oakes understands perfectly well that, however Lincoln viewed blacks, he had long hated slavery—with as much conviction, Oakes claims, as the radical ex-slave Douglass. Their differences had to do with their respective political positions. Douglass, the radical reformer, had no formal power, and could agitate as he pleased to proclaim his principles and persuade others. Lincoln had enormous power and enjoyed its possession, and accepted the mottled responsibilities of the presidency. Those duties, in his understanding, necessitated pragmatic compromise and negotiation in step with public opinion, as well as adherence to his oath to preserve, protect, and defend the Constitution. "It is important to democracy that reformers like Frederick Douglass could say what needed to be said," Oakes wisely observes, "but it is indispensable to democracy that politicians like Abraham Lincoln could do only what the law and the people allowed them to do." And, he might have added, it was indispensable for the nation, and above all the slaves, that Lincoln performed as president as well as he did.

Stauffer approaches Douglass and Lincoln, and defines his task, very differently. The ex-slave and the politician, he asserts, were oddly similar, despite the racial difference. Both were self-made men in the nineteenth-century American mold. Douglass escaped the vicious world of bondage and rose, through self-education and hard work, to become one of the greatest American orators and intellectuals of his time or any other. Lincoln escaped the vicious world of white rural poverty and rose, through self-education and hard work, to become one of the greatest American orators and intellectuals of his time or any other. As young men, they read many of the same books. Both turned to humor to overcome despair.

To be sure, Stauffer claims, Douglass "brilliantly exposed Lincoln's limitations as a champion of freedom." And this is really the book's central argument: that once the sectional crisis began, Douglass, the fearless and uncompromising social revolutionary, by turns denounced and encouraged the antislavery conservative Republican Lincoln—and Lincoln finally saw the light. Stauffer also notes that the two men were able to put aside their political differences and become friends who "genuinely liked and admired each other." Douglass and Lincoln only met on three occasions, the last time fleetingly at a crowded East Room reception at the White House after Lincoln's second inauguration. There is abundant evidence, from 1863 through 1865, that they truly held each other in high mutual esteem; and Lincoln, during their second meeting as well as in the East Room, referred to Douglass as "my friend." This is enough to persuade Stauffer that he has located another rare but singularly important interracial friendship in antebellum America.

But casting that friendship in terms of the parallel lives of two "self-made" men is highly problematic. Millions of Americans shared Douglass's and Lincoln's belief in hard work and education as the keys to self-improvement. Frederick Douglass, by contrast, was one of only a handful of slaves who successfully escaped to freedom to become a self-made man. This distinction vitiates the superficial similarities between his life and Lincoln's—and that of any other white American. Stauffer nevertheless devotes the first part of his book to an examination of what he makes of the parallels. He departs most vigorously from the standard accounts by pushing hard what evidence he can muster in an excursion into Douglass's and Lincoln's sexual lives and proclivities, and especially about what he imagines were their homoerotic tendencies.

Douglass lived through an unsatisfying marriage with another ex-slave, established prolonged extramarital liaisons with at least two white women, and finally found connubial bliss late in life with a much younger woman, a former secretary, who also was white. He evinced no sexual desires at all for other men. But Stauffer, the student of transgressive self-fashioning and all the rest, is on the lookout, and he brings up an incident in 1838 that fleetingly appears promising. Recently escaped from slavery, standing near the Tombs prison in New York City, and disguised in what looked like a sailors' outfit, Douglass was approached by a sailor named Stuart. The two struck up a conversation, in what Stauffer says "seemed almost like a pickup." In the end, though, Stauffer admits, "the pickup stemmed more from sympathy than any desire for sex," and he drops the story.

Lincoln is another matter. Since Carl Sandburg wrote of the "streak of lavender" that he detected in Lincoln, there has been speculation about Lincoln's affection for men, and Stauffer is determined to give it one more whirl. He notes an intellectual debt to C. A. Tripp's *The Intimate World of Abraham Lincoln*, a discredited hodgepodge of supposition and deception which appeared in 2003, though he does not endorse Tripp's sensational claim that Lincoln was "predominantly homosexual." Stauffer favors the more diffuse argument, adapted from Michel Foucault and now generally accepted in the academy, that until the words "homosexuality" and "heterosexuality" were invented (some say in 1868, others in 1886 or 1892), sexual love between men was a repertory of acts and not a trait of personality. In America, so the argument goes, sexuality was much more polymorphous before the Civil War than after. Yet if Stauffer sees the antebellum sexual universe as, in his words, "very blurry indeed," he is adamant about one thing: "Lincoln's soul mate and the love of his life was a man named Joshua Speed."

Stauffer's rehearsal of the old Speed story illustrates the difference between a historian and a professor with an agenda. Joshua Speed was a young storeowner and the son of a wealthy Kentucky planter. Between 1837 and 1841, he roomed with Lincoln above Speed's store in Springfield. As was then the custom, they shared a bed ("a very large double-bed," Speed later recalled), and they became, according to numerous accounts, intimate friends, confessing to each other their hopes, fears, and ambitions, while musing aloud and gossiping about politics and (especially) literature. Stauffer works hard to suggest that what he calls this "romantic friendship" included loving sexual contact. As evidence, he presents a mishmash of strained analogies and literary references (including, inevitably, Ishmael and Queequeg) as somehow telling. He notes that "male–male sex was also common in the military." He dismisses as "rhetorical gymnastics" David Herbert Donald's detailed denial of homoeroticism in Lincoln's and Speed's friendship. And so he concludes that "there is no reason to suppose that [Lincoln] didn't also have carnal relations with Joshua Speed."

The trouble is there is no reason to suppose that they did. Speed's letters to Lincoln during the years in question, Stauffer records, "have sadly been lost"; but Lincoln's letters to Speed betray no signs of any passion or romance, let alone a sexual bond, apart from some pledges of undying friendship. (Lincoln did, as Stauffer notes, close one letter to Speed "Yours forever"—but David Herbert Donald pointed out that Lincoln used the same phrase in letters to his law partner and an Illinois congressman.) As Stauffer does not bring Lincoln's sexuality to bear either on his relations to Douglass or on any other later aspect of his life, including his marriage, it is difficult to see why the Speed story arises at all, especially given how fragmentary the evidence is. It is also difficult to understand why Stauffer would devote so much energy, even in passing, to the imputation of a profound homoeroticism that, by his own admission, cannot be proved, at least with the available documentation.

Stauffer's remarks on Douglass's and Lincoln's sexual lives look like nods to current academic styles. Most of *Giants* instead presents a variation on the familiar populist arguments about Lincoln—whom Stauffer repeatedly derides as a conservative, deeply reluctant about undertaking emancipation—and how circumstances repeatedly forced him into the kind of greatness that Douglass embodied. Stauffer's account, though, is almost completely devoid of politics, except in trying to make Douglass and the radicals look brilliant, and Lincoln either begrudging or benighted. This approach flattens crucial complexities and badly misrepresents Lincoln's politics and his ideas. The confusion is particularly severe when Stauffer considers constitutional issues, beginning with the Supreme Court's proslavery ruling in the *Dred Scott* case in 1857.

According to Stauffer, Lincoln, prior to *Dred Scott*, believed in the absolute supremacy of the Supreme Court as the final arbiter of all constitutional issues—but Chief Justice Taney's ruling in *Dred Scott*, Stauffer claims, changed everything. By opposing the decision, Stauffer writes, Lincoln "rejected the Court as the nation's supreme authority," redoubled his support for the non-extension of slavery, which flew in the face of that decision, and suddenly began to rely "on a natural (or 'higher' law) and follow the path that Frederick Douglass had long ago taken." Lincoln the lawyer now "repudiated the Constitution and legal precedent and defined the Declaration [of Independence] to be the centerpiece of government." Not for the first time, and not for the last, in Stauffer's telling, Lincoln belatedly approached Douglass's principled position.

This is nonsense. Of course Lincoln believed and had long insisted that the federal courts must be obeyed. Yet when, in 1856, he asserted that the Supreme Court was the proper body to decide constitutional issues, and that he would abide by the court's decisions, he did not say that all its decisions were settled law (let alone what he called "well-settled" law), or that abiding by those decisions ruled out seeking their undoing. The *Dred Scott* decision certainly moved Lincoln to clarify his thinking about the legitimacy of Supreme Court decisions, to himself as well as to the public—but, contrary to Stauffer, Lincoln rejected the

Dred Scott ruling not because he thought it violated a "higher law," but because he thought it was erroneous and unconstitutional (as well as unjust), and he called for constitutional and democratic action to overturn it. "We know the court that made it has often over-ruled its own decisions," Lincoln declared, "and we shall do what we can to have it over-rule this."

Lincoln hardly "repudiated" the Constitution. Lincoln repudiated the Taney Court's interpretation of the Constitution as flagrantly unsound. The best way to remedy the situation, he believed, would be to hold fast to the antislavery principles that Chief Justice Taney had wrongly declared unconstitutional, and elect officials (including a president and a Senate majority) who would uphold accurate constitutional interpretation. Once in office, those men would legislate and execute accordingly, and start to change the composition of the Supreme Court, and finally succeed in overturning *Dred Scott*.

This was the democratic political path that Lincoln took (which eventually led him to the presidency), at the very moment when Douglass and the "black hearts" of the erstwhile Radical Abolition Party were pondering violence in the name of a "higher law," including violence directed against the federal government. The difference between them was not small, nor was Lincoln's constitutional reasoning abstruse. The great mass of American citizens understood the difference (even if Southern proslavery extremists tried to equate Lincoln's views with those of the radicals). But Stauffer misunderstands some elementary historical and political distinctions.

Stauffer's readings of other basic constitutional and political facts repeatedly diminish Lincoln by turning him into a craven compromiser and worse. This is precisely the caricature of him that was cultivated by radical Republicans and immediatist abolitionists. Stauffer endorses Douglass's denunciation of Lincoln's first inaugural address as "double-tongued," and he likewise endorses what he calls Douglass's view that, by appealing to the South for reconciliation, Lincoln cruelly "ignored the cries of blacks in chains." Stauffer might have paused to remember that, on March 4, 1861, when Lincoln was inaugurated, the war had not yet begun. Lincoln's bid for reconciliation was a politically crafted way of giving the South a chance to renounce secession and recognize the legitimacy of his own election—and the legitimacy of the duly elected representatives of the antislavery Republican Party. It is understandable that the radical abolitionist Douglass reacted to Lincoln's speech with a harsh polemic. But for a scholar to say that Lincoln callously "sacrificed the humanity of blacks" distorts his political circumstances and intentions.

Lincoln's address did give tepid, provisional backing to a constitutional amendment that had passed Congress and that would have prohibited any future amendment banning slavery in the states where it existed. At first, the incoming president opposed the idea as needless conciliation. But as Lincoln believed, like most Americans, that Congress already lacked the power to ban slavery in the states, he also construed the amendment as an unthreatening effort to make explicit a provision which was, he said, "now implied constitutional law." In any event, he believed, quite soundly, that the amendment did nothing to interfere with his bedrock conviction about Congress's power to halt the spread of slavery, and thereby to commence its elimination. But Stauffer, horrified, misdescribes the proposal flatly as "an unamendable amendment guaranteeing slavery in the states forever," and falsely charges that Lincoln's "intellectually and morally dishonest" stance "negated his belief in the 'ultimate extinction of slavery.'" He then paraphrases, in apparent agreement, Douglass's wild charge that as soon as Lincoln made this concession the "nickname 'Honest Abe' sank into the sewers of Washington."

Stauffer, like Gates, does allow that President Lincoln eventually enlarged his antislavery convictions. Yet also like Gates—and in line with the rest of the "two Lincolns" literature—he sometimes explains that development in terms of some sort of individual epiphany, once again devoid of politics. Concerning Lincoln's eventual decision to issue the Emancipation Proclamation, Stauffer offers the far-fetched assertion that Lincoln "experienced the equivalent of a conversion" that may have started with Willie's death in February 1862. "Perhaps Willie's death fueled Lincoln's sympathies for parents throughout the North who had lost a son. . . . The need to emancipate the slaves in order to save the Union weighed upon Lincoln, a heavy burden." No historian doubts that Lincoln was haunted by death and deeply moved by the war's carnage, or that he underwent what he called "a process of crystallization" in his thinking about religion between 1862 and 1865 (although there is no evidence that he ever became a believing Christian). But the idea that sentimental or religious feelings motivated Lincoln's evolving views about so crucial and hazardous an issue as emancipation is sheer fantasy.

No less so is Stauffer's broader point that the story of the politics that led to the Emancipation Proclamation offers the greatest example of Lincoln finally catching up to and heeding the wisdom of Frederick Douglass and the radicals. In fact, that there is only one slight example of Douglass directly affecting any of Lincoln's decisions about slavery and conducting the war, and even that example is debatable. It occurred in 1864, late in the war, during the second of their three meetings.

★   ★   ★

LINCOLN AND DOUGLASS first met in August 1863, when Douglass came to the White House to register various complaints about the mistreatment of black soldiers. The president quickly impressed the radical by making a fuss over him (which, given the racial implications, meant a great deal to Douglass) and by otherwise handling the situation like a master politician. Instead of expressing anger or affecting condescension over Douglass's attacks on him, Lincoln calmly listened to Douglass's concerns about the administration's tardiness, explained his own position about the need sometimes to go slowly, and forthrightly insisted that he had never vacillated on emancipation or any other important decision. (Lincoln also endorsed, with his own signature, an official pass through Union lines issued to Douglass earlier in the day by Secretary of War Stanton. The pass came with a promise from Stanton, which delighted Douglass, of a formal commission to aid in the raising of black troops in Mississippi.)

Having come to Washington full of grievances, Douglass departed smitten by Lincoln, writing that the "wise, great, and eloquent" president would "go down to posterity, if the nation is saved, as Honest Abraham." Even when the promised Mississippi commission never actually materialized, the disappointed Douglass refused to blame the president. Having met the man, he was now persuaded that his anxieties about what he regarded as Lincoln's equivocations about slavery and freedom had been misplaced. Lincoln had conceded nothing.

A year later Lincoln was in deep political trouble, and he invited Douglass, whose enthusiasm for the president had waned, to confer with him at the White House—their second meeting. Earlier in the year, radical Republicans, seeking a candidate publicly committed to racial equality, tried to deny Lincoln renomination and replace him with John C. Frémont. Douglass, returning to his earlier criticisms of the president, backed Frémont and his radical program for redistributing rebels' lands to freed slaves, which Stauffer, recalling his earlier book, likens to the Radical Abolition Party platform of 1855. It was, Stauffer observes favorably, a firm rebuke of what he derides as Lincoln's "misguided policies."

Lincoln handily fended off the radicals and won renomination in early July. The main threat now came from the Democrats, who, along with some skittish moderate Republicans, were calling for a negotiated peace with the Confederacy. Lincoln released a public letter stating that he could no longer consider restoring the Union unless the slaves were emancipated, which pleased some of the radicals but further riled the opposition. Lincoln next considered issuing a second letter in order to clarify his position and openly recognize that public opinion prevented him from ever fighting the war purely in order to achieve abolition. He began the second meeting with Douglass by asking him if he should release this second letter. Douglass, not surprisingly, said no.

Lincoln laid the letter aside for good, which may have been Douglass's most direct contribution of consequence in the war—although it is also possible that Lincoln had made his decision before he met with Douglass, and was simply trying to make the radical feel important.

Lincoln wanted more out of the meeting. He told Douglass that the slaves were not flocking to Union lines as quickly as he had hoped, and he asked Douglass to undertake a new assignment: devising some means to spread the word of emancipation to the slaves on the plantations. Douglass was stunned that Lincoln would approve of what looked to him like inciting a slave uprising—a move that he deemed similar to John Brown's insurrectionary plot a few years earlier. Douglass eagerly agreed to come up with a proposal, and quickly went to work on drafting specifics.

In fact, apart from its ultimate goal of liberating slaves, Lincoln's proposal was exactly the opposite of John Brown's crusade. Brown, contemptuous of mainstream politics and politicians, aimed to overthrow slavery by first seizing the federal arsenal at Harpers Ferry, which was a mission doomed from the start. Lincoln, the president of the very government that Brown had attacked, was using his full force as commander-in-chief to impose emancipation on Southern rebels, which was a mission with a reasonable chance of some success. Still, it made no difference to Lincoln that Douglass was deluding himself into thinking that he was reenacting Brown's revolution—just so long as the radical worked with him on emancipation and remained loyal to him in a dismal political season.

General Sherman's victory at Atlanta several weeks later dramatically changed the political as well as the military situation, helping lift Lincoln to reelection while rendering it unnecessary to take special measures to encourage the slaves to flee to Union lines. Once again, an administration offer to enlist Douglass came to nothing. But Douglass was greatly relieved, persuaded now more than ever that Lincoln was not just a personal friend but a true friend to his people. Only weeks before, Douglass had ridiculed the president as an unprincipled politician who had to be forced by circumstances to do the right thing. Now he considered Lincoln's reelection imperative, having seen in him "a deeper moral conviction against slavery than I had ever seen before in anything spoken or written by him." Here is the real conversion story: the conversion of Frederick Douglass into a believer in Abraham Lincoln. It had required no divine intervention, only Lincoln's sincerity and political skill.

Less than seven months later, Douglass and Lincoln met for the last time. Approaching the White House reception following Lincoln's second inauguration, Douglass found his entrance barred by guards who claimed that they had been told to admit no persons of color. But after Lincoln was alerted, Douglass gained admission. "Here comes my friend Douglass," exclaimed Lincoln, who took him by the hand and asked him what he thought of his speech earlier in the day, insisting (or so Douglass proudly recounted) that "there is no man in the country whose opinion I value more than yours." Douglass replied that he thought it had been "a sacred effort," and Lincoln said he was glad to hear it. Douglass then returned to his home in Rochester, New York, deeply honored—just as anyone, he later wrote, "would regard himself honored by such expressions, from such a man." Six weeks later Lincoln was dead. To the grief-stricken Douglass, as to countless others, Lincoln had become something like America's Christ, whose martyrdom, he said, "will be the salvation of our country," by uniting blacks and whites in reconciliation. It was not to be.

Douglass outlived Lincoln by thirty years, which leaves Stauffer with a good deal of ground to cover without his gimmick of parallel lives. Interestingly, though, Stauffer finds a parallel, although he may not have realized that he did so. Many historians have offered an exaggerated "two Lincolns" interpretation of the president, but Stauffer, who presents his own version of the "two Lincolns" story, comes up with what might be called a "two Douglasses" interpretation. The chief difference is that although the historians (and Stauffer) claim that Lincoln changed from bad to good, Stauffer argues that Douglass changed from good to bad.

According to Stauffer, the years of Reconstruction after 1865, and Reconstruction's eventual failure, coincided with Douglass's increasing quietude. "Like most other black and white abolitionists," he remarks, "Douglass saw the end of the war as the endpoint of an era and of his life's work." The intrepid radical became a Republican Party loyalist. (For black Americans, Douglass would say, there was a simple rule in electoral politics: "The Republican Party is the ship, all else is the sea.") But Douglass, in Stauffer's account, also became fixed in the past, once Congress had beaten back the reactionary presidency of Andrew Johnson. Having "declared victory," Stauffer writes, President Ulysses S. Grant and other Republican leaders turned "a blind eye" to the murder and terror by former Confederates that eventually destroyed Reconstruction. "So too did Douglass," Stauffer argues, noting Douglass's increasingly comfortable economic circumstances, his appointment to party patronage positions—and, not least, his failure to recognize "the new outrages [being] perpetrated against blacks" in his famous speech about Lincoln in 1876.

Stauffer concludes his book with an anecdote about Douglass in 1895, just before his death. A young black student asked the old eminence for advice about what Negroes just starting out ought to be thinking about doing: "Agitate! Agitate! Agitate!" Douglass proclaimed, with all the might he had left in him. Yet Stauffer also leaves the impression that Douglass was for the most part a burned-out case for the last thirty years of his life, a black bourgeois Republican blind to the poverty of the mass of blacks—like "a retired athlete or political leader . . . unable to reenter the fray with the same passion and in the same way." In this way, Stauffer remarks, Douglass's politics came ironically to resemble Lincoln's in their "gradual and comparatively conservative approach to reform." The former radical giant had shriveled: "Not once in the postwar period did Douglass endorse extralegal means to end oppression."

Stauffer's blanket condemnation of Republicans such as Grant for turning their backs on Southern blacks is, at the very least, unfair. As

Stauffer himself notes, Grant, as president, crushed the Ku Klux Klan in 1871. He might also have mentioned Grant's support for the successful ratification of the Fifteenth Amendment in 1870, and for the full range of the enforcement acts that he signed in 1870 and 1871, and for the Civil Rights Act of 1875—taken together, the strongest civil rights record of any president between Abraham Lincoln and Lyndon B. Johnson. Even after the economic panic of 1873 and a Democratic resurgence in the midterm elections of 1874 sharply reduced his options, Grant remained committed to enforcing the Fourteenth and Fifteenth Amendments, and doing what he could to protect Unionists and freedmen in the South.

Stauffer's portrait of a complacent, conservative Douglass after the war is perverse. Even as the Republican Party's support for Reconstruction receded in the mid-1870s, Douglass remained firmly committed to using the ballot box as the central instrument for advancing Southern black interests. When, in the 1880s and 1890s, black disenfranchisement spread throughout the former Confederacy, Douglass raised his voice in fierce indignation, denouncing the "suppression of the legal vote in the south" as a "national problem," "as much a problem for Maine and Massachusetts as it is for the Carolinas and Georgia." He went so far as to declare, in 1888, that the emancipation intended by Lincoln had not actually come to pass—and that the Negro in the South was "worse off, in many ways, than when he was a slave."

Douglass in his later years did indeed become more like Lincoln—not because he turned "conservative," but because he came to recognize, as Lincoln did almost instinctively, the difference between the role of a radical reformer and the role of a politician. He arrived at a moral and historical appreciation of politics. James Oakes puts it well: "[Douglass] did not claim that the abolitionist perspective was invalid, only that it was partial and therefore inadequate. Lincoln was an elected official, a politician, not a reformer; he was responsible to a broad public that no abolitionist crusader had to worry about." Douglass, that is, had come to see politics as more complex than he had before the war. It is a kind of wisdom lost on political moralists of all generations, for whom revolution or radical reform is the ship, and virtually everything else is a corrupting bog of compromise.

Without an appreciation of this complexity, it becomes easy to view Douglass as a backslider, just as it is easy to see Lincoln as a hopelessly cautious politician—or, as Stauffer puts it, a "conservative"—who only began to transcend politics in 1862 or 1863. In fact, it was Lincoln's pragmatic, at times cold-blooded, but always practical insistence on not transcending politics that enabled him, as Douglass put it in 1876, to restore the Union and "free his country from the great crime of slavery":

> Had he put the abolition of slavery before the salvation of the Union, he would have inevitably driven from him a powerful class of the American people and rendered resistance to rebellion impossible. Viewed from the genuine abolition ground, Mr. Lincoln seemed tardy, cold, dull, and indifferent; but measuring him by the sentiment of his country, a sentiment he was bound as a statesman to consult, he was swift, zealous, radical, and determined.

Had Lincoln as president been the radical that Stauffer would have preferred, the slaveholders would almost surely have won the Civil War.

★ ★ ★

THE ADAGE THAT understanding history requires understanding the historian also applies to literary critics who write history. Despite differences in methods and conclusions, much recent writing on Lincoln reflects a common mood among a portion of the intelligentsia, one that cannot be ascribed to Lincoln's bicentennial in 2009 and the 150th anniversary of the Civil War from 2011 to 2015. It might seem political, but this is imprecise: it cares about politics only so as to demote it and repudiate it and transcend it. The mood to which I refer is in truth profoundly antipolitical. It runs deeper than conventional election loyalties, touching what has become a ganglion of contemporary hopes and dreams about America, about its past, its present, and its future. And it has nothing to do with Abraham Lincoln.

As a state legislator in 1837, Lincoln rose to object to a Democratic resolution on the Illinois State Bank—and, it seemed at first, to attack the very profession of politics. "Mr. Chairman," he said, "this movement is exclusively the work of politicians; a set of men who have interests aside from the interests of the people, and who, to say the most of them are, taken as a mass, at least one long step removed from being honest men." Then he threw in his kicker: "I say this with greater freedom because, being a politician myself, none can regard it as personal."

The candor of Lincoln's language, the ease with which he accurately describes his real vocation, is bracing. He saw no shame in the practice of politics, and experienced no priggish discomfort about what it takes to get great things done. He was never too good for politics. Quite the contrary: for him, politics—ordinary, grimy, unelevating politics—was itself a good, and an instrument for good. Lincoln knew who he was. He knew that his colleagues knew who he was. He would never renounce who he was. It would take the earnest historians and critics of a later age to do that for him—or, taking him at his word, to slight his achievements while vaunting their own radical heroes. In misunderstanding Abraham Lincoln, these writers misunderstand American democratic politics, in Lincoln's day as well as in our own.

8

★ ★ ★ ★ ★ ▬▬▬▬▬▬▬▬

Democracy at Gettysburg, 1863

IN HIS GETTYSBURG ADDRESS, HISTORIANS RELATE, ABRAham Lincoln dedicated a cemetery for the Union dead by proclaiming the expanded goals for which the North was fighting in 1863. The speech's mention of "a new birth of freedom" affirmed the nation's commitment to abolishing slavery, which had become a second war aim alongside preserving the Union. And in doing this, the Address also changed the very meaning of America. By citing the Declaration of Independence and not the U.S. Constitution as the nation's cornerstone—defined, he said, by "the proposition that all men are created equal"—Lincoln singlehandedly (and sneakily) recast the American creed along the Declaration's more egalitarian lines.

The second of these claims, though, is erroneous, and the first is incomplete. Whatever else Lincoln may have said at Gettysburg, the idea that the Declaration contained the nation's fundamental political principles had been a staple of antislavery politics at least since the outbreak of the Missouri crisis in 1819. The second plank of the Republican platform on which Lincoln ran in 1860 repeated the assertion. As president, Lincoln entrenched the idea as no other previous figure had or could, but he neither invented it nor smuggled it into his remarks at Gettysburg. Rather, he repeated yet again what had long since become a set piece in his speeches as well as in the politics of the Republican Party. The Gettysburg Address was not at all what one writer has called it, "one of the most daring acts of open-air sleight-of-hand ever witnessed by the unsuspecting."

As for Northern war aims, the Address is in fact remarkably circumspect with regard to both the Union and slavery. It contains not a single explicit reference to saving the Union, although no one could doubt that this remained one of Lincoln's overriding goals. Its one allusion to slavery seems nearly as clear-cut as it was important, yet Lincoln did not use the word. This is not surprising given the continuing displeasure among many Northerners about the Emancipation Proclamation he had issued nearly eleven months earlier.

Lincoln opened the Address with the now iconic statement that the founding fathers had created a government dedicated to equality, meaning equality of rights. But the Address's most emphatic passage comes at the very end, and it concerns neither the Union nor slavery per se: the great cause for which the Union dead had given the last full measure of devotion, Lincoln said, was to prevent government of, by, and for the people from perishing with them. A familiar word for this form of government, then and (even more) now, is democracy. For Lincoln, equality and democracy were essential and inseparable features of American government. And although the three were entwined, preserving the Union and abolishing slavery were not exactly the same as securing democracy. Abolishing slavery had become in itself a crucial explicit goal by 1863, but it also served as a means to vindicate democracy. And although the concepts of democracy and the Union were tightly linked, they were also distinct: Union, in the American context, was an indispensable condition for the practice and preservation of democratic government.

Much as with the word "slavery," Lincoln had his reasons to avoid "democracy" at Gettysburg. But whatever word or words he used, Lincoln took the occasion to proclaim that he and his administration were determined to preserve democracy. It was a point that he and many other Northerners had made often, even before the attack on Fort Sumter. But never, before or after, would Lincoln make the point as forcefully as he did at Gettysburg. Here, at the core of the Gettysburg Address, was something akin to a third transcendent war aim—saving democracy—that, if it was to be achieved, required crushing secession and freeing the slaves.

★ ★ ★

THE ADDRESS'S AVOIDANCE of the word "democracy" is not mysterious. Since the election of Andrew Jackson in 1828, the political party that Jackson and his supporters established had been known as the Democratic Party or, more familiarly, the Democracy. Lincoln, a lifelong Whig partisan until the Whig Party ceased to exist in 1854, had little if anything good to say about Jackson's Democracy. As a Republican, he had nothing good to say about the slaveholder-dominated Democracy of the 1850s, stripped of its Northern antislavery adherents.

So thoroughly had the Democratic Party blurred the distinction, though, that a veteran party man like Lincoln found it difficult to refer to democracy as a form of government without creating confusion. Lincoln's published collected works contain 527 separate entries using the word "democracy" or "democratic." Virtually all refer to the political party and not a political system. "But great is Democracy in its resources," he wrote to his friend and supporter Anson G. Henry as the 1860 campaign heated up, "and it may yet give its fortunes a turn." As ever, Lincoln meant the Democracy, and not democracy.

Lincoln preferred terms like "self-government," "free government," or "popular government," which also frequently appeared in other political leaders' speeches and in the partisan press. "Allow ALL the governed an equal voice in the government," he said in his famous Peoria speech in 1854, "and that, and that only, is self-government." The "common object" of the slaveholders and their political supporters, he wrote in some fragmentary notes, probably in 1858, "is to subvert, in the public mind, and in the practical administration, our old and only standard of free government, that 'all men are created equal.'" The Southern rebellion, he charged in his first Annual Message to Congress, "is largely, if not exclusively, a war upon the first principle of popular government—the rights of the people."

One of the rare occasions when Lincoln departed from his usual practice came when he spoke as president, in his message to the special session of Congress that convened on July 4, 1861. Lincoln used the word almost offhandedly, but the example was telling. The issue of secession, Lincoln wrote, "presents to the whole family of man, the question, whether a constitutional republic, or a democracy—a government of the people, by the same people—can, or cannot, maintain its territorial integrity, against its own domestic foes." By using "constitutional republic" and "democracy" as bywords, as if testing out which fit best, Lincoln affirmed the inexactness and multiplicity of the American political vocabulary in 1861. Without question, though, more than two years before the Gettysburg Address, Lincoln had begun devising his famous phrase about "government of" and "by the people"—he had only to include the "for"—in order to describe democracy. He also made it clear that, from the very start of the conflict, he had perceived secession and the crisis of the Union as a crisis of democracy.

At Gettysburg, Lincoln connected democracy's preservation with "a new birth of freedom," and on one earlier occasion, Lincoln appears to have defined the word "democracy" in direct opposition to slavery. The provenance of the tantalizing document is questionable, as is the date, although the editors of his collected works conjectured that he wrote it on August 1, 1858. "As I would not be a *slave*, so I would not be a *master*," the scrap of paper reads, apparently in Lincoln's handwriting. "This expresses my idea of democracy. Whatever differs from this, to the extent of the difference, is no democracy."

If Lincoln indeed wrote these words, he understood the meaning of democracy to embrace legal and social relations between humans as well as a political system: a democratic polity could never tolerate the essentially undemocratic condition of masters and slaves. By this definition, the slave South was no democracy. And by this definition, the crisis of democracy predated Southern secession. Six weeks before he purportedly wrote these words, Lincoln commenced his senatorial campaign against Stephen A. Douglas. Just as "a house divided against itself cannot stand," he declared, he believed that "this government cannot endure, permanently, half *slave* and half *free*." According to the later definition of democracy, this also would have meant that the government could not endure half *democratic* and half *nondemocratic*. The growing conflict over slavery in the 1850s would inherently have been a struggle for democracy, as it would have been since the nation's founding.

Lincoln expressed this particular formulation about slavery and democracy nowhere else in his writings. Yet at Gettysburg, he concluded by extolling both the nation's "new birth of freedom" and democracy's preservation, as if one followed from the other. And the idea that slavery was undemocratic—both the relation between master and slave, and the polity and legal structures built on that relation—was commonplace among antislavery Northerners before war began as well as after. The slave South was an oligarchy that oppressed black slaves and the "great mass" of its white population, Horace Greeley's influential *New-York Daily Tribune* observed, and so the war involved a collision "between democracy on the one hand, and this foreign element and doubly aristocratical institution of negro slavery on the other."

Slaveholders, while sometimes holding to less-than-democratic ideals of an organic and hierarchical social order, responded that they had built a perfect representative democracy, in which the bondage of inferior blacks enabled white equality. "There is no proposition clearer to my mind, than this—banish African Slavery from among us and you destroy Democratic liberty," a delegate to the Alabama secession convention observed in January 1861. Americans, and not just Americans, could easily interpret the Gettysburg Address, in light of these clashing ideas, as the latest defense of what Lincoln considered the Northern states' true democracy in contrast to the slaveholders' sham democracy.

Quite apart from the contest between slavery and democracy, though, Lincoln had ample cause at Gettysburg to describe securing democracy as the North's great purpose, even if, as was his habit, he did not use the word. Ensuring democratic government had in fact been at the heart of the matter at least since the slaveholding states began mobilizing to secede, not simply in the context of American politics but in the eyes of the world, "the whole family of man."

★ ★ ★

THE ADDRESS DESCRIBES democracy not only as the American form of government but as a universal ideal—an ideal in great danger of being extinguished. America may have provided Lincoln, as it did Alexis de Tocqueville, with what Tocqueville called "the image of democracy itself." But elsewhere in the Atlantic world, in the middle of the nineteenth century, democracy was in retreat. Disorder into mayhem seemed the inevitable result of popular government. The French Revolution's degeneration into the Reign of Terror and Bonapartism, followed by the Bourbon restoration, had tainted antimonarchism as well as democracy. Periodic republican and democratic uprisings, culminating in the revolutions that swept Europe in 1848, had been suppressed. Even in the United States, conservative Whigs bemoaned the effects of Andrew Jackson's democratic politics and what they called, behind closed doors, "the democracy of numbers and radicalism." And in the Old World, the outbreak of a civil war in America delighted old-line tories, aristocrats, and legitimists as proof positive that republicanism and thus democracy were doomed to failure—a failure made all the more striking in the American case because it was tied to the institution of human bondage. "We were now witnessing the bursting of the great republican bubble which had so often been held up to us as a model on which to cast our British Constitution," Sir John Ramsden, MP, told the House of Commons in May 1861.

At Gettysburg, as before, Lincoln was acutely aware of these stakes. Not just American democracy was on trial, he said in the Address; democracy itself as a political proposition was on trial. (Indeed, given the blows dealt to democratic movements in the Old World, it was easy enough for Lincoln and others to see America as a singular and even providential nation: if democracy failed in America, it could never succeed anywhere else.) Northern newspapers had repeatedly observed how cynical aristocrats, in one Illinois editor's words, "affect to read in the pregnant events of the day the complete and irredeemable failure of Democracy." An Ohio newspaper spelled out the larger hazards: "It is not only a question of whether we have a government or not, here, but we believe what is now being decided is whether a free government shall again spring up in any quarter of the globe." Ordinary Northern soldiers said much the same thing in their letters home: if the Southern "traitors" destroyed the government, one private in the 27th Connecticut Regiment wrote, "all the hope and confidence in the capacity of men for self government will be lost." Or, as Lincoln put it at Gettysburg, the war called into question not simply the American democratic experiment but whether any nation conceived in liberty and dedicated to equality could last for long. The testing had begun with Southern secession, the great unmentioned trigger for what the Address simply called "a great civil war."

Secession came in direct response to Lincoln's election in 1860. The election's outcome conformed to the Constitution to the letter: having obtained a commanding majority of votes in the Electoral College, Lincoln was duly chosen president. But Southern secessionists would not have it. Lincoln had won only a plurality of the national popular tally in a purely sectional vote. He had run on a party platform pledged to commence slavery's eradication, which the slaveholders charged would violate what they insisted were the Constitution's guarantees of slave property as a nationally sanctioned institution. An electoral majority was about to commence trouncing the constitutional rights of a minority, which would ruin the republic. "A mere partizan election by a majority of voters," the *Richmond Semi-Weekly Examiner* contended, ". . . will be the actual destruction of the political institutions of the United States." (Had the *Examiner* recalled that Lincoln's margin of victory in the popular vote was only a plurality, it could have made its point even more forcefully.) After what the pro-secession slaveholders described as a partisan electoral coup d'état, the only course left was to dissolve the Union.

The essential clash was over slavery, but framed as a constitutional question: Did the Constitution recognize property-holding in slaves as a national institution? The slaveholders asserted that it did, basing their arguments in part on federal judicial decisions that had culminated in Chief Justice Roger Taney's majority ruling in *Dred Scott v. Sandford* in 1857. Any effort to restrict slavery's expansion, they charged, was unconstitutional, as it would abrogate the slaveholders' rights to hold their human property anywhere—even, some argued, in states where slavery had been abolished.

Lincoln and his supporters denounced Taney's ruling as unconstitutional. They asserted that the Constitution regarded slaves as persons not as property, that slavery was purely a state-sanctioned and not a national institution, and that claims to slave property had no force outside those states that had not abolished slavery. Accordingly, they insisted, Congress had ample authority to restrict slavery in the territories or anywhere else that fell under its jurisdiction.

Lincoln and the Republicans were determined to overturn what the party's 1860 platform called "the new dogma" and the "dangerous political heresy" contained in Taney's decision, which the platform deemed "revolutionary in its tendency, and subversive of the peace and harmony of the country." Having rejected the slaveholders' property claims under the Constitution, they dismissed any argument for "car-r[ying] Slavery into all or any of the Territories of the United States." Here was the crucial constitutional question over which the Southern secessionists led their states out of the Union.

The legitimacy of secession, in turn, became the second pivotal constitutional issue. The secessionists argued that they were acting as their revolutionary forebears had in 1776, freeing themselves from what had become tyranny, which they commonly described, as one leading Alabaman did, as "a consolidated, centralized General Government." Some secessionists, basing their claims on the so-called compact theory of the Constitution as restated by John C. Calhoun, asserted that the separate sovereign states actually had the clear constitutional right to withdraw. Lincoln and the Republicans, as well as Union Democrats and anti-secession Southerners, repudiated both arguments. There had been, they said, no abrogation or revision of the Constitution, nor would there be; there had only been successive resolutions of the political and moral questions concerning slavery's expansion. "[T]he only substantial dispute," Lincoln said in his first inaugural address, was over whether slavery was right or wrong, and whether it ought to be extended.

For seventy years, the slaveholding South had enjoyed the upper hand. The electoral success of Lincoln and the Republicans had shifted the politics of the controversy by turning what had been a minority into a majority, but that legitimate change was not fixed by some illusory consolidated tyranny. What the secessionists deemed intolerable centralization basically amounted to the possibility that the *Dred Scott* decision would be overturned—a reversal that would be no more permanent than the original decision had been.

The compact theory, meanwhile, was, to Lincoln and his supporters, a constitutionally flimsy yet dangerous artifice. They upheld instead the nationalist ideas previously propounded in different ways by leaders as diverse as Daniel Webster and Andrew Jackson. By these lights, the American people, and not the states, had created the nation, as an improvement of the union that predated the Constitution. Instituted by and for "We, the People," the nation was distinct from any association of states, with powers that the states had ceded to it. The Union, far from a contingent compact, was perpetual. Secession, one Rhode Island editor observed, did not follow "the character of the American constitution" but was instead "a departure from the obligations of that instrument," a treasonous display of "violent contempt of popular authority."

With the states of the lower South having already issued their ordinances of secession, Lincoln devoted a good deal of his first inaugural address to refuting the secessionists' rationales. "Plainly," he said, "the central idea of secession is the essence of anarchy." As in all constitutional disputes, either the majority would acquiesce to the will of the minority or vice versa. So long as the majority was subject to constitutional constraints and limitations, and so long as its predominance could be easily ended "with deliberate changes of popular opinions and sentiments," majority rule was "the only true sovereign of a free people." Permit a minority to secede and it would only be a matter of time before a minority within that minority would secede—a formula for chaos. "Rejecting the majority principle," Lincoln concluded, would mean that "anarchy or despotism in some form is all that is left."

Lincoln's logic deserves amplification. The destruction of the Union, he said, was an act of rebellion, based on an untenable theory of government in general and of the U.S. Constitution in particular. Elsewhere in his first inaugural address, Lincoln dwelled on the virtues of the Union itself, above and beyond its primacy to the American constitutional order. The speech's famous peroration, on the "mystic chords of memory" swelling "the chorus of the Union," contain the most striking images of this kind of nationalist sentiment of the entire Civil War era, as an appeal to national unity and identity. But Lincoln's dissection of secession consisted chiefly of a defense not of national unity but of government by majority rule, which is to say of democracy. Secession flouted the bonds of nationality, but even more important, it repudiated democracy.

Lincoln's democratic argument was no more peculiar to him than were his views on slavery and the Declaration of Independence. Nearly three months earlier, the *Iowa State Register* of Des Moines, contemplating the impeding secession of South Carolina, stated that "if the will of the majority is no longer the governing power in this country, free government is at an end." Similar declarations appeared in pro-Republican newspapers across the North during the secession crisis. Lincoln simply stated, with eloquence and presidential force, what had become the common sense of the subject among his fellow Unionists. In doing so, he completed a shift toward an increasingly pointed defense of democracy that appeared full-blown elsewhere in his first inaugural address, which he would restate, even more eloquently, at Gettysburg.

★   ★   ★

BEFORE THE GETTYSBURG ADDRESS, Lincoln's thoughts about democracy had evolved in response to changing political circumstances. Over the half decade before 1860, his pronouncements on the subject turned largely on the concept of popular sovereignty. In 1847 and 1848, mainstream Northern Democrats, faced with rising opposition to extending slavery, seized upon the phrase to denote what they posited as a moderating democratic solution to the sectional controversy. Antislavery forces were demanding slavery's prohibition in the territories; proslavery forces were demanding no restrictions at all. If, though, the federal government granted to territorial residents what Democratic senator and 1848 presidential nominee Lewis Cass called the right "to regulate their concerns in their own way," then the slavery question could be settled in, allegedly, the most directly democratic manner imaginable. Cass lost in 1848, but the idea of "popular sovereignty" became a primary organizing principle of the Northern Democracy in the 1850s, especially after the passage of the Kansas-Nebraska Act in 1854. Lincoln's Illinois rival, Senator Stephen A. Douglas, became popular sovereignty's greatest champion.

For Lincoln, this appropriation of a democratic principle was as much a fraud as the idea of a slaveholders' democracy. Ostensibly democratic, the "popular sovereignty" proclaimed by Cass, Douglas, and their supporters imagined democracy as a kind of micropolitics, in which local assemblies of citizens made decisions on the basis of majority rule. But the micropolitics of popular sovereignty slighted the macropolitics of the democratic nation. Specifically, it conferred rights to self-government to settlers in territories where, under the Constitution, those rights were severely constrained. Article IV, Section 2, after all, expressly granted to Congress, and not to territorial settlers, the power "to dispose of and make all needful Rules and Regulations respecting the Territory or other Property belonging to the United States."

In plain violation of that provision, "popular sovereignty" would, on Lincoln's view, permit slaveholders to rush into new territories and give slavery the foothold it needed to become intractable. Democratic verbiage would cloak the spread of slavery by acknowledging, he wrote to one supporter, "that slavery has equal rights with liberty." And when put to the test, as it was in "Bleeding" Kansas after the passage of the Kansas-Nebraska Act in 1854, "popular sovereignty" deteriorated into territorial civil war. Far from democratic, the idea, Lincoln charged during his debates with Douglas in 1858, was "nothing but a living, creeping lie from the time of its introduction, till to-day."

Lincoln propounded what he called "genuine popular sovereignty," which involved the constitutional norms of the larger national democracy. "A general government," he explained in 1859, "shall do all those things which pertain to it, and all the local governments shall do precisely as they please in respect to those matters which exclusively concern them." In accord with his insistence that the federal government enjoyed, under the Constitution, certain exclusive powers over slavery, this rendering of popular sovereignty upheld the divided sovereignty that was a hallmark of the American democratic republic. But Lincoln's divided and divisive election to the presidency, which sparked off Southern secession, in time forced him to think more directly about democracy and majority rule. During the weeks before the election of 1860, as Lincoln's victory appeared increasingly certain, Southern disunionists made it clear that were he to be elected, secession would quickly follow. Pro-Republican newspapers responded forcefully. Would it be shown, a Connecticut editor wrote, "that the will of a peaceful voting majority can no longer govern the nation; that any minority wicked enough and desperate enough can govern us on the great principle of a pirate in a powder magazine, who will blow the ship to atoms if his orders are not complied with?" The election, according to the *Daily Pittsburgh Gazette*, was "no longer a mere contest between four men, but a struggle for the maintenance of the great majority principle in this Government. Shall the people rule?" Nearly two months after the election, and four days after South Carolina issued the first ordinance of secession, a West Virginia newspaper commented on Lincoln's disunionist Southern Democratic foes with mock surprise: "They were beaten—fairly, honorably, constitutionally, overwhelmingly beaten.—What is the sequel? They submit, of course. No; they do not."

Lincoln maintained a strategic silence between election day and his inauguration, although he made it clear that he now considered himself, as he wrote to New York's governor Edwin D. Morgan, "the representative for the time being of the majority of the nation." Preparing what would become his inaugural address's democratic refutation of secession, he fixed on the legitimacy of his election as a clear expression of the majority's constitutional as well as democratic will. A number of voices had urged him, in the face of the crisis, to support some sort of compromise that would stave off secession by forcing him to relent on his (and his party's) opposition to the extension of slavery. Such surrender, he wrote in a draft of the address, would mark the ruin not just of a man or a party but also "the ruin of the government itself." If a president-elect felt duty-bound suddenly to abandon the most essential principles and promises on which he had run, what was the use of holding a democratic election in the first place? As for his selection as president being a coup d'état, Lincoln allowed that people could err in any election, including his own, but he would also remind the public that under a popular government, "the true cure is in the next election; and not in the treachery of the party elected."

In the inaugural address's final text, Lincoln, defending his presidency's legitimacy, delivered the most stirring defense of democratic politics and government offered by any American president since Thomas Jefferson. "Why should there not be a patient confidence in the ultimate justice of the people?" he asked. "Is there any better or equal hope in the world? In our present differences, is either party without faith of being in the right? If the Almighty Ruler of Nations, with His eternal truth and justice, be on your side of the North, or yours of the South, that truth and that justice will surely prevail by the judgment of this great tribunal of the American people."

In 1801, Jefferson had called the national government, founded on the will of the majority, "the world's best hope." Silently citing Jefferson and then updating him, Lincoln spoke in even loftier terms about the democratic citizenry—"this great tribunal of the American people"—while he reemphasized how the destiny of all mankind hung in the balance of American democracy's success. He would make both points again at Gettysburg, after more than two and a half years of carnage, and with an even sharper sense of the threat that the slaveholders and the war posed to democracy.

★   ★   ★

AT GETTYSBURG, Lincoln did not envisage democracy's possible death simply in terms of the collapse of the government created by the American Revolution. He also perceived the Confederate foe as an embodiment of antidemocratic principles in the very structure of the government they were trying to establish—the first republic in world history created in order to uphold racial slavery. Undemocratic slavery, he thought, fostered undemocratic political institutions that preserved, protected, and defended the power of a slaveholding oligarchy.

Secession, a crisis for American democracy, rattled democratic institutions within the insurgent South. Designing new national and state governments posed a dilemma to the slaveholders. How were the proudly sovereign states of the new Confederacy to handle the tensions between the states' existing liberal democratic institutions and the hierarchy and order of a slaveholders' republic? For some secessionists, the issue came down to preserving the existing democracy by explicitly excluding all but adult white males from active citizenship. The seceding states did exactly that, replicating, in the most conspicuous ways, the prewar institutional status quo. But difficult questions remained.

Throughout the South, secession had been hotly disputed, especially in areas dominated by slaveless small farmers' households. Accordingly, would the state secession conventions run the risk of permitting the citizenry at large to approve or disapprove of their work? Although adult white male suffrage was the norm, some slaveholding state governments, above all South Carolina, were far less democratic than others. (South Carolina demanded high property qualifications to serve as governor, gave the power to elect governors and presidential electors to the state legislature, and apportioned representation unequally in enormous favor of affluent slaveholders' districts.) Would the revised state constitutions, without changing prominent institutions like suffrage, look to the less democratic models and adopt subtler restrictions?

Even before secession, spokesmen in areas controlled by large plantation slaveholders, most of them one-time Whigs, had expressed concern about what they considered the ignorant and possibly fractious non-slaveholding yeomanry. The unease intensified as secession created a temporary yet possibly turbulent period of transition from one political order to another. Would the latent suspicions of democracy lead the new state governments to restrict popular government?

As the Southern state conventions turned to reforming their state constitutions as well as writing and approving ordinances of secession, antidemocratic voices found an opening to shout at the top of their lungs. "Some of the wisest and best citizens propose a hereditary monarchy," one Georgia editor exclaimed; less monarchical sages, he said, favored what he called "additional safeguards," including "an *Executive for life, a vastly restricted suffrage*," and senators elected for life. As if responding to these outbursts, a county public meeting in November 1860 declared its adamant opposition "to the overthrow of our present republican form of Government and the establishment in lieu thereof of a 'Constitutional Monarchy' in these Southern States."

The convening of the Georgia secession convention inspired one newspaper reader to bid the delegates to "check the radical tendencies of the age," chiefly by giving all high court appointments to the governor, subject to approval by two-thirds of the state senate. Without those reforms, he wrote, "the transitive state through which we are now passing" might lead to anarchy and mob rule. Still other commentators desired modifications that would rid the legislatures of "mere wrangling demagogues" and "county politicians," in favor of "better legislators" who were truly "representative of the honor and the interests of the State." Some of the more temperate delegates grew worried about what one Mississippian called "crude opinions" concerning the conventions' authority to redesign state governments, fostering an "absolutism" inside the conventions that "changed the form of our government from a representative democracy to an oligarchy."

Temperate voices prevailed at the state conventions, and the shifts in the new constitutions toward a less democratic system were fairly minor. Still, the antidemocratic strain in Southern politics was unmistakable. "Property does not have the proper constitutional influence," the antidemocratic South Carolina planter David Gavin complained about his state's revised constitution. Only three of the seceding states—Virginia, Tennessee, and Texas—held public referenda on their respective ordinances of secession. And the Constitution of the Confederate States of America, adopted on March 11, 1861, enshrined the fear of possibly divisive democracy in other ways, particularly with respect to party politics.

Since the nation's founding, a strong animus against parties and party conflict had shaped American politics, especially conservative politics. Lincoln and his fellow liberal New School Whigs wholly rejected such thinking; Lincoln climbed up the ladder in Illinois as a masterful party pol; the Republican Party's great achievement was to combine Jacksonian democratic ideas and Whig ideas about economic development together with antislavery politics. But the antiparty animus and its elitist tone remained strong in much of the country, above all in the slaveholding South with its vaunted ideals of honor, harmony, and disinterested virtue.

In 1850, a typical article in the *Southern Quarterly Review*, while contrasting the South and the North, had lambasted "the systematic immoralities of political parties, and the utter shamelessness with which they grasp at power, in the teeth of principle." In February 1861, as delegates gathered both for the Confederate constitutional convention and the Louisiana state convention, a writer for the *New Orleans Daily Picayune* warned against heeding the "party spirit." The Confederate constitutional convention, which gathered in Montgomery that same month, crafted provisions designed to limit electioneering and the dispensing of party patronage, including a one-term, six-year presidency. Curbing the machinations of parties and party politicians, the prominent Alabaman Robert H. Smith declared, would help prevent the Confederacy from degenerating into something "much worse than . . . a pure democracy . . . a mere oligarchy, and that not of intelligence and virtue but of low ambition."

The reactionary effusions and antiparty principles of the seceding South affirmed Northern arguments about the basically undemocratic character of the slaveholding states—and Abraham Lincoln took special notice. "It continues to develop that the insurrection is largely, if not exclusively, a war upon the first principle of popular government—the rights of the people," he remarked in his first Annual Message to Congress, delivered on December 3, 1861. Pointing to "grave and maturely considered public documents" along with "the general tone of the insurgents," Lincoln charged that Southerners were now propounding abridgment of the existing rights of suffrage and selection of public officers, and advancing "labored arguments to prove that large control of people in government, is the source of all political evil." The Southerners' antidemocratic zeal knew no bounds: "Monarchy itself," Lincoln observed, "is sometimes hinted at as a possible refuge from the power of the people." What had begun as an attempt to repudiate a democratic national election had evolved into a "returning despotism," against which, as president, Lincoln said he had no choice but to raise his voice in warning.

Lincoln exaggerated: the Southern antidemocratic upsurge was not nearly as strong as his rhetoric suggested. Unquestionably, though, fear and loathing of democracy was a political force inside the slaveholders' ranks, and Lincoln described it as an emblem of all that the Union was up against. "This is, essentially, a People's contest," Lincoln had told a special session of Congress five months earlier, with the Union struggling to maintain "that form, and substance of government, whose leading object is, to elevate the condition of men." In his first Annual Message, he described that form and substance as "the popular principle applied to government." A year later, in his second Annual Message, having announced the preliminary Emancipation Proclamation, Lincoln turned his earlier emendation of "the world's best hope"—Jefferson's phrase about democratic government—into "the last best hope of earth." At Gettysburg, with astonishing concision, he would complete the evolution of his democratic thinking.

★ ★ ★

THE GETTYSBURG ADDRESS builds in a mighty crescendo. It begins calmly, in a scriptural cadence, relating that "four score and seven years ago"—that is, in 1776, not 1787—the founding generation put forth "a new nation, conceived in Liberty" and dedicated to equality. Here, compressed into a single sentence, is the crux of the political argument that Lincoln and the Republicans had been making since 1854: that the egalitarian liberty proclaimed in the Declaration is the taproot of American politics and government. Implied in those thirty words is the basic justification for the national government ensuring that slavery would remain, as Lincoln had phrased it in his "House Divided" speech, "in the course of ultimate extinction."

The next four sentences describe the consequences of Southern resistance and disunion: "a great civil war," which would decide the fate of egalitarian government. Having specified the bitter fruits of secession, the Address then pauses to honor all those, living and dead, who fought to resist disunion and vindicate the Declaration. Suddenly, though, the speech enlarges its scope and heightens the emotional tension, focusing now on the honored dead, and placing upon Lincoln's listeners and the entire Union the burden of completing the work that the slain had advanced.

Then the tension peaks. A question instantly flashes to mind: What, exactly, is the unfinished work demanding rededication that Lincoln is talking about; what are the tasks that remain? A listener or reader might expect the speech to return to where it began, to the tasks of safeguarding liberty and equality. But instead, in sonorous litany and conclusion, the speech reaches a still more exalted level: what remains are two momentous goals as yet unmentioned, the destruction of slavery in nothing less than "a new birth of freedom," and beyond that, encompassing all, the defense and validation of American democracy, the last best hope of earth.

Between the Revolution and the Civil War, American politics at bottom involved struggles over democracy—over how democratic the nation should be, and over what sort of democracy was best. Abraham Lincoln had played a leading role in those struggles beginning in 1854, and he had helped mightily in shaping the outcomes. The seemingly democratic idea of "popular sovereignty," invented and touted by partisans of what was still called the Democracy, was not democratic at all, he charged, but a shill, an evasion of the Constitution intended not to secure the people's will but instead to spread slavery. The idea of a proslavery democracy was an oxymoron; secession, while claiming to be resistance to tyranny, was in fact an anarchic repudiation of democracy. Anyone who doubted the despotic character of the self-declared republic of slavery had only to listen hard to some of its adherents propound every conceivable curtailment of popular government, up to and including hereditary monarchy.

The exigencies of secession and civil war had deepened the crisis of American democracy, which was a crisis for democracy the world over. In that deepening, the separate strands of Lincoln's thinking about liberty, equality, and democracy had pulled together, ever tighter. Undemocratic secession had severed the Union; reclaiming that Union would require crushing an ever more despotic threat; repulsing that threat would come to require, in time, military emancipation of the slaves, whose abominable status as human property had been the fundamental reason behind undemocratic secession. By the autumn of 1863, the war for the Union had become a radicalized war of liberation, and from that Union and that liberation would come the salvation of democracy. This was the point of Lincoln's Gettysburg Address.

9

★ ★ ★ ★ ★ ══════════════

The Steel Town and the Gilded Age

THE LOCKOUT AND STRIKE AT THE CARNEGIE STEELWORKS in Homestead, Pennsylvania, in 1892 was a culminating event of the Gilded Age. The stakes were enormous, in a fight that pitted the world's mightiest steel corporation against the nation's strongest trade union. Several of its episodes—the workers' pitched battles with the Pinkerton strikebreakers, the arrival of the Pennsylvania state militia, the shooting of Henry Clay Frick by Alexander Berkman—these are set pieces in the history of the American labor movement.

Not that the Homestead strike was the only dramatic labor upheaval of its time, or anywhere near the bloodiest. The nationwide railroad strike fifteen years earlier had far greater economic repercussions and cost many times the number of lives. After 1877, factories and mines across America became armed camps, as industrial strife reached levels unmatched anywhere in the world in the nineteenth century. In 1892 alone, state militias intervened in twenty-three separate labor disputes, from the docks of New Orleans to the iron mines of Minnesota. Labor turmoil would not reach its peak for another two years, with coal miners' strikes and the Pullman strike and boycott, in which railroad management, the nation's judiciary, and federal troops ordered by President Grover Cleveland combined forces and dealt organized labor a lasting defeat.

Still, the Homestead strike stands out as one of the most dramatic and bitter industrial conflicts of the era, a parable of the bewildering economic and political forces that were rapidly expanding corporate authority over American life. On one side were the skilled, relatively well-paid members of the Amalgamated Association of Iron and Steel Workers, who had long-established rights as industrial craftsmen and a large degree of control at work. The Amalgamated also had the support of thousands of other Homestead workers, including hundreds of immigrant laborers who had recently arrived from Central Europe filled with high expectations of the New World.

On the opposite side were Andrew Carnegie and Henry Clay Frick, determined to eradicate the union in order to gain complete control of the Homestead Works and affirm the principle that the property rights of a United States corporation were absolute. In this aim, they asked for, and got, the powerful backing of county authorities, the state courts, and some of Pennsylvania's leading elected officials, thus forging an alliance between government and capital that augured a repressive era in the politics of industrial America. "Never heretofore," one labor journalist concluded after the union's defeat, "has civil authority permitted itself to be employed as a tool to a corporation so palpably." Whatever the view, it became clear to observers that something alarming had happened at Homestead.

Because of the intensity of public reaction, the Homestead struggle left an unusually rich documentary record. *"The River Ran Red,"* edited by David P. Demarest and first published to commemorate the strike's centenary, collects newspaper clippings, sermons, photographs, cartoons, and other contemporary sources, all testifying to the shocking effect the events had on the nation. Dozens of out-of-town journalists and sketch artists were on the scene. Committees of both the House and the Senate began convening hearings into the causes of the lockout and strike even before the five-month battle was over.

Fifteen years later, teams of sociologists from the Pittsburgh Survey, a pioneering social research project funded by the Russell Sage Foundation and other progressive organizations, descended on Homestead to gather information about the strike's impact and consequences. Some of the frenzied, confidential cables and memoranda from 1892 that historians later discovered in the Carnegie and Frick papers are also included in the anthology.

Building on these sources, Paul Krause's *The Battle for Homestead*, also published in 1992 and still the most thorough historical study of the conflict, examines Homestead from the bottom up, and particularly through the testimony of numerous, now forgotten labor leaders, local politicians, and Homestead workers. More deeply than any previous account, Krause's explores the political ideas of the period and the cultural assumptions of the town's polyglot workforce. Krause's command of European history and his fluency in Slovak—rare among American historians of the immigrant experience—are an enormous help here, giving him access to testimony that had before been closed. Although he is entirely on the union's side, Krause's treatment of Carnegie, Frick, and their political allies seems fair. One can debate some of his historical judgments, especially about the workers' political ideas, but his book is the most reliable account available so far of how Homestead happened, and why it had such a powerful, even traumatic, impact.

The ostensible cause of the lockout and strike was a dispute over wages, but everyone in Homestead knew that the roots were deeper. Twenty years earlier, when iron was still the industrial metal of choice, skilled workers virtually controlled production. Puddling the molten iron and rolling the finished product required a mastery of arcane craft lore and enormous physical strength, along with an ability to lead crews of up to sixteen men through their tasks. There were only a few ways to do the work correctly in these mills and foundries. The skilled workers knew what these were, management did not, and power over day-to-day operations was distributed accordingly. In the

1860s and 1870s disputes arose over wages and working conditions, but the ironworkers managed to sustain their craft unions, which merged in 1876 to form the Amalgamated, a union of nearly four thousand members—strong enough to force their employers to take them seriously. The puddlers, who stood at the apex of the labor hierarchy, referred to the iron industry as "our trade" without much fear of being contradicted. Manufacturers, they believed, were free to sell their products at whatever prices they pleased, but they had no right to set the price of labor.

Power began to shift in the 1870s and 1880s, when the Bessemer process and the open-hearth furnace revolutionized the industry. By changing the chemistry of metal-making, the inventors of these new processes vastly improved the methods for removing impurities from iron and mixing the purified product with alloys in order to make steel. They then perfected the technology required to apply their discoveries and produce industrial steel far more cheaply than iron. A new generation of steel manufacturers, particularly the young Scottish immigrant Andrew Carnegie, invested heavily in the new equipment. Having made a small fortune in railroad and iron investments in the 1860s, Carnegie steadily acquired new Bessemer facilities and, in the mid-1880s, built the nation's premier open-hearth furnace at Homestead.

Much of the savings in the switch from iron to steel involved labor: the new technology allowed manufacturers to replace highly skilled workers with machines tended by newcomers with indifferent skills. Open-hearth steelmaking eventually eliminated puddling altogether. By the end of the century, the president of the Carnegie Steel Company, Charles Schwab, would boast that he needed only six weeks to turn a raw farm boy into a competent melder, and melding was one of the few skilled jobs by then remaining.

The changes affected much more than wage bills and profit margins. By transforming the work process, the new steel methods also undermined the skilled workers' monopoly on expertise, and thus enabled management to assert its control over the work rules as well as over wages. Henceforth, the owners and managers expected to dictate all the industry's decisions, which the workers would either have to accept or lose their jobs.

Once management installed the new machines, the first step for the new regime was to cripple or destroy the craft unions. And here, once again, Andrew Carnegie was expert. In 1876, Carnegie had broken a strike at his immense Bessemer steelworks in Braddock, Pennsylvania, and ousted the local chapter of the newly united Amalgamated. When in the 1880s labor organizations (first the Amalgamated, then the Knights of Labor) tried to reestablish a foothold at Braddock, Carnegie was powerful enough to prevent it.

It was the Carnegie plant at Homestead, however, that posed the ultimate test of the new managerial power. After he purchased the already technologically advanced Homestead steelworks in 1883, Carnegie made it the jewel of his growing corporate empire: the American answer, he believed, to the gargantuan Krupp plants at Essen. By the end of the decade, Carnegie had added the latest in open-hearth technology, built new finishing mills (including an enormous and sophisticated department for manufacturing armor plate), and pushed overall production to unprecedented levels. Spread out over some ninety acres of land beside the Monongahela River, and manned, in 1892, by 3,800 workers, the Homestead Works was an industrial marvel where the latest machines required only a minimum of skilled labor. To visit the place, astonished trade journals reported, was to see steelmaking's future.

But Homestead also had the best-organized workforce in the industry: the Homestead branch of the Amalgamated, which kept pace with industrial expansion by enrolling additional skilled and semi-skilled workers and enlarging the number of local lodges, or chapters, from six to eight. Although the national body tended toward cautious craft unionism, dedicated exclusively to serving the interests of the more skilled and better-paid men, the Homestead Amalgamated, in defiance of the national union's policy, enlisted unskilled Slovak immigrants on the eve of the lockout, in order to solidify its bargaining position. All told, in 1892, about one quarter of all the steelworks' employees were members of the Amalgamated, while a local assembly of the less powerful Knights of Labor was also admitting laborers as well as skilled men from Carnegie's mills, and from the nearby Homestead Glass Works.

Homestead's organized workers denied they were aiming to obstruct the steelmaking revolution or to force the company to preserve redundant jobs. Repeatedly, the union proved tolerant of technological replacement. The Amalgamated's national president, William Weihe, asserted that the skilled men considered themselves industrial innovators of a sort and welcomed the new methods, believing "in the American idea that the genius of the country should not be retarded." So long as the Amalgamated's lodges controlled the work rules and looked after the membership's wages, the men appeared satisfied.

This is not to idealize conditions in the Homestead Works, or in the town generally. The mills never closed, and most employees worked either a ten- or a fourteen-hour shift. The heat from the converters and furnaces was so intense that the men's tobacco spittle sizzled when it hit the floor. The Pittsburgh Survey later reported that Homestead employees reached their peak at thirty and were worn out at forty. The men often labored in a state of exhaustion, continually scorched by cinders, their throats parched by the tiny particles of steel that filled the air. Not surprisingly, horrifying accidents were commonplace: on payday at the plant gate, the men on their way home would pass groups of ex-workmates begging with cups and carrying signs that explained exactly how they had been mutilated.

But the men of the Amalgamated were able to tolerate these conditions, largely thanks to the union. The local lodges were authentically democratic and enjoyed considerable autonomy. Individual workers could depend on their elected leaders—steelworkers like themselves—to hear their complaints and present them to management effectively.

In 1889, Carnegie himself and his company chairman, William Abbott, decided to test the union's strength with a lockout, only to discover how formidable the union was. With almost military precision, and with the support of nonunion men and their families, the Amalgamated sealed off the town to outsiders, scared away sheriff's deputies and scab black and immigrant steelworkers brought in by train to work the mills, and forced Carnegie's representatives to negotiate a new three-year contract. The eventual compromise settlement that was reached included wage cuts, according to a sliding scale that pegged the skilled men's rates to the market price of steel. But it also recognized the Amalgamated as the workers' bargaining representative; it kept the skilled men's wages one-third higher than those in neighboring mills; it tied laborers' rates to the skilled men's wages; and it preserved the union's control in directing work operations on the mill floor. Amicably or not, labor and capital were still partners, each side dependent on the other.

There were plenty of other reminders of labor's strong position in Homestead. Living in a tightly enclosed community, bordered on one side by the Monongahela and by the hills that overlooked the back end of town, everyone in Homestead not employed by Carnegie was connected in one way or another with the steelworkers, either by family or friendship. The Amalgamated, the Knights of Labor, and a number of working-class fraternal associations and church groups were the town's cultural centers, coordinating dances, picnics, and funerals for members and their families. Local politics, not surprisingly, were pro-labor, and municipal officials tended to be well disposed toward the men. In 1890, a year after the abortive lockout, the citizens of Homestead elected one "Honest" John McLuckie, a veteran steelworker and union champion, as their burgess (or mayor) almost unanimously. As the incumbent in 1892, McLuckie would be important to the unionists when Andrew Carnegie again tried to break the Homestead Amalgamated.

★ ★ ★

CARNEGIE WAS RANKLED by the failure of his lockout in 1889, and he was well prepared for what he expected would be a showdown. But he wanted to get his way without unduly damaging his considerable public reputation. The son of a Scottish weaver and democratic activist, and himself an enemy of aristocratic privilege, Carnegie was a complex man, widely thought of as an enlightened employer, a robber baron of the best sort. His endowments of libraries and other philanthropies had already set him apart from other industrial magnates, and he had recently written a political tract, *Triumphant Democracy*, which celebrated the blessings of popular, democratic government. He loved praise and was addicted to celebrity. He had grand literary aspirations, and he also had talent. In 1886, he went so far as to publish two articles in *The Forum* that extolled the mutual interests of labor and capital and defended the trade unions' right to exist.

But Carnegie's idea of a democratic union was a compliant union working in the company's interests, not an independent organization like the Amalgamated. Such unions, with their work rules and strike threats, were, in his view, undemocratic fetters on production, relics of the bygone age of iron that restricted progress—"a tax on improvements," as one of his partners later remarked. After the debacle of 1889, Carnegie was convinced of the necessity of ridding his company of the Amalgamated, and he took careful note of strategic errors in order to avoid them in future. He would not, as he had in 1889, allow orders to pile up on the eve of a lockout, lest his customers' complaints add to the pressure for a quick settlement. Above all, he would have a shrewd and implacable commander in charge of implementing company policy. In 1892, the year the 1889 Homestead contract was about to expire, the Carnegie Steel Corporation had been reorganized, with Carnegie's old associate Henry Clay Frick now chief executive—the ideal man to take on a union.

If the union men distrusted Carnegie as a hypocrite, they regarded Frick as a monster. Krause, perhaps in the interest of fairness, tends to understate the hatred Frick inspired. The son of a poor Pennsylvania farmer, Frick in his youth was determined to amass half a million dollars before he died. On his thirtieth birthday he estimated that he was worth twice that sum, thanks largely to his benefactor, Thomas Mellon, the patriarch of the Mellon banking clan, who had helped him make some brilliant investments in the coke industry, which supplied the iron and steel companies with their all-important fuel. Soon thereafter, Frick became the King of Coke, and merged his holdings with those of Carnegie, the King of Steel, to create an unusually cohesive industrial combination. Whereas Carnegie was gregarious, with an instinct for public relations, and still loosely identified with his radical background, Frick was a solitary man, an autocrat who had a nearly obsessive hatred of trade unions. Indeed, Carnegie's conciliatory writings on organized labor angered Frick and placed a strain on their partnership. In the late 1880s and 1890s, Frick suppressed union organizing in the coke fields, using hired gunmen and strikebreakers, and endured criticism without a sign of embarrassment.

Carnegie hoped that the Homestead Amalgamated could be destroyed peacefully, but he gave Frick total authority to make sure that it was done, and left for his annual grouse-hunting holiday in Scotland. Frick assumed from the start that there could be no peace and erected a wooden wall topped with barbed wire around the Homestead Works, with twelve-foot searchlight towers and slots which, the workers feared, would permit Frick's men to fire on any troublemakers. When negotiations began, management reiterated its terms to the union representatives, a complicated formula that would drastically lower the minimum wage rates and asserted management's right to enforce wage reductions throughout Homestead's workforce. In his careful account of the baffling contract talks, Krause convincingly shows that management's offer was not really serious. Frick intended to make his terms so odious that the union would not accept, creating an impasse that would allow him to lock out the workers, and then break the Amalgamated.

As had been expected, the union turned down Frick's offer. On June 25, Frick announced that the company would no longer deal with the Amalgamated, and that each employee would now have to negotiate individually. Three days later, management shut down one of Homestead's open-hearth departments and the entire armor plate mill, and started laying off the men. Almost immediately an undisclosed number of laborers in the steelworks—many, Krause believes, affiliated with the Knights of Labor—struck in support of the locked-out workers. On June 29, the company closed the entire plant.

An elected executive board of all the Homestead Amalgamated lodges, known as the advisory committee in deference to the union's democratic structure, reacted methodically, relying on many of the same techniques that had been successful three years before. After a mass meeting which rejected Frick's ultimatum, the committee's leader, a highly respected Irish immigrant steel roller named Hugh O'Donnell, announced that the men wanted no violence and would "very gently, but very firmly" push back the scabs, whose arrival seemed imminent. Still, after Frick's ominous fortification of the steelworks, the committee had no choice but to organize, as O'Donnell put it, on "a truly military basis."

With the support of Burgess McLuckie, who was also a member of the advisory committee, the union posted scouts at lookout points along the river, took control of the local utilities, and sealed off the town. The men—skilled and unskilled, American-born Protestants and Slovak Catholics—were remarkably united, and began to win support from neighboring steel towns and from the other inhabitants of Homestead. Frick's aggressive measures proved a unifying force: in Homestead, local businessmen helped the strikers' families; barkeeps stopped selling liquor and opened their doors to union meetings; even cooks and waiters in the local hotel joined the strike by refusing to serve food to management. Critics have sometimes assailed recent writing in labor history for sentimentalizing working-class solidarity; Krause shows that, at least among the Homestead strikers and their supporters, the solidarity was genuine.

Krause also believes that the protest at Homestead exemplified a distinct American working-class republicanism, rich in political associations with the American Revolution. It is not always easy to follow this part of his argument, for Krause tries to assimilate disparate ideas and traditions to a singular republican point of view: a neoclassical civic humanism derived from Machiavelli and James Harrington, the democratic republican ideas of Thomas Paine, the labor republicanism of the Jacksonian era, a "Christian republicanism" he never adequately defines, combined with the Slovak notion of *za chlebom* (which, roughly translated, means the right to one's daily bread). Too often, Krause deploys republicanism as the all-purpose antonym of acquisitive self-interest, making the labor movement sound almost saintly, a view more appropriate for monks than for hardbitten trade unionists.

Yet if Krause misreads labor's goals as selflessly virtuous, there is abundant evidence that Homestead's workers, like other workers throughout the country during the Gilded Age, understood their individual self-interest as part of a larger, collective, democratic ideal and an American egalitarian tradition. Above all, they believed that, in a democracy, productive labor should be a guarantee of dignity and economic security, and much of this belief was a direct legacy of the Civil War. Krause quotes one Homestead steelworker from 1882, reacting to his anti-union employers: "Just think of it, my fellow workmen living in a land where not twenty years ago we had a war against slavery . . . that we . . . would go in our right minds and sober senses and sign away our rights as free-born American citizens." To such men, the war had destroyed the slave system, with its bondage and its arrogant elite of wealth and power, and had upheld the principle that one was entitled to the fruits of one's labor. But their employers had a different view of autonomy, endorsing a universal submission to what one union newspaper called "the empirical and cruel law of supply and demand." Since Carnegie and many of his friends had made their original fortunes from the Civil War, it seemed especially outrageous that they were considering violent means to crush anyone who now stood in their way. At Homestead, the word that the future of American equality and democracy was at stake helped to bolster resistance throughout the strike, with tragic results.

Sometime between 1 and 2:30 AM, on July 6, eight days after the company began its lockout, union scouts spotted two barges on the Monongahela, packed with Winchester rifles and with three hundred uniformed special guards from the Pinkerton Detective Agency on board. The Pinkertons had acquired notoriety as thugs for hire. In 1888, Carnegie had employed them in a strike at the Braddock works; Frick had used Pinkerton men in the coke fields with offhand efficiency. Their presence seemed again an invitation to bloodshed.

The scouts' alarm brought thousands of strikers and other Homesteaders to the river, carrying rifles, pistols, dynamite, even fireworks left over from the Fourth of July, as well as two artillery pieces, one of them an old Union army cannon that was said to have been fired at the battle of Antietam. Throughout the day, thousands more workingmen began arriving as reinforcements from the surrounding Carnegie steel towns. For nearly fourteen hours, workers and Pinkertons traded gunfire, as the workers, crouched behind steel beam barricades, pinned down the detectives at the water's edge. The strikers attempted, unsuccessfully, to slaughter the invaders in their barges, by the use of various flaming contraptions filled with oil. By the time the exhausted Pinkertons, themselves mostly unemployed workers and college boys from the large eastern cities, surrendered to union officials and Burgess McLuckie, three detectives and seven workers lay dead or dying.

Krause describes what happened next as a "carnival of revenge," a phrase he lifts from a contemporary journalist's dispatch. He cannot resist interpreting this "carnival" in the anthropological way currently fashionable among historians, as a violent acting out of social reversals followed by an expected restoration of the established order. The analogy, with its nod to Mikhail Bakhtin and Emmanuel Le Roy Ladurie, seems strained. Homestead's workers and their friends were angry beyond the breaking point and certainly wanted revenge, but their actions seem very different from the contrived, ritualistic anarchy normally associated with carnival. In a spontaneous eruption of hatred, mixed with the relief and satisfaction of victory, a six-hundred-yard-long gauntlet of Homesteaders beat the disarmed Pinkertons and pulled off their blue-and-white uniforms. Women assaulted the guards with rocks, sticks, umbrellas, whips, and anything else close to hand. A group of Central Europeans, shrieking with grief over the body of a worker, called for a general massacre, a not unpopular position in the crowd.

It was a miracle that no additional detectives were killed: by the time Hugh O'Donnell, the head of the advisory committee, restored calm, the battered Pinkertons resembled, according to one eyewitness, the most degraded of the immigrants who passed through Ellis Island. At last, before dawn, a train arrived to carry them back to the safety of Philadelphia and New York.

Having routed the barges, the Homestead strikers had reason to be confident. They had no way of knowing fully about the continuing consultations behind the scenes of Frick, the Carnegie Steel Company's chief lawyer, Philander Knox, and the principal political leaders of Allegheny County, including the Pittsburgh Republican Party boss, Christopher Magee. At first Frick and Knox had demanded that local officials keep the works open to strikebreakers; it was when the county sheriff and his deputies failed to do so that Frick sent in the Pinkertons. Meanwhile, Magee (who was also a business associate of Frick's) pressed Governor Robert Pattison to dispatch the state militia.

Pattison, a Democrat in normally Republican Pennsylvania, had been elected two years earlier with important help from Magee, who crossed party lines in order to undo one of his GOP rivals. Pattison had run reasonably well in labor districts, and he was aware that if he sent in the soldiers he would lose thousands of votes. On July 8, two days after the Pinkertons were repulsed, a union delegation from Homestead traveled to Harrisburg, the state capital, conferred, and departed, convinced that the governor would not send in troops. But on July 10, after the local sheriff reported that the situation was out of control, Pattison yielded.

Eight thousand five hundred well-drilled soldiers set off for Homestead. The union leaders, sensing impending disaster, hastily prepared a patriotic brass band reception, in the frail hope that a friendly public demonstration might persuade the militia to remain neutral. But the commanding officer, General George Snowden, rejected the union's welcome: "I do not recognize your association, sir," Snowden curtly informed O'Donnell, before announcing that, as "master of this situation," he intended to reopen the works and restore law and order. The Homesteaders could barely believe their eyes when, on July 15, the first streams of smoke curled up from the Carnegie furnaces, manned by scab labor. Worse news came three days later, when several prominent Homesteaders, including O'Donnell and McLuckie, were charged with murder.

Alexander Berkman's attempt to assassinate Frick on July 23 was another blow to the workers. Berkman, an anarchist, had emigrated from Vilnius to the United States in 1888, and at the outbreak of the Homestead strike was running a lunchroom and ice cream parlor in Worcester, Massachusetts, with his lover, the young Emma Goldman. For several days before he arrived in Pennsylvania, rumors were spreading of an impending anarchist attack. European anarchist terrorism was then at its peak, and memories of the Haymarket bombing and the anarchist scare in Chicago six years earlier remained fresh. Although radical influence on the Homestead union was negligible, known anarchists from Pittsburgh were distributing crude handbills in the town calling for an insurrection.

Still, Berkman was acting on his own when he took a train to Pittsburgh, gained admission to Frick's office, and started shooting, in the belief that his bravery would arouse the masses. Incredibly, Frick survived and was back at his desk the same afternoon. Instead of igniting a revolution, Berkman managed to win public sympathy for the man who, in the previous six weeks, had become the most hated employer in the country. (Convicted, Berkman spent fourteen years in prison, after which he resumed his anarchist work with Goldman, was imprisoned again, and, in 1919, was deported to Russia. In 1925, he wrote *The Bolshevik Myth*, a denunciation of the Soviets' use of terror and repression of fellow revolutionaries.)

Once the steelworks resumed limited production, the strike was doomed, but it took four months before the workers gave in. Hugh O'Donnell was alarmed at the public reaction to Berkman's deed and secretly approached that year's GOP vice presidential nominee, Whitelaw Reid, to act as an intermediary with the company and reopen negotiations. Reid, himself no friend of labor, saw that the conflict at Homestead would cost the incumbent Republican President, Benjamin Harrison, votes in the autumn elections, and he sent Carnegie a cable advising him to negotiate. But Carnegie, like Frick, saw O'Donnell's mission as the sign of a split in labor's ranks and rejected further talks.

In late September, the chief justice of the Pennsylvania Supreme Court announced another round of indictments, charging nearly three dozen of the strike leaders with treason—thereby equating alleged crimes against Andrew Carnegie's property with crimes against the commonwealth. Few of the accused ever stood trial and those few were not convicted, but for a critical three weeks, the union's leaders were effectively cut off from the membership. The strikebreakers— many of them black men, the hated "nigger black sheep" brought in by a cynical management—restored production to acceptable levels, filling, among others, government military orders. Racism, provoked by Carnegie and Frick, redirected the desperate workers' fury, and the solidarity of the strike's early phases degenerated into attacks on the blacks, including a riot on November 13 that left several men badly wounded. A week after the riot, the unionists, penniless and demoralized, voted to end the walkout and return to work on the company's terms. Only about one-fifth of the old workforce was reinstated, and the union leaders were banned from every mining and metal firm in the country.

The Amalgamated's collapse in Homestead sealed the union's fate throughout the industry. When the rising young writer Hamlin Garland visited the town in 1894, he found it a squalid and brutalized place, its residents resigned and miserable, "urged on by necessity, blinded and dulled." An elaborate spy system was in place to detect any incipient organizing. Andrew Carnegie, who had wired Frick his encouragement during the lockout, returned to America to face public disapproval and expressed his sadness at what had happened in his absence. But over the next few years, Carnegie, free of the union, increased his empire's productivity while steadily lowering wages. In 1899, he confided to a friend, "Ashamed to tell you profits these days. Prodigious!" Two years later, still voicing regret over the way management had handled the strike, Carnegie sold the company to J. P. Morgan for $400 million, then devoted himself wholly to philanthropy, endowing libraries and other charities, including a relief fund for Homestead employees.

Carnegie's exultation testified to the liberated prospects of American big business at the end of the nineteenth century. In the wake of the events at Homestead, a new American economic and political order was born, founded on a new alliance between industry and the national government. Among the contracts filled by the Homestead plate department was one for sheet armor for the United States Navy, designed for state-of-the-art battleships and cruisers—proud emblems of the nation's resurgent military might. (Six years later, one of the battleships already outfitted by Carnegie, the *Maine*, exploded and sank to the bottom of Havana harbor, ushering in the Spanish–American War.) The new corporate order of the 1890s eventually brought spectacular technological innovations and greater national output, visible everywhere from the great urban skyscrapers to the swell of mass-produced durable consumer goods. It also brought new social dislocation and suffering to industrial workers, who had lost any measure of power in the workplace.

General Snowden, the militia commander, accurately described the Homestead strikers when he exclaimed in his official report that it was hard to appreciate their audacity: "They believe the works are theirs quite as much as Carnegie's." It was not until half a century later, when the CIO began organizing during the New Deal, that Homestead's steelworkers regained a durable union presence. In 1941, the local CIO dedicated a granite monument in Homestead in memory of the slain strikers, as if to mark the successful completion of a hard decades-long battle. Unionized by the United Steelworkers of America, the Homestead Works, absorbed into U.S. Steel, remained a keystone of the American steel industry and the envy of the world into the late 1950s. It looked as if it would go on forever.

But the historical memory of the Homestead strike faded as smokestack capitalism gave way to yet another America, where organized labor and its principles were severely hobbled. Beginning with a bitter strike in 1959, during which the Eisenhower administration invoked the anti-labor Taft–Hartley act, the United Steelworkers fell on the defensive, and steel imports from abroad began steadily to rise. A century after the Homestead strike, William Serrin, the former labor reporter for the *New York Times*, eloquently recounted in his book *Homestead: The Glory and Tragedy of an American Steel Town* how the steel industry, amid corporate buyouts and mergers, adversarial financial conditions, foreign competition, and plant closings, reorganized yet again in the 1970s and 1980s and abandoned the Monongahela Valley. Brave resistance by community groups and the unions proved futile—a harbinger of what awaited the labor movement generally into the early twenty-first century. Like Garland in 1892, Serrin recorded voices of bitterness and resignation, as a different reality and a different symbolism attached themselves to labor's old battleground. Today, about all that is left of the Homestead Works are a couple of preserved water pump buildings and some modest historical monuments. The great steel mills, demolished in the early 1990s, were replaced in 1999 by a shopping mall.

10

★ ★ ★ ★ ★ ▬▬▬▬▬

W. E. B. Du Bois:
A Heroic Education

IN HIS MYSTERIOUS *EDUCATION*, PRINTED IN 1907, THE AGING Henry Adams belatedly ushered in the twentieth century with a scientific prophecy of expanding chaos and accelerated historical time. A few years earlier, his fellow New Englander and Harvard man, the young W. E. B. Du Bois, ushered in the new century with his poetic, equally mysterious *The Souls of Black Folk*, and with a prophecy of his own: "The problem of the twentieth century is the problem of the color line." Both prophecies still live, with as many portents for the rest of the century ahead as for the one just passed.

The two men apparently never met or corresponded. (Adams left his teaching post in the Harvard history department eleven years before Du Bois arrived to complete his second undergraduate degree in 1888, although Du Bois did in time wind up working with Adams's disciple, Albert Bushnell Hart.) Their temperaments and their generational experiences were utterly different: one was the chronicler of insiderhood, the other was the chronicler of marginality. Yet their careers and their legacies bear comparison. Both trained in Berlin as well as at Harvard, absorbing the new spirit of Germanic scholarship without enslaving themselves to its ponderous prose style. Neither intended to become a historian, and both wrote masterworks of American history, fixed on what each believed was the crucial passage in the nation's political development (for Adams, the administrations of Jefferson and Madison, for Du Bois, Reconstruction). Both wrote novels in which a woman was the protagonist. More famously, both were men of autobiographical imagination, who wrote achingly of leading doubled lives, grandly equating the burdens of that doubleness with America itself.

Long after his death, Adams was remembered as an important historian but was read mainly by professionals. His reputation revived roughly sixty years ago, nearly achieving cultish proportions, mainly because of the *Education*. The post–World War II vogue for American studies picked up Adams as the great ironist of the Gilded Age and after, and the *Education* became an undergraduate talisman of bookish sensitivity in the Beat 1950s, a declaration of sophisticated alienation and the quest for illumination—the refined sophomore's *On the Road*.

Du Bois, who lived until 1963, has been enjoying a different kind of extended revival over the last thirty years. Instantly celebrated for *The Souls of Black Folk*, always admired as an architect of what became the modern civil rights movement, Du Bois suffered in America for his fellow traveling (capped by his formal enlistment, at age ninety-three, in the Communist Party), as well as for his pan-African nationalism. By a cosmic coincidence, he died in Ghana on the eve of the March on Washington, and the next day, Roy Wilkins—the head of the National Association for the Advancement of Colored People, which Du Bois had helped to found in 1909—respectfully informed the marchers of the news while carefully remarking that "in his later years, Dr. Du Bois chose another path" from theirs. (Less measured tributes arrived in Accra from Gus Hall, Jomo Kenyatta, Walter Ulbricht, and Mao Zedong.) It took the upheavals of the late 1960s and two decades of continuing racial turmoil for a new generation of professors and activists to repair Du Bois's reputation, not simply as a propagandist and organizer but as an intellectual. Along with its other accomplishments, the early incarnation of what has become the African American studies movement deserves great credit for retrieving *The Souls of Black Folk* and *Black Reconstruction in America*, which belong prominently in any collection of American classics.

Indeed, on campus and off, Du Bois and his writings have become so respectable that they are almost impossible to avoid. Du Bois's major books and essays (although not, curiously, *Black Reconstruction in America*) are enshrined in the Library of America. There are endless conferences, symposia, and lectures dedicated to race consciousness and the color line, often with Du Bois's work as their touchstone. And his life is the subject of a major full-dress biography by the eminent scholar David Levering Lewis, both volumes of which, separately, won the Pulitzer Prize.

The great strengths of Lewis's massive work are its thoroughness and its tone. Because Du Bois lived so long and wrote so often about himself—in three full autobiographies, one briefer memoir, and numerous shorter pieces—his biographer is faced with an unusually large amount of detective work. He must first gather the facts and then judge them against his subject's own not always reliable accounts. Lewis is an expert gatherer; he presents more information than the average reader needs to know, right down to Du Bois's college courses and grades. The trickier task, which Lewis performs well, is to avoid either debunking or apologizing. His Du Bois is a man of stark polarities and contradictions, not least the double standards of his Victorian private life and his genuine commitments to sexual as well as racial equality. Lewis reports faithfully and gracefully, keeping as his main narrative line Du Bois's complex rise to political and intellectual leadership, beginning, in his early years, as a scholar and agitator, then as the editor of the NAACP monthly *The Crisis* and as a budding pan-Africanist.

Lewis's accounts of Du Bois's central writings are less energetic. Their appearance is noted, as is their reception and connection to Du Bois's personal formation and political views; their main points are explicated alongside some interesting judgments (not all of them friendly). But Lewis prefers not to dally too long before picking up his narration of Du Bois's life. His contribution lies not so much in advancing the case for Du Bois as a major American thinker (which Lewis plainly believes he was) as in helping his readers approach Du Bois's thought historically. Given the superheated air that seems inevitably to surround conversations about race, and the frequency with which Du Bois's observations on race, especially in *The Souls of Black Folk*, are invoked as timeless and authoritative, that contribution is not small.

★ ★ ★

FROM THE MOMENT it appeared in April 1903, *The Souls of Black Folk* caused a sensation. Among black readers, James Weldon Johnson later claimed, it had the greatest impact of any book since *Uncle Tom's Cabin*. William James, Du Bois's undergraduate mentor at Harvard, dispatched a copy to his brother Henry, who privately praised it (a little backhandedly) as "the only 'Southern' book of any distinction published in many a year." In Germany, Max Weber, whose lectures Du Bois attended in his Berlin days, pronounced it a "splendid" effort and went to work finding a translator. Within two months, Du Bois's American publishers had to arrange for a third printing, as the book became the subject of discussion in periodicals across the country, with the conspicuous exception of most white Southern newspapers and those controlled by the friends and supporters of Du Bois's antagonist, Booker T. Washington. For a collection of mainly reworked, previously published essays on race relations and the Negro by a young black sociologist and historian at Atlanta University, it was an extraordinary success, unprecedented in the history of American letters.

The flashpoint of controversy was the book's third essay, "Of Mr. Booker T. Washington and Others." Du Bois had once been an admirer of Washington—he had praised him for his famous Atlanta Compromise speech urging racial accommodation in 1895—but he had moved in a more radical direction over the previous five years.

Du Bois's objections were political: he was scornful of Washington's circumspection about racial equality. But they were also cultural. Like Washington, Du Bois was dismayed by the debased condition of the Negro masses, barely one generation out of slavery, but Washington's view was tainted by a fundamental pessimism about the worth of black people's cultural resources. He had little faith that their potential extended beyond gaining the most practical knowledge about raising pigs and getting on in the world. To Du Bois, who was all for practical knowledge, Washington's pessimism was a lie, elevating a philistine materialism that denied black folks' soul.

Or, more precisely, their souls. The plural was critical to the book's larger purpose of establishing black America's cultural presence and identity. Du Bois, who as Lewis points out mounted his essays with a jeweler's precision, was very exact about the title: *The Souls of Black Folk*, not *The Soul of Black Folks*. "After the Egyptian and Indian, the Greek and Roman, the Teuton and Mongolian," he asserted in the book's most cited passage:

> the Negro is a sort of seventh son, born with a veil, and gifted with second-sight in this American world,— a world which yields him no true self-consciousness, but only lets him see himself through the revelation of the other world. It is a peculiar sensation, this double-consciousness, this sense of always looking at one's self through the eyes of others, of measuring one's soul by the tape of a world that looks on in amused contempt and pity. One ever feels his two-ness,—an American, a Negro; two souls, two thoughts, two unreconciled strivings; two warring ideals in one dark body, whose dogged strength alone keeps it from being torn asunder.
>
> The history of the American Negro is the history of this strife,— this longing to attain self-conscious manhood, to merge his double self into a better and truer self. In this merging he wishes neither of the older selves to be lost. He would not Africanize America, for America has too much to teach the world and Africa. He would

not bleach his Negro soul in a flood of white Americanism, for he knows that Negro blood has a message for the world. He simply wishes to make it possible for a man to be both a Negro and an American, without being cursed and spit upon by his fellows, without having the doors of Opportunity closed roughly in his face.

These are heartfelt, brave, and seductive words, an anatomy of racial alienation unlike any that preceded it, and they thrilled and persuaded Du Bois's admirers. Indeed, they are so seductive that even today it is easy to miss their intense ambiguity—and how they blend a painful self-consciousness and stirring forthrightness with a muddled, late-Victorian mysticism.

At the core of Du Bois's thinking was the fiction of the folk—"the unifying ideal of Race" that would elevate the Negro people and redeem America. In his early writings, Du Bois's racialist categories were deeply beholden to racial science, reinforced by his reading in the Anglo-Saxon school of American historiography and in the German Romantic nationalists from Herder to Treitschke, his teacher in Berlin. His first important foray into the subject, in an address to the newly-established American Negro Academy in 1897, posited the existence of no fewer than three primordial and eight historic races; by the time he wrote *Souls*, he had reduced the number to seven.

White racism, he acknowledged, had led many blacks to minimize race distinctions and seek instead full participation in a reformed, color-blind American democracy. But Du Bois thought it was absurd for blacks in America, no less than for Mongolians on the Asian steppes, to deny the realities of race. "The history of the world is the history not of individuals but of groups, not of nations but of races," he stated emphatically. American blacks could, however, undo the unjust and unnatural subordination of their race. And for the purposes of such a transformation, Du Bois espoused, as Kwame Anthony Appiah has observed, "what Sartre once called . . . an 'anti-racist racism.'"

The themes of racial solidarity and pride, and the rejection of integration and its supposed corollary, assimilationism, were hardly new at the start of the twentieth century. As Lewis notes, Du Bois's remarks belonged to "an old love-hate tradition" among black writers and activists that stretched back before the Civil War and had become, by Du Bois's time, two distinct tendencies: an integrationist tendency, upheld most eloquently by the aging Frederick Douglass, and a nationalist tendency, associated with Martin Delany, James Holly, and one of Du Bois's mentors, the Rev. Alexander Crummell. (Washington, with his outward placating of whites and his ideology of self-help for blacks, stood apart from both tendencies.) In his declarations on the indissolubility of race, Du Bois aligned himself with the nationalists, gathering their scattered perceptions into a statement of racial theory, raising that theory to the level of conventional racial philosophy, and then overturning all conventions by celebrating the Negro race's capacities, achievements, and strivings.

It was in these celebrations that *The Souls of Black Folk* reached its lyrical heights, foreshadowed by the pairing, as the epigraph of each chapter, of a portion of high verse (from Byron, the Bible, and so on) with a musical transcription from the black spirituals. Writing in a melange of genres—history, fiction, biography, memoir—Du Bois turned the everyday white racist characterizations of the black peasantry on their heads. Where white Americans (and some blacks) saw indolence, mindless sensuality, and an imitative culture, Du Bois discerned deep spirituality, historical purpose, and sublime artistic gifts, especially in the Negro's religious music—"the rhythmic cry of the slave" and the plaintive melodies of the spirituals (or Sorrow Songs) which, despite caricature and defilement, remained "the most beautiful expression of human experience born this side of the seas."

Not that Du Bois romanticized black people's condition, either in the North or in the South. Slavery, he wrote, had bred a "dark fatalism" and "a spirit of revolt and revenge" in the Negro. After Reconstruction's demise, the despair reappeared, driving the black masses into dissipated self-destructiveness while goading the better-off to flee from any sense of consanguinity and responsibility. It would take extraordinary, cultivated, prophetic heroes such as Crummell (to whom he devoted an essay in *Souls*) to raise the race. The notion of individual leadership was in tune with Du Bois's Germanic philosophical proclivities (especially as translated into Anglo-American letters by one of his intellectual heroes, Thomas Carlyle), and it would quickly develop into his doctrine of the Talented Tenth, that "[t]he Negro race, like all races, is going to be saved by its exceptional men." Yet without turning sentimental, Du Bois's retrieval of the cultural gifts of the most ordinary folk underwrote his case for their cultural potential and their essential unity and separateness.

Separateness was not, however, the only fact of American racial life, as Du Bois beheld America. Instead of settling for a choice of nationalism over assimilation, Du Bois offered his dialectic of doubleness; he wrote of a divided American Negro soul, part American, part Negro, the two parts ever in conflict with each other but headed for an eventual merging. Although the intellectual origins of the doubleness idea remain obscure in the text, various scholars have had little difficulty in recovering them.

Emerson's essay "The Transcendentalist," written in 1843, had fixed the term "double consciousness" in New England letters as a division between contemplation and the clatter of everyday thought. A more direct influence on Du Bois was almost certainly his beloved William James, whose lectures and writings on psychology used the term in a medical sense (borrowed from the French psychologist Binet) to denote the simultaneous existence of more than one consciousness in a single brain—what today is known familiarly as a split personality. And in college, Du Bois would have encountered the word "consciousness" used interchangeably with "soul," in any number of idealist philosophical works. But none of his teachers and predecessors applied the idea to the social psychology of race relations; nor did they fully anticipate Du Bois's stress on the Negro's intense and constant awareness of his doubleness.

Around this ultimately optimistic Sturm und Drang, Du Bois spun a paradoxical racial mysticism, blending Romantic motifs, black folklore, and more—possibly including, as the critic Eric Sundquist has suggested, the spiritualist Madame Blavatsky's occult bestseller *Isis Unveiled*, which appeared a quarter-century earlier. As a double-souled self, Du Bois's Negro was born with a veil, the seventh son of the races, and thus was blessed with second sight, "an intuitive quality," Lewis calls it, which enabled him to see things denied to other— and to do so, Du Bois implied, with a unique moral acuity. But this was Du Bois's most poignant point: the veil also blocked the Negro's sight and strivings, permitting him to see himself reflected only second-hand, "through the revelation of the other world," the world of whites. Thus the veil was a tragic gift, the mythic rendering of the color line.

Living behind the veil made blacks obscure to the point of invisibility in America. It united the Negro race but kept it from truly knowing itself, from enjoying American opportunity, from soaring to the blue sky of eternal and ideal knowledge that hung over the races of man. And so, unlike the crass Booker T. Washington, Du Bois would have the Negro rip away the veil to stand "free, free as the sunshine trickling down the morning . . . swelling with song, instinct with life, tremulous treble and darkening bass." Then, in America, there would dwell "two world-races," distinct but existing in human brotherhood, the old America enriched by "lighthearted but determined Negro humility," by "loving, jovial good humor," by "the soul of the Sorrow Songs."

★ ★ ★

LEWIS FINDS "profoundly radical" significance in all of this portentousness, and it is important to see in what respects he is correct. When Du Bois spoke of America, he meant white America, by which we would mean white Anglo-Saxon America. In 1903, the United States was still pre-pluralist: the official approving recognition of ethnicity was still half a century away. Instead, a variety of racial categories, not unlike Du Bois's, was spread carelessly over the hordes of immigrants who had arrived from Russia, central and southern Europe, and Asia. Americanness remained reserved to the Anglo-Saxons (or, in some cases, an awkward concession to the second-generation Irish, the Anglo-Saxon-Celts).

Within a decade of Du Bois's writing, Anglo-Saxon-Celtism would come under assault from numerous directions, as a younger generation of essayists, newspapermen, painters, and bohemians—Lewis calls them "mainstream," but most were on the leftish edge of liberalism—found what Randolph Bourne called "trans-national America" in the immigrant big-city slums and factory towns. With no example to embolden him, Du Bois, the first African American to take a doctorate from Harvard, anticipated this cultural revolt, and he may even have directly helped to inspire it.

The impact of *The Souls of Black Folk* on black American writing, and on writing about black America, is all the clearer. The descent of the imaginative treatments of two-ness, invisibility, and the magic behind the veil, from Ellison to Baldwin to Morrison, has by now become a stock theme in accounts of modern American literature. But the book's radicalism, its astonishing precocity, hardly ends there. It would take more than fifty years for mainstream American historical writing to catch up with Du Bois's insight about the resilience and spiritual depth of the slaves' culture, and about the benefits of Reconstruction and the ex-slaves' role in achieving those benefits (matters Du Bois would later develop at length but sketched out in *Souls'* second essay, "On the Dawn of Freedom"). And historians have only begun to comprehend and amplify Du Bois's claim (always in tension with his racial dualisms) that American culture has been marked, indeed defined, by black people's presence: "Your country? How came it yours? Before the Pilgrims landed we were here. . . . Would America have been America without her Negro people?"

Still, for all of its radical prescience, *The Souls of Black Folk* is also an intensely peculiar and Victorian work. Its poetic myth-making provides an alluring cover for ideas bounded in time and by their thinkers' experience. From the perspective of our identity-obsessed times, even undergraduates can start to pick away at the simplicities of Du Bois's "double consciousness." (Why only double? What about black *women's* consciousness? Or consciousness of region or class, or skin tone, or sexuality? Or whatever other variable comes to mind?) By such lights, Du Bois was on the right track, but he didn't get nearly far enough.

A different and far more challenging criticism arises from taking *The Souls of Black Folk* out of its American context and assessing Du Bois, in his own terms, as "a co-worker in the kingdom of culture." On this view, Du Bois looks less like a precursor of American cosmopolitanism and more like an African American Herzl (or even an American Yeats), who transmuted Germanic nationalist romance into a nationalism of and for the vilified. Yet here lie some of the more disturbing ambiguities and anachronisms of Du Bois's antiracist racism. If part of Du Bois's glory was to fashion an inspired myth of the Race, a myth as compelling as anything the Anglo-Saxonists had devised, that myth was trapped by its confused and dubious origins, a trap Du Bois himself came to realize and would struggle with over the rest of his life.

Initially, Du Bois's thoughts on race amounted to a jumble of received scientific opinion and cultural enthusiasm, held together by the sheer bravura of his uncompromising challenge to white supremacy. "Just exactly what race was," Lewis writes of his important 1897 address to the Negro Academy, "Du Bois never said clearly." In fact, Du Bois said that race was many things: in part, a biological fact, but also something more important, something akin to history or culture, arising from "differences—subtle, delicate, and elusive, though they may be—which have silently but definitely separated men into groups." Yet when he came to discuss those elusive differences, Du Bois fell back on national stereotypes—the Germans as philosophers, the French as artists—that undercut his grandiose racial taxonomy. A common language, the usual Herderian line of cultural demarcation, did not forge the world's blacks in a Negro race; moreover, the strivings and historical experiences that Du Bois tried at times to equate with a racial essence were attributes that, according to even vaguely coherent racial theory, emanated *from* racial identity, not the other way around. Although he worked very hard to avoid it, Du Bois's racializing depended on precisely the biological factors that he wished to mute, positing race as "a vast family of human beings" generally "of common blood."

Unfortunately for such projections of the black *Volksgeist*, the scholarly and popular consensus on race science was beginning to crumble at the very time that Du Bois was writing. That consensus was the victim of fresh anthropological departures that would eventually sever the linkage between physical characteristics and moral qualities and intellectual capacities. In his helpful review of Du Bois's racial ideas, Appiah shows that he was well aware that thinking on the subject was changing, and that, at least by 1911, he came to reject outright any biological grounding for nonphysical racial differences. "So far at least as intellectual and moral aptitudes are concerned," Du Bois wrote in *The Crisis*, "we ought to speak of civilizations where we now speak of races."

But what was the Negro civilization? What did the high-flown talk about "the shadow of a mighty Negro past" that "flits through the tale of Ethiopia the Shadowy and of Egypt the Sphinx" have to do with Americans who were descended from bondsmen born at the other end of the continent from Egypt and Ethiopia? What was it that bound Du Bois to an African fatherland when (as he would allow in his autobiographical *Dusk of Dawn*), neither his father nor his father's father had seen or cared for Africa, and when his mother's folk's ties, though closer, were still tenuous? What was it, that is, beyond the heritage of suffering and white racism—a heritage that would seem to link American Indians, Africans, Asians, and all the non-white people of the world in a single civilization?

If the "folk" part of *The Souls of Black Folk* was deeply flawed, the part about "souls" was a mighty projection of a racial theme from a more circumscribed set of social and personal concerns. "Between me and the other world there is ever an unasked question:" Du Bois wrote, "unasked by some through feelings of delicacy, by others through the difficulty of rightly framing it. All, nevertheless, flutter round it. . . . To the real question, How does it feel to be a problem. I seldom utter a word." Out of this, he constructed his account of the great black dilemma: the refraction, and the consequent doubling, of consciousness.

But what did the vast majority of American blacks, still living in the rural South in 1903, know of unasked questions, or of existing as a problem, or of any kind of two-ness at all? Identity, for them, as post-Emancipation white supremacy reached its zenith, was fixed by the all too straightforward realities of Southern racism, violence, and poverty. As numerous contemporaries and subsequent historians would detail, their collective identity owed little enough to the white man's world, or to any complicated refraction of it. Rather, that identity had complications of its own, elaborated among themselves in a range of social distinctions—between "dicty" snobs and "no 'counts," "better folk" and "common folk"—that confounded the mounting white racist insistence that all the world was simply and eternally divided between themselves on the one hand and "niggers" on the other.

Indeed, as Lewis repeatedly reminds us, Du Bois spoke most forcefully for, and to, a tiny segment of black America and not to black America generally—the sorts of people who turn up in *Souls* as the exemplary leaders of the race, from the educator John Hope to the novelist Charles W. Chesnutt, to the anti-lynching organizer Ida B. Wells-Barnett. Most of them had either been born in the North or had resettled there, and had come of age in the aftermath of Reconstruction. Many were college-educated. In adulthood, they formed a small, highly accomplished, professional black upper crust, "whose parents," as Lewis puts it, "had made a successful go of it in slavery times and had family silver to go with their genteel manners." By no means did they uniformly thrill to *The Souls of Black Folk*—least of all, those allied with Booker T. Washington. But although some of them backed Washington, it was precisely among these professionals that black resentment of Washington's admixture of uplift and resignation ran deepest, among those who had never flinched from believing that their capacities and achievements and backgrounds made them the equal of any white person. And it was among this minority of the black minority that Du Bois's theme of doubleness hit a nerve.

Framed in this way, *The Souls of Black Folk* emerges as the testament to an important divide in black American life nearly a century ago, a divide shaped by starkly different regional contexts of white racism. Du Bois, the man of the expansive, industrializing, polyglot, racially divided North, could not imagine any kind of racial progress short of a full-scale assault on the most formidable citadels of politics and learning. Such an assault, however, made the most sense to those in conditions fundamentally unlike those of the rural, sharecropping, one-party South. To the extent that Du Bois and Washington spoke to these different realities, Lewis argues that they effectively argued past each other. But their Manichean struggle would have taken place "in one form or another" even if neither man had surfaced.

★   ★   ★

FINALLY, THE STRANGENESS and the audacity of *The Souls of Black Folk* arose less from broad historical circumstances than from the strangeness and audacity of its author. Du Bois pitched his arguments to his intended Talented Tenth, the "quality folk" who prided themselves on being "representative Negroes." As his ideas took shape, however, the young Du Bois may have been—and may have felt himself to be—the most marginal man in America.

The future prophet of the color line had been born, after all, a mulatto ("in blood, about one-half or more Negro and the rest French and Dutch" he claimed in one letter) in Massachusetts, the Northern state widely considered the cradle of abolitionism; but it was a state, he learned early in life, that was hardly free of racial prejudice. At

Harvard—only the seventh man of African descent admitted—he won abundant praise from his teachers, but he felt distanced from his fellow students, by his humble class background as well as by his color. He would later write that he was "at but not of" the place.

In Berlin—where, Lewis observes, Du Bois spent some of the most exuberant and carefree days of his life—he soaked up all he could in the classroom, awestruck, proud, determined to make the most of his miraculous if fully merited opportunity. Yet in Germany, the division in Du Bois's soul deepened, as he heard his teacher Heinrich von Treitschke, one of the intellectual founders of Prussian Aryan nationalism—"the greatest of all the professors," in Du Bois's estimation—explode from the lecture podium, *"Die Mullatten sind niedrig! Sie fuhlen sich niedrig!"* ("The mulattoes are inferior! They feel themselves inferior!") Du Bois's Berlin notebook is filled with the generic self-conscious angst of a precocious graduate student abroad, but with special twists and turns. Descriptions of solitary midnight ceremonies by candlelight, with prayer to the zeitgeist about fulfilling his destiny, sit alongside descriptions of mornings given over to contemplation and singing to himself, in his German boardinghouse, "America the Beautiful" and "Steal Away to Jesus." And then, after his return, and as he completed his doctorate at Harvard, America's foremost young black scholar found himself confined in his first teaching post to the lower reaches of the black academy, at what was then the third-rate Wilberforce College in Ohio, knowing he would never teach in any white college or university.

Du Bois, in short, suffered a singular fate: raised by his heroic education to scholarly levels unreached by all but a handful of American whites, he still lived in a civilization where his color marked him as a nonperson, one who, when he traveled, rode the Jim Crow car. A man of reason, he would not forsake his reason's achievements; but the world of reason turned out to be utterly unreasonable, casting him, of all people, as a pariah. Here, with all of its idiosyncrasies, was the matrix of double consciousness, and it was as untypical an experience as could be imagined. But brilliant and arrogant as he was, and with the prestige he could command among his fellow blacks and sympathetic whites, Du Bois was able, in *The Souls of Black Folk*, to translate his personal dilemma into a universal drama of race, and render it convincing.

He did not stop here. Lewis's first volume describes Du Bois's departure from academic life and his early career as a movement leader, and closes with his intervention on behalf of the colonized colored races at Versailles in 1919. The second volume is even more crowded with events, from Du Bois's bruising bouts with Marcus Garvey, his break with the NAACP, and his turn to Marxism (and the writing of *Black Reconstruction in America*), on to the admixture of civil rights work, Stalinist apologetics, Third Worldism, and persecution by federal authorities than eventually led him to Ghana in 1961. Never satisfied, never at rest, Du Bois kept refashioning his alienated consciousness (and, in his continuing autobiographical works, his view of himself), carrying his wounded sensibilities and strivings to the eve of segregation's downfall. Over these momentous decades, however, *The Souls of Black Folk* won Du Bois the most admirers, as it does today.

And so, with its dated racialism and its mythohistorical fantasies, it will surely endure. In its endurance, however, lie some of its greatest ironies. If, in its own time, *Souls* was a peculiar thing, Jim Crow's subsequent demise has made its themes of doubleness and identity far more prominent, not just for black intellectuals but for a newly expanded black middle class, on whom the competing claims of particularism and acceptance in an America where racism powerfully abides bear down all the harder. Du Bois's double consciousness may prove inadequate to these pressures—simplistic in its dualism, reducing universal ambivalences and anxieties to purely racial terms. But if *Souls* imparts a heady, uplifting love of blacknesss and the soul of the Sorrow Songs—and with that (in its more dubious passages) a fabricated racial mysticism—it also describes an act of refusal, a refusal to allow alienation to become a surrender to self-reference or to any cramped conception of race.

I sit with Shakespeare and he winces not. Across the color line I move arm in arm with Balzac and Dumas, where smiling men and welcoming women glide in gilded halls. From out of the caves of evening that swing between the strong-limbed earth and the tracery of the stars, I summon Aurelius and Aristotle and what soul I will, and they come graciously with no scorn or condescension.

In his reclamation of the spirituality of the oppressed and the despised, Du Bois also wrote a paean to what nowadays is sometimes glibly stigmatized as the culture of the oppressors. For all of their orotund phrasing, it took a beautiful defiance to write these words in 1903. They were an assertion of individuality and genius as well as of race pride. Today, in a very different but still racialized America, their beauty has not dimmed.

11

★ ★ ★ ★ ★ ====

Theodore Roosevelt: Politics and Folly

THEODORE ROOSEVELT, THE YOUNGEST MAN TO SERVE AS president of the United States, and the youngest ex-president, also died young, at the age of sixty, in 1919. Apart from the four presidents who have been assassinated, only two of Roosevelt's predecessors, James K. Polk and Chester A. Arthur, died younger than he did, as has only one of his successors, Warren G. Harding. The asthmatic child who grew to become the foremost American exponent of strenuous, combative virility lived at full throttle, even during the ten years after he left the White House—and he paid for it.

Edmund Morris's *Colonel Roosevelt* covers those last ten years, concluding Morris's three-volume biography and displaying the same penchant for detailed storytelling that dominated the first two volumes. Morris spares his readers little about Roosevelt's dramas, including his physical torments. Recurrences of tropical malaria, a gunshot wound from a would-be assassin, painful abscesses from old injuries, a gruesome rectal hemorrhage (and subsequent surgery), bouts with rheumatism—Morris describes each one at length, until Roosevelt finally succumbs to a pulmonary embolism (or more likely, Morris contends, a heart attack). For Morris, Roosevelt's bravery in courting and suffering these agonies testifies to his outsized personality. Yet as Morris also recognizes, Roosevelt's will to power—which enabled him, as president, to transform the office—came with awful physical and emotional costs.

Theodore Roosevelt's dogged courage and toughness are beyond dispute, and they did not fade in his later years. In 1912, while he was headed for a campaign stop in Milwaukee during his schismatic third-party run for the presidency, a lunatic shot him in the chest at close range. After refusing medical attention, TR proceeded to the rally, climbed to the podium, and gestured for silence as the blood soaked through his exposed shirtfront. Morris writes:

> Waiting for the noise to subside, he reached into his jacket pocket for his speech. The fifty-page typescript was folded in half. He did not notice that it had been shot through until he began to read. For some reason, the sight of the double starburst perforation seemed to shock him more than the blood he had seen on his fingertips. He hesitated, temporarily wordless, then tried to make the crowd laugh again with his humorous falsetto: "You see, I was going to make quite a long speech."

More than an hour later, Roosevelt came to the last page of his prepared remarks, and only then did he agree to be taken to the hospital. He survived because the bullet, which was headed straight for his heart, had had to pass through a heavy overcoat and a steel-reinforced eyeglass case as well as the lengthy typescript, before it nestled against his fourth right rib.

Formidable as he was, though, Roosevelt could not ward off the unsteadiness and pathos of his final years, and he brought a good deal of it on himself. After he voluntarily left the White House in 1909—he had conveniently, and in retrospect unwisely, adhered to custom and forsworn a third term four years earlier—Roosevelt preferred to be addressed not as Mr. President but simply as Colonel, the army rank he had earned with the Rough Riders in Cuba during the Spanish-American War (hence the title of Morris's book). President no longer, Roosevelt proclaimed that he was determined to be an ordinary private citizen. But he was a proud and energetic man, still in the prime of life, and he took poorly to powerlessness.

Roosevelt's idea of gentlemanly retirement was immediately to commence a perilous year-long safari to Africa with one of his sons, funded in part by Andrew Carnegie, on which it was estimated that he personally killed nine lions, eight elephants, twenty zebras, seven giraffes, and six buffaloes. (Those carcasses and hundreds more of big-game animals slaughtered by the expedition were duly salted and shipped home to be stuffed and displayed at the Smithsonian Institution and American Museum of Natural History, burnishing Roosevelt's reputation as one of America's most intrepid hunting naturalists.) Before he returned to the United States, he completed a tumultuous six-week public speaking tour that took him from Khartoum through the major capitals of Europe.

Once back in America, Roosevelt came to regard his anointed successor, William Howard Taft, as the betrayer of his Square Deal policies, and so he set forth to regain his job. But by the time Roosevelt broke publicly with the White House, at the end of 1911, the sitting president with all the perquisites of patronage had already sewn up the support of Republican Party leaders. Roosevelt won the overwhelming majority of the vote in the ensuing nonbinding Republican primaries, but it was insufficient to deny Taft renomination. Infuriated, TR bolted from the GOP to run on the Progressive Party ticket and advance a program of governmental activism that he called the New Nationalism, which he had started propounding two years earlier.

Roosevelt had the pleasure of finishing second and seeing Taft trounced in 1912—TR regarded the Democrat Woodrow Wilson's victory as a foregone conclusion after Taft won the Republican nomination—but his Bull Moose candidacy ruined his reputation with the old-guard bosses and big-business conservatives who controlled the GOP. Morris does not speculate, but had Roosevelt tempered his outrage and grandiosity and bided his time, he almost certainly would have won the Republican nomination four years later. Instead, he spent a good part of those four years assailing President Wilson from the sidelines as a weakling in foreign affairs, only to be passed over by the Republicans once again in 1916. Roosevelt then had to suffer the humiliation of campaigning in support of the dull, cautious, moderately progressive GOP candidate Charles Evans Hughes, even as the crowds shouted "We Want Teddy!" (Drab though he was, Evans very nearly defeated Wilson, as Roosevelt surely would have done had he been the nominee.)

When the United States at last entered the Great War in 1917, Roosevelt lobbied hard for a military commission to lead a volunteer regiment in France, but the administration he had denounced for years turned him down. In his own place, Roosevelt proudly sent two of his sons off to fight, only to be devastated when his youngest boy, Quentin, was killed flying a combat mission over France.

Above and beyond his run at the presidency, Roosevelt had done his utmost, after he left the White House, to remain, as he put it famously, "the man in the arena." Yet he lacked a firm political mooring and lurched furiously between safaris of one sort or another—joining another tropical expedition in 1914, this time along the uncharted Rio da Dúvida in Brazil, and very nearly perishing; delivering hundreds of political speeches and public lectures; writing an autobiography along with seven other books, as well as hundreds of articles, essays, and speeches on whatever artistic, literary, scientific, or political topic struck his fancy. Even as his body began seriously to fail, Roosevelt set his sights on yet another presidential campaign in 1920. But his ferocity of spirit could not make up for his accumulated political mistakes, and he was left to public and private exertions that succeeded chiefly in exhausting him. Quentin's death was the last crushing blow: the Rough Rider who had loudly romanticized war as uplifting and even ennobling sobbed over his poor "Quentyquee." "What made this loss so devastating to him," Morris observes, "was the truth it conveyed: that death in battle was no more glamorous than death in an abattoir."

This is Morris's writing at its best: compact and psychologically astute. Having lived with Theodore Roosevelt for half as long as Roosevelt himself actually lived, and having immersed himself in Roosevelt's enormous output of writings, Morris knows the details of the man's life and grasps his temperament better than any other biographer or historian ever has. With a few deft strokes, offset by dry wit, Morris brings TR alive—and even though he greatly admires his subject, he does not always place him in the most flattering light. "He used the strongest language," Morris observes of Roosevelt's martial instincts, "to emasculate men who hated militarism, or recoiled like women from the chance to prove themselves in armed action: 'aunties' and 'sublimated sweetbreads,' shrilly piping for peace. (The tendency of his own voice to break into the treble register was an embarrassment in that regard.)"

On TR's attitudes toward the poverty-stricken, Morris writes shrewdly that "like many well-born men with a social conscience, Roosevelt liked to think that he empathized with the poor. He was democratic, in a detached, affable way." But if Roosevelt deluded himself, Morris continues, his aristocratic confidence also meant that "he lacked some of the neuroses of progressives—economic envy and race hatred especially. His radicalism was a matter of energy rather than urgency."

The major drawbacks in *Colonel Roosevelt*, as in the other two volumes, have to do with Morris's uneven handling of Roosevelt's true vocation, which was that of a professional party politician. Roosevelt's adventures as an explorer, his writings as an amateur historian and naturalist, his gargantuan appetites for art, literature, and science, are all very interesting, and they are essential topics in any full-length biography. But what makes Roosevelt worthy of three monumental volumes is his political career and its legacy. Unfortunately, Morris the discerning biographer and skilled teller of stories is less helpful in explaining why Roosevelt succeeded and why he failed in public life. Not that Morris skimps on politics: election campaigns, factional rivalries, competing programs and philosophies, backroom machinations, all (or mostly) get related in full. Roosevelt's drive, enthusiasm, and toothy grin—as well as his capacity to hate, and his insistence on seeing any social or political problem as cause for combat—helped define the man's politics, and Morris describes them well. But Morris is less sure-handed—and at moments he seems uncomfortable—when he comes up against Roosevelt the calculating, contradictory, and cunning politician.

It is a fascinating and, finally, tragic tale. Roosevelt could never have become a successful president, let alone a statesman, had he not been a supremely successful party politician—a point that the historian John Morton Blum made more than sixty years ago in his classic study, *The Republican Roosevelt*. During his presidency, Roosevelt's political resourcefulness helped him earn his eventual place on Mount Rushmore. Thereafter, though, he squandered his political gifts, having lost the discipline required to use them effectively, and his pride and ambition undid him.

★ ★ ★

IT WAS UNUSUAL for a young man of Roosevelt's background to choose politics as a lifelong career. Born in Manhattan in 1858 to genteel wealth, with a father who propounded the do-good Christianity that would eventually flower as the Social Gospel, "Teedie" could have been expected to join a high-minded private civic association or perhaps to turn his literary interests toward excoriating the vulgar parvenus of the Gilded Age. All the while he could have established himself as a well-heeled New York lawyer, his initial profession of choice. But the law bored young Roosevelt and he gravitated to the rough-and-tumble of electoral politics, which offered opportunities to fight for and then exert real power. (He would claim for years that his motives for entering politics were entirely altruistic, but his fellow politicians knew better than to accept an altruist on his own stated terms.)

Roosevelt naturally became a Republican, and as an ambitious young state assemblyman, he advanced the conventional ideas of his class, above all that the chief problems besetting American government were the callous and corrupt Democratic urban machines with their low immigrant voters, and the only slightly less offensive graft-hungry politicos inside the Republican Party. When it looked as if one of the latter, the spoilsman and rogue senator James G. Blaine of Maine, would win the GOP presidential nomination in 1884, Roosevelt fiercely helped lead the fight against him. After Blaine prevailed, disgusted high-minded reformers, who became known as Mugwumps, left the party and backed the Democratic candidate, New York's governor Grover Cleveland. Whatever his drawbacks, the Mugwumps asserted, Cleveland at least was a man of decency and integrity—and sound economic conservatism. Roosevelt paused, swallowed his bitterness—and backed Blaine.

In the first important test of his political mettle, Roosevelt had apparently violated every standard of political honor. He himself said in private that he thought Blaine unfit for the presidency (although he had been a particularly effective secretary of state). His closest political associates—except for his friend and mentor Henry Cabot Lodge, who also supported Blaine—condemned him as a selfish, misguided conniver. And in the first volume of his trilogy, Morris also sounds bewildered and offended by Roosevelt's decision. Morris does observe that Roosevelt may simply have been acting as a professional politician, but this doesn't offset his dismay at what he calls TR's flagrant immorality: "No adulterer," Morris writes, "could more adroitly combine illicit lovemaking with matrimonial obligations than Roosevelt in his relations with both wings of the party in 1884." Morris mugwumpishly concludes that Roosevelt must have acted out of self-interest.

In fact, it was far from clear that supporting Blaine was in Roosevelt's best political interest, especially after Cleveland won the election. The Mugwumps claimed the credit, and the young assemblyman looked like a loser as well as a tool of corruption. Roosevelt thought that his party loyalty "meant to me pretty sure political death," and for a time he assumed that his political career was over. Nor was Roosevelt, in choosing his party above his personal preference, thinking only about himself.

Roosevelt was absolutely certain that, like it or not, most Republican voters favored Blaine. He respected the process by which the party had made its decision and thus felt bound to respect that decision. Pursuing power in a democracy meant working by the means of organized political parties; party success required allegiance and discipline that surmounted personal opinions and considerations; breaking that discipline betrayed an unserious commitment to pursuing power. The only professional course for Roosevelt—and, on this view, the only democratic course—was to abide by and support the party's nominee, with the hope that down the road, his own side, and perhaps he himself, would command the party.

The Blaine episode was Roosevelt's coming-of-age as a professional politician. (Only in time did TR's good fortune at Blaine's defeat become apparent; Morris mystically says this shows that "fate, as usual, was on [Roosevelt's] side.") Soon after, he openly proclaimed party loyalty as a democratic virtue, and described elevated nonpartisanship as "not only fantastic, but absolutely wrong." The Mugwumps, Roosevelt later wrote, were dangerous elitists who "distrusted the average citizen and shuddered over the 'coarseness' of the professional politicians." Nonpartisan do-gooders lacked virility—the quality he prized above all others and equated with courage—and in their ambivalence about the hard realities of political power were "almost or quite as hostile to manliness as they were to unrefined vice." Roosevelt would press for reforms that served the public good, even if they displeased some of his fellow Republicans, but he would also strike and sustain the requisite alliances with practical, hard-nosed party bosses.

By 1898, when he won the Republican nomination for governor of

New York, Roosevelt had earned a reputation not simply as a hero in the Spanish-American War, but as a progressive who was a reliable party man. Once elected, Roosevelt pushed successfully for reforms, including stricter taxation of public utilities franchises, and antago- nized Thomas "Boss" Platt, the head of the state's GOP machine; but he also worked closely with Platt on patronage and legislation. Nei- ther the Boss's creature nor his enemy, Roosevelt exhibited enough independence that Platt was happy to back TR's nomination for vice president in 1900—a booby prize that would conveniently remove Roosevelt from Albany. Roosevelt dutifully accepted his assignment, but also saw its advantages. Based on his experience as governor, he was coming to believe that only the federal government had sufficient power to tame the dynamic new forces of industrial America, and from the start, he coolly regarded the vice presidency as a stepping stone to the White House. When McKinley's assassination in 1901 shockingly made him an accidental president, Roosevelt was prepared to exercise the office with the political finesse and, if necessary, merci- lessness required of any successful president.

An important party leader who had opposed putting Roosevelt on the ticket, McKinley's political manager, Mark Hanna of Ohio, reportedly said in frustration to TR's backers, "Don't any of you realize that there's only one life between this madman and the Presidency?" Now that he was president, Roosevelt would refute such slanders. No radical, let alone a madman, he believed mainly in the gospel of social works and upright conduct he had learned from his father. At a time when genuine radicals were preaching some variant of state socialism, Roosevelt insisted that "the true function of the State, as it interferes in social life, should be to make the chances of competition more even, not to abolish them." Abraham Lincoln, whom Roosevelt venerated, could have said as much.

But Republican Party orthodoxy had changed since the Civil War, as the democratic nationalism of Lincoln and Ulysses S. Grant gave way to a doctrine of laissez-faire that in theory abjured any role for government in society except to act as an impartial umpire in times of friction and conflict, but in reality simply cleared the path for large industrial and financial interests. Roosevelt, on the contrary, looked back to the Civil War era, understood the federal government's potential capacity to serve the common good, and insisted that "the sphere of the State's action may be vastly increased without in any way diminishing the happiness of either the many or the few." He naturally viewed the presidency as the center of that action: "I believe in a strong executive," he said. "I believe in power." In government as in business, he believed, "the guiding intelligence of the man at the top" determined success or failure. He would later describe the president, with no false modesty, as "merely the most important among a large number of public servants," but the president still had "more power than in any other office in any great republic or constitutional monarchy of modern times."

Guided by a moral code of duty and personal honor instead of any political ideology, Roosevelt took up the fight against what he called "the selfish individual" who needed to learn that "we must now shackle cunning by law exactly as a few centuries back we shackled force by law." Extremes of poverty and wealth appalled him and he ascribed these disorders not to impersonal social forces but to sly, effete men who combined selfishness with willful ignorance. Roosevelt's great domestic achievements as president included prosecuting the antitrust *Northern Securities* case, settling the anthracite coal strike in 1902, winning passage of the Meat Inspection Act and the Pure Food and Drug Act, and regulating railroad rates under the Elkins and Hepburn Acts. None sprang from any social theory greater than what he called "social efficiency," which he said derived loosely from a "love of order, ability to fight well and breed well, capacity to subordinate the interests of the individual to the interests of the community." In foreign policy he translated "social efficiency" to mean military preparedness and active participation in global affairs, in order to ensure international orderliness and virtue—a civilizing mission that, especially in the Caribbean and the Pacific, can only be described as imperialist.

Yet Roosevelt's pursuit of "social efficiency," with all of its noble and dubious implications, would have been fruitless without his expert handling of the intricacies of partisan and presidential politics. Confronted, upon entering the White House, with a powerful rival in the kingmaker, Senator Hanna, who fancied himself a possible presidential contender in 1904, Roosevelt moved swiftly and relentlessly to assert his control over his party, regionally and locally as well as in Washington. The contest with Hanna, Roosevelt would later observe, was regrettable since they agreed about a great deal, not least on securing the Panama Canal treaty in 1903. TR considered the senator overall a force for good. But politics was politics. Concerning his takeover of the state party in South Carolina, one of many, Roosevelt remarked on how he "ruthlessly threw out all the old republican politicians" and substituted his own loyalists. Hanna died suddenly of typhoid fever early in 1904, and the threat to Roosevelt's renomination disappeared; but by then, he fully commanded the levers of power inside the GOP.

Morris nicely describes the Roosevelt–Hanna rivalry in his second volume, although he focuses too much on TR's shrewd use of Booker T. Washington as both a symbol and an adviser in order to undermine Hanna's crucial Southern base of support. Morris's blow-by-blow account of Roosevelt's mastery of Congress likewise shows off TR's political guile to good effect. But Morris's fascination with personalities and stories detracts from an understanding of Roosevelt's purposeful strategizing in, for example, playing off Republican divisions over revising tariff rates (about which he cared little) in order to secure regulation of the railroads (about which he cared a great deal).

Morris describes the twists and turns of Roosevelt's foreign policy copiously, but he could have accounted more exactly for how TR's presumptions about the presidency and congressional indifference to international affairs repeatedly led him to bypass checks on executive power. Neither the Panama Canal negotiations nor the later Santo

Domingo crisis (which led TR to promulgate unilaterally the expansive so-called Roosevelt Corollary to the Monroe Doctrine) affected much of the American public, and the outcomes can be justified. But Roosevelt's conduct of "Big Stick" diplomacy called into question his oft-declared reverence for the Constitution.

Once he left the presidency, however, Roosevelt the political master was bereft. That he thought he could live without power was his greatest miscalculation. His hubris in believing that the good of the nation, indeed the world, hinged on his getting it back caused his tragic downfall. There are historians who take a kinder view and see in Roosevelt's New Nationalist presidential campaign in 1912 the redeeming prophetic elements of what would become the heart of American liberalism through the New Deal and beyond. Those elements are certainly there to be found: Roosevelt made proposals for social insurance, workers' compensation, women's suffrage, an inheritance tax, and more, including a national health service drawn from existing government medical agencies.

Morris ventures no such connections between the New Nationalism and the New Deal. But he describes well the unreality of the Progressive Party convention, its delegates "scrubbed and prosperous looking, well dressed and well behaved, churchgoing, charitable, bourgeois to a fault." The high-mindedness of 1884 had become the respectable crusading purity of 1912. But more to the point, Theodore Roosevelt, the hardheaded young pol, had become, out of his personal dejection and hurt pride, the latest crusader-in-chief, making the one move, defying an incumbent president of his own party, that was guaranteed to seal the end of his political career. In doing so, he guaranteed, despite himself, that the Republican Party would be an agent not of progressive reform, let alone "social efficiency," but of the laissez-faire, pro-business conservatism of the Harding–Coolidge era—the era that brought the rampant speculation and growing inequality that laid the groundwork for the Great Depression.

Here, in Roosevelt's lifelong search for power gone haywire, is the key to his tragic later years and their lasting importance to American politics. After the Progressive Party debacle of 1912 left the old guard in charge of the GOP, it would take a Democrat whom Roosevelt despised, Woodrow Wilson, to carry out some of the party's reform proposals of 1912, including a federal workmen's compensation law, votes for women, and the establishment of a federal income tax. Only many years later, after a Democratic Party led by Northern liberals made an alliance with the remnants of TR's progressive Republicans, would other reforms, including Social Security, come to pass, during the presidency of Roosevelt's slyer, more enduring, and less egoistic distant cousin, Franklin. Even then, the conservatism emboldened by TR's prideful miscalculations, now fully entrenched among Republicans, would resist change ferociously and succeed in blocking some of the social reforms of 1912 until our own time. Just as modern liberalism has been built, in part, on the first President Roosevelt's achievements, so the history of the modern conservative Republican Party owes something to Colonel Roosevelt's blunders in attempting to reclaim his place.

12

★ ★ ★ ★ ★ ══════════

The Liberals
and the Leftists

THE RISE AND FALL OF THE PROGRESSIVES AND THE ADVENT
of the New Deal redirected the American egalitarian tradition, building on but also greatly enlarging the democratic nationalism of the
Lincoln Republicans. As the locus of egalitarian politics changed,
so did the character of American dissent. Lodged more than ever in
national organizations, accorded a legitimacy and power forcefully
denied it for much of the nineteenth century (above all in the realm of
organized labor), a more coherent if endlessly contentious and squabbling American left emerged. The Bolshevik Revolution in Russia created an international political and ideological force with which, until
the late twentieth century, American dissenters of every kind would
have to come to terms, for better or worse. In the wake of these developments, and especially the victories of the civil rights movement of
the 1950s and 1960s, scholars as well as activists began rewriting the
history of American egalitarianism, emphasizing the primacy of the
radical left, as well as of ordinary, powerless Americans, as the chief
agents of equality and justice.

Michael Kazin's book *American Dreamers* surveys the history of
American leftists and their impact on the nation over the last two cen-

turies, and it presupposes that this impact has been enormous. But Kazin is a judicious scholar without bluster, a professor of history at Georgetown and coeditor of *Dissent*, and his assessments are carefully measured. Kazin concedes that radical leftists have often been out of touch with prevailing values, including those of the people they wish to liberate. He concludes that American radicals have done more to change what he calls the nation's "moral culture" than to change its politics.

And yet, even as Kazin tries to avoid romanticizing the left, and even as he emphasizes how leftists have repeatedly failed to achieve their radical goals, his book still gives the left the lion's share of the credit for pushing the great reforms that have been enacted. In doing so, it leaves unchallenged some conventional conceptions about American politics and how change happens. These conventions begin with a presumption about who controls American political life, what C. Wright Mills called the "power elite," an interlocking directorate of wealth and bureaucracy at the top. Kazin refers to this directorate interchangeably as the "establishment" or the "governing elite." Unless challenged by radicals, this elite, in his view, is slow to right social wrongs, but without the support of the elite's more enlightened elements, the radicals remain in the political wilderness.

Auspiciously—as with the abolition of slavery, the rise of the New Deal, and the victories of the civil rights movement—momentous changes supported by radicals have indeed come to pass. Yet Kazin argues that the liberal components of the governing elite have supported major reforms strictly in order to advance purposes of their own. Abraham Lincoln and the Republicans, he writes, embraced emancipation only halfway through the Civil War, when it became clear that doing so "could speed victory for the North" and save the Union, their true goal. Franklin D. Roosevelt endorsed labor's rights only when he needed to court labor's votes. Even when they are successful, Kazin writes, the radicals—"decidedly junior partners in a coalition driven by establishment reformers"—end up shoved aside as the liberals enact their more limited programs and take all of the credit. Prophets without honor, the leftists return to the political margins where they and later radicals dream new and bigger dreams— and, Kazin argues, enrich the moral culture—until another social movement jars the establishment.

Some radical historians, most conspicuously Howard Zinn, have described this pattern as a chronicle of thoroughgoing oppression. In their view, the reforms initiated by radicals have practically always turned into scams, orchestrated by clever rulers to preserve and even reinforce their power. Kazin has strongly criticized Zinn's writing, assailing his best-known book, *A People's History of the United States* (more than two million copies sold) as "bad history." Zinn's ideological animus, Kazin charges, "reduces the past to a Manichean fable" of evil tyrants and the noble downtrodden. Zinn, Kazin complains, fails to explain why most Americans have accepted, indeed, celebrated the capitalist United States. And Kazin pointedly rejects Zinn's jaundiced view of liberal reformers and their reforms: the Emancipation Proclamation and the Voting Rights Act, he insists, were important political advances and not merely establishment ruses.

Yet if *American Dreamers* is far sounder history than Zinn's work, they both follow a basic design: radicals challenge the privileged and, when successful, move liberals to action, but then the liberals co-opt them, undercutting radical transformation while claiming credit for advancing social justice. Unlike conservatives, liberals accede to pressure from below, but they do so out of calculated, often selfish necessity rather than high principle, devoted to salvaging a distressed, existing status quo and heading off fundamental political change.

The basic problem with this approach lies in its overidentification of dissent with protest to the exclusion of politics. For Kazin, the left consists of anyone who has sought to achieve, in his words, "a radically egalitarian transformation of society." The definition embraces an enormous array of spokesmen and causes, and Kazin's account runs from the abolitionists and workingmen radicals of the Jacksonian era through a succession of socialists, women's suffragists, Greenwich Village bohemians, and civil rights protesters, down to today's left-wing professoriat. But it excludes what might be called the political egalitarians, from pragmatic social democrats to committed liberals, who actually effected radical transformations, including the most radical transformation of all in American history, slavery's destruction. Because Kazin lumps these advocates with the "establishment," his left is always bound for glorious political defeat. Because he regards reformers as grudging and half-hearted, lacking in purity and prone to pursuing their political self-interest, he misconstrues how much of American history has been driven not by co-optation and frustration on the left but by convergences of protest and politics.

★ ★ ★

MOST OF *AMERICAN DREAMERS* consists of crisp and useful summaries of nearly four decades' worth of historical research about American radical movements, including Kazin's own work on the amorphous populist strain in American politics. The lives of both long-forgotten radicals and the better-known—such as Emma Goldman—were usually similar to those movements: a season or two, and sometimes several seasons, of fame (or notoriety) and even of influence, followed by a return to the fringe.

After the Civil War, for example, various radicals tried to move beyond emancipation to ensure full economic as well as political equality for ex-slaves, and they gained some support in Congress. Most of the ex-slaves, however, hoped that Reconstruction would provide, Kazin writes, "a chance to exercise the same rights white citizens had long taken for granted"—hopes that were "hardly revolutionary" but aimed instead "to fulfill the promise of liberal capitalism." Those hopes meshed well with the aims of Southern black political leaders who "generally fit the classic model of the self-made man."

Reconstruction did achieve major victories, including the ratification of the Fourteenth and Fifteenth Amendments, but there were limits, and these limits thwarted the sweeping plans, advanced by Congressman Thaddeus Stevens and a band of Republican radicals in Washington, to confiscate the lands of ex-Confederates and distribute them to the freedmen. As it turned out, securing even basic civil and political rights for Southern blacks required exerting federal military force for more than a decade after Appomattox. Liberal reformism finally slackened, and a violent counterrevolution by Southern whites overthrew Reconstruction in the 1870s. It would take another three generations before a Second Reconstruction emerged.

Even at the zenith of its popularity, during the decade before World War I, the Socialist Party, led by the charismatic Eugene V. Debs, failed to turn itself into an enduring mass movement. Something about America—especially its overarching ideals of classless individualism—blunted the Socialists' appeal and led workers to support the so-called "bread-and-butter" unionism of Samuel Gompers and the American Federation of Labor, which would fight for maximum gain within the system. And some things about American radicals, including the Socialists—their inability to handle what Daniel Bell called America's "give-and-take, political world," their chronic penchant for self-righteous dogmatism and sectarian squabbling—repeatedly undermined left-wing campaigns. Instead, Progressive Era liberals and New Dealers enacted reforms that frustrated radical change. Debs's successor, Norman Thomas, famously quipped, when asked by a reporter whether Franklin D. Roosevelt was actually carrying out his socialist program, "Yes, he is carrying it out in a coffin."

"And yet," Kazin seems to say. The familiar explanations for radicalism's political failures proposed decades ago by Bell and Irving Howe still have merit, but, Kazin believes, they cannot tell the entire story. "Without political power or honor as prophets," he insists, "leftists still helped to make the United States a more humane society." They have done so largely outside of conventional politics, building what he calls an evolving "culture of rebellion."

Alienated novelists, poets, playwrights, filmmakers, and songwriters, Kazin argues, as well as muckraking journalists and left-wing historians, have influenced many more Americans than would ever embrace a radical political movement. From Harriet Beecher Stowe to Bruce Springsteen, he finds a persistent radical artistic imagination that he believes has been the left's mightiest weapon. To understand American radicalism's humanizing power, and how the left changed the nation, it is less important, in Kazin's view, to consider how Americans voted than to consider what books and magazines they read, what plays and movies they attended, and what songs they heard and sang.

The point is perceptive even if it is not especially novel: recall Abraham Lincoln's famous if apocryphal remark to Stowe calling her the little woman who wrote the book that started the great Civil War. Kazin is at his most effective when he discusses the impact of fiction like John Steinbeck's *The Grapes of Wrath* or, more ironically, the lifelong Republican Frank Capra's populist films of the 1930s and 1940s. Without question, imagined archetypes like Tom Joad or Jefferson Smith have left stronger and more lasting impressions on American perceptions than any radical tract.

As Kazin himself remarks, though, some of the artists promoted by the left—he mentions Richard Wright and could have included Bob Dylan—did eventually find the constraints of what Dylan called "finger pointing" oppressive. Kazin has much to say about the ways in which left-wing political impulses have inspired American artists, but too little to say about how leftism can reduce art to agitprop or smothering political kitsch, telling in its day but lasting only as artifact, like Clifford Odets's play *Waiting for Lefty*.

More troubling is how, even as *American Dreamers* concedes the left's political weaknesses and emphasizes left-wing cultural influence, it also clings to the post-1960s story line and inflates the radicals' political importance at crucial moments. Measured by their own terms of success, Kazin's leftists may have continually failed in politics. But Kazin also claims that the left has been responsible for those great reforms which have succeeded, more so than the grudging establishment reformers.

Kazin understands that liberal reformism has existed independently of radical agitation—he cursorily calls the New Deal reforms "liberal achievements," and mentions a stillborn liberal "new age of reform" in the 1960s. But his book chiefly makes liberalism's ideas seem like weaker versions of the radicals' ideals, advanced as responses to the radicals' protests. Slighting the politics of reformers who actually had power and used it, Kazin holds to the familiar distinction between idealistic if sometimes wrongheaded radicals and craven or merely opportunistic establishment liberals. He thereby exaggerates the radicals' significance while he drains liberal politics of intellectual potency and political integrity. And because he emphasizes protest over politics, he ignores those radicals who, working in collaboration with his establishment reformers, achieved a great deal.

Kazin's oddly brief discussion of the Civil War and emancipation is a case in point. Few if any historians would dispute the enormous importance of the abolitionists in provoking the sectional conflict over slavery. Yet Kazin thinks that the abolitionists had more to do with achieving emancipation than they actually did. As early as 1859, he writes, John Brown's raid on Harpers Ferry persuaded abolitionist leaders, although not the cautious moderate Abraham Lincoln, "that war was now the only solution." Kazin neglects to mention that when the Southern states actually began seceding in 1860 and 1861, most radical abolitionists were eager to let them depart and regarded all efforts to save the Union as, in William Lloyd Garrison's words, "simply idiotic." In fact, Lincoln's election, his refusal to compromise over barring the expansion of slavery, and his determination to crush secession if necessary—and nothing the radical abolitionists said or did—set off the war.

Kazin observes that the abolitionists enjoyed a newfound popularity and legitimacy after Fort Sumter, but he also calls that popularity the major political factor in clearing the way for the Emancipation

Proclamation, which is inaccurate. He disregards almost the entire history preceding the proclamation, including the ways that Lincoln skillfully played the fractious radicals off against formidable conservative Northern opinion in order to ensure that his proclamation did not destroy the Union cause. Kazin also gives Frederick Douglass much of the credit for convincing Lincoln to allow the enlistment of black troops, a pivotal decision in which Douglass and other radical abolitionists actually had no direct part at all.

Lincoln appears only fleetingly in Kazin's book, as a stereotyped moderate who believed in the ballot over the bullet and opposed giving ex-slaves confiscated rebel land, and yet who somehow changed to the point where, in his second inaugural address, he delivered an attack on the sin of slavery that Kazin deems worthy of John Brown himself. Kazin lacks a deeper appreciation of Lincoln's antislavery politics going back to the 1850s and earlier, or the antislavery politics of his party, and of how the abolitionists affected the intricate mainstream politics that really mattered. His portrayal of the most convulsive event in American history is a skimpy caricature.

Kazin's account of the New Deal years focuses on the Communist Party, and argues that the Party's influence far exceeded its tiny membership (at its peak, perhaps about 75,000 members). Paradoxically, Kazin writes, the more the Communists proclaimed their genuine Stalinist ideology, the more distrusted and despised they became, whereas "the more they delayed and diluted their ultimate ends, the better they did." The Popular Front, which dropped ultra-revolutionary rhetoric and embraced patriotic populist themes—coincidental with Stalin's Great Terror—was, as Howe described it, "a brilliant masquerade." Yet Kazin notes the successes of the Communist Party's cadres as labor organizers for the Congress of Industrial Organizations in the late 1930s. And then, returning to his point about the power of left-wing culture, he lists popular Party or pro-Party artists, including Woody Guthrie and Paul Robeson, and hails their contributions—wrongly dismissed by critics, he says, as "crowd-pleasing banalities or Stalinist apologetics"—as essential to the history of their time.

The link Kazin makes here between art and politics is hazy. "This Land Is Your Land" and "Pretty Boy Floyd" should not be written off as a Stalinist apologetics, but their value exists above and beyond Woody Guthrie's pro-Communist politics. More important, Kazin's slighting of the liberal reformers who supposedly wanted to snatch labor's votes for President Roosevelt minimizes how the New Deal did a great deal more to open the way for the left than vice versa.

The decisive pressure for the New Deal measures, as Kazin knows but understates, came not from Communists or even the CIO's leader, John L. Lewis (a Republican), but from FDR's own advisers as well as from urban liberals like Senator Robert Wagner of New York. The urban liberals had been working on labor issues long before the Great Depression or, for that matter, the Bolshevik Revolution. Wagner became galvanized by the Triangle Shirtwaist Factory fire in 1911. His efforts on behalf of labor reform began while he was president pro tempore of the New York state senate and a regular Tammany Hall Democrat; that work culminated, with the advice of young liberal counselors such as Leon Keyserling, in the landmark National Labor Relations Act of 1935 that bears Wagner's name.

Labor protests surely helped heighten the sense of emergency early in 1935—when the Communist Party, still denouncing FDR and the New Dealers as "social fascists," opposed the Wagner Act—but they were not the principal inspiration of the reformers, who had begun shaping their ideas and goals decades earlier. Those goals were not to pass piecemeal reforms that would placate or restrain radical labor. The Wagner Act, for example, explicitly protected and encouraged industrial unionism and, as Kazin notes in passing, "enabled industrial unions to gain a sturdy foothold in factories and mines and on the docks."

New Deal social legislation certainly had its shortcomings, as Kazin points out: conservative Democrats from the South and West were able to exempt agricultural workers from the Wagner Act's provisions, while, chiefly for administrative reasons, casual laborers, domestic servants, and federal employees as well as agricultural workers failed to gain coverage under the Social Security Act, signed into law by Roosevelt a few weeks later. Overall, though, New Deal liberals like Wagner and Keyserling did far more for the subsequent rise of radical labor than Kazin describes.

Kazin's overemphasis on the Communists, meanwhile, leads him to omit entirely some of the left's genuine triumphs during the 1930s and 1940s, and in the generation after. He seems uninterested in those who gained actual political influence. *American Dreamers* contains not a single reference to the socialists Walter and Victor Reuther, who courageously both opposed Communists and made the United Auto Workers one of the strongest forces in the American labor movement and the Democratic Party. Nor does Kazin mention the left-wing clothing workers' leader Sidney Hillman, whom FDR relied upon for campaign organization ("Clear it with Sidney"), and was an important figure in Roosevelt's 1944 victory and in labor's integration into the Democratic Party. Kazin excludes the other anti-Communist social democrats who became major forces inside the mainstream trade unions and left-liberal political efforts like the Farmer-Labor Party of Minnesota—the organization that, following its merger with the state's Democratic Party in 1944, became the base for the youthful Hubert Humphrey, who became a leader of the national party's pro-civil rights wing.

After the Eisenhower interregnum, these various streams emerged to make possible the enormous policy achievements of the Great Society. The anti-Communist unions, moreover, helped create and support, among other things, a stalwart movement of labor solidarity against Communism in Poland and throughout Eastern and Central Europe—a movement that in time was instrumental in overthrowing Soviet totalitarianism. There is a great deal to criticize in the work of the anti-Communist social democrats, including the stubborn and tragic support that some of them gave to the disastrous American war in Vietnam—but to ignore them and their contributions altogether truncates, flattens, and simplifies the history of the American left.

The civil rights movement in many ways fits most closely with the contemporary academic left's conception of political change. Kazin calls it the one radical commitment of the era "that has stood up well over time," and here he describes the contributions of black anti-Communist leftists like A. Philip Randolph and Bayard Rustin. He also makes the case that Martin Luther King, Jr., was just as committed as the avowed socialists were to what he calls "radical structural change."

Yet Kazin fails to describe how the movement won its major political victories. The 1964 Civil Rights Act and the 1965 Voting Rights Act receive only brief mentions. President Lyndon Johnson—who praised civil rights protestors for forcing lawmakers to act—is presented almost entirely as the engineer of the Vietnam catastrophe. Instead of explaining the sources of the Great Society and the workings of presidential leadership, Kazin writes at length about the Student Non-Violent Coordinating Committee's turn to black nationalism and the rise of the Black Panthers. He credits Black Power militants with prodding millions of blacks "to comprehend themselves and their society in assertive and candid ways." He has some criticism of the Panthers, but his praise for how black radicals supposedly emboldened African Americans culturally becomes a substitute for analysis of the left's role in the complicated politics of civil rights reform. If the cultural factor is all-important, why slight Berry Gordy and the rise of Motown?

Kazin's treatment of the left since the 1960s is particularly incomplete. He astutely appraises the antiwar New Left and its revival of older radical conceptions of ethical responsibility. Kazin's argument about the left's cultural impact helps explain the lasting effects of the feminist and gay rights movements, with their insistence on "the expansion of individual liberty into every sphere of private life"—an insistence that, as in the case of *Roe v. Wade*, he observes, led to more than cultural changes. But here, too, his thesis that the advancement of women's and gay rights demonstrates the cultural reach of a politically thwarted left neglects the indispensable legal efforts of untiring liberals. (He makes no mention, for example, of Ruth Bader Ginsburg, who was director of the Women's Rights Project of the American Civil Liberties Union before President Bill Clinton appointed her to the Supreme Court.)

Kazin then describes how the New Left degenerated into ferocious and abiding contempt for liberals and liberalism, which sent some of its adherents spiraling into the violence and neo-Leninist sectarianism of the Weather Underground. And with the New Left's demise, Kazin avers, "for the first time in 150 years, no American radical movement survived that was worthy of the name"—an amnesia attack that forgets modern feminism and the gay rights movement after 1973.

Here, though, Kazin's analysis begins to get fuddled, as he returns to his basic presumptions about the left and American politics. He unsurprisingly ignores those influential and productive groups—ranging from the Children's Defense Fund to the National Resources Defense Council—that by his definition are insufficiently radical. Instead, Kazin discusses various single-issue left-wing campaigns of the last thirty years, including those that opposed President Reagan's nuclear weapons buildup and policies in Central America, and laments how almost all of them failed. Crediting social critics including Michael Moore with gaining "a foothold in popular culture," he yearns for much more, yet cannot say what that might be.

And so he repeats his refrain: "Reformers from above," he writes, "always needed the pressure of left-wing movements from below." Lacking that pressure, Bill Clinton could not be "the transformative figure" Kazin says he wanted to be, and Barack Obama will not become one. Lacking that pressure, liberalism will retain "the baleful image it acquired in the 1970s: as an ideology out of touch with the interests and beliefs of ordinary Americans."

Out of touch? Kazin's gloomy account of the last three decades sidesteps the fact that for eight years, the Clinton administration—although it rarely used the demonized label "liberal," preferring "progressive"—attempted to reinvent the New Deal liberalism of the 1930s and make it relevant to the changed world of the 1990s and the new century. To be sure, many liberals as well as leftists criticized Clinton's policies, sometimes harshly, not least the welfare reform legislation of 1996. But whatever Kazin might think of Clinton's record, he owes his readers a fair-minded statement of its actual strengths and weaknesses, if only to show how his notion of a left-wing social movement would and could realistically have made it better. He fails to acknowledge, let alone explain, the Clinton administration's accomplishments which included overseeing the longest period of economic growth in modern times, one that significantly raised family income and real wages for the first time in a generation. And in glossing over the Clinton years, Kazin ignores how American leftists retained contempt for liberalism, a late-1960s' turn of mind that led a portion of the left to the single act that did more to change the nation's politics than any it had done since the civil rights years.

Angered by, among other things, Clinton's support of the North American Free Trade Agreement—a pact endorsed by such economists as Paul Krugman—the left largely abandoned Clinton, and had little to offer in the bitter fight over his comprehensive health care reform in 1994, after which Newt Gingrich and right-wing Republicans seized control of the House of Representatives. Clinton outwitted Gingrich in a confrontation over a debt limit bill (preventing the savaging of Medicare and Medicaid and leading to passage of a host of progressive policies), but leftists condemned Clinton as the smarmy practitioner of "triangulation." When the infuriated Republicans responded to Clinton's successes by manipulating the Monica Lewinsky scandal and conducting an unconstitutional impeachment drive, leftists like Christopher Hitchens and Barbara Ehrenreich continued to deride Clinton (and his wife) as serial liars and mountebanks, and sometimes repeated groundless Republican confabulations.

Then came the great political achievement of a prominent part of the left: ensuring the election of George W. Bush over Al Gore in 2000. Kazin devotes only one-third of a paragraph to Ralph Nader's three third-party campaigns for the presidency, and only a lone sentence to how, in 2000, the former consumer advocate carefully and consciously drew votes away from Democrats in key swing states and thereby enabled Bush to win Florida "and, with it, the White House." Kazin now plainly disapproves of the debacle, but even in the obvious light of what a turning point Bush's election proved to be, he slights it.

Several of the leftists whom Kazin praises as cultural celebrities supported Nader, and some of them recycled false Republican attacks on Gore as, in Ehrenreich's words, an "inveterate bribe-seeker." Kazin himself lamented at the time that Nader had not managed to build a stronger third-party challenge to what he called the Democrats' disgusting "poll-driven moderation." He conceded that Nader's candidacy was helping Bush, but what truly disturbed him was Nader's failure to stir mass enthusiasm and break through the latest ridiculous competition "between two men in dark suits and red ties who keep their fingers in the air and their brains on automatic pilot." Thus Al Gore, one of the most experienced and creative liberal policy leaders of his generation, was painted as the moral and political equivalent of George W. Bush.

By 2008, Bush and the Republicans had wreaked so much havoc and become so discredited that the Democrats' chance came around again—and the left persuaded itself that a young, center-left African American with little national political or government experience was the "transformative" movement president for whom they had been waiting for decades. But leftists' enthusiasm faded when President Barack Obama undertook to initiate what Kazin calls "a new era of modest reform." *American Dreamers* went to press before Kazin could mention Occupy Wall Street and the left's disillusionment and displeasure with Obama, although he subsequently described OWS's anarchist fervor as bracing in its egalitarianism but unlikely "to make the leap from visionary protest to sensible politics." More recently, he has, with justice, credited Occupy and the agitation demanding a $15-per-hour minimum wage with helping "to turn economic inequality into an issue no one in public life can ignore." (The loose-knit Black Lives Matter campaign and the presidential candidacy of Bernie Sanders were still too new to assess.) Kazin remains hopeful, as he was at the conclusion of *American Dreamers*, that radical egalitarian ideas and rhetoric might yet inspire an effective social movement. But it is all as yet undefined. Kazin's left is "TBD."

As a historian, Kazin, despite his sober judgments, exaggerates the importance of some radicals even as he ignores others' genuine achievements—and does so at liberalism's expense. His view of history acknowledges but diminishes the debt radicals have owed to liberals —just as it blinds him to the damage some leftists have willfully done over the last thirty years to liberal ideals and, ironically, to their own.

13

★ ★ ★ ★ ★ ═══════════

The Cold War and the
Perils of Junk History

THE HIGHLY-TOUTED BOOK ON AMERICAN HISTORY BY OLI-
ver Stone and his coauthor Peter Kuznick, and the accompanying ten-
part televised documentary, have a misleading title. Most, if not all, of
the interpretations that they present in *The Untold History of the United
States*—from the war in the Philippines to the one in Afghanistan—
have appeared in revisionist histories of American foreign policy written over the last fifty years. Challenged by early reviewers, Stone and
Kuznick essentially conceded the point about their sources and claimed
that what they call the "revisionist narrative" that informs their book
has in truth become "the dominant narrative among university-based
historians."

The real problem, they say, is that this revisionism has yet to pen-
etrate the public schools, the mainstream media, and "those parts of
America that cling to the notion of American exceptionalism." Their
version of history may not be untold, but "it has been almost entirely
'unlearned.'" And so what originally sounded like a startling account
of a suppressed history is in fact largely a recapitulation and popular-
ization of a particular stream of academic work, in a book that would
more properly be called *The Unlearned History of the United States*—if

the scholarship and the authors' reworking of it were thorough, factually accurate, and historically convincing.

Far from producing a history of the United States, either untold or unlearned, Stone and Kuznick devote themselves almost entirely to America's role in world affairs since 1900 and particularly since 1939. (Although Kuznick, a professor at American University, is responsible for the historical research, virtually all of it in secondary sources, Stone the celebrity filmmaker gets top billing, and his is the narrator's voice in the television series.) Their basic aim is to describe the nation's malevolent seizure of global supremacy during and after World War II, and its imperial exploits through the first term of Barack Obama's presidency.

It is largely a tale of great men—good and bad. By the 1920s, the democratic republic of Jefferson, Lincoln, Whitman, and the youthful William Jennings Bryan "had ceased to exist," and had been replaced by an America whose "unique mixture of idealism, militarism, avarice, and realpolitik propelled [it] toward becoming a world power." The paradoxical but bad Woodrow Wilson promised to spread democracy and end colonialism, but his policies mocked the first and advanced the second. He spouted high-minded rhetoric while bankers and munitions manufacturers dragged the country under false pretenses into World War I. Wilson's subsequent ineptness about the World War I settlement and the League of Nations fostered an abiding skepticism about international involvement that disastrously slowed America's response to the threat of Germany, Italy, and Japan in the 1930s.

Led by the good Franklin D. Roosevelt, the United States eventually enlisted against Fascism and gained what Stone and Kuznick call "an opportunity to reclaim some of that democratic, egalitarian heritage on which its earlier greatness and moral leadership had rested." But the nation squandered the opportunity by needlessly dropping atomic bombs on Hiroshima and Nagasaki and instigating a vicious Cold War with the Soviet Union. The calamitous turning point came in 1944 and 1945, when Harry Truman (very bad) ascended to the vice presidency and, after FDR's death, to the presidency. Maligned by Stone and Kuznick as a neurotic, corrupt, racist demagogue, Truman made all of the wrong decisions.

Stone and Kuznick's greatest hero is FDR's secretary of agriculture and third-term vice president Henry Wallace (very good), who futilely opposed Truman's policies. Their next hero, two decades later, is President John F. Kennedy. Startled by the Bay of Pigs fiasco two years earlier, Kennedy in 1963 was supposedly on the verge of rejecting Cold War orthodoxy and leading "the United States and the world down a . . . path of peace and prosperity" along the lines that Wallace had prophetically laid out. But JFK, like Wallace before him, "had many enemies who deplored progressive change." Stone and Kuznick stop just short of blaming Kennedy's assassination on those hidden enemies, as Stone did in his conspiracy film *JFK* (1991). But they say his death handed the country back to those who "would systematically destroy the promise of the Kennedy years as they returned the country to war and repression."

The United States, according to Stone and Kuznick, has remained in the malefic grip of the militarists and empire-builders to this day. Even well-intentioned leaders like Barack Obama have been brainwashed into sustaining the repressive national security state that oversees US domination of the world. It is a bleak assessment, but Stone and Kuznick do not entirely lack hope. They detect in Obama's performance since 2010 some dim signs that the president "might be undergoing a Kennedyesque road-to-Damascus conversion" about American militarism and imperialism. But like many left-leaning historians, Stone and Kuznick look for deliverance not to any elected officials but to an ill-defined social movement, one they envisage as "US citizens joining with the rebellious masses everywhere to deploy the lessons of history, their history, the people's history, which is no longer untold"—a worldwide rebellion at least partly inspired, the authors imply modestly, by *The Untold History of the United States*.

Although Stone and Kuznick claim that their efforts reflect the dominant view of American history inside the universities, the work of many highly distinguished and influential scholars ranging from the traditionalist John Lewis Gaddis to the revisionist-influenced Melvyn P. Leffler indicates otherwise. The soundness of Stone and Kuznick's work, though, depends not on its intellectual pedigree but on how the authors render the historical record.

One persistent feature of that rendering is Stone and Kuznick's partiality to Joseph Stalin and the Soviet Union in world affairs. They don't deny Stalin's crimes, although they don't say much about them either. But they are always ready with a euphemism or a justification for the Soviets' actions, no matter how dubious or immoral. Had the United States, they say, been more willing to aid Stalin in the late 1930s—that is, at the height of Stalin's Great Terror—then Stalin never would have struck his notorious nonaggression pact with Nazi Germany in 1939. That alliance was a matter of necessity, Stone and Kuznick insist, buying Stalin time before Germany's invasion of the Soviet Union, which Stalin had foreseen. Stone and Kuznick say nothing about Nazi–Soviet military cooperation. They say virtually nothing about the pact's rapacious partition of Poland, or the Soviet invasion of the Baltic states in 1940 and the decades of brutal occupation that followed. They do briefly chide Stalin's policies in Eastern Europe as "heavy-handed."

In a review of *The Untold History* for the *Daily Beast*, Michael Moynihan pointed out the book's twisted accounts of Soviet actions and intentions, and a great deal more: the authors' manipulation of reliable sources, their reliance on untrustworthy sources, their tailoring of quotations, their reporting of long-debunked apocrypha as true, and a slew of other crimes and misdemeanors against scholarship. These willful lapses make the book a prime example of what Moynihan called "junk history," useless for historians and harmful for historians' students and readers. A closer look at how Stone and Kuznick mishandle what they call a key event in modern American history affirms Moynihan's judgment. As it happens, the momentous episode involved not the history of American foreign policy but the machinations of American party politics, against the backdrop of the opening of the Cold War.

★ ★ ★

IN 1940, Stone and Kuznick write, President Roosevelt named his brilliant secretary of agriculture, Henry Wallace, "a champion of freedom and democracy," as his running mate, overruling reluctant party bosses and conservatives. Four years later, the hacks got their revenge. With Roosevelt's health declining, the bosses knew that the nominee for vice president might well soon become president, so they conspired to dump Wallace and replace him with the crude but malleable Missourian Harry Truman.

According to Stone and Kuznick, FDR, too enfeebled and politically dependent to put up a fight, made it clear to Wallace and, in an open letter, to the Democratic convention delegates that he preferred to run with him again. "Rank-and-file Democrats" rose up against "the bosses' stranglehold over the [convention] proceedings and strong-arm tactics," mounted a raucous demonstration, and very nearly nominated Wallace, but were cut short when "the bosses forced adjournment against the will of the delegates." The bosses' puppet, Truman, prevailed, "the first major setback to hopes for a peaceful postwar world."

Following FDR's death in April 1945, with the "small man" Truman in the White House, disaster followed disaster. "To err is Truman," as the Republicans put it at the time. The United States dropped atomic bombs on Japan even though, according to the authors, the Japanese themselves already knew they had been defeated. Truman, they believe, hoped this would scare Stalin and the Soviets into postwar submission. When the Soviets refused to be intimidated, an insecure Truman resolved to "stand up to Stalin and show him who was boss." The Truman Doctrine, the Berlin airlift, and the Marshall Plan nefariously bullied Stalin into a Cold War that he didn't want, a conflict that soon escalated into a nuclear arms race that would imperil civilization itself. The great naysayer was again Henry Wallace, whom FDR, before his death, had salvaged from the bosses' conspiracy and appointed secretary of commerce.

In making this case, Stone and Kuznick simply ignore the facts and the scholarship that contradict their basic assumptions. It is hardly clear, for example, that the Japanese government was close to surrendering on the Allies' terms in the summer of 1945. American analysts believed that, short of a bloody invasion of its shores, Japanese leaders would fight hard, holding out for a much milder negotiated settlement, and scholarship since the 1990s has rejected the revisionist claim that the war might have ended just as quickly had the atomic bombs not been dropped. This negates Stone and Kuznick's contention that Truman was misleading about his motive for using the bombs: that they would spare the lives of untold thousands of American GIs. Nor did Truman shift away from FDR's incomplete vision of a grand bargain with the Soviets until he fitfully became convinced that Stalin's violations of solemn agreements and encroachments in Eastern and Central Europe posed a threat to Western security.

When, in September 1946, Wallace publicly attacked Truman's foreign policy and advocated recognition of Soviet control in Eastern Europe, Truman forced him out of the cabinet. "With Wallace gone," the authors write, "the United States plunged headlong into Cold War both at home and abroad." An aroused Wallace challenged Truman and what he called "the bipartisan reactionary war policy" in the 1948 election, calling for unilateral disarmament. But Red-baiting, feints to the left by Truman, and Democratic voters' fears of a Republican victory destroyed Wallace and his Progressive Party.

History, though, might have turned out much more happily, if only . . . "Few people remember," Stone and Kuznick observe, "how close Wallace came to getting the vice presidential nomination on that steamy Chicago night in July 1944." In a book full of auspicious turning points, none looms larger than this one. Yet the thinly sourced account of that night in 1944 by Stone and Kuznick and of the events that surrounded it distorts, to put it mildly, what actually occurred.

"A virtual conspiracy" of party leaders did, indeed, work to dump Wallace from the ticket, as the historian Robert H. Ferrell has shown, but not chiefly as anti-Communists fearing Wallace's pro-Soviet politics. Henry Wallace was a brilliant agronomist, probably the greatest secretary of agriculture the nation has ever had. His efforts to help down-and-out farmers during the Great Depression revolutionized rural America. But as vice president and presiding officer of the Senate, Wallace—"aloof, even ethereal," in Ferrell's words—had antagonized nearly every member of the upper chamber, which made him a major political liability for FDR. Wallace was also, as he described himself, "a searcher for methods of bringing the 'inner light' to outward manifestation," and his searches led him to fall under the influence of some oddball prophets. These included, for a time, a White Russian émigré, theosophist, and confidence man named Nicholas Roerich, whom—before he turned against him—Wallace addressed as "Dear Guru." Wallace's esoteric interests, notorious in Washington, as well as his political incapacities rendered him, to his critics, unfit for the presidency. Opposition to his renomination was virtually universal among FDR's closest advisers.

Months before the Democratic convention, in consultation with the determined party leaders, Roosevelt, aware of the damage Wallace could do to the ticket, decided to jettison him. A week before the convention, at a White House meeting, Roosevelt and the party chieftains considered several possible options but settled on Truman. Although the president barely knew the Missourian, he was comforted by his support of the New Deal and his leadership in the Senate in rooting out waste and profiteering in the war production industries. Truman, coming from a traditional North-South border state, also would do the most of any possible choice to balance the ticket, in what was shaping up as a tough campaign against the young New York Republican Thomas E. Dewey.

But the wily Roosevelt—as ever eager to dominate but reluctant to offend, and willing to tell people what he knew they wanted to hear—withheld his decisions from Wallace and the other aspirants for the nomination, including the powerful former senator James F. Byrnes of South Carolina. FDR even told Wallace airily that he hoped to run with him again, a message that any astute politician would have understood was the kiss of death; once the convention had commenced, Roosevelt released the highly ambiguous message that Stone and Kuznick describe simply as pro-Wallace.

Wallace, for his own part, came to realize that Roosevelt was being duplicitous, recording in his diary his certainty that, as the convention approached, the president "wanted to ditch me as noiselessly as possible." He was unwilling to go quietly. His supporters, using bogus tickets, packed the convention hall, hoping to stampede the convention. Wallace might have been nominated had party leaders not hastily adjourned the proceedings. Wallace was unaware that FDR had forcefully ordered the party bosses to get Truman's acceptance as his running mate at once—"Have you got that fellow lined up yet?" he asked—while cajoling Truman by appealing to his sense of patriotic duty. The day after the failed stampede, Truman's friends spread the word that Roosevelt was backing their man, and he was nominated on the second ballot. Wallace had indeed been thwarted—from forcing himself onto a ticket where Roosevelt had decided he did not belong.

Stone and Kuznick's idolization of Wallace and demonization of Truman similarly inspire their gauzy coverage of the Progressive Party campaign four years later. In the intervening years, Wallace's opposition to Truman's policies had broadened to include a defense of the Soviet coup in Czechoslovakia in 1948. "The men in Moscow, from their viewpoint, would be utter morons if they failed to respond with acts of pro-Russian consolidation," he declared. When Wallace finally ran against Truman as leader of the Progressive Party, the president's supporters noted Wallace's convergence with the Kremlin's party line. Stone and Kuznick, though—echoing Wallace's supporters at the time—repeat Wallace's contemporary denials that the Communist Party USA had any involvement with his campaign.

Stone and Kuznick cannot explain why, two years after the 1948 campaign, the radical journalist I. F. Stone—no defender, to say the least, of Harry Truman—wrote matter-of-factly, "The Communists have been the dominant influence in the Progressive Party. . . . If it had not been for the Communists, there would have been no Progressive Party." Nor does Stone and Kuznick's analysis adequately account for the views of Wallace's former supporter Eleanor Roosevelt, who repeatedly denounced Wallace and his movement in 1948, charging that "the American Communists will be the nucleus of Mr. Wallace's third party," and proclaiming that "any use of my husband's name in connection with that party is from my point of view entirely dishonest."

(Any lingering doubts about the Communists' control of the Progressive Party have been dispelled by Thomas W. Devine's thorough and devastating book *Henry Wallace's 1948 Presidential Campaign and the Future of Postwar Liberalism*, which appeared shortly after Stone and Kuznick's *Untold History*. Devine confirms that the Progressive Party's top command, dominated by Communists, ensured that the party's politics and political interests hewed closely to those of the Communist Party. The "nucleus" of American Communists, as Eleanor Roosevelt put it, included Wallace's close aide and confidant Calvin "Beanie" Baldwin and Baldwin's wife, Lillian Traugott, both concealed Communists; Traugott even worked for Soviet intelligence. Some of Devine's information, including Baldwin's Communist ties, was well-known to scholars long before Stone and Kuznick chose to evade it.)

Stone and Kuznick's claim that Wallace and the Progressive Party's challenge prompted Truman's "progressive strategy" on domestic issues cannot explain the historic civil rights initiatives undertaken by Truman well before the campaign that provoked the Dixiecrat presidential candidacy of Governor Strom Thurmond of South Carolina in 1948. Nor does their book explain why non-Communist leaders of black organizations, including Walter White and Roy Wilkins of the NAACP attacked Wallace as vigorously as they supported Truman.

(It goes almost without saying that black anti-Communist radicals such as Bayard Rustin make no appearance in these pages.)

There are ample grounds for criticizing and even condemning some of Truman's actions in the Cold War, not least the loyalty oath program he instituted in 1947. But by glorifying the Henry Wallace of the mid- to late 1940s, Stone and Kuznick indulge in a Manicheanism that inadvertently recalls the long political and intellectual antecedents behind their interpretation. That "untold" history began not in the 1960s and the Vietnam era with which Stone—Oliver, not just I. F.—became so closely identified, as anyone who has seen *Platoon* (1986) and his other Vietnam movies instantly grasps. It began in the 1940s, when the beginning of the Cold War divided American liberals and leftists of various stripes.

On one side stood those such as Reinhold Niebuhr, J. K. Galbraith, Walter Reuther, Chester Bowles, and Eleanor Roosevelt, who believed that liberalism and Communism were fundamentally opposed, with respect both to social ends and political means. On the other side stood those who believed that liberalism and Communism existed on a continuum, with political freedom at one end and economic freedom on the other, and who believed further that, through peaceful coexistence and competition, each side could learn from the other. And there was a third group, of Communists who believed that liberalism was an underdeveloped politics, useful as a cover for their own higher ends.

The first group, the liberal anti-Communists, included the great majority of New Deal liberals, and gravitated to organizations such as Americans for Democratic Action, which sought to expand the reforms of the New Deal while isolating Communists at home and supporting the containment of Soviet influence abroad. The second group, the anti-anti-Communists, included liberals who found their voice in the Progressive Party, who saw the West and especially the United States as the aggressor in the Cold War, and who regarded liberal anti-Communism as virtually indistinguishable from—indeed, as complicit with—the anti-Communism of the right.

Defeated in 1948, the Progressive Party carried no states and received fewer votes than the Dixiecrats, who carried four states. The Progressive Party's outlook made something of a comeback during the late 1960s, though under drastically different circumstances, when Cold War liberalism as well as the administration of Lyndon Johnson became tainted, both fairly and unfairly, by the Vietnam catastrophe.

Liberal anti-Communists indeed waged and supported the war, but a variety of other liberal anti-Communists—George Ball, Clark Clifford, Eugene McCarthy, and Stanley Hoffman, to name only a few—became cogent critics and opponents of the Vietnam War both inside and outside the government, a division Stone and Kuznick note but do not fully discuss or explain. The Vietnam experience led historians to undertake long-overdue critical evaluations of America's part in the Cold War. But it also revived a "progressive" frame of mind that, with some superficial modifications—chiefly, ritualistic denunciations of the Stalinist terror coupled with insistence on Stalin's benign postwar motives—has treated the Cold War as the driving force of American empire and sometimes indicted the whole of liberal politics for timidity and worse in the face of global social injustice.

With a few twists, above all its defense of the liberal anti-Communist (but Oliver Stone's longtime personal hero) John F. Kennedy, *The Untold History of the United States*, both the book and the televised series, is a quirky summa of the old Progressive rhetoric as proclaimed by Stone and Kuznick's other hero, Henry Wallace, but presented as brand new. They fail to say that in 1952 Wallace published his article "Where I Was Wrong," writing that during the 1948 campaign, as during the rest of the 1940s, he had been inadequately informed about Stalin's crimes and

did not see . . . the Soviet determination to enslave the common man morally, mentally and physically for its own imperial purposes. . . .

More and more I am convinced that Russian Communism in its total disregard of truth, in its fanaticism, its intolerance and its resolute denial of God and religion is something utterly evil.

He supported Dwight Eisenhower and, in 1960, Richard Nixon for president.

Although the book by Stone and Kuznick is heavily footnoted, the sourcing, as the example of Wallace's 1952 article suggests, recalls nothing so much as Dick Cheney's cherry-picking of intelligence, particularly about the origins and early years of the Cold War. The authors also devote many thousands of words to criticism of such destructive American policies as Ronald Reagan's in Central America and George W. Bush's in Iraq, but much of this will be familiar to readers of the *New York Review of Books* and other organs of liberal opinion, as will their objections to Barack Obama's use of predator drones. This book is less a work of history than a skewed political document, restating and updating a view of the world that the independent radical Dwight Macdonald once identified with what he called "Wallaceland," "a region of perpetual fogs caused by the warm winds of the liberal Gulf Stream coming in contact with the Soviet glacier"—but now more than twenty years after the dissolution of the Soviet empire.

14

★ ★ ★ ★ ★ ▬▬▬▬

Lyndon B. Johnson:
The Triumph of Politics

IN HISTORY, AS IN HIS OWN LIFETIME, LYNDON B. JOHNSON seems trapped by his sharp contradictions. There was—and there remains in memory—a "good" Lyndon, the surprisingly compassionate white Southerner addressing a joint session of Congress and exclaiming the civil rights movement's protest refrain, "We shall overcome." The "good" Lyndon masterminded passage of the Civil Rights Act of 1964 and the Voting Rights Act of 1965, and envisaged and then enacted the landmark programs of the Great Society. But there was also the "bad" Lyndon of Vietnam and the credibility gap. By the time Johnson abandoned the White House in 1968, the "bad" LBJ had thoroughly displaced the "good" LBJ, at least as far as many reformist Democratic Party liberals were concerned. Less than three years after he signed the Civil Rights Act, Johnson, the champion of social protest, had become the reviled target of protests: "Hey, hey, LBJ / How many kids did you kill today?" The "good" Lyndon was willing to alienate the white solid South from the Democratic Party in the name of racial justice, but the "bad" Lyndon's Vietnam disaster finished off the updated New Deal coalition that had been resoundingly affirmed in 1964.

For some liberal Democrats, Vietnam was not Johnson's only offense. Even before the 1960s, a strong strain of high-minded liberalism mistrusted Johnson for cunningly practicing power politics. Born of the old good-government tradition of the antiparty Mugwumps, reinforced by the liberal *bien pensants'* adoration of their icon Adlai Stevenson, and solidified by the cool John F. Kennedy followers' disdain of the professional pol (a disdain not shared by JFK), this reformist outlook classified glad-handing politicians, with their party machines, arm-twisting, and smoke-filled rooms, not as agents of democracy but as corrupt evils thwarting the pursuit of open, efficient, and rational public policy. A matter of style as well as ideology, this sensibility endures today among better-educated and more affluent liberal Democrats. Just as Lyndon Johnson, the supremely expert practitioner of old-school party politics, made many liberals uneasy in the 1950s and 1960s, so his history discomfits many liberals—and many historians—today.

Inspired by a "Dump Johnson" movement launched in 1967, antiwar liberals flocked first to Johnson's challenger, Senator Eugene McCarthy, who attacked the president's Vietnam policies with a waspish wit and a gloss of detached Stevensonian erudition. Then, to Johnson's furious dismay, much of the liberal base bolted to Senator Robert Kennedy when he finally entered the primaries—the displaced prince of Camelot who would not just end the war but reclaim the presidency from the vulgar Texas usurper.

The contest between McCarthy and Kennedy provoked further liberal disquiets, which have endured over the decades. Johnson despised Kennedy for a multitude of personal and political slights dating back to the 1960 campaign and before. It was a case of mutual contempt, to borrow the title of Jeff Shesol's fine book about their rivalry. After President Kennedy's assassination, Johnson feared, with ample reason, that Bobby and his coterie were plotting to remove him from the presidency. But many liberals, including McCarthy's most ardent supporters (original Stevensonians who saw JFK as the usurper), also loathed

Bobby, nearly as much as they loathed Johnson. For them, there was a "bad" Bobby, memorably caricatured by the popular *Village Voice* cartoonist Jules Feiffer—an unscrupulously ambitious ruffian who had been his martyred brother's henchman. As campaign manager and political adviser, RFK exposed the sharp-edged political side of the Kennedy operation—and because JFK was imagined personally to be above such sordidness, Bobby became the evil one. "We believe that he is anti-liberal and disturbingly authoritarian," said the Bobby-hater par excellence Gore Vidal.

The fights between McCarthy's and Kennedy's supporters in 1968 were fierce, and the differences in political sensibility of those days are still very much alive, at least among liberals of a certain age. Over time, however, Johnson has become the supremely vexing figure in the modern history of the Democratic Party, honored for his domestic achievements but disgraced for his destructiveness and deceit over Vietnam, and for his cynical political arts—the president, as the *New York Times* editorial page had occasion to describe him in 2008, "who escalated the war in Vietnam into a generational disaster."

In that same year, 2008, an enormous wave of postpartisan anticipation helped elect to the presidency Barack Obama, who hoped to overcome the embittered ideological stalemate that had poisoned national politics over the previous two decades. Less than four years later, though, many liberal Democrats, including some of President Obama's erstwhile enthusiasts, were complaining about the administration's compromises and attempted compromises, and wishing Obama was more like, well, Lyndon Johnson. "Along with the inevitable FDR," Benjamin Dueholm, a blogger for the *Washington Monthly*, wrote, "Johnson has become an unlikely touchstone for progressive discontent with President Obama." In winning civil rights reform along with Medicare, Medicaid, and the rest of the Great Society programs, "Johnson is now admired for masterfully deploying methods of persuasion that Obama appears to disdain." Johnson had no use for the kind of high-minded postpartisanship that Obama seemed genuinely to have believed in even after it was exposed as a self-defeating conceit. Johnson, so the argument went, understood as Obama did not that the best arguments and the loftiest rhetoric do not necessarily get much done by themselves. Johnson, in short, was a thoroughgoing politician, whereas Obama, supposedly, felt distaste for any kind of politics other than the electoral.

The president's defenders replied that changed structural realities and a pathological Republican partisanship, unknown in the mid-1960s, were preventing Obama from accomplishing as much as he would like, and that, even then, Obama won a historic, even monumental liberal victory with the Affordable Care Act—all true. Johnson, unlike Obama, was able to count on a working liberal majority in Congress to enact the Voting Rights Act and many of the hallmark Great Society measures. Still, in order to win the Civil Rights Bill in 1964, his signal victory, LBJ had to overcome unstinting opposition, led by the segregationist Democratic bulls of the Senate, for whom the filibuster was a favored and lethal weapon. In the light of the political frustrations of Obama's first term, Johnson's political craftiness suddenly looked virtuous. LBJ's example, Dueholm contended, showed that, no matter the constraints, "the true genius of power can circumvent those limits to a degree, through fair means or foul."

★   ★   ★

IT WAS IRONIC that Barack Obama's early travails as president prompted some liberals, at least momentarily, to reassess Lyndon Johnson more positively than they had in forty years. Adding to the irony, a catalyst for this reevaluation was the publication of Robert A. Caro's *The Passage of Power*, the fourth enormous volume of his colossal biography of Johnson.

Caro has labored under certain analytical constrictions as he has built his masterwork. Having declared, long ago, his basically hostile interpretation of Johnson, Caro is stuck with it. The suspense in reading Caro's successive volumes has been to see not how Johnson fares, but how Caro fits his subject's sprawling and stormy life into his own established and unforgiving view of the man.

Caro opened his first volume, in 1982, with a summary prospectus of Johnson's presidency—a topic that his narrative would reach, barely, three volumes and thirty years later. The Johnson administration, he argued, was a "watershed in America's history, one of the great divides in the evolution of its foreign and domestic policies." On one side were "the tides of social change that had begun flowing during the New Deal" and that crested with Johnson's Great Society. On the other was disaster—"the widespread mistrust of the President that was symbolized by the phrase . . . 'credibility gap,'" as well as the decisive moment in the shift "from a 'constitutional' to an 'imperial' Presidency." And there was more: Johnson, he wrote, was the "most effective instrument" of a rising ascendancy of Sunbelt robber barons in oil, gas, aerospace, and other new industries that, having despoiled the riches of their own region, used their stunning wealth "to bend government to their ends."

Lyndon Johnson, in other words, not only oversaw the demise of liberalism as Caro's generation had come to know it; he caused it. By sapping the public's trust in government, undermining the separation of powers, and abetting the Sunbelt buccaneers, his misdeeds paved the way for the abuses of power by Richard M. Nixon and then for the rise of Ronald Reagan, who won the presidency two years before Caro's first Johnson volume appeared. And Johnson's offenses, Caro insisted, stemmed less from foolish decisions, political pressures, unintended consequences, and chance occurrences—key factors in most historical writing—than they did from Johnson's foul character and personality, shaped by the drama of his own life. Character was destiny—not only LBJ's, but ours as well.

Along with his view of Johnson's politics, Caro fully formed his interpretation of Johnson's character thirty years ago. Johnson, he explained in volume one, always displayed a bright "thread of achievement," exemplified by his efforts as a young congressman in the 1930s to secure electrification for the Texas Hill Country—but that thread was entwined with, and usually obscured by, another thread, "as dark as the other is bright." This latter impulse Caro described as "a hunger for power in its most naked form, for power not to improve the lives of others but to manipulate and dominate them, to bend them to his will." If ordinary citizens' lives happened to be improved as a result of or in tandem with Johnson's sinister ambition, so much the better. But the will to dominate, and the insecurity that fueled it, was always primary for LBJ, to the point of defying rationality. Johnson's hunger for power, Caro contended, linked to his bad personal and business ethics, was "a constant throughout his life," something "so fierce and consuming that no consideration of morality or ethics, no cost to himself—or to anyone else—could stand before it." The moralistic good Lyndon/ bad Lyndon distinction that liberals seized upon in the 1960s became, in Caro's hands, a deep-seated dualism—a case of turning the political into the personal and then explaining Johnson's political career on the basis of those alleged personal drives.

Caro ascribed Johnson's will to power, rather reductively, to a combination of heredity and boyhood trauma, specifically to young Lyndon's shame at watching the humiliating failure of his father, Sam Ealy Johnson, Jr., a sometime state legislator. Caro was certain that Johnson's mostly appalling personality had been completely shaped by the time he finished his studies at Southwest Texas State Teachers' College in 1930. "Some men—perhaps most men—who attain great power are altered by that power," he asserted. "Not Lyndon Johnson. The fire in which he had been shaped . . . had forged the metal of his being, a metal hard to begin with, into a metal much harder." And so, in the 882 pages of volume one (which took the story through 1941) and in the 1,673 pages of the two succeeding volumes (taking the story through 1958), Caro poured an astonishing wealth of fascinating detail, much of it newly discovered, into a simple analytical structure involving the eternal oscillation between good and evil—never quite a struggle—that defined Johnson's inner self and then changed the course of history.

This is not to say that Caro has viewed LBJ, in isolation, as an ogre with some notable saving graces. Indeed, Caro has dramatized the vileness of Johnson's character by playing him off against noble foes or allies who serve as moral foils. Most unfortunate, for Caro's readers, was his prolonged encomium in his second volume to Coke Stevenson, Johnson's opponent for a U.S. Senate seat from Texas in 1948. Stevenson was a charismatic ex-governor, political reactionary, and racist whom Caro ennobled as a larger-than-life, rugged, incorruptible hero—"the Abraham Lincoln of Texas," as one of his enthusiasts wrote. Before and after Stevenson, Caro found Johnson's chief foils not in his rivals but in his mentors: the lonely, wise, and truly honorable Speaker of the House Sam Rayburn, and the equally lonely, wise, and honorable (although staunchly pro-segregationist) Senator Richard B. Russell of Georgia.

The Passage of Power presents a very different foil for Johnson, neither a contrasting hero nor a noble mentor: Robert F. Kennedy. Herein lay a major reason why several early reviewers described the book as far less hard on Johnson than Caro's earlier volumes. Describing Bobby Kennedy, Caro returns to his dualism of darkness and light: "The portrait that was Robert Kennedy has always been heavily layered, with the harsh, dark colors—the rudeness, the ruthlessness, the rage; the desire to please and emulate his father—so dominant that it had been hard to see the glimpses of brighter hues. But they were there." In glimpses, anyway: although Caro's book discusses his compassion and gentleness, Kennedy's darker hues dominate—no metal, no threads, just painted "colors."

The Passage of Power shows Johnson becoming locked in a political death struggle with a man whose damaged, ambitious, and repulsive character easily matched his own—and whose mean-spirited competence actually frightened Johnson himself. The contrast with Bobby Kennedy helps enormously in making Caro's Lyndon Johnson appear in this volume, if not wholly decent and honorable, then at least sympathetic. Much as with his treatment of Johnson, Caro's disparagement of Kennedy recalls reformist liberals' disparagements of him from fifty years ago. As the "bad" Bobby becomes a major protagonist, the "good" Lyndon emerges valiantly as never before in Robert Caro's pages. As terrible as Lyndon was, it seems, Bobby could sometimes be the worse of the two.

★ ★ ★

CARO FORESHADOWED the "good" Lyndon's appearance at the conclusion of *Master of the Senate*, his third volume, with a dramatic extended narrative on the passage of the Civil Rights Bill in 1957. Many officials had a hand in that achievement—including, somewhat oddly in retrospect, Vice President Richard Nixon—but Senate Majority Leader Johnson was the indispensable man. It was LBJ who achieved a compromise between "the incorrigible right and the immovable left"—Caro here aptly quoted the great Southern historian C. Vann Woodward—with a "political astuteness . . . amounting to genius."

Liberals, to be sure, complained with good reason that the final bill was weak. As Caro's book makes clear, Johnson was initially moved by the assurance that failure to get some sort of legislation through the obdurate Senate would damage his leadership and kill his chances of winning the Democratic presidential nomination. But LBJ, Caro wrote, had "done all he could" in the fight for civil rights, "the most he could do in the position—Majority Leader of one of the two houses of Congress—in which he was situated." And the piecemeal victory of 1957 beckoned to a presidency in which Johnson, "among all the white government officials in twentieth-century America," would do "the most to help America's black men and women in their fight for equality and justice"—but not before Johnson had to suffer the many indignities of his vice presidency, not least the indignities of his vicious battles with Robert Kennedy.

The hatred between Johnson and Kennedy is unavoidable in any full account of either man or of the politics of the 1960s, and several books have examined it (above all Shesol's *Mutual Contempt*, which Caro acknowledges). There can only be so much for Caro to add. Still, Caro finds some intriguing new nuggets, including the story of the first nasty encounter, in the Senate dining room in 1953, between Johnson, then the minority leader of the Senate, and Kennedy, a young staffer for the irresponsible, loutish, Red-baiting Senator Joseph McCarthy.

Johnson had been telling unkind jokes around Washington about President Franklin D. Roosevelt's savvy handling, back in 1940, of Kennedy's troublesome father, the former ambassador Joseph P. Kennedy. The elder Kennedy, a supporter of McCarthy, had obtained for Robert his position in McCarthy's office, and Robert was extremely touchy about criticism, let alone ridicule, directed at his family. Bidden by McCarthy after he entered the dining room, Johnson stopped at McCarthy's table and shook hands with him and his staffers, but Kennedy, seething, refused to offer even a perfunctory pleasantry. Alert to the smallest slight, Johnson practically tackled Kennedy into shaking his hand. A minor, forgettable incident at the time—although not to Johnson's aides, from whom Caro ferreted it out—it backdates the bad feeling by a decade before Johnson succeeded Kennedy's murdered brother to the presidency. And although, in the event, Johnson acted, as ever, the thin-skinned bully, it was young Kennedy's implacable resentment that sparked the feud.

The feud recurs in *The Passage of Power*, from the 1960 campaign through the assassination in Dallas and beyond, with Kennedy generally the aggressor. After Johnson made his maladroit bid for the Democratic nomination in 1960, John Kennedy considered him for the vice presidency and offered him a place on the ticket—only to have an exasperated Bobby repeatedly try to persuade him to back away. Johnson finally got the nod, but thereafter, Caro relates, he would reply to the merest mention of Robert Kennedy's name by moving one hand swiftly across his neck, sometimes saying outright that "I'll cut his throat if it's the last thing I do." And throughout his brother's administration, Attorney General Kennedy made no pretense about his scorn for Vice President Johnson.

On one famous evening in 1962, after a White House social function, the anxious Johnson confronted Kennedy directly, asking him over and over to explain the reasons for his dislike, before he supplied his own explanation: that Kennedy thought he had attacked his father and tried to stop his brother's nomination at the 1960 convention. Of course, Johnson had done both of those things, but to try and smooth things over he clumsily denied them, which only deepened Kennedy's contempt. Johnson, he complained, "lies all the time. . . He lies even when he doesn't have to lie."

Caro's RFK is not uniformly loathsome. *The Passage of Power*'s account of the greatest crisis of the Kennedy administration, the Soviet deployment of nuclear missiles in Cuba, describes the attorney general as thoughtful and restrained, compared to the deceitful and bellicose Johnson. But Kennedy's hostility toward Johnson brought out the worst in him—and the gap between the two men was unbridgeable.

★   ★   ★

PRIOR TO HIS becoming vice president, part of Johnson's genius had been to take offices previously accorded little influence and turn them into staging grounds for his gargantuan ambitions, notably the position of Senate majority leader. "Power is where power goes," he would remark. But unlike certain of his successors, above all Dick Cheney, Johnson found himself defeated by the vice presidency and by the men he called the "Harvards" inside the Kennedy White House, the closest to the president being Robert Kennedy. After failing in awkward efforts to retain his powers as party leader in the Senate—an abrogation of the separation of powers that his former colleagues would not abide—and then to expand his role in the White House, Johnson became virtually a forgotten man in Washington. Cut out of important decision-making, reduced to performing on ceremonial occasions while presiding as the figurehead president of the Senate that had once been virtually his instrument,

Johnson came to realize that, whether or not President Kennedy kept him on the ticket in 1964, his political future looked bleak. Deflated, he retreated into a sullen funk. "My future is behind me," he told his aide Horace Busby.

Caro does not try to turn Johnson into an injured saint, which would all but repudiate what he has thus far written. Prone to self-pity, Johnson nursed slights, especially those dealt him by Robert Kennedy. Caro also shows Johnson brazenly trying to throttle the press when a reporter got too nosy about his private financial dealings. And some of Johnson's more dubious past activities and relations, copiously described with dogged zeal in Caro's earlier volumes, continued to haunt him, notably his mentorship of the shady Capitol Hill fixer Bobby Baker.

Otherwise, though, Caro presents Johnson's isolation as a terrible waste of his talents, not least on the burning issue of civil rights. Despite his segregationist voting record, Johnson's bright thread, according to Caro, had always included what he calls a "genuine empathy and compassion for Americans of color," which dated back to his days in the 1920s as a schoolteacher among poverty-stricken Mexican children in desolate South Texas. Having first worked himself up over the Civil Rights Bill in 1957—when, Caro writes, "compassion had, for the first time, coincided with ambition"—Johnson worked himself up all over again as the civil rights movement surged in 1962 and 1963.

In February 1963, after he had delivered pro-civil rights speeches in Detroit and Cleveland, Johnson visited strife-torn St. Augustine, Florida, and addressed racially integrated audiences, achieving what his aide George Reedy called "a major breakthrough on the color line." In a Memorial Day speech at Gettysburg, nearly a century after Lincoln's address, Johnson echoed Dr. Martin Luther King, Jr.'s eloquent but controversial "Letter from a Birmingham Jail," written just six weeks earlier: "The Negro today asks justice. We do not answer him—we do not answer those who lie beneath this soil—when we reply to the Negro by asking 'Patience.' . . . To ask for patience from the Negro is to ask him to give more of what he has already given enough." Thereafter, an invigorated Johnson ceased his sulking and, refusing to be put off, demanded a meeting with President Kennedy to discuss a major civil rights bill that the administration had drafted without consulting him and was about to introduce in Congress.

Johnson soon found himself at the center of the action at last. He offered sage tactical advice, urging the president not to send up a civil rights bill prematurely lest the Southern power-brokers in the Senate hold the rest of the administration's legislative agenda hostage and force the rights bill to be ignominiously withdrawn. He pleaded for Kennedy to give blacks a firm and eloquent moral commitment. He declaimed about civil rights at top-level White House meetings with influential business and labor leaders, impressing even the skeptical Arthur Schlesinger, Jr., the historian and special assistant to the president, who thought he outperformed both of the Kennedy brothers. JFK began addressing Johnson, in RFK's presence, with a respect that exceeded civil courtesy and at times approached deference. "For a couple of weeks there, he started to look almost like the old Lyndon," Reedy later recalled.

But then the "bad" Bobby intervened, showing up the vice president at a White House meeting with civil rights leaders, personally and ostentatiously undermining his authority over the Committee on Equal Employment Opportunity, and generally humiliating him. Kennedy acknowledged that Johnson had some sound points to make on dealing with Congress, but he described his caution as obstructionist. Outmaneuvered, Johnson retreated once again into depression, probably worsened by heavy drinking, which scared his closest aides. Rumors were spreading around Washington that with the administration, including the vice president, now firmly on the record in favor of civil rights, Johnson's electoral usefulness in the South had evaporated and he would be dumped in 1964— rumors that JFK stoutly denied but that redoubled Johnson's gloom.

The Senate Rules Committee had undertaken an investigation

of Bobby Baker that was moving uncomfortably close to Johnson. Despised by the "Harvards" and mistrusted by Northern liberals, estranged from his longtime Southern conservative allies over civil rights, Johnson still had powerful friends in Washington, but he was beginning to resemble a political party of one. Finally, in the fall of 1963, the vice president's inability to heal a political division in Texas between his former protégé Governor John Connally and Senator Ralph Yarborough signaled how badly his influence had waned even in his native state. It was left to the president to try and clean up the Texas mess on a four-day political and fundraising trip that would take him to Dallas.

Aboard Air Force One, after it landed at Andrews Air Force Base with his slain brother's body, Robert Kennedy brusquely ignored President Johnson, and over the coming days, Johnson came to believe, Bobby "seriously considered whether he would let me be president." Nor was Kennedy the only devastated New Frontiersmen who regarded Johnson as a usurper. Caro repeats the story reported by Shesol of how, a day after the assassination—with the late president lying in state in the East Room—Schlesinger convened a private lunch to discuss the possibility of dumping Johnson in 1964 in favor of a ticket of Robert Kennedy and Hubert Humphrey. Somehow, they thought LBJ was still the utterly irrelevant vice president. Yet if Robert Kennedy did not single-handedly create the revulsion at Johnson, he quickly became the focal point of the Kennedy loyalists' quest for the restoration of Camelot.

Johnson, for his part, faced the devastation not simply of his bitter rivals but of the entire nation. At the hour of Kennedy's death, official and journalistic investigations were about to unleash storms of controversy about Johnson's connections with the unsavory Baker as well as about his own dubious finances that might well have driven him from public life entirely. Instead, he rose to the presidency through tragedy. And astonishingly, after his years in purgatory, Johnson curbed his instinctual excesses and assumed office with composed authority, sensing clearly what needed to be done once the nation's nerves began to settle down. Martyrs need to die for causes, he would later tell Doris Kearns Goodwin, the young White House fellow whom he picked as his assistant, but JFK had never quite defined what his cause was: "That was my job. I had to take the dead man's program and turn it into a martyr's cause."

★   ★   ★

IN DECIDING TO CLOSE *The Passage of Power* with neither President Kennedy's assassination nor the events immediately thereafter, but nearly seven weeks later, in early January 1964, Caro displayed excellent historian's instincts. At the time, and ever since, there was a great deal written about how the anguished but successful transition from President Kennedy to President Johnson testified to the resiliency of the American constitutional order. Although this is true enough, Caro understands that constitutional order depends on the actions of real-life, flawed human beings. And, tested by unimaginable burdens, Lyndon Johnson performed magnificently. "For a period of time, a brief but crucial moment in history," Caro writes, Johnson held his destructive impulses in check, and, in overcoming them, "in a way conquered himself." For just less than seven weeks, the "good" Lyndon was resplendent—and inside those weeks he began blasting open the logjam that had trapped the Kennedy administration's legislative agenda, including the Civil Rights Bill.

There is something almost spooky in Caro's presentation of Johnson's sudden reawakening and powers restored. Even before he has reached Parkland Hospital, riding behind the dying president's limousine, Caro depicts Johnson as almost preternaturally calm, fully in control of himself and, as far as possible, tempering the chaos all about him. Despite the embarrassment he had suffered, the new president had to project humbleness and deference to all the late president's men, many of whom disliked or despised him, while also getting himself fully up to speed on the domestic and foreign policy issues about which he had been purposefully kept out of the loop. He wore what Caro describes as a mask of humility, "a mask," he writes, "that in those crucial days, never slipped." With skill and even with grace, Johnson turned that mask of humility into a mask of command.

He began with a carefully modulated speech before a joint session of Congress two days after Kennedy's funeral, in which he pledged to continue the slain leader's programs and singled out the Civil Rights Bill as a fitting memorial. ("We have talked long enough in this country about equal rights," he insisted.) Johnson had proved capable of delivering strong speeches and delivering them well, but the nation, knowing him chiefly as a Capitol Hill pol from Texas, was unprepared for his skillful weaving together of Kennedy's legacy with his own sense of purpose. "The formidable and elusive Majority Leader of the United States Senate sounded like a President," *Time* magazine observed.

What the country and its national leaders were even less prepared for was a president who could combine forceful rhetoric with an immense knowledge of how power worked in Washington and an immense skill at putting that knowledge to use. President Kennedy had not been at his best when it came to legislative arm-twisting. "Kennedy was not naïve, but as a legislator he was very green," the civil rights leader Roy Wilkins remembered. "He saw himself as being dry-eyed, realistic. In retrospect, I think that for all of his talk about the art of the possible, he didn't really know what was possible and what wasn't in Congress. . . . Johnson knew exactly what was possible."

Much, probably too much, has been written about the so-called "Johnson treatment," whereby LBJ would tower over, glower at, and almost smother whomever he was trying to persuade. As Caro recognizes, these tactics were appendages to Johnson's vast store of institutional acumen, his talent for sizing up men as well as political situations, and his understanding that all political situations came down to sizing up men. If Kennedy felt most comfortable dealing in foreign affairs, and best showed his mettle when dealing with crises, Johnson's genius was to take a legislative proposal and, as he vowed to do with the Civil Rights Bill, "write it in the books of law."

The last third of *The Passage of Power* shows Johnson pulling off one bravura presidential performance after another. He knew that Kennedy's murder demanded an official and authoritative investigation: "the atmosphere was poisonous and had to be cleared," he later recalled. Caro does a fine job of narrating how Johnson persuaded two key figures, Chief Justice Earl Warren and Senator Richard Russell, to serve despite their initial strong refusals to do so, playing on their sense of patriotism and, in Russell's case, boxing him in with a fait accompli by announcing his appointment to the press, behind his back.

Caro's most stirring, even inspiring chapters detail how Johnson, surpassing his performance in 1957, began pushing long-stalled legislation forward while breaking down the formidable Southern resistance to the Civil Rights Bill which, against his advice, the Kennedy administration had sent up to the Hill. As Johnson predicted, the senior Southern senators were making trouble for most of what the White House had asked for, above all a tax cut bill designed to stimulate a sluggish economy. But with the Civil Rights Bill on the agenda, nothing would be done unless and until the administration removed it. So Johnson, suddenly and without preparation, was thrown into the battles over the budget and the tax cut. He fixed his attention on Senator Harry Byrd of Virginia, chairman of the powerful Senate Finance Committee, a courteous, polite, but unyielding fiscal conservative. Caro's account of how Johnson handled Byrd—with concessions wrapped in words and gestures of respect, designed to flatter the old man's ego—is a small masterpiece of political history and political psychology from as close to the inside as Caro can get. In the end, Johnson "got" the ungettable Byrd—and with Byrd on board, he also got the tax cut bill through the Senate before the Civil Rights Bill came over from the House for debate.

The Civil Rights Bill, meanwhile, seemed to be withering on the vine, its supporters unable even to get it through the House Rules Committee, let alone the full House and Senate. After backing the unusual strategy of forcing the bill out of committee with a discharge petition signed by the House majority, Johnson took the even riskier step of placing the full force of his office and his considerable political skills behind the effort, mixing appeals to conscience with promises of political pelf, including a grant of handsome government contracts to Purdue University, which happened to be in the district of House Minority Leader Charles Halleck.

By the end of January the bill had cleared the Rules Committee, and eleven days later the House passed it and sent it to the Senate. The denouement involved Johnson marshaling liberal forces, led by Senator Hubert Humphrey, who were strong on oratory but weak on working the rules of the Senate, and an intense courtship of Senate Minority Leader Everett Dirksen, which paid off when Republican votes broke the longest filibuster in Senate history. Finally, the amended bill was approved by the House, taking until early July, well beyond the opening weeks that Caro says marked the passage of power to Lyndon Johnson. But as Caro notes, it all stemmed from Johnson's decision, only ten days after President Kennedy's death, to support the gambit of a discharge petition, the only possible instrument for saving the bill, and to press forward with that gambit with every political tool at hand and every ounce of strength.

Of course, as Caro would have it, Johnson's dark thread did not disappear completely. Before the end of 1963, Johnson's views on the deteriorating military situation in Vietnam were hardening, as were his linking of his thoughts on the conflict to the domestic political situation and his insistence on hiding his true intentions from Congress and the public. To John Knight of Knight Ridder newspapers, a skeptic on the war, Johnson remarked that he saw three options: to stay and fight, to try and neutralize North Vietnam (which he thought "totally impractical"), or to "run and let the dominoes start falling over. And God almighty, what they said about us leaving China would just be warming up compared to what they'd say now." No one would ever accuse President Lyndon Johnson of "losing" Vietnam, but with an election coming in November, Johnson was not about to show his cards. Among these cards was a relatively minor escalation, which Johnson secretly approved on January 16, authorizing stepped-up covert operations in a variety of strategic sites—including a place, then known only to area specialists, called the Gulf of Tonkin. Alongside his early triumphs, Caro shows, President Johnson was quietly laying the foundation for disaster.

Meanwhile, the feud with Robert Kennedy assumed new proportions, with Kennedy violently robbed of both the brother he adored and the power that had come with serving him. Completely shattered, Kennedy nevertheless stayed on at the Justice Department, if only to preserve some sense of continuity with his brother's glory. But he bitterly resented how Johnson was getting the credit for achievements on civil rights that the Kennedy White House had initiated. And Johnson, always fearful that Bobby would one day try and reclaim the presidency, resented that, despite all of the achievements that were very much his, he still had to deal with the "snot-nosed little runt" upholding the family honor and glamour. "Every day as soon as I opened the papers or turned on the television, there was something about Bobby Kennedy," Johnson remarked years later. "Somehow or other it just didn't seem fair." For the time being, both men kept up a show of mutual allegiance, but the hatreds were unaltered—except that now Johnson held all the power.

Caro, who is fond of adumbration, is plainly hinting at his final volume to come. Crowding so much of the "good" Lyndon and his landmark works into this volume—ascribing them to a fleeting few weeks, his "life's finest moment," when the "good" Lyndon managed to keep the "bad" Lyndon at bay—Caro enhances the moralism that underlies his entire approach to politics, history, and biography. Caro actually promises that the "bad" Lyndon—with what he calls "the elements of his personality [that were] absent during the transition"—is "shortly to reappear." One gets the sense that the "good" Bobby, likewise already revealed along the way in *The Passage of Power*, will eventually emerge in counterpoint, the brighter and gentler angels of his nature finally overcoming his rude and ruthless passions—although he might also at least sometimes turn into a Jules Feiffer cartoon when stacked up against Eugene McCarthy.

For the moment, though, the image that lingers is of Lyndon Johnson in the political and spiritual culmination of his transition to the presidency, delivering the State of the Union address on January 8, 1964, plumping for the tax cut (and the reduction in federal spending that was part of Harry Byrd's price for agreement), but also raising the stakes of social reform, moving beyond the Civil Rights Bill that still had yet to pass, moving beyond anything that any liberal Democrat could have imagined he would fight for, beyond anything any liberal Democratic chief executive, including the sainted Franklin Delano Roosevelt, could have even proposed in earnest. "This administration," he said—and then threw in, for emphasis, "today, here and now," before he completed the vow—"declares unconditional war on poverty in America." With those words, Johnson claimed the presidency as his own with the most sweeping call for social and economic justice ever uttered by a modern American president. But the words would have meant nothing without what Walter Lippmann called, quoted by Caro, "the political gifts for which Lyndon Johnson is celebrated."

★ ★ ★

WHAT MIGHT ANY of this have to do with our own times? It is obviously absurd to imagine that Caro designed *The Passage of Power*— a book ten years in the making—as a commentary on current events. When some liberals claimed to see in Caro's description of Johnson's expert dealings with a difficult Congress a reproach, intended or not, of President Barack Obama, Caro sharply denied it. "I happen to think he's made great strides," he told an interviewer about Obama in 2012; indeed, for all of the obvious differences in their political styles, he sees something of Johnson in his successor. "People find a lot wrong with [Obama's] health care legislation, as do I, the bill that's passed," he observes, "but I keep remembering something that Lyndon Johnson said. Once we pass it, we can always go back and amend it. And I feel it was an accomplishment to get a health care bill." Besides, he points out that LBJ's civil rights reforms opened the way for an African American to be elected president: "Obama really is Lyndon Johnson's legacy."

If, however, there are any contemporary lessons in Caro's story of Lyndon Johnson's triumphs of early 1964—and if we are to understand why some liberals have come to assess Johnson more positively—it is not enough to seize on legacies or to dwell on political tactics and style, important as they may be. It is more important to take account of the political situation in 1963, and Johnson's historical understanding of and grappling with the immediate realities he faced in the presidency.

Lyndon Johnson arrived in Washington in 1937, a young New Dealer congressman—and the following year, he witnessed and survived a conservative revolution that redefined national politics. The recession of 1937–38, along with the failure of FDR's court-packing scheme and his effort to purge conservative Democratic candidates in favor of New Dealers, cost the Democrats a net loss of seventy-two seats in the House and seven seats in the Senate in the elections of 1938. Those results signaled the beginnings of a new bipartisan conservative working majority of Midwestern Republicans and Southern segregationist Democrats that would thwart liberal politics for decades.

Johnson made his way in the world of that majority, rising to the highest levels of the Democratic leadership by accommodating himself to its limits. As Senate minority and then majority leader in the 1950s, he learned to work with the so-called "Modern Republicans" in and around the administration of Dwight D. Eisenhower who had made their peace with the New Deal. He also learned to offset the rise of the hard Republican right epitomized by Senator Joseph McCarthy. He even learned, in 1957, how to secure passage of the weak but symbolically important Civil Rights Bill. Elected vice president three years later, Johnson understood as well as anyone the power of the enduring bipartisan conservative coalition and the imperative of attacking it head on in order to win any reform legislation—and he understood how it might best be done. John Kennedy, who failed to pass a single important piece of domestic legislation in nearly three years in office, could have put that understanding to good use, but instead he froze Johnson out.

After Dallas, when he would turn a dead man's program into a martyr's cause, fastening once again on civil rights, Johnson was more than well-prepared. He would, in effect, need to create his own majorities in Congress—not in the name of an ideology, personal branding, or a dream of some new fanciful bipartisanship, but piecemeal. He would do so as each ever-shifting political situation arose, relying on a thorough knowledge of the rules of both houses of Congress and just as thorough a knowledge of the men he needed to persuade. Thus, to pass the tax cut bill and clear the way for the Civil Rights Bill, he picked the lock of the Senate Finance Committee by winning over Harry Byrd, the senior Democratic member of the venerable conservative majority; and to secure the Civil Rights Bill, with Humphrey's help, he seduced the Republican leader, Everett Dirksen. By the end of the year, thanks in part to the Republicans' overreaction in nominating Barry Goldwater for the presidency, Johnson had obliterated the bipartisan antireform alliance and swept in the enormous, liberal Democratic majorities of the eightieth Congress that would swiftly approve, by lopsided margins, the Voting Rights Bill, Medicare, Medicaid, Project Head Start, and the other programs of the Great Society.

The overriding realities of national politics over the last twenty years bear comparison with the rise of the conservative counterrevolution of 1938. After Ronald Reagan departed the presidency in 1989, the Republicans on Capitol Hill, and especially in the House of Representatives, began lurching fitfully further to the right, their caucus centered in the white conservative South that Johnson and the Democrats had abandoned when they fought for civil rights and which Goldwater first gathered up for the GOP. Then, following the defeat of President Bill Clinton's health care reform early in his first term, the Republicans regained the House majority for the first time since 1955, led by the right-wing firebrand Newt Gingrich. Reagan's election had marked the start of a new political era, but it took another fourteen years for the counterrevolution against LBJ's Great Society to seize command of Congress. Yet the latest reaction did not stop there. After Clinton recovered to outwit Gingrich and then win reelection in 1996, the Republicans on Capitol Hill pushed ever further to the right, under the command of House Majority Leader Tom DeLay, who oversaw the impeachment farce and then forced Gingrich out.

The conservative five-to-four majority on the Supreme Court placed George W. Bush in the White House in 2000, but Bush's "compassionate conservatism" quickly gave way to the fiercely politicized methods of Dick Cheney and Karl Rove. The DeLay-led right-wing Republican Congress was happy to go along, even after DeLay was caught up in a money-laundering scandal, after which the Democrats regained the House majority in 2006. By then, most of the country had turned fiercely against Bush—and so would the irreducible hard-right base, over his desperate effort to stanch the worst financial crisis since the Great Depression with a massive bailout of financial institutions. This right-wing revulsion against Bush as a secret "big-government" betrayer would in time explode as the Tea Party. In the meantime, the voters turned to a remarkable Democratic newcomer, Barack Obama, who, in the teeth of the white Dixie-driven Republican march to the right, became the first African American to win the White House.

Looking back on this history, the respected centrist political scientists Norman J. Ornstein and Thomas E. Mann observed in 2012 that the undeniable actuality for decades—obscured, they said, by a press intent on proving its objectivity—was that right-wing Republicans, especially in Congress, had been the cause of the intensified polarization in Washington, turning their party into "an insurgent outlier in American politics." Yet Obama initially propagated the idea that both parties were responsible for the acidulous politics of the 1990s, that "politics as usual" and "the old Washington games with the same old Washington players" had produced stalemate. He offered instead a transcendent and "transformative" postpartisanship that would carry the country to the higher ground of peace, prosperity, and social justice. He would be the latest antidote not just to radicalized Reaganism but to the kind of low political scheming that an earlier generation of reform Democrats had seen and detested in Lyndon Johnson and, in many cases, in Robert Kennedy as well.

The prospects for postpartisan transformation were, in reality, nil. By the time Obama became president, the sort of right-wing revanchism and even paranoia that in Johnson's day occupied the margins of American politics, in groups such as the John Birch Society, had become part of the mainstream inside the Republican Party as well as on television and the Internet. At the same time, though, Obama at first enjoyed certain political advantages over the Republicans. Unlike the long-entrenched bipartisan conservative majority that Johnson confronted in 1964, Obama, in 2009, faced a fractured opposition party that had lost its House majority in 2006, that was in public disgrace after the eight-year Bush regime, and whose candidate, Senator John McCain, had just conducted the feeblest presidential campaign since the Michael Dukakis campaign in 1988.

Soon after he took office, Johnson, the accidental president who carried the mantel of the martyred Kennedy, had enjoyed a stunning 77 percent public approval rating. Yet he had run on a ticket that barely squeaked by three years earlier, and he began his presidency in political loneliness, detested by Kennedy liberals, alienated from Southern Democrats, and deeply mistrusted by Republicans. Out of this isolation he produced the transformative presidency that began with his work on the Civil Rights Bill. Obama, by contrast, was elected in 2008 with the first presidential popular majority that his party had enjoyed in more than thirty years and the largest in more than forty. On Inauguration Day, he enjoyed an impressive 69 percent public approval rating, substantially better than his four predecessors, including Ronald Reagan, when they took office. More important, he enjoyed a seventy-nine-seat Democratic majority in the House and an eight-seat Democratic majority in the Senate—very close to a working party majority, which he would enjoy, briefly, during the summer of 2009, without the bipartisan Southern–Midwestern conservative axis that Johnson confronted.

Faced with the worst financial crisis since the Great Depression, Obama went right to work, salvaging the auto industry and then addressing the economic emergency with a modest stimulus plan. Yet despite the president's sweet reason, the stimulus won not a single Republican vote. Obama then turned to health care reform, his signal effort, and after more than a year of struggle came away with a major piece of legislation, the Affordable Care Act—the most ambitious social reform of its kind since the heyday of Lyndon Johnson's Great Society. But the White House pursued health care reform first by handing the issue in the Senate over to the dilatory Senator Max Baucus of Montana and the so-called Gang of Six. By the time Obama finally signed what had become the ACA, the White House had either backed off from early avowals, above all its support for a public option, or negotiated away important provisions to the big pharmaceutical and insurance lobbies. And still, after all the tussling, only a single Republican in either chamber voted for the amended bill.

Winning the health care act hardly paved the way either for a closing of the partisan gap or a public endorsement of Obama's achievement. Whipped up by Republican charges that health care reform proved Obama was a fearsome "socialist," the electorate handed the House majority back to the GOP in 2010 and whittled down to six the Democratic majority in the Senate. The White House and Senate leadership had the chance to alter the rules on filibustering, before the new Congress began its work—the kind of maneuver that Lyndon

Johnson could have been counted on to pull off. Instead, boxed in, Obama pursued a "grand bargain" when the Republicans threatened to throw the already fragile economy into utter chaos during the debt ceiling crisis over the summer of 2011. Some influential Democrats urged the president to shut down the entire phony crisis by invoking the Fourteenth Amendment that prohibits shenanigans with the full faith and credit of the United States. It was, again, the kind of thing that Lyndon Johnson would conceivably have done, if only to show his opponents that the president of the United States—"your President," he would have said, with an edge—would not put up with zealous, posturing partisans threatening the nation's security.

After winning reelection in 2012 but seeing the Democrats lose the Senate as well in 2014, Obama seemed finally to give up on postpartisanship, vowing to press his agenda as far as possible through executive actions, and doing precisely that despite Republican charges that he was abusing his constitutional powers. In 2015, he proclaimed in his State of the Union address a program of bold domestic reforms that would never win approval but that served as a kind of harbinger of what some future Democratic White House might accomplish. Although he clung to some postpartisan rhetoric—promising Republicans he would seek out their ideas and "to work with you to make this country stronger"—there were no illusions that any grand bargains were in the offing, or would be for the remainder of his presidency.

It is at this intersection of past and present that *The Passage of Power* connects with our own political problems. But finally, comparisons between Obama and Johnson—the sort of presentism that is always a temptation—are beside the historical point. In its final third, *The Passage of Power* shows Caro's atrocious Lyndon Johnson getting a grip on his baser drives just long enough to pull the country through its trauma and undertake what would become his greatest political achievements. The book leaves us assured that, like a golfer teeing up, Caro is preparing his readers for the full force of what he will undoubtedly show as the revived hateful Johnson ruining everything in Vietnam, driven by his dark psychology and vile character. But this volume offers a primer about the sources and uses of executive power as understood by one of the truly formidable presidents in our history. Thomas Jefferson, Abraham Lincoln, and Franklin Roosevelt all combined keen historical awareness with a gift for sizing up political situations inside Washington and pursuing their goals with deeply effective governing skills, tactical as well as strategic. These qualities are no guarantee of success, let alone of sound policies, but they have been essential to securing the greater good. And these were qualities that Lyndon Johnson possessed in abundance.

Bibliographic Notes
and References

Introduction

The quotations from Walt Whitman appear in "Democratic Vistas," in *Two Rivulets* (Camden, NJ, 1876), 27, and "When I Read the Book," in *Leaves of Grass* (Philadelphia, 1892), 14.

1: The Postpartisan Style in American Politics

An earlier version of this chapter appeared as "The Mirage," *New Republic*, November 17, 2011, pp. 25–33. Basic primary sources on parties in the Revolutionary and early national periods include three indispensable collections of papers: Julian P. Boyd et al., eds., *The Papers of Thomas Jefferson* (41 vols. to date; Princeton, NJ, 1950–), Harold C. Syrett, ed., *The Papers of Alexander Hamilton* (27 vols.; New York, 1961–87), and William T. Hutchinson and William M. E. Rachal, eds., *The Papers of James Madison* (17 vols.; Chicago, 1962–91). The case for the rise of professional parties in the 1820s and 1830s, as written by one of its architects, appears in Martin Van Buren, *Inquiry into the Origins and Course of Political Parties in the United States* (New York, 1867), quotations on pp. 4, 166. Richard Hofstadter, *The Idea of a Party System: The Rise of Legitimate Opposition in the United States, 1780–1840* (Berkeley, 1969; quotation on p. 17), redirected historians' attention to the issue of partisanship and antipartisanship, while David Hackett Fischer, *The Revolution of American Conservatism: The*

Federalist Party in the Era of Jeffersonian Democracy (New York, 1965), is richly detailed and informative on early antipartisanship and includes, on p. 159, the quotation here on p. 8, "*Office-holders, Office-seekers, Pimps,*" originally in *Constitutionalist and Weekly Magazine* (Exeter, NH), March 1, 1814. On the Jacksonian and antebellum periods, Mark Voss-Hubbard, *Beyond Party: Cultures of Antipartisanship in Northern Politics before the Civil War* (Baltimore, 2002), illuminates how antipartisanship shaped the nativist Know-Nothing movement, with larger implications for antipartisanship generally. On the Whigs, see Michael F. Holt, *The Rise and Fall of the American Whig Party: Jacksonian Politics and the Onset of the Civil War* (New York, 2003). The "shoeblacks" quotation on p. 11 appears in the *Daily Intelligencer* (Washington, DC), June 13, 1835. *The Junius Tracts. Number VI: Democracy* (New York, 1844), written by the minister turned political writer Calvin Colton, is a concise statement of Whig antiparty partisanship; quotations on pp. 5, 12. On the slave South and the Confederacy, George C. Rable, *The Confederate Republic: A Revolution Against Politics* (Chapel Hill, 1994), is essential; quotation on p. 215. See also "The Southern Convention," *Southern Quarterly Review*, new series, II (July 1850): 191–232, quotation on p. 198; and "Characteristics of the Statesman," *Southern Quarterly Review* VI (July 1844): 95–129, quotation on p. 126. On antiparty sentiments and the Confederate Constitution, see especially Robert H. Smith, *An Address to the Citizens of Alabama on the Constitution and Laws of the Confederate States of America* (Mobile, 1861), quotations on pp. 13–14.

John G. Sproat, "*The Best Men": Liberal Reformers in the Gilded Age* (1968; Chicago, 1982) is the classic account of the Liberal Republicans and Mugwumps, but should be supplemented with Gerald W. McFarland, *Mugwumps, Morals, and Politics, 1884–1920* (Amherst, MA, 1975), and Michael E. McGerr, *The Decline of Popular Politics: The American North, 1865–1928* (New York, 1988). The files of *The Nation* are an excellent primary source; quotations from April 16, 1874, and April 26, 1877. Two other telling sources, also quoted here, are Henry Adams, "The Independents in the Canvas," *North American Review* 123 (1876): 463; and [Jonathan Baxter Harrison], "Limited Sovereignty in the United States," *Atlantic Monthly* 43 (1879): 186. James J. Connolly. *An Elusive Unity: Urban Democracy and Machine Politics in Industrializing America* (Ithaca, NY, 2010), examines with insight the politics which the genteel reformers sought to eradicate. On Theodore Roosevelt as politician, John Morton Blum, *The Republican Roosevelt* (1954; Cambridge, MA, 1977) is particularly incisive. A fresh appraisal of Progressive Era politics appears in Michael E. McGerr, *A Fierce Discontent: The Rise and Fall of the Progressive Movement in America, 1870–1920* (New York, 2005); and for a different view, see Jackson Lears, *The Remaking of a Nation: The Making of Modern America, 1877–1920* (New York, 2009). Woodrow Wilson presented his mature ideas about parties and partisanship in *Constitu-*

tional Government in the United States (New York, 1908), quotations on pp. 208, 218; also see John Milton Cooper, *Woodrow Wilson: A Biography* (New York, 2009). On Herbert Hoover, see above all Joan Hoff Wilson, *Herbert Hoover: Forgotten Progressive* (Boston, 1975), quotation on p. 209. Important studies in the strong and voluminous literature on the decline of Progressivism and the advent of the New Deal include Barry Karl, *The Uneasy State: The United States from 1915 to 1945* (Chicago, 1983), quotation on pp. 234–35. On the New Deal itself, see Alan Brinkley, *The End of Reform: New Deal Liberalism in Recession and Reform* (New York, 1995), Alexander J. Field, *A Great Leap Forward: 1930s Depression and U.S. Economic Growth* (New Haven, 2011), and Ira Katznelson, *Fear Itself: The New Deal and the Origins of Our Time* (New York, 2013). The quotation from Hymie Schorenstein about Franklin D. Roosevelt appears in William Safire, *Safire's Political Dictionary* (1968; New York, 2008), 333. The themes of partisanship and antipartisanship are less well covered over the period since 1945, but see James T. Patterson, *Great Expectations: The United States, 1945–1974* (New York, 1996), and Sean Wilentz, *The Age of Reagan: A History, 1974–2008* (New York, 2008). John F. Kennedy's observations quoted on pp. 29–30 appear in "The Presidency in 1960—National Press Club, Washington, D.C., January 14 1960," made available online by Gerhard Peters and John T. Woolley in The American Presidency Project, http://www.presidency.ucsb.edu/ ws/?pid=25795. On recent distempers, two books are especially informative: Larry M. Bartels, *Unequal Democracy: The Political Economy of the New Gilded Age* (Princeton, NJ, 2008), and Thomas E. Mann and Norman J. Ornstein, *It's Even Worse Than It Looks: How the American Constitutional System Collided with the New Politics of Extremism* (New York, 2012). For a perceptive defense of parties and partisanship as an antidote to hyperpartisanship, see Russell Muirhead, *The Promise of Party in a Polarized Age* (Cambridge, MA, 2014).

2: America's Forgotten Egalitarian Tradition

An earlier version of this chapter appeared as "America's Lost Egalitarian Tradition," *Daedalus* 131:1 (Winter 2002), pp. 66–80. Copyright © 2002 by the American Academy of Arts and Sciences. This chapter's framing and discussion of the issues of inequality and American egalitarianism draws on an important book by James L. Huston, *Securing the Fruits of Labor: The American Concept of Wealth Distribution, 1765–1900* (1998; Baton Rouge, 2015). See also Sir Henry Phelps Brown, *Egalitarianism and the Generation of Inequality* (Oxford, 1988), a magisterial comparative overview of the history of economic egalitarianism since the Renaissance. In addition to the basic primary sources cited for chapter 1, see Sam B. Smith and Harriet Chappell Owsley, eds., *The Papers of Andrew*

Jackson (9 vols. to date; Knoxville, TN, 1980–); John Spencer Barrett, ed., *Correspondence of Andrew Jackson* (7 vols.; Washington, DC, 1926–35), Robert I. Meriwether et al., eds., *Papers of John C. Calhoun* (28 vols.; Columbia, SC, 1959–2003), and Roy C. Basler, ed., *The Collected Works of Abraham Lincoln* (8 vols.; New Brunswick, NJ, 1953). The quotation on p. 36 appears in Eric Foner, *Tom Paine and Revolutionary America* (New York, 1976), 93. For statistics on American inequality before 1913, see Jeffrey G. Williamson and Peter H. Lindert, *American Inequality: A Macroeconomic History* (New York, 1980); Peter H. Lindert and Jeffrey G. Williamson, "American Incomes, 1774–1860," National Bureau of Economic Research Working Paper No. 18396, September 2012, available at http://www.nber.org/papers/w18396; and Edward Pessen, *Riches, Class, and Power before the Civil War* (Lexington, MA, 1973). But see also, for contrasting views, Lee Soltow, *Men and Wealth in the United States, 1850–1870* (New Haven, 1975); Richard H. Steckel, "Poverty and Prosperity: A Longitudinal Study of Wealth Accumulation, 1850–1860," *Review of Economics and Statistics* 72 (1990): 275–85; and Carole Shammas, "A New Look at Long-Term Wealth Trends in the United States," *American Historical Review* 98 (1993): 412–31. On the period since 1913, see Thomas Piketty and Emmanuel Saez, "Income Inequality in the United States, 1913–1998," *Quarterly Journal of Economics* 118 (2003): 1–39; Emmanuel Saez and Gabriel Zucman, "Wealth Inequality since 1913: Evidence from Capitalized Income Tax Data," Bureau of Economic Research Working Paper No. 20625, October 2014, available at http://gabriel-zucman.eu/files/SaezZucman2014.pdf.   On fluctuations from the 1980s to the present, see Robert J. Shapiro, "Income Growth and Decline under Recent U.S. Presidents and the New Challenge to Restore Broad Economic Prosperity," Center for Effective Public Management, Brookings Institution, March 2015, available at http://www.brookings.edu/~/media/research/files/papers/2015/03/05-income-growth-decline-economic-prosperity-shapiro/shapirov3.pdf.

On "Anglicization," see John M. Murrin, "A Roof without Walls: The Dilemma of American National Identity," in Richard Beemen, Stephen Botein, and Edward C. Carter II, eds., *Beyond Confederation: Origins of the Constitution and American Identity* (Chapel Hill, NC, 1987), 333–48. On equality and the American Revolution, see especially Gordon S. Wood, *The Radicalism of the American Revolution* (New York, 1991), and Michael Merrill and Sean Wilentz, *The Key of Liberty: The Life and Democratic Writings of William Manning, "A Laborer," 1747–1814* (Cambridge, MA, 1994). The quotation from Joyce Appleby appears in her *Thomas Jefferson* (New York, 2003), 85. On the Jacksonian period, see Michael F. Holt, *The Rise and Fall of the American Whig Party: Jacksonian Politics and the Onset of the Civil War* (New York, 2003), and Sean Wilentz, *The Rise of American Democracy: Jefferson to Lincoln* (New York, 2005). The National

Republican/Whig view of social mobility and the harmony of interests are concisely presented in Tristam Burges, *Address of the Hon. Tristam Burges Delivered at the Third Annual Fair of the American Institute of the City of New York* (New York, 1830), quotation on pp. 16–17; and Edward Everett, *An Address Delivered before the Mercantile Library Association* (Boston, 1838), quotations on pp. 12–13. On the Republicans and Lincoln, see Eric Foner, *Free Soil, Free Labor, Free Men: The Ideology of the Republican Party before the Civil War* (New York, 1970), and Gabor H. Boritt, *Lincoln and the Economics of the American Dream* (Memphis, 1978). George Fitzhugh, *Cannibals All!; or, Slaves without Masters* (Richmond, 1857; quotation on p. ix), is a peculiar but telling look at proslavery ideology; for a more expansive view of slaveholder thought, see Michael O'Brien's indispensable *Conjectures of Order: Intellectual Life and the American South, 1810–1860* (2 vols.; Chapel Hill, NC, 2004). On Reconstruction, see above all Eric Foner, *Reconstruction: America's Unfinished Revolution* (New York, 1988). For the period after 1877, see the books by Lears, McGerr, Karl, Brinkley, Katznelson, Patterson, and Wilentz cited for chapter 1. For an admiring look at FDR's "second bill of rights," see Cass Sunstein, *The Second Bill of Rights: FDR's Unfinished Revolution and Why We Need It More Than Ever* (New York, 2004). On the "great compression," see Claudia Goldin and Robert A. Margo, "The Great Compression: The Wage Structure in the United States at Mid-Century," National Bureau of Economic Research Working Paper No. 3817, August 1991, available at http://www.nber.org/papers/w3817. The quotation from Larry Bartels appears in his *Unequal Democracy: The Political Economy of the New Gilded Age* (Princeton, NJ, 2008), 60.

3: Thomas Paine: The Origins of American Egalitarianism

An earlier version of this chapter appeared as "The Air Around Tom Paine," *New Republic*, April 24, 1995, pp. 34–41. The most accessible volume of Paine's writings is Thomas Paine, *Collected Writings*, ed. Eric Foner (New York, 1995). The quotation on p. 79 is from the most thorough biography to date, John Keane, *Tom Paine: A Political Life* (1995; New York, 2003), 190. Among the other important studies to appear in recent decades are Eric Foner, *Tom Paine and Revolutionary America* (New York, 1976); Jack Fruchtman, Jr., *Thomas Paine and the Religion of Nature* (Baltimore, 1995); Gregory Claeys, *Thomas Paine: Social and Political Thought* (Boston, 1989), Harvey J. Kaye, *Thomas Paine and the Promise of America* (New York, 2005); Craig Nelson, *Thomas Paine: Enlightenment, Revolution, and the Birth of Modern Nations* (New York, 2006); Seth Cotlar, *Tom Paine's America: The Rise and Fall of Transatlantic Radicalism in the Early Republic* (Charlottesville, VA, 2011); and W.A. Speck, *A Political Biography of Thomas Paine* (London, 2013).

4: Life, Liberty, and the Pursuit of Thomas Jefferson

This chapter draws on essays published originally as "Life, Liberty, and the Pursuit of Thomas Jefferson," *New Republic*, March 10, 1997, pp. 32–42, and "The Details of Greatness," *New Republic*, March 29, 2004, pp. 27–35. The essential sources are Julian P. Boyd et al., eds., *The Papers of Thomas Jefferson* (41 vols. to date; Princeton, NJ, 1950–); J. Jefferson Looney, ed., *The Papers of Thomas Jefferson: Retirement Series* (10 vols. to date; Princeton, NJ, 2005–); Andrew Lipscomb, ed., *The Writings of Thomas Jefferson* (20 vols.; Washington, DC, 1903–04). The books discussed in this chapter are Conor Cruise O'Brien, *The Long Affair: Thomas Jefferson and the French Revolution* (Chicago, 1998); Garry Wills, *"Negro President": Jefferson and the Slave Power* (New York, 2003); Annette Gordon-Reed, *Thomas Jefferson and Sally Hemings: An American Controversy* (Charlottesville, VA, 1997); and Gordon-Reed, *The Hemingses of Monticello: An American Family* (New York, 2008). See also Robert McColley, *Slavery and Jeffersonian Virginia* (1964; Urbana, IL, 1973), and Joseph Ellis, *American Sphinx: The Character of Thomas Jefferson* (New York, 1997), quotations on pp. 21–22, 353. The quotations on p. 85 are from Forrest McDonald's dust-jacket blurb for Richard K. Matthews, *The Radical Politics of Thomas Jefferson: A Revisionist View* (Lawrence, KS, 1984, and Michael Zuckerman, *Almost Chosen People: Oblique Biographies in the American Grain* (Berkeley, 1993), 196. For Franklin D. Roosevelt's appreciation of Jefferson, see his "Address at Jefferson Day Dinner in St. Paul, Minnesota, April 18, 1932," made available online by Gerhard Peters and John T. Woolley in the American Presidency Project, at http://www.presidency.ucsb.edu/ws/?pid=88409. David Brion Davis's remarks on Jefferson and Burke appear in *The Problem of Slavery in the Age of Revolution, 1770–1823* (Ithaca, NY, 1974), quotation on p. 174. The quotations from William Loughton Smith and John Rutledge, Jr., on pp. 94 and 96 appear in *Annals of Congress,* 1st Cong., 2nd sess., House, 1505, and ibid., 6th Cong., 1st sess., House, 230, and in Smith's anonymously authored pamphlet *The Pretentions of Thomas Jefferson to the Presidency Examined* (Philadelphia, 1796), 16. The quotation from Ezra Stiles on p. 96 appears in a letter from Stiles to Jacob Richardson dated July 9, 1794, quoted in Edmund S. Morgan, *The Gentle Puritan: A Life of Ezra Stiles, 1727–1795* (New Haven, 1962), 456. The letter from Thomas Pickering to Rufus King dated March 4, 1804, appears in Henry Adams, ed., *Documents Relating to New England Federalism, 1800–1815* (Boston, 1877), 351–3. On the New England Federalists and slavery, see James Banner, *To the Hartford Convention: The Federalists and the Origins of Party Politics in Massachusetts, 1789–1815* (New York, 1970), quotations on pp. 106–7. My discussion of the three-fifths clause draws on Brian D. Humes, Elaine K. Swift, Richard

Valelly, Kenneth Finegold, and Evelyn C. Fink, "Representation of the Ante-bellum South in the House of Representatives: Measuring the Impact of the Three-Fifths Clause," in David W. Brady and Matthew D. McCubbins, eds., *Party, Process, and Political Change in Congress: New Perspectives on the History of Congress* (Stanford, 2002), 452–69. The authors' quantitative methodology undercuts some of their conclusions, but their findings are highly informative. The quotation from William Loughton Smith on p. 102 appears in a letter from Smith to Edward Rutledge dated February 28, 1790, in George C. Rogers, Jr., ed., "The Letters of William Loughton Smith to Edward Rutledge: June 8, 1790 to April 28, 1794," *South Carolina Historical Magazine* 69 (1968): 107. Matthew E. Mason, "Slavery Overshadowed: Congress Debates Prohibiting the Atlantic Slave Trade to the United States," *Journal of the Early Republic* 20 (2000): 59–81, is the closest study of its subject and points out that Jefferson, whatever the shortcomings of his record on slavery, "proved effective and deci-sive in his opposition to the international slave trade" (63). On Plumer and Pickering, see Gerald H. Clarfield, *Timothy Pickering and the American Repub-lic* (Pittsburgh, 1980), 220–22. For a shrewd, devastating portrait of Picker-ing as a "glowering hack," see Stanley M. Elkins and Eric L. McKitrick, *The Age of Federalism: The Early American Republic, 1788–1800* (New York, 1993), 623–26. Edmund Bacon is quoted in Hamilton W. Pierson, *Jefferson at Monti-cello: The Private Life of Thomas Jefferson* (New York, 1862), 38. More favorable recent assessments, emphasizing Jefferson's democratic politics, include Joyce Appleby, *Thomas Jefferson* (New York, 2003), and Jon Meacham, *Thomas Jef-ferson: The Art of Power* (New York, 2012). See also Jeffrey L. Pasley's bracing review of the literature, "Politics and the Misadventures of Thomas Jefferson's Modern Reputation," *Journal of Southern History* 72 (2006): 871–901, quotation on p. 894.

5: John Quincy Adams: Slavery's Arch-Enemy

An earlier version of this chapter appeared as "The Mandarin and the Rebel," *New Republic*, December 22, 1997, pp. 25–34. The most thorough edition of John Quincy Adams's diary to date is *Memoirs of John Quincy Adams, Compris-ing Portions of His Diary from 1795 to 1848*, ed. Charles Francis Adams (12 vols.; Philadelphia, 1874–77), but see also Allan Nevins's edition, *The Diary of John Quincy Adams, 1794–1845: American Political, Social, and Intellectual Life from Washington to Polk* (New York, 1928), quotation on p. xxiv. The entirety of the manuscript diary is now available online, courtesy of the Massachusetts His-torical Society, at http://www.masshist.org/jqadiaries/php/. In addition to the book discussed here, Paul C. Nagel, *John Quincy Adams: A Public Life, A Private Life* (New York, 1997), see Samuel Flagg Bemis's standard works, *John Quincy Adams and the Foundations of American Foreign Policy* (New York, 1949) and *John Quincy Adams and the Union* (New York, 1956), quotation on p. 303; Leonard L. Richards, *The Life and Times of Congressman John Quincy Adams* (New York, 1986), quotation on p. 99; Gary V. Wood, *Heir to the Fathers: John Quincy Adams and the Spirit of Constitutional Government* (Lanham, MD, 2004); Fred Kaplan, *John Quincy Adams: American Visionary* (New York, 2014); and Charles Edel, *Nation Builder: John Quincy Adams and the Grand Strategy of the Republic* (Cambridge, MA, 2014). The quotation from the Virginia legislator on p. 125 appears in the *Richmond Enquirer*, March 14, 1848. Adams's thoughts on Masonry, as contained in his correspondence, are collected in Adams, *Letters on the Masonic Institution* (Boston, 1847), quotation on p. 68. On anti-Masonry, see Paul Goodman, *Towards a Christian Republic: Antimasonry and the Great Transition in New England, 1826–1836* (New York, 1988). On Adams and the fight over the gag rule, see William Lee Miller, *Arguing about Slavery: John Quincy Adams and the Great Battle in the United States Congress* (New York, 1995).

6: John Brown: The Temptation of Terror

An earlier version of this chapter appeared as "Homegrown Terrorist," *New Republic*, October 24, 2005, pp. 23–30. The book discussed in this chapter is David S. Reynolds, *John Brown, Abolitionist: The Man Who Killed Slavery, Sparked the Civil War, and Seeded Civil Rights* (New York, 2005). Highlights in the voluminous literature on Brown include W. E. B. Du Bois, *John Brown* (Philadelphia, 1909); Oswald Garrison Villard, *John Brown, 1800–1859: A Biography Fifty Years After* (Boston, 1910); Robert Penn Warren, *John Brown: The Making of a Martyr* (New York, 1929); Stephen B. Oates, *To Purge This Land with Blood; A Biography of John Brown* (New York, 1970); Benjamin Quarles, *Allies for Freedom: Blacks and John Brown* (New York, 1974); Merrill D. Peterson, *John Brown: The Legend Revisited* (Charlottesville, VA, 2002); and Tony Horwitz, *Midnight Rising: John Brown and the Raid that Sparked the Civil War* (New York, 2011). Jonathan Halperin Earle, *John Brown's Raid on Harpers Ferry: A Brief History with Documents* (Boston, 2008), is a fine collection of sources that covers Brown's career over the entire 1850s. The quotation from Charles Francis Adams on p. 166 appears in the Charles Francis Adams Diary, November 7, 1860, Massachusetts Historical Society.

7: *Abraham Lincoln: Egalitarian Politician*

An earlier version of this chapter appeared as "Who Lincoln Was," *New Republic*, July 15, 2009, pp. 24–47. That original essay produced a sharp debate, all of which is available at http://www.newrepublic.com/article/books-and-arts/who-lincoln-was. The books discussed here are Michael Burlingame, *Abraham Lincoln: A Life* (2 vols.; Baltimore, 2008); Ronald C. White, *A. Lincoln: A Biography* (New York, 2009); Fred Kaplan, *Lincoln: The Biography of a Writer* (New York, 2008); Henry Louis Gates, Jr., and Donald Yacovone, eds., *Lincoln on Race & Slavery* (Princeton, 2009); and John Stauffer, *Giants: The Parallel Lives of Frederick Douglass and Abraham Lincoln* (New York, 2008). As these works attest, serious study of Lincoln begins with Roy C. Basler, ed., *The Collected Works of Abraham Lincoln* (8 vols.; New Brunswick, NJ, 1953). For important treatments of Lincoln as a politician, see Richard N. Current, "The Master Politician," *The Lincoln Nobody Knows* (New York, 1958); David Herbert Donald, "A. Lincoln, Politician," *Lincoln Reconsidered: Essays on the Civil War Era* (1956; New York, 2001); and David Herbert Donald, *Lincoln* (New York, 1995). The quotation from John Hay on p. 179 appears in "Hay to William Herndon, September 3, 1866," in Douglas L. Wilson and Rodney O. Davis, eds., *Herndon's Informants: Letters, Interviews, and Statements about Abraham Lincoln* (Urbana, IL, 1998), p. 332. The quotation from Hay and John G. Nicolay on p. 194 appears in Nicolay and Hay, *Abraham Lincoln: A History* (1890; 10 vols.; New York, 1906), pp. vi, 156. The quotation from Everett Dirksen on p. 196 appears in Donald, *Lincoln Reconsidered*, p. 13. For a corrective to some of the arguments criticized here, in line with my own view, see James Oakes, *The Radical and the Republican: Frederick Douglass, Abraham Lincoln, and the Triumph of Antislavery Politics* (New York, 2007), quotations on pp. 170, 172.

8: *Democracy at Gettysburg, 1863*

An earlier version of this chapter appeared as "Democracy at Gettysburg," in Sean Conant, ed., *The Gettysburg Address: Perspectives in Lincoln's Greatest Speech* (New York, 2015), 51–71. The final text of the Gettysburg Address appears in Roy C. Basler, ed., *The Collected Works of Abraham Lincoln* (8 vols.; New Brunswick, NJ, 1953), VII:23. On the Declaration, the Constitution, and the Gettysburg Address, see above all Garry Wills, *Lincoln at Gettysburg: The Words That Remade America* (New York, 1992), quotation on p. 38. The argument about the Address and the redefinition of Union war aims appears more widely;

for an excellent formulation, see David Herbert Donald, *Lincoln* (New York, 1995), 460–66. Historians have not been blind to the importance of democracy in the Gettysburg Address; see, for example, the essays in Mario M. Cuomo and Harold Holzer, eds., *Lincoln on Democracy* (1990; New York, 1991), including Hans Trefousse's remark on how the Address affirmed that "the war was a struggle for democracy, for if a popular decision by ballots could be challenged by bullets, democratic government was at an end" (302). The trouble, I think, is that historians too often elide democracy with the Union and antislavery in Lincoln's thought and in pro-Union political thinking more generally. We have thus neglected how, at Gettysburg, Lincoln built on long-standing disputes over what, in fact, democracy was and ought to be. The Gettysburg Address declared the war a struggle for democracy but also declared what had become Lincoln's conception of democracy. For an interesting recent treatment of democracy and the Gettysburg Address, see Allen Guelzo's essay "Lincoln's Sound Bite: Have Faith in Democracy," *New York Times*, November 17, 2013. The quotation from Horace Greeley's *Tribune* on p. 217 appears in the *New-York Daily Tribune*, November 27, 1860. The Ramsden quotation on p. 219 appears in Amanda Foreman, *A World on Fire: Britain's Crucial Role in the American Civil War* (New York, 2010), 98–99; the complementary quotations on American views of the crisis of democracy appear in *Daily Whig and Republican* (Quincy, IL), May 3, 1861; *Gazette* (Columbus, OH), June 21, 1861; *Newport* (RI) *Mercury*, May 25, 1861; *Iowa State Register* (Des Moines), December 12, 1860; *Evening Press* (Hartford, CT), October 26, 1860; *Daily Pittsburgh Gazette*, November 2, 1860; *Daily Intelligencer* (Wheeling, VA), December 24, 1860; and James M. McPherson, *For Cause and Comrades: Why Men Fought in the Civil War* (New York, 1997), 113. On the Southern antiparty temperament, see the sources given for chapter 1. For some soundings in the most antidemocratic currents of Southern political thinking, see William Russell Smith, *The History and Debates of the Convention of the People of Alabama* (Montgomery, AL, 1861), quotations on pp. 224, 441; and the sources in Michael P. Johnson, *Toward a Patriarchal Republic: The Secession of Georgia* (Baton Rouge, 1977); and Stephanie McCurry, *Confederate Reckoning: Power and Politics in the Civil War South* (Cambridge, MA, 2010).

9: The Steel Town and the Gilded Age

An earlier version of this chapter appeared as "A Triumph of the Gilded Age," *New York Review of Books*, October 22, 1992. The books discussed here are David Demarest, Jr., ed., *"The River Ran Red": Homestead 1892* (Pittsburgh,

1992), and Paul Krause, *The Battle for Homestead, 1880–1892: Politics, Culture, and Steel* (Pittsburgh, 1992). Other studies well worth consulting include J. Bernard Hogg, "The Homestead Strike of 1892" (PhD dissertation, University of Chicago, 1943), and Paul Kahan, *The Homestead Strike: Labor, Violence, and American Industry* (New York, 2014). Arthur G. Burgoyne's dramatic pro-labor journalistic account, *Homestead* (1893; Pittsburgh, 1979) includes valuable detail. On management's response see Joseph Frazier Wall, *Andrew Carnegie* (1970; Pittsburgh, 1989), and David Nasaw, *Andrew Carnegie* (New York, 2006). On labor in Pittsburgh, see also Francis G. Couvares, *The Remaking of Pittsburgh: Class and Culture in an Industrializing City, 1877–1919* (Albany, NY, 1984). Two essential works on American labor in this period are Herbert G. Gutman, *Work, Culture, and Society in Industrializing America* (New York, 1976), and David Montgomery, *The Fall of the House of Labor: The Workplace, the State, and American Labor Activism, 1865–1925* (New York, 1987).

10: W. E. B. Du Bois: A Heroic Education

An earlier version of this chapter appeared as "Hearts and Souls," *New Republic*, April 4, 1994, pp. 28–35. David Levering Lewis, *W. E. B. Du Bois, 1868–1919: Biography of a Race* (New York, 1993), discussed here, and David Levering Lewis, *W. E. B. Du Bois: The Fight for Equality and the American Century 1919–1963* (New York, 2000), are indispensable. W. E. B. Du Bois, *Writings*, ed. Nathan Huggins (New York, 1996) includes *The Souls of Black Folk* although not, regrettably, *Black Reconstruction in America*. A standout amid the spate of books on Du Bois in recent years is Kwame Anthony Appiah, *Lines of Descent: W. E. B. Du Bois and the Emergence of Identity* (Cambridge, MA, 2014). On Du Bois and Madame Blavatsky, mentioned on p. 258, see Eric Sundquist, *Race in the Making of American Literature* (Cambridge, MA, 1993), 576.

11: Theodore Roosevelt: Politics and Folly

An earlier version of this chapter appeared as "The Pride of Teddy Roosevelt," *New York Review of Books*, May 12, 2011. Edmund Morris, *Colonel Roosevelt* (New York, 2010), completes Morris's massively detailed three-volume biography. Readers should also consult John Morton Blum, *The Republican Roosevelt* (1954, Cambridge, MA, 1977); William Harbaugh, *Power and Responsibility: The Life and Times of Theodore Roosevelt* (New York, 1961); and Kathleen Dalton,

Theodore Roosevelt: A Strenuous Life (New York, 2002). Roosevelt's own *Auto-biography* (New York, 1910), for all of its historical limitations, is a source of insight. Roosevelt's voluminous writings and official papers are collected as *The Works of Theodore Roosevelt* (24 vols.; New York, 1923–26). An excellent selection of Roosevelt's correspondence is skillfully presented in Elting E. Morison, ed., *The Letters of Theodore Roosevelt* (8 vols.; Cambridge, MA, 1951–54).

12: The Liberals and the Leftists

An earlier version of this chapter appeared as "The Left vs. the Liberals," *New York Review of Books*, August 16, 2012. This chapter discusses Michael Kazin, *American Dreamers: How the Left Changed a Nation* (New York, 2011). For earlier influential assessments of the American left, see Daniel Bell, *Marxian Socialism in the United States* (Princeton, NJ, 1952), and *The End of Ideology: The Exhaustion of Political Ideas in the Fifties* (Glencoe, IL, 1960); Irving Howe and Lewis Coser, *The American Communist Party: A Critical History, 1919–1957* (Boston, 1957); and Irving Howe, *Socialism and America* (Orlando, FL, 1986). See also Seymour Martin Lipset and Gary Marks, *It Didn't Happen Here: Why Socialism Failed in the United States* (New York, 2001). Kazin's critique of Howard Zinn, *A People's History of the United States* (1980; New York, 2003) appears in *Dissent*, Spring 2004, available at https://www.dissentmagazine.org/article/howard-zinns-history-lessons. See also Barbara Ehrenreich, "Vote for Nader," *The Nation*, August 21, 2000, as well as Kazin's articles, "Where's Perot When We Need Him?" *Los Angeles Times*, October 29, 2000; "Anarchism Now: Occupy Wall Street Revives an Ideology," *New Republic*, November 7, 2011; and "The Radical Left: Always a Bridesmaid," *Daily Beast*, August 8, 2015, available at http://www.thedailybeast.com/articles/2015/08/08/the-radical-left-always-a-bridesmaid.html. The quotation from William Lloyd Garrison on p. 286 appears in James M. McPherson, *The Struggle for Equality: The Abolitionists and the Negro in the Civil War and Reconstruction* (Princeton, NJ, 1964), 33.

13: The Cold War and the Perils of Junk History

An earlier version of this chapter appeared as "Cherry-Picking Our History," *New York Review of Books*, February 21, 2013. Oliver Stone and Peter Kuznick, *The Untold History of the United* States (New York, 2012), accompanied a ten-episode release marketed by Showtime as *Oliver Stone's Untold History of the United States*. For a recent overview of the Soviet repressive record in Eastern Europe, which allows for American exaggerations of Stalin's aggressive intentions, see Anne Applebaum, *Iron Curtain: The Crushing of Eastern Europe, 1945–1956* (New York, 2012). Michael Moynihan's review, "Oliver Stone's Junk History Debunked," *Daily Beast*, November 19, 2012, is available at http://www.thedailybeast.com/articles/2012/11/19/oliver-stone-s-junk-history-of-the-united-states-debunked.html. For a judicious review of the literature on Truman's decision to drop the atomic bomb, see J. Samuel Walker, "Recent Literature on Truman's Atomic Bomb Decision: A Search for Middle Ground," *Diplomatic History* 29 (2005): 311–34. The most thorough study of the 1944 convention is Robert H. Ferrell, *Choosing Truman: The Democratic Convention of 1944* (Columbia, MO, 1994), quotation on p. 3, but see also James MacGregor Burns, *Roosevelt: The Soldier of Freedom* (New York 1970), 503–7. The quotations from Wallace on "Dear Guru" and FDR's decision to dump him appear in John C. Culver and John Hyde, *American Dreamer: The Life and Times of Henry A. Wallace* (New York, 2000), 82, and John Morton Blum, ed., *The Price of Vision: The Diary of Henry A. Wallace, 1942–1946,* (Boston, 1973), 371. The quotations from I. F. Stone and Eleanor Roosevelt on p. 303 appear in Arthur M. Schlesinger, Jr., *A Life in the Twentieth Century: Innocent Beginnings, 1917–1950* (Boston, 2000), 456–57. On black civil rights leaders' opposition to Wallace, see Manfred Berg, "Black Civil Rights and Liberal Anticommunism: The NAACP in the Early Cold War," *Journal of American History* 94 (2007): 86. On the Progressive Party's 1948 campaign, see Thomas W. Devine, *Henry Wallace's 1948 Campaign and the Future of Postwar Liberalism* (Chapel Hill, NC, 2013). Wallace's mea culpa came in his article "Where I Was Wrong," *The Week Magazine*, September 7, 1952. Dwight Macdonald's oft-quoted remark about Wallaceland appears in his *Henry Wallace: The Man and the Myth* (New York, 1948), 24.

14: Lyndon B. Johnson: The Triumph of Politics

An earlier version of this chapter appeared as "Efficacy and Democracy," *New Republic*, July 12, 2012, pp. 30–39. Robert A. Caro, *The Passage of Power* (New York, 2012), is the fourth volume of Caro's grand work, collectively entitled *The Years of Lyndon Johnson*. For a different view, see the second volume of Robert Dallek's two-volume life of Johnson, *Flawed Giant: Lyndon Johnson and His Times* (New York, 1998). Gore Vidal is quoted in Mary Perot Nichols, "Bobby is Not 'Best Man' for Playwright Vidal," *Village Voice*, October 1, 1964. The comment about Johnson and the "generational disaster" of Vietnam appeared in the *New York Times*, January 9, 2008. On liberals contrasting Johnson and

Obama, see Benjamin Duehold, "Does Obama Lack LBJ's Cunning?" *Wash-ington Monthly*, May 2, 2012, available at http://www.washingtonmonthly.com/ten-miles-square/2012/05/_in_the_passage_of037065.php.

On Johnson and Robert F. Kennedy, see Jeff Shesol, *Mutual Contempt: Lyndon Johnson, Robert Kennedy, and the Feud that Defined a Decade* (New York, 1998). Caro's comments about Obama appear in "CNN Transcript: Fareed Zakaria GPS, Interview with Robert Caro, August 26, 2012," available at http://www.cnn.com/TRANSCRIPTS/1208/26/fzgps.01.html. On the Republican Party as an "insurgent outlier," see Thomas E. Mann and Norman J. Ornstein, *It's Even Worse Than It Looks: How the American Constitutional System Collided with the New Politics of Extremism* (New York, 2012), xxiv, 185.

ACKNOWLEDGMENTS

This book exists because my longtime editor and even longer-time friend Drake McFeely at W. W. Norton saw that I had been writing it over the years piece by piece. My abiding thanks to him and to his assistant, Jeff Shreve, as well as to Bob Weil and Steve Forman at Norton for expert advice on various matters. Allegra Huston copyedited the manuscript with precision and flair. Andrew Wylie, as ever, has been a valuable sounding board and literary cornerman as well as my agent.

I am deeply grateful to three institutions, two of which provided the resources to complete the book during the academic year 2014–15. The New-York Historical Society granted me the Leah and Michael Weisberg Fellowship and with it came the peace and quiet to write and revise while drawing on the society's rich holdings. My thanks go to the society's president and CEO, Louise Mirrer, and her staff, as well as to Leah and Michael Weisberg. I was also fortunate to spend a month as the Siemens Berlin Prize Fellow at the American Academy in Berlin, amid a wonderful group of musicians, poets, artists, novelists, and scholars, for which I am grateful to acting director Gahl Burt and her staff. As ever, I owe an enormous debt to everyone at my home base, the Princeton University History Department, especially its current chair, William Chester Jordan, as well as to the librarians and staff at Princeton's Firestone Library.

Earlier versions of about half of these chapters appeared in the *New Republic* at the instigation of Leon Wieseltier, who edited them with vigor, sympathy, and style. His friendship and encouragement have been great blessings. My work for the magazine early on also benefited from the sharp editorial eye and high expectations of Ann Hulbert. Most of the other chapters first appeared in the *New York Review of Books* thanks to Robert Silvers and the late Barbara Epstein, whose intellectual energy and impeccable standards were and are inspiring. I am also grateful to James Miller and Sean Conant for inviting me to write essays that forced me to think anew about big subjects, and for then helping me make those essays better.

Chapter 1 began as the Robert G. Wesson Lectures on Problems in Democracy, delivered at Stanford University in 2010. I am grateful to the McCoy Family Center for Ethics in Society at Stanford, then directed by Debra Satz, for the honor of the invitation, and to Bruce Cain for his probing response to what I had to say. I was delighted to deliver a condensed version of the Wesson Lectures in 2011 as part of the President's Lecture Series at Princeton, for which I am grateful to then-president Shirley M. Tilghman.

Three old friends helped me beyond measure, both in writing the original essays and then in rewriting them for this book. Countless hours of conversation with Sidney Blumenthal, over two decades, about politics and history and just about everything else, have shaped my thinking and sharpened my prose, while giving me a continuing education on how American politics really works as seen from the inside. Paul Berman, a fearless exemplar as a writer, helped me with the very oldest essay here nearly a quarter century ago, chipped in generously on several of the others, and offered indispensable advice in the final stages. Michael Merrill, a model labor educator and my sometime coauthor, read drafts of chapter 2 and forthrightly pushed me to say things I couldn't have figured out, let alone said, on my own. I am also grateful to Andrew Edwards of the graduate history program at Princeton, who gave chapter 2 a close and helpful reading.

INDEX

Abbott, William, 238–39
abolitionists, abolitionism, 12, 13, 48, 49,
    110, 149, 151, 155, 189, 191, 204,
    286–87
Adams, Abigail, 129
Adams, Charles Francis, 128, 138, 141, 166
Adams, George Washington, 135
Adams, Henry, 17, 18, 19, 28, 176, 177,
    250–51
Adams, John, 6, 28, 39, 72, 73, 74, 93, 104–
    5, 108, 111, 121, 129, 130, 136
    inequality denounced by, 32–33
    McCullough's view of, 88
    recent rehabilitation of, 88
Adams, John Quincy, 10, 28, 99, 103,
    125–47, 182–83
    and acquisition of Florida, 132
    amiability of, 131–32
    in *Amistad* affair, 142, 145
    and anti-Masonic movement, 135–42,
        144, 145, 146
    anti-slavery views of, xxiv, 125, 127,
        142–47
    death of, 125
    in election of 1824, 133–34
    in election of 1828, 127–28, 137, 140,
        141, 215
    emotional life of, 128–31, 132, 135
    federal spending by, 133
    and Monroe Doctrine, 132–33
    paradox of, 127–28
    partisanship disdained by, 141, 146
    party line voted by, 141–42
    on party strife, 9
    religious outlook of, 139
    writings of, 130
Adams, Louisa Johnson, 131
Adams, Samuel, 34
Aesop, 182
Affordable Care Act (2010), 31, 65, 310,
    330
Afghanistan War, 205
Africa, 107
African Americans, 24, 65, 79
    and colonization plans, 94, 95, 187–89
    culture of, 290
    voting rights for, 54–55, 210
    see also Du Bois, W. E. B.
agrarianism, 35, 57
Agrarian Justice (Paine), 77, 82
Alabama, 109
Alien Act (1798), 101, 106
Amalgamated Association of Iron and Steel
    Workers, 233, 236, 238–39, 240–42,
    247–48
amalgamation policy, 9
American Anti-Slavery Society, 152, 154
American Civil Liberties Union, 291
American Crisis, The (Paine), 70, 71–72
American Dreamers (Kazin), 280–89,
    290–94
American Federation of Labor, 284
American Museum of National History, 269
American Peace Society, 159–60

American Review, 12, 142
American Revolution, 37, 38, 58, 71, 82,
    129, 191, 226, 231
Americans for Democratic Action, 304
Ames, Fisher, 6, 8, 122
Amistad, 142, 145
Anderson, John B., 26
Anglo-Saxon-Celts, 259, 260
Antietam, battle of, 244
anti-Masonic movement, 135–42, 144, 145,
    146
Anti-Masonic Party, 137
anti-monarchial politics, 33–34, 37
apartheid, 85
Appiah, Kwame Anthony, 255
Appleby, Joyce, 41, 118
Arthur, Chester A., 267
asylums, 45
Atlanta, Ga., 185, 207
Atlanta Compromise speech, 253
Atlantic Monthly, 17
auto industry, 330

Bacon, Edmund, 113
Bailey, Gamaliel, 49
Baker, Bobby, 317, 319
Bakhtin, Mikhail, 244
Baldwin, Calvin "Beanie," 303
Baldwin, James, 259
Ball, George, 305
ballot reform, 19
Baltic states, 298
Bank of North America, 79, 80
Bankruptcy Act (1800), 101
Bank of the United States, 42n
banks, banking, 40, 44
    Jackson's war on, 43–44, 45–46
Banner, James M., Jr., 110
Bartels, Larry M., 64
Barzun, Jacques, 175, 181
Battle for Homestead, The (Krause), 235
Baucus, Max, 330
Bayard, James A., 140
Bay of Pigs invasion, 297
Beard, Charles A., 107
Bell, Daniel, 284
Bemis, Samuel Flagg, 141
Benton, Thomas Hart, 125
Berkman, Alexander, 233, 246–47

Berlin, 264
Berlin airlift, 299
Bessemer process, 236
Bessemer steelworks, 237
Bible, 179, 181, 183, 185, 256
Bidwell, Barnabas, 108n
Bill of Rights, xxi
Binet, Alfred, 257
bin Laden, Osama, 168
Bishop, Abraham, 37
Black Hearts of Men, The (Stauffer), 196–98
Black Lives Matter, 294
Black Panthers, 290
Black Power, 290
Black Reconstruction in America (Du Bois),
    252, 265
Blackstone, William, 179
Blaine, James G., 19, 273–74
Blavatsky, Madame, 258
Blum, John Morton, 272
Bolingbroke, Lord, 5
Bolívar, Simón, 134
Bolshevik Myth, The (Berkman), 247
Bolshevik Revolution, 61, 280, 288
Bourne, Randolph, 259
Bowker, R. R., 18
Bowles, Chester, 304
Braddock works, 237, 244
Bragg, Braxton, 17
Brains Trust, 23
Braintree, Mass., 129
Breckenridge, John C., 164
Brodie, Fawn, 114
Brook Farm, 42
Brown, Albert Gallatin, 14
Brown, H. Rap, 150
Brown, John, xxiv, 148–69, 196–97, 207, 287
    in Harpers Ferry attack, 148, 149, 151,
        160–62, 166, 197, 207, 286
    historical assessment of, 148–51
    insanity allegation against, 152–53
    reaction to raid of, 162–64, 166–67
    reasons for raid of, 153–55
    religious background of, 152, 153
    as viewed by black nationalists, 150
Brown, Joseph E., 16, 17
Bryan, William Jennings, 296
Buchanan, James, 158, 159
Bull Moose Party, 22, 269–70

Bunker Hill, 129
Burges, Tristam, 44
Burke, Edmund, 72, 73, 74, 75, 91, 93, 130
Burlingame, Michael, 177–79
Burns, James MacGregor, 29
Burns, Ken, 89
Burns, Robert, 179
Busby, Horace, 317
Bush, George W., 26–27, 64, 169, 293, 306
  hyper-partisan presidency of, 3, 4
Butler, Pierce, 100
Byrd, Harry, 322, 325, 327
Byrnes, James F., 302
Byron, George Gordon, Lord, 179, 256

Cabot, George, 7
Calhoun, John C., 13, 34, 88, 142–43, 144
  concurrent majority theory of, 13, 14
  on states' rights, 52, 221
Callender, James, 114, 116
Calvin, John, 153
canals, 133
"Candid State of Parties" (Madison), 5, 6
Capra, Frank, 285
Caribbean, 192, 277
Carlyle, Thomas, 257
Carnegie, Andrew, 234, 235, 237, 238–41, 243, 248, 249, 269
Carnegie Steel Corporation, 240, 245
Carnegie steelworks, *see* Homestead works
Caro, Robert A., xxv, 310–16, 320–21, 324–26, 331
Carter, Jimmy, 25, 27, 30, 62, 63
Cass, Lewis, 243–44
Catherine the Great, 126
Central America, 291, 306
Chase, Salmon P., 49
Cheetham, James, 73
Cheney, Dick, 306, 316, 328
Chernow, Ron, 88
Chesnutt, Charles W., 262
Children's Defense Fund, 291
China, 323–24
Citizen Tom Paine (Fast), 69
Civil Rights Act (1875), 210
Civil Rights Act (1957), 314, 327

Civil Rights Act (1964), 60, 290, 307, 310, 318, 320, 321, 322–23, 325, 327, 329
civil rights movement, 24–25, 60–62, 86, 150, 174, 280, 281, 283
civil service, 19
Civil War, U.S., xxi, 16, 17, 65, 104, 119, 149, 151, 167, 168, 173, 176, 192, 281, 283, 286
  black troops in, 287
  Lincoln's importance in, 178–79
Clark, John Bates, 55
Clark, John Maurice, 55
Clay, Henry, 103–4, 133, 134, 138, 140, 141, 144, 156, 184, 189
Cleveland, Grover, 19, 28, 234, 273, 274
Clifford, Clark, 305
Clinton, Bill, 26, 28, 64, 291, 292, 328
Clinton, Hillary Rodham, 292
Cobbett, William, 83
Cold War, 119, 296–306
  start of, xxv
Coles, Edward, 111
collective bargaining, 57
Colonel Roosevelt (Morris), 267–68, 271–72
Colton, Calvin, 46
Commentaries (Blackstone), 179
Committee on Equal Employment Opportunity, 318
Common Sense (Paine), 62, 70, 71, 72, 75–76, 77, 78
Communism, 24, 61, 289–90
Communist Party, 251, 287, 289, 303
compact theory, 221
"compassionate conservatism," 27, 328
Compromise of 1850, 155
concurrent majority theory, 13, 14
Confederate States of America, 14, 15–17, 28, 52–53, 61, 170, 226
  constitutional convention of, 15, 228–29
  democracy in, 227–30
Confederation Congress, 109
Congregationalism, 98
Congress, U.S., slave trade ended by, 108
Congress of Industrial Organizations (CIO), 174, 249, 287, 288
Connally, John, 319
Connecticut, 98
Conscience Whigs, 146

Constitution, U.S., xxi, xxiii, 33, 37, 49, 120,
    144, 145, 158, 159, 175, 188, 190–91,
    192, 193, 198, 203, 213, 220, 224
  compact theory of, 221
Constitutional Convention, 100
Constitutional framers, partisanship dis-
    dained by, xix
consumer safety, 57
Coolidge, Calvin, 22, 58, 278
Cooper Institute address (Lincoln), 182,
    185
Copperheads, 16
Corcoran, Thomas, 23
corporate economy, 55–56
corporations, xxiv, 63
cotton, 47, 81, 107, 112, 191
Crash of 1929, 58
Crawford, William H., 133, 140
Crisis, 252
Croly, Herbert, 57, 86
Crummell, Alexander, 256, 257
Cuban Missile Crisis, 316
currency, 19
Czechoslovakia, 302

Daily Beast, 298
Daily Pittsburgh Gazette, 225
Davis, David Brion, 85, 93
Davis, Jefferson, 16, 17, 88
Davis, John, 140
Debs, Eugene V., 149, 284
Declaration of Independence, xxi, 78, 84,
    87–88, 89, 97, 108, 110, 124, 202, 213,
    231
deficit, 64
Defoe, Daniel, 73
Delany, Martin, 256
Delaware, 106
DeLay, Tom, 27, 328
Demarest, David P., 234
democracy, xx–xxi, 110, 214–32, 244
Democratic National Convention, (2004), 3
democratic nationalism, xxv, 53, 57, 275,
    280
Democratic Party, U.S.:
  anti-slavery sentiments in, 48
  doughface, 170
  FDR's conservative purge of, 23–24
  inequality denounced by, xxii, 42–43

  1980s problems of, 26
  as pro-slavery, 12
  proslavery sentiment in, 50
  rise of, 10, 13, 42, 215
  segregation faced by, 59
  in South, 14, 24–25, 62, 329
Democratic-Republicans, *see* Jeffersonians
Democratic Republican societies, 5
depression of 1870s, 55
depressions, 57
deregulation, 64
Devine, Thomas W., 303
Dewey, Thomas E., 301
Diary in America, A (Marryat), 182
Dirksen, Everett, 196, 323, 327
Dissent, 281
Dixiecrats, 24, 25, 59, 61, 303, 305
Dixon, Thomas, 186
Dodd-Frank reforms, 65
Donald, David Herbert, 173, 201
double consciousness, 254–55, 257–58, 260,
    264, 265
Douglas, Stephen A., 50, 156, 158, 159, 165,
    166, 182, 185, 188, 192, 217, 243–44
Douglass, Frederick, 173, 190, 192, 196–
    200, 203, 204, 256
  black troops and, 287
  Brown's raid and, 160, 161
  after Civil War, 208–11
  Fugitive Slave Law denounced by, 155
  Lincoln's meetings with, 205–8
  Thirteenth Amendment praised by, 186
Doyle, James, 157
Dred Scott v. Sanford, 104, 159, 165, 202–3,
    220, 221
Du Bois, W. E. B., xxiv, 149, 250–66
  Booker T. Washington vs., 253–54, 258,
    263
  death of, 251
  education of, 250–51
  influences on, 258
  Marxism of, 265
  racial ideas of, 255–58, 260–61, 265–66
Dueholm, Benjamin, 309, 310
Dukakis, Michael, 26, 64, 329
Dunn, Oscar J., 54–55
Dusk of Dawn, 261
Dwight, Theodore, 122
Dylan, Bob, 69, 285

Eastern Pennsylvania Anti-Slavery Society, 12
economic growth, recent, 63
economic stimulus, 27
Education of Henry Adams, The (Adams), 250, 251
Edwards, Jonathan, 153
Efficiency Movement, 22
egalitarianism, xxv, 31–66, 280–81
  in aftermath of Civil War, 53–54
  in early republic, 32–37, 40–42
  fueled by anti-monarchial politics, 33–34
  future of, 65–66
  in Jacksonian era, 42–44, 46
  and labor theory of value, 34–35, 36–37, 42, 44, 49–50, 51, 55
  of Paine, xxiv, 36, 66
  racism and, 51–52, 60–62
  slavery and, 47–53
  see also inequality, economic
Ehrenreich, Barbara, 292, 293
Eisenhower, Dwight D., 24, 306, 326
Elkins Act (1903), 276
Ellis, Joseph, 90, 119
Ellison, Ralph, 259
Emancipation Proclamation, 167–68, 174, 186, 195, 204, 205, 214, 282
embargo, 84, 132, 140
Emerson, Ralph Waldo, 128, 160, 163, 257
enforcement acts, 210
Enlightenment, 34, 69, 74, 85, 120, 122
environmental conservation, 58
Era of Good Feelings, 9
Eumenes, 33
Evening Post, 7
Everett, Edward, 44, 185
ex-slaves, 53–54

Fables (Aesop), 182
Farley, James A., 23
Farmer-Labor Party, 289
Fast, Howard, 69
Federalist Papers, 82
Federalist Party, U.S., 7–9, 11, 28, 37, 52, 96, 104–5, 106
  death of, 41
  inequality and, 39, 40, 44
  Jefferson vs., 99–101, 122–23
  Pickering's defense of, 98, 99

politicians denounced by, 8
slavery and, 47, 48, 110
federal workmen's compensation, 279
Fehrenbacher, Don E., 181
Feiffer, Jules, 309
Ferrell, Robert H., 301
Fifteenth Amendment, 210, 283
financial panic of 1819, 134
Finney, Charles, 139
fire-eaters, 28, 159
Fitzhugh, George, 50–51
Flint, Charles R., 56
Florida, 132, 293
Foner, Eric, 80, 190
Forum, 240
Foucault, Michel, 200
founders, parties distrusted by, xix
Fourteenth Amendment, 210, 283
Fox, Charles James, 74
France, 109, 121
Francis of Assisi, xvii
Franklin, Benjamin, 5, 74, 102
Franklin, John Hope, 89
Freehling, William W., 105
Free Soil Party, 104, 155, 158
free trade, 17
Frémont, John C., 158, 206
French Directory, 92
French Revolution, 79, 90–92, 136, 218
  Jefferson's support for, 90–92, 96–97
  Northern Jeffersonians' support for, 92–93
Frick, Henry Clay, 233, 234, 235, 240–42, 244, 245, 247, 248
Fugitive Slave Law, 155–56, 160, 171, 172

Gaddis, John Lewis, 298
Galbraith, J. K., 304
Gallatin, Albert, 40, 107, 121
Garland, Hamlin, 248, 249
Garrison, William Lloyd, xvii, 12, 42, 143, 149, 150, 152, 159, 191, 286
Garvey, Marcus, 265
Gates, Henry Louis, Jr., 187–95, 204
Gavin, David, 228
Genêt, Edmond, 92, 131
Gentz, Friedrich von, 130
Georgia, 108, 228
Germany, 41, 61, 296, 298
Gettysburg, Pa., 317

Gettysburg Address, 182, 185, 213
  misunderstandings of, 213–14
  and preservation of democracy, 214–15,
    216, 218, 219, 230–32
Giants (Stauffer), 196, 198–99, 201–5
Gibbon, Edward, 80
Gilded Age, 20, 243, 251
  see also Homestead works
Giles, W. B., 140
Gingrich, Newt, 27, 64, 292, 328
Ginsburg, Ruth Bader, 291
Godkin, E. L., 18, 28
Godwin, William, 122
Goldin, Claudia, 59
Goldman, Emma, 246, 247
Goldwater, Barry, 24, 25, 327, 328
Gompers, Samuel, 22, 284
Goodwin, Doris Kearns, 320
Gordon-Reed, Annette, 114–15, 116–18
Gordy, Berry, 290
Gore, Al, 26, 293
Grant, Ulysses S., 18, 209–10, 275
Grapes of Wrath, The (Steinbeck), 285
Great Britain, 36–37, 39, 121
Great Crash of 2008, xxii, 27, 31, 64, 330
Great Depression, 22, 31, 278, 301
  egalitarian politics unleashed by, xxii
great divergence, 63
Great Society, 60, 64, 65, 289, 290, 309,
    310, 311, 327, 330
  fraying of, 31–32, 61, 62
  inequality and, xxii
  partisanship's creation of, xx, 29
Great Terror, 287, 298
Greeley, Horace, 18, 195, 217
Grégoire, Abbé Henri, 93–94, 190
Griffith, D. W., 186
Gulf of Tonkin, 324
Gurley, Phineas Densmore, 180–81
Guthrie, Woody, 287, 288

Haitian Revolution, 85, 106, 108–9
Hall, Gus, 251
Halleck, Charles, 323
Hamilton, Alexander, 42*n*, 52, 72, 77, 86,
    103, 121
  fiscal policies of, 5
  inequality seen as inevitable by, xxi,
    38–39, 40, 44

Jefferson vs., xxi, 90, 91, 92, 95–96
organized politics embraced by, 7
Pickering's plot opposed by, 99
recent rehabilitation of, 70, 88
Washington's Farewell Address cowritten
  by, 6
Hammond, James Henry, 51, 143
Hanna, Mark, 275, 277
Harding, Warren G., 42, 58, 267, 278
Harper, Robert Goodloe, 101–2
Harpers Ferry attack, 148, 149, 151, 160–
  62, 166, 197, 207, 286
Harrington, James, 243
Harris, James, 157
Harrison, Benjamin, 247
Hart, Albert Bushnell, 250
Harvard University, 264
Hay, John, 179, 194
Haymarket bombing, 246
Hayne, Robert, 183
health care, 31, 58, 65, 278, 326, 328
  see also Affordable Care Act; Medicaid;
  Medicare
Hemings, Eston, 115
Hemings, Madison, 114, 115, 116, 117
Hemings, Sally, 90, 113–18, 189
Hemingses of Monticello, The (Gordon-Reed),
  116
Hemings family, 112
Henry IV, Part 2 (Shakespeare), 131
*Henry Wallace's 1948 Presidential Campaign
  and the Future of Postwar Liberalism*
  (Devine), 303
Hepburn Act (1906), 276
Herndon, William, 180
Higginson, Thomas Wentworth, 160
Hillhouse, James, 102–3, 110
Hillman, Sidney, 289
Hiroshima bombing, 296
Hispanics, xxiii
Hitchens, Christopher, 292
Hodge, Charles, 180
Hoffman, Stanley, 305
Hofstadter, Richard, 5, 186
Holly, James, 256
Holzer, Harold, 176, 193
Homestead (Serrin), 249
Homestead Act (1862), 53
Homestead Glass Works, 238

Homestead Works, xxiv, 233, 234–38, 241–46, 247–48, 249
Hoover, Herbert, 22–23, 58
Hope, John, 262
"House Divided" speech, 180, 183, 185, 217, 231
House of Commons, U.K., 219
House of Representatives, U.S., 101, 102–3, 134, 142, 158, 292
    Rules Committee of, 323
Howe, Irving, 284
Hugh, Charles Evans, 270
Hume, David, 34
Humphrey, Hubert, 289, 319, 323
Hyland, William G., Jr., 116

IBM, 56
Illinois, 166
Illinois State Bank, 212
Illuminati, 136
immigrants, immigration, 18, 19, 41, 69, 259
"Impartial Examiner," 33
income inequality, 59, 63, 64
income tax, 42, 57, 58, 279
In Defense of Thomas Jefferson (Hyland), 116
independency, 20
Indiana, 166
industrial workers, xxi
inequality, economic:
    current political fight against, xxii
    Democrats' denunciation of, xxii, 42–43
    economists' changing views of, 55–56
    Federalists and, 39, 40, 44
    growth in 1920s of, 58
    historical fight against, xx–xxii
    Jackson and, xxi, 34, 47
    Jefferson and, xxi, xxiv, 32, 35, 39–40, 42, 47
    John Adams's denunciation of, 32–33
    Lincoln and, 134
    Madison and, xxi, 32, 39, 78
    in market revolution, 41
    New Deal and, xxii, xxv, 57, 280
    in Progressive Era, xxi–xxii
    racism and, xxi, 60
    recent acceptance of, 31
    recent growth in, 63–64
    Republicans' denunciation of, xxii
    in Revolutionary America, 35–36

seen as inevitable by Hamilton, xxi, 38–39, 40, 44
slavery and, xxi, 34, 46–53
through twentieth century, 59
as viewed in 1920s, 56
Whigs' denunciation of, 44–46
see also egalitarianism
inheritance tax, 278
Innocent III, Pope, xvii
internal improvements, 45, 57, 133
Intimate World of Abraham Lincoln, The (Tripp), 200
Inventing America (Wills), 117
investments:
    of Carnegie, 236
    of Frick, 240–41
    speculative, 38, 40–41
Iowa State Register, 223
Iraq War, 306
Ireland, 41
iron, 235–36
Isis Unveiled (Blavatsky), 258
Italy, 296

Jackson, Andrew, 28, 127, 129, 133–34, 139, 170, 184, 215, 218, 221
    in bank war, 43–44, 45–46, 186
    in dispute with South, 52
    in election of 1828, 127, 129, 137
    inequality and, xxi, 34, 47
    as Mason, 136, 137
    in nullification dispute, 184, 187
    Southern support for, 14
Jackson, Thomas J., 162
Jacksonians, 53, 142
    labor defined by, 44
    partisan rationale of, 10–11, 14, 17
    protectionism opposed by, 45
Jacobins, 74, 79, 85, 92, 96
James, Henry, 253
James, William, 253, 257
James I, King of England, 82
Japan, 296, 300
Jefferson, Martha, 113–14
Jefferson, Thomas, 49, 50, 66, 84–124, 130, 251, 296, 332
    African American view of, 88–89
    amalgamation denounced by, 9
    in appeal to city democrats, 122–23

Jefferson, Thomas (*continued*)
  black colonization schemes of, 94, 95
  colonialism denounced by, 37
  in election of 1800, 7, 96, 99, 104–5, 136
  embargo of, 84, 132, 140
  first inaugural address of, 7, 16, 121, 184,
    226, 230
  French Revolution supported by, 90–92,
    96–97
  on gradual emancipation, 111
  Hamilton vs., xxi, 90, 91, 92, 95–96
  hate mail received by, 84
  Hemings's relationship with, 90, 113–18
  ideal republican empire of, 75, 80
  individual sovereignty and, 119–22
  inequality and, xxi, xxiv, 32, 35, 39–40,
    42, 47
  Paine compared to, 74–75, 80
  party machinery and, 5–6, 7, 9, 21, 28
  prose mastery of, 182
  racism of, 87, 89, 90, 93–94, 189, 190
  Republican admiration of, 119
  reputation of, 84–92, 94, 95, 96, 97–106,
    107–18, 119
  as slaveholder, 87, 90, 92, 112–18, 123
  slavery opposed by, 87–88, 93–95, 107–8,
    111–12
  slave trade closing pushed by, 107–8
Jeffersonians, 5–8, 9–10, 11, 37, 42, 98, 101, 103
  as abolitionists, 110
  French Revolution supported by, 92–93
  inequality opposed by, 39–40
  labor defined by, 44
  in mid-Atlantic states, 122
  and partisanship, 17, 29
Jefferson Memorial, 85
Jews, 24
JFK (film), 297
Jim Crow, xxii, 23, 55, 57, 60, 61–62, 65,
    149, 264, 265
John Birch Society, 329
John Quincy Adams (Nagel), 128–29
Johnson, Andrew, 209
Johnson, James Weldon, 253
Johnson, Lyndon B., xxii, xxv, 28, 29, 65,
    305, 307–32
  civil rights embraced by, 24, 60–61, 174,
    307, 309, 317, 318, 321, 322
  contradictions of, 307–8

cynical view of, 174
  and election of 1968, 308–9
  partisanship disdained by, 309–10
  Vietnam escalated by, 25, 290
Johnson, Sam Early, Jr., 312
Jones, Alice Hanson, 35
Jones, Mother, 149
Jordan, Winthrop D., 85
Judiciary Act (1801), 101
Julian, George, 54
Justice Department, U.S., 324

Kansas, 150, 156–58, 159–60
Kansas-Nebraska Act (1854), 108n, 156,
    158, 173, 243
Kaplan, Fred, 182–83, 184–85, 186
Karl, Barry, 21
Kazin, Michael, xxv, 280–89, 290–94
Kennedy, John F., 297, 305, 308, 313–14,
    317, 320, 327
  assassination of, 308, 320
  civil rights embraced by, 24–25, 60, 318
  partisanship of, 24, 28, 29–30
Kennedy, Joseph P., 315
Kennedy, Robert F., 308–9, 313–14, 315–
    16, 317, 318, 319, 324–25, 329
Kentucky, 109, 126
Kenyatta, Jomo, 251
King, Martin Luther, Jr., 60, 61, 89, 174,
    290, 317–18
King, Rufus, 98, 99, 103
Knight, John, 323
Knights of Labor, 19, 56–57, 237, 238, 239,
    242
Know Nothings, 12
Knox, Philander, 245
Krause, Paul, 235, 241, 243
Krugman, Paul, 63, 292
Ku Klux Klan, 85, 91, 186, 210
Kuznick, Peter, 295–306

labor, 24, 281, 288
  organized, xxi, xxiv, 57, 62, 289
labor theory of value, 34–35, 36–37, 42, 44,
    49–50, 51, 55
labor violence, 57
Ladurie, Emmanuel Le Roy, 244
Lafayette, Marquis de, 9, 74
La Follette, Robert M., 56

laissez-faire, 17–18, 19, 58, 64, 81, 275–76
land, sold by federal governments, 40–41
Latin America, 192
Latinos, xxiii
League of Nations, 22, 296
Lee, Robert E., 161
Leffler, Melvyn P., 298
"Letter from a Birmingham Jail," 317–18
Letters from Silesia (J. Q. Adams), 130
Levy, Leonard W., 85
Lewinsky, Monica, 292
Lewis, David Levering, 252–53, 254, 256, 258–59
Lewis, John L., 174, 288
liberalism, classical, 17–18, 19, 71
Liberal Republican Party, U.S., 18
Liberty Guards, 156
Liberty Party, U.S., 49, 155, 158
Lincoln, Abraham, xvii, 21, 29, 60, 81, 120, 159, 170–212, 275, 281, 286, 296, 332
  apotheosis of, 175–76, 178–79
  assassination of, 179, 186
  black colonization plan of, 95, 187–89
  cynical view of, 173–74
  on democracy, 214–17, 222–32
  Douglas's debates with, 50, 185, 192, 244
  early political career of, 172–73
  1852 anti-Pierce speech of, 170–71
  election of 1860 won by, 52, 151, 219–20
  Emancipation Proclamation drafted and issued by, 167–68, 174, 186, 195, 204, 205, 214
  "empathic" interpretation of, 174–75
  first inaugural of, 165, 184, 185, 194, 203, 204, 222, 226
  inequality and, 34
  on John Brown, 167
  on labor theory of value, 49–50
  as master party politician, xxiv, 13–14, 28, 30
  Paine admired by, 73
  Peoria speech of, 171, 215
  on politics, 212
  as president-elect, 176–77, 225–26
  psychology of, 177–78
  racial views of, 171–72, 182, 187–96
  ranked as best president, 170
  religious views of, 180–81, 205
  rhetoric of, 174–75, 179–87

second inaugural address of, 185–86, 199, 287
  sexuality of, 200–201
  slavery opposed by, 48, 49, 149, 151, 172, 177, 187–96
  on Wilmot Proviso, 104
  see also Gettysburg Address
Lincoln, Willie, 181, 205
Lincoln on Race & Slavery (Gates), 187–95, 204
Lincoln President-Elect (Holzer), 176
Lindert, Peter H., 35, 41
Lippmann, Walter, 325
Locke, John, 34, 36, 50
Lodge, Henry Cabot, 273
Logan, George, 35
Long Affair, The (O'Brien), 89–91, 94, 95, 96, 97, 111, 114, 116
Louisiana Purchase, 104, 107, 110, 121, 140, 191
Louisiana Territory, 102–3
Louis XVI, King of France, 72, 91, 92, 96
Lovejoy, Elijah, 154, 155

Macdonald, Dwight, 306
Machiavelli, Niccolò, 243
Macon, Nathaniel, 108*n*
Madison, James, 72, 77, 82, 94, 100, 119, 120, 132, 133, 175, 251
  inequality and, xxi, 32, 39, 78
  on plebian many vs. wealthy few, 8
  two party system proposed by, 5, 6
Magee, Christopher, 245
Mailer, Norman, 197
Maine, 248
Malcolm X, 150
Malone, Dumas, 85, 90, 115
Manifest Destiny, 127
Mann, Thomas E., 328
Manning, William, 37
Mao Zedong, 251
March on Washington (1963), 251
Margo, Robert, 59
market revolution, 41, 46
Marryat, Frederick, 171, 172, 182
Marshall, John, 6, 94
Marshall Plan, 299
Maryland, 106, 135
Mason, George, 108

Massachusetts, 105, 137
Master of the Senate (Caro), 314
McCain, John, 329
McCarthy, Eugene, 305, 308–9, 325
McCarthy, Joseph, 24, 315, 326
McColley, Robert, 87
McCullough, David, 88
McDonald, Forrest, 85
McKinley, William, 275
McLuckie, "Honest" John, 239, 242, 244, 246
McVeigh, Timothy, 97
Meacham, Jon, 118
Meat Inspection Act (1906), 276
Medicaid, 292, 309, 327
Medicare, 292, 309, 327
Mellon, Andrew, 58
Mellon, Thomas, 241
Memminger, Christopher G., 53
mercantilism, 38
Mexican War, 126, 127, 146, 155, 191
Mexico, 100, 104
Mills, C. Wright, 281
minimum wage, 294
Minneapolis Journal, 20
Minnesota Labor, 233
Mississippi, 164, 206
Mississippi Territory, 106–7, 109–10
Missouri, 47, 100, 103–4, 112
Missouri Compromise (1820), 10, 104, 129, 134, 142–43
Missouri crisis, 47, 104, 142–43, 213
Mondale, Walter, 26
monopolies, 42, 43, 55, 56
Monroe, James, 9, 10, 13, 28, 94, 127
Monroe Doctrine, 132–33
    Roosevelt Corollary to, 278
Monticello, 112–13, 115, 121
Moore, Michael, 291
Morgan, Edmund S., 85
Morgan, Edwin D., 225
Morgan, J. P., 248
Morgan, William, 136, 139
Morrill Act (1862), 53
Morris, Edmund, 267–68, 271–72, 273, 277
Morris, Thomas, 48–49
Morrison, Toni, 259
Morse, Jedidiah, 136
Motown, 290

Mount Rushmore, 272
Moynihan, Michael, 298
Mugwumps, 17, 19, 28, 273, 274, 308
Murrin, John M., 36
Mutual Contempt (Shesol), 314–15

Nader, Ralph, 26, 293
Nagasaki bombing, 296
Nagel, Paul C., 128–29, 131–32
Napoleon I, Emperor of the French, 155
Nation, 18
National Association for the Advancement of Colored People (NAACP), 149, 251, 252, 265, 303
national bank, 42, 45, 121
National Banking Acts (1863, 1864), 53
National Convention (Paris), 72
national debt assumption plan, 38
nationalization of railroads, 57
National Labor Relations Act (1935), 288
National Republicans, 42, 44–45, 47, 135, 137
National Resources Defense Council, 291
National Socialism, 61
Native Americans, 34, 35, 36, 85
Navy Department, U.S., 101
Negro Academy, 260
Negro President (Wills), 97–106, 107, 109–10, 111
Nevins, Allan, 129
New Deal, 24, 26, 58, 59–60, 61, 62, 64, 65, 86, 119, 174, 249, 278, 281, 284, 286, 287, 288–89, 301, 304, 307, 310, 326
    fraying of, 31–32, 61, 62
    inequality and, xxii, xxv, 57, 280
    partisanship's creation of, xx, 29
New England, 98, 106, 138–39
New Frontier, 319
New Harmony, 42
New Jersey, 98, 135
New Left, 290
New Nationists, 278
New Orleans, La., 233
New Orleans *Daily Picayune*, 15
New Politics reformers, 25
New Rochelle, N.Y., 70, 83
New School Whigs, 12, 229
New York, N.Y., 110, 122

New-York Daily Tribune, 217

New-York Manumission Society, 88*n*, 109

New York State, 98, 126, 152, 160, 166
  machine politics in, 9–10

New York Times, 249, 309

Nicolay, John, 194

Niebuhr, Reinhold, xvii, 304

Nixon, Richard M., 25, 27, 28, 306, 311, 314

North, U.S., 14, 15, 16, 18, 47, 48–49, 158–59
  inequality in, 50–51
  and proposals to redistribute land, 54

North American Free Trade Agreement, 292

Northern Democratic Party, 104, 166–67, 188, 243

Northern Securities case, 276

North Vietnam, 323

Northwest Ordinance, 109–10

Northwest Territory, 109–10

Notes on the State of Virginia (Jefferson), 87, 89, 90, 190

nullification, 62, 184, 187

Oakes, James, 198, 210

Oates, Stephen, 150

Obama, Barack, 64–65, 70, 291, 293–94, 296, 297, 306, 309, 325–26, 328
  election of, 293–94, 309, 329–30
  fraying of social compact denounced by, 31–32
  partisanship and, 3–4, 27–28, 30, 308–9, 329, 330–31
  as polarizing, 4

O'Brien, Conor Cruise, 85, 89–91, 94, 95, 96, 97, 111, 114, 116

observatories, 133

Occupy Wall Street, 293–94

Odets, Clifford, 285

O'Donnell, Hugh, 242, 245, 247

Ohio, 126, 152, 166

oil-price crises, 62

Ornstein, Norman J., 328

Otis, Harrison Gray, 107, 140

Pacific Ocean, 277

Pacific Railway Act (1862), 53

Paine, Thomas, 46, 62, 66, 69–83, 120, 122, 123, 243
  conservative fondness for, 70, 78–79
  democratic edge of, 75–77, 130
  as egalitarian, xxiv, 36, 66
  French Revolution defended by, 72, 79
  importance of, 71–72
  Jefferson compared to, 74–75, 80
  legacy of, 69–70, 79
  as optimistic about reason, 77, 80, 82
  revival of interest in, 70
  scholarship on, 70–71
  style of, 72–74
  as unremembered at death, 69

Panama Canal, 277–78

panic of 1873, 210

Parsons, Theophilus, 130, 140

partisanship, xxii, xxiv–xxv, 3–30
  in colonial America, 4–5
  concurrent majority theory and, 13, 14
  as consistent in U.S. history, 28–29
  denounced by Washington, 5, 6–7, 8, 11, 13, 17, 28
  Jacksonians' rationale for, 10–11, 17
  J. Q. Adams's disdain for, 141
  in 1950s, 24
  Obama and, 3–4
  in Progressive Era, 20–21
  recent optimism about, 3–4
  slavery and, xx, xxii
  South and, 14–15
  as well-functioning, xx
  Whig opposition to, 11–12

Pasley, Jeffrey L., 111, 122

Passage of Power, The (Caro), 310, 313, 315–16, 320–21, 325, 331

Pattison, Robert, 245–46

Peninsular Wars, 155

Pennsylvania, 105, 126, 137, 151, 152
  colonial, 5

Pennsylvania Abolition Society, 71, 102

People's History of the United States, The (Zinn), 282

People's (Populist) Party, 19
  founding platform of, 56

Perot, Ross, 26

Petersburg, Va., 54

Phi Beta Kappa, 137

Philadelphia, Pa., 110, 122

Philippines, 295
Phillips, Wendell, 160
Pickering, Timothy, 97–99, 101, 106, 110–
    11, 121, 122, 140
    Haitian Revolution supported by, 108–9
    Hillhouse amendment vote of, 103
    Northwest Ordinance and, 109–10
    in plot against Jeffersonians, 98–99
    slavery denounced by, 109
    and slavery in Mississippi, 107
Pierce, Franklin, 156, 170, 171, 172, 182
Piketty, Thomas, 59
Pinckney, Charles, 100, 122
Pinckney, Charles Cotesworth, 100, 122
Pinkerton Detective Agency, 244, 245
Pittsburgh Survey, 235, 238
Platoon (film), 304
Platt, Thomas, 275
"Plea for Captain Brown, A" (Thoreau), 163
Plumer, William, 111
Pocock, J. G. A., 71
Poland, 289
political parties:
    as absent from Confederacy, 14, 15–17
    distrust of, xix, xx, 6–7, 8, 11, 17,
        28–29
    Madison's proposal of, 5
    rise of, xviii–xx
    see also specific parties
Polk, James K., 267
Pol Pot, 85
Popular Front, 287
popular sovereignty, 243–44
Populist Party, *see* People's (Populist) Party
Port Folio, 122
"Pretty Boy Floyd" (song), 288
price regulation, 57
prison construction, 45
Progressive Era, 21–22, 57–58, 86
    inequality in, xxi–xxii
    parties distrusted in, xix
    partisanship in, 20–21
    partisanship's creation of, xx
Progressive Party, 21, 269, 279, 302, 303,
        304–5
Project Head Start, 327
property rights, 35, 53, 77
proportional representation, 19
Proprietary Party, 5

protectionism, 45
public works projects, 57
Pullman strike, 233–34
Pure Food and Drug Act (1906), 276
Purge This Land with Blood, The (Oates), 150

Quakers, 5

racism, xxiv, 31, 65, 71
    inequality and, xxi, 60
Radical Abolition Party, 197, 206
Radical and the Republican, The (Oakes), 198
Radical Republicans, 54, 64, 203, 206
railroads, 57, 276, 277
Ramsay, David, 47
Ramsden, John, 219
Randolph, A. Philip, 60, 61, 290
Randolph, John, 140
Rayburn, Sam, 313
Raymond, Daniel, 45
Reagan, Ronald, 25, 27, 28, 29, 306, 311,
        327, 328, 330
    economic policies of, 62–63
    election of, xxii
    nuclear buildup of, 291
    Paine cited by, 70, 79
Reconstruction, 54, 55, 57, 209, 251, 256–
        57, 283–84
    overthrow of, xxi, 18, 60, 149, 284
    Second, 119, 284
Reedy, George, 317
reformatories, 45
reformism, 20–21
Reid, Whitelaw, 247
Reign of Terror, 72, 74, 75, 92, 96, 218
religious freedom, 77, 86
rents, 38
Republican Party, U.S., 51
    antipartisanship of, 17
    black suffrage pushed by, 54
    conservative coup in, 24
    election of, 52
    formation of, 12, 172
    Hoover as symbol of, 23
    inequality denounced by, xxii
    Jefferson admired by, 119
    Obama's reelection and, 32
    opposed to slavery, 48–49, 148, 158, 159,
        177

partisanship of, 13–14
recent transformation of, 4
rightward shift of, 327–28
Rove's desire for permanent majority of, 27
southern whites in, 24–25, 62
Republican Party, U.S. (Jeffersonian), *see* Jeffersonians
Republican Roosevelt, The (Blum), 272
Reuther, Victor, 289
Reuther, Walter, 289, 304
revolutions of 1848, 218
Reynolds, David S., 148–49, 150–51, 153, 157–58, 164, 166, 168, 169
Richards, Leonard L., 143
Richmond Semi-Weekly Examiner, 220
Rights of Man (Paine), 72, 74, 77, 82
right-wing militias, 85, 91
Rio da Dúvida, 270
"River Ran Red, The" (Demarest, ed.), 234–35
roads, 133
Robeson, Paul, 287
Robespierre, Maximilien, 92
Roerich, Nicholas, 301
Roe v. Wade, 290–91
Romney, Mitt, 65
Roof, Dylann Storm, 97
Roosevelt, Eleanor, 303, 304
Roosevelt, Franklin Delano, xxv, 29, 60, 284, 288, 296, 299, 300, 315, 325, 332
as comfortable with party system, 23, 28
conservative purge by, 23–24
cynical view of, 174
death of, 299
fireside chats of, 187
first inaugural of, 187
labor supported by, 281
second bill of rights desired by, 58
Social Security Act signed by, 289
Truman chosen as vice president by, 299, 301–2
see also New Deal
Roosevelt, Quentin, 270–71
Roosevelt, Theodore, 29, 30, 57, 267–79
courage of, 267–68
imperialism of, 277–78
in New York gubernatorial campaign, 274–75

Paine denounced by, 70
as partisan politician, xxiv–xxv, 19, 28
reforms pressed by, 19–20, 21, 58, 276–77, 278
third-party candidacy in 1912 of, 22
Rough Riders, 269
Rove, Karl, 27, 328
Ruffin, Edmund, 162
Russell, Jonathan, 140
Russell, Richard B., 313, 322
Russell Sage Foundation, 235
Russia, 126, 129, 132, 259
Rustin, Bayard, 290, 304
Rutledge, John, 34
Rutledge, John, Jr., 96, 101–2

Saez, Emmanuel, 59, 63
Saint-Dominique, 109
Sanborn, Franklin B., 160
Sandburg, Carl, 179, 200
Sanders, Bernie, 294
Santo Domingo, 277–78
Sartre, Jean-Paul, 255
Schlesinger, Arthur, Jr., 318, 319
Schorenstein, Hymie, 23
Schwab, Charles, 256
Scott, Winfield, 171
secession, xxi, 62, 94, 99, 104, 111, 147, 148, 151, 164, 165, 167, 170, 176, 177, 184, 192–94, 204, 215, 216–23, 225, 227, 232
Second Bank of the United States, 42*n*, 43, 134, 186
Second Great Awakening, 45, 136, 152
Sedgwick, Theodore, 7, 110
Sedition Act (1798), 101, 106, 111
segregation, 310
Selma, Ala., 60
Senate, U.S., 103
Rules Committee of, 318–19
Seneca Falls convention (1848), 196
September 11, 2001, terrorist attacks, 27, 168
September Massacres, 91
Serrin, William, 249
Seward, William Henry, 12, 138, 156, 166, 167
Shakespeare, William, 130, 179, 183, 184, 185

Sherman, William, 157, 185, 207
Shesol, Jeff, 308, 314–15, 319
Short, William, 9, 91, 96, 97
silent majority, 25
Slade, William, 144
slaves, slavery, 10, 38, 44, 46, 65, 71, 81,
    82, 107–8, 217, 256, 259, 281, 283,
    286
  concentration of wealth in, 41
  as cornerstone of Confederacy, 14, 15,
    166
  criticisms of, 46–47, 48
  defenses of, 13, 71–72
  expansion of, 177, 193; *see also*
    Mississippi Territory; Missouri
    Compromise
  inequality and, xxi, 34, 46–53
  Jefferson's opposition to, 87–88, 93–95,
    111–12
  Mississippi territory and, 106–7, 109–
    10
  partisanship and, xx, xxii
  Pickering and, 98, 109–10
  post-1815 revival of, 112
  see also three-fifths clause
Smith, Adam, 34, 80–81
Smith, Gerrit, 155, 159–60, 197
Smith, James McCune, 197
Smith, Robert H., 15, 229
Smith, William Loughton, 94, 96, 102
Smithsonian Institute, 269
Snowden, George, 246
Socialist Party, 284
socialists, 283
Social Security Act (1935), 289
Souls of Black Folk, The (Du Bois), xxiv, 250,
    251, 252, 253, 254–56, 257, 259–63,
    265
South, U.S., 13, 14–15, 18, 23, 47, 49, 50,
    143, 191
  inequality in, 50–51
  Jackson vs., 52
  proposals to redistribute land in, 54
  reaction to Brown raid in, 162–64
  see also Dixiecrats
South Africa, 85
South Carolina, 13, 14, 108, 163, 184, 227
  secession of, 193–94, 225
Southern Quarterly Review, 15, 229

Soviet Union, 302
  missiles deployed in Cuba by, 316
  see also Cold War
Spain, 132
Spanish-American War, 248, 269, 275
Speed, Joshua, 200–201
spoilsmanship, 13, 18, 29, 139
Springsteen, Bruce, 285
Square Deal, xxv, 29, 269
Stalin, Joseph, 287, 288, 298, 299–300,
    305
Stanton, Edwin, 205–6
state banks, 40
state corporations, 40
Stauffer, John, 196–205, 208–10, 211
Steinbeck, John, 285
Stephens, Alexander Hamilton, 14, 166
Stevens, Thaddeus, 54, 141
Stevenson, Adlai, 308
Stevenson, Coke, 313
Stickney, Albert, 18
Stiles, Ezra, 35, 96
stimulus plan, 330
Stone, I. F., 303, 304
Stone, Oliver, xxv, 295–306
Stowe, Harriet Beecher, 171, 285
Stuart, J. E. B., 161
Stuart (sailor), 200
Student Non-Violent Coordinating
    Committee, 290
*Summary View of the Rights of British
    America* (Jefferson), 37
Sumner, Charles, 157
Sundquist, Eric, 258
Swift, Jonathan, 73

Taft, William Howard, 21, 269
Taft-Hartley Act (1947), 249
Talented Tenth, 257, 263
Talleyrand, Charles Maurice de, 92
Tallmadge, James, Jr., 103
Taney, Roger B., 202, 203, 220
Tappan, Lewis, 143, 145
tariff reform, 19, 43, 45, 277
tax cuts, 322, 325, 327
  of George W. Bush, 4, 64
taxes, 16, 45, 52, 64, 121, 240, 275
  income, 42, 57, 58, 279
  inheritance, 278

Taylor, John, 44
Tea Party, 29, 328
Tennessee, 109, 228
Tennyson, Alfred, Lord, 183
Texas, 146, 164, 228
Thatcher, George, 106–7, 110
third parties, 26
Thirteenth Amendment, 151, 186
"This Land Is Your Land" (song), 288
Thomas, Norman, 284
Thomas Jefferson (documentary), 89
Thomas Jefferson and Sally Hemings
    (Gordon-Reed), 114–15, 116
Thomas Jefferson Foundation, 116
Thomas Paine Memorial Association, 70
Thoreau, Henry David, 163
three-fifths clause, 47, 98, 99, 100–105, 106,
    108*n*
Thurmond, Strom, 59, 303
Time, 321
Tocqueville, Alexis de, 218
trade unions, xxi, xxiv, 62, 289
"Transcendentalist, The" (Emerson), 257
transportation, 57
Traugott, Lillian, 303
Treaty of Ghent, 129, 132
Treaty of Paris, 129
Treitschke, Heinrich von, 255, 264
Triangle Shirtwaist Factory fire, 288
Tripp, C. A., 200
Triumphant Democracy, 240
Truman, Harry, 59, 297, 299, 300–303
Truman Doctrine, 299
Trumbull, Lyman, 18, 177
Tucker, St. George, 87
Tugwell, Rexford, 23
Turner, Nat, 155, 164
Two Treatises on Government (Locke), 34

Ulbricht, Walter, 251
"Ulysses" (Tennyson), 183
Uncle Tom's Cabin (Stowe), 171, 253
unemployment, 64
United Auto Workers, 289
United League of Gileadites, 155
United Steelworkers of America, 249
Untold History of the United States, The
    (Stone and Kuznick), 295–306
Upshur, Abel, 50

U.S. Steel, 249
utopian communities, 42

Van Buren, Martin, 10, 13, 141
    on need for moneyed oligarchy, 10–11
Vance, Zebulon, 16
Verwoerd, Hendrik, 85
Vesey, Denmark, 164
Vietnam War, 25, 62, 290, 304, 305, 307–8,
    323–24, 331
Village Voice, 309
Villard, Oswald Garrison, 149
Virginia, 107, 228
    legal codes of, 94
Volker, Paul, 63
Volney, Comte de, 34
voting rights, 52, 54–55, 95–96, 210, 283
Voting Rights Act (1965), 60, 290, 307,
    310, 327

wages, 59, 64
Wagner, Robert, 288–89
Wagner Act (1935), 288
Waiting for Lefty (Odets), 285
Wallace, George C., 25, 60
Wallace, Henry A., xxv, 297, 299–300, 301,
    302–4, 305–6
War of 1812, 9, 41, 42*n*, 47
Warren, Earl, 322
Warren, Joseph, 129
Washington, Booker T., 253–54, 258, 263
Washington, George, 28, 94, 121, 131,
    136
    Farewell Address of, 5, 6–7, 8, 11, 17
    as slaveholder, 13, 87
Washington Monthly, 309
Watergate, 25, 62
wealth, 59, 63
Wealth of Nations, The (Smith), 80–81
Weather Underground, 150
Weber, Max, 253
Webster, Daniel, 125, 140–41, 144, 183,
    184, 221
Webster, Noah, 33
Weed, Thurlow, 12, 127–28, 136, 141
Weihe, William, 238
Weld, Theodore Dwight, 144
welfare reform, 292
Wells-Barnett, Ida B., 262

westward expansion, 46
"Where I Was Wrong" (Wallace), 305–6
Whig Party, British, 93
Whig Party, U.S., 51, 142, 144–45, 146, 215
    collapse of, 158, 170
    inequality opposed by, 44–46
    partisanship opposed by, 11–12
    rise of, 42, 141
    slavery and, 47, 48
    in South, 14
White, Ronald C., Jr., 179–81, 183
White, Walter, 303
white supremacy, xxi, 188
Whitman, Walt, xx, xxiii, 69, 126, 296
Wieland, Christoph Martin, 130
Wilkins, Roy, 251, 303, 321
Wilkinson, Allen, 157
Williamson, Jeffrey G., 35, 41
Wills, Garry, 97–106, 107, 109–10, 111
Wilmot, David, 104
Wilmot Proviso, 100

Wilson, Joan Hoff, 23
Wilson, Woodrow, 21, 22, 23, 28, 58, 269,
    270, 279, 296
Wise, Henry A., 125, 162
women's rights, 24, 31, 283
Woodward, C. Vann, 314
worker safety, 57
working hours, 57
World War I, 61, 270, 284, 296
World War II, 59, 296, 300
Wright, Richard, 285
Wythe, George, 87

XYZ Affair, 92

Yacovone, Donald, 187
Yarborough, Ralph, 319

Zinn, Howard, 282
Zuckerman, Michael, 85
Zucman, Gabriel, 59